Portugal

A twentieth-century interpretation

Portugal and the system of provinces, 1936–76

Portugal

A twentieth-century interpretation

Tom Gallagher

Manchester University Press

Published by
Manchester University Press
Oxford Road, Manchester M13 9PL

British Library cataloguing in publication data

Gallagher, Tom
  Portugal.
  1. Portugal—History—1910–1974
  2. Portugal—History—1974–
  I. Title
  946.9'042   DP680

  ISBN 0-7190-0876-X

Library of Congress Cataloging in Publication Data

Gallagher, Tom, 1954–
  Portugal: a twentieth-century interpretation.
  Bibliography: p.
  Includes index.
  1. Portugal—Politics and government—1910–1974.
  2. Portugal—Politics and government—1974–
I. Title.
DP675.G34   1982   946.9'04   82-20379

Typeset by
Northern Phototypesetting Co, Bolton
Printed in Great Britain by
Butler & Tanner Ltd
Frome and London

CONTENTS

PREFACE

From time to time, books on Portugal are published looking at the port-wine trade, Portugal's overseas empire, or else tracing the development of the 'Perpetual Alliance' between England and Portugal whose 600th anniversary falls in May 1986. Portuguese history is rich in excitement and drama and earlier periods will undoubtedly continue to attract foreign writers.

In comparison, very little of value has emerged on modern and contemporary Portuguese history and life. Why should this be so? Is Portugal the New Zealand or Sweden of twentieth-century southern Europe, with a history that is simply too bland to attract external interest? Until the revolution of 1974–75 which toppled the long established *Estado Novo* regime, this was what many people thought, if they thought of Portugal at all. From the early 1930s to the late 1960s Portugal had only one head of government, a shy but marvellously clever university professor called Dr Salazar who often told visiting foreigners that politics had been abolished in his land. 'Happy countries have no history,' was his reply to a journalist who once asked why nothing ever seemed to happen in Portugal. Compared to the turbulent era which preceded the onset of dictatorial rule in 1926 (dubbed by one observer as the 'nightmare republic') and to the uncertain 1970s when democracy was restored, Portugal seemed an oasis of calm in the second and third quarters of this century, when Dr Salazar controlled her destinies. Political crises, strikes, riots and inflation seemed to pass Portugal by and years could pass without political stories from Lisbon ever appearing in the newspapers.

This suited Portugal's hermit leader well. His enemies compared him with Mussolini or Franco, but this west European dictator had more in common with pre-Vatican Council pontiffs or the Dalai Lama of Tibet. His aim, no less, was to keep much of the twentieth century at bay in Portugal and resist modern trends which would undermine his traditionalist goals and values. Among other things, Salazar was a confirmed opponent of consumerism, urbanisation, secularism, women's rights, trade unionism and dynamic capitalism. Portugal experienced a long political and social ice age between 1926 and 1974 but it would be a mistake to believe that she was completely insulated from the outside world. In the 1960s and early 1970s well over a million people emigrated (many clandestinely) in the greatest movement of population witnessed in Portugal's 800-year history. By voting with their feet in such numbers the Portuguese demonstrated their opposition to Salazar's claustrophobic rule in the most direct way possible. Inside the country, a wide range of political opinions could be found among supporters and opponents of the *Estado Novo*, and it was thanks to his brilliant political footwork, not to popular acquiescence or fear, that Salazar was able to rule so long and so successfully. In 1968, while having his hair cut, he suffered an accident after a (British-made) deckchair collapsed under him, but nobody could fill his place, and within six years his unique political experiment had foundered. With his distrust of materialism and belief in ecology Salazar was, in some ways, rather ahead of his time but, in most other respects, he was very much a figure from the past.

Only since the emergence of a new democratic order which has linked Portugal with the rest of western Europe has it been possible to explore the curious *travail* Portugal has embarked upon during the present century. Beforehand, information was a precious resource in a land where the censor was far more ubiquitous than the secret policeman or the political commissar. Today some (though not all) historical archives are open and people are quite often willing to talk about the past. It is unfortunate that Salazar's own papers will not be made available to the scholar until some time in the twenty-first century (according to a Portuguese newspaper in 1981), a pace Salazar might not have quarrelled with.

This book endeavours to be a general history of Portugal in what was a fairly remarkable time. In ascending order of importance, it explores economic, social and political developments over the last eighty years. Chapter one fills in the historical background and argues that the Portuguese political tradition has not always been authoritarian or despotic. Portugal was one of the first southern European countries to evolve from oligarchical rule to pluralist democracy. However, divisions in the political elite and the economic backwardness of society doomed the experiment with liberal democracy. Chapter two examines how the spirit of the age ceased to be liberal and secular, with counter-revolution finally triumphant by 1926.

About the first phase of authoritarian rule, the military dictatorship (1926–32), very little has been published. Chapter three attempts to unravel the hidden history of the *ditadura militar*. It examines the political ideas of Portugal's military rulers alongside their failure to establish new enduring political structures.

It was Dr Salazar, a civilian, who brought stability and coherence to the new authoritarian order. Chapters four and five trace his career, personality and political philosophy. The political institutions of the *Estado Novo*, economic policies, and the nature of the political elite are examined. Salazar's relationship with Fascism and Portugal's role in both the Spanish Civil War and the Second World War are assessed along with the methods used by the dictator to bolster his rule.

The nature and extent of opposition are analysed in chapter six along with the fluctuating state of civil–military relations, and the role of the Church in Salazar's Portugal. The stagnation and immobilism which the *Estado Novo* eventually became a byword for are looked at in chapter seven, which also looks at the challenge posed to Salazar by dissension within the elite, unrest among the masses and revolt in the colonies, and why he survived these challenges. The last phase of authoritarian rule, between 1968 and 1974, when Marcelo Caetano was prime minister, is the subject of chapter eight. The eighteen-month upheaval of 1974–75 when Portugal went down the path of revolution perhaps further than any other west European country in the last hundred years is scrutinised in chapter nine. A final chapter then assesses the shortcomings and achievements of Portuguese democracy up to the early 1980s.

It has taken a number of years to research and write this book, and I would like to thank the following institutions for providing me with generous assistance which enabled me to do fieldwork in Portugal over a number of years: the Gulbenkian Foundation for enabling me to do preliminary research in 1977 with the help of a *bolsa*; the Nuffield Foundation, who helped fund a trip to Portugal in September 1980 to observe the general election campaign of that month; and the Twenty-seven Foundation of the Institute of Historical Research in London, who awarded me a grant in 1981 which enabled me to do further research on opposition and repression in Salazar's Portugal.

Several colleagues and friends have been unstinting with advice and practical help, and I would like to take this opportunity to thank them. I benefited greatly from Professor Kenneth Medhurst's advice and knowledge of the Hispanic world when he was latterly senior lecturer in the Government Department at Manchester University and I remain deeply grateful to him for having helped to clarify my mind in key respects and for his general backing. Let me also thank Dr Clive Willis of the Spanish and Portuguese Department at Manchester University for providing me with another Gulbenkian grant that enabled me to spend two months studying Portuguese at the University of Lisbon's Faculty of Letters in 1976. Dr Willis has also checked the Portuguese spelling and phraseology employed here, for which I am also grateful. Thanks are also due to his former colleague Amélia Pereira Hutchinson, who first introduced me to the Portuguese language in 1975–76 and who provided me with useful background knowledge of her own country. I would also like to thank Custódia Martins, her successor as Portuguese assistant, for allowing me to make off with the Portuguese newspapers.

At Bradford University, I would like to thank Professor James O'Connell for his backing as the project was being completed. Two other people I ought not to forget are Brian Carlin and Dr Michael Elliott-Bateman.

Above all, I would like to record my appreciation for the hospitality extended to me by Patricia McGowan and also Carlos Lança during past visits to Portugal. But for Pat's knowledge and unceasing help there would be many gaps in this book. She was also kind enough to read part of the manuscript, but of course any mistakes or slips are my responsibility.

Thanks are also due to the many other people in Portugal who consented to be interviewed or were otherwise free with information and advice. I will always remember the many kindnesses done to me by strangers and friends on various trips. Let me finally thank the staff of the various libraries which I have used while researching this book. These include the staff of John Rylands University Library of Manchester, the Central Reference Library (Manchester), the Social Science Staff of Bradford University Library, the staff of the Public Record Office (Kew) and those of the Biblioteca Nacional (Lisbon).

ABBREVIATIONS

AD	Democratic Alliance (1979–)
AEV	Acção Escolar Vanguarda (1934–36)
ANP	Acção Nacional Popular (1969–74)
APU	United People's Alliance (1979–)
CADC	Academic Centre for Christian Democracy (1901–03 – ?)
CAP	Confederation of Portuguese Farmers (1975–)
CCP	Portuguese Catholic Centre (1917–34)
CDE	Democratic Electoral Committee
CDS	Party of the Social Democratic Centre (1974–)
CEUD	Electoral Committee of Democratic Unity (1969–73)
CGTP-IS	General Confederation of Portuguese Workers – Intersindical (1977–)
CIA	Central Intelligence Agency, USA
COPCON	Operational Command for Continental Portugal (1974–75)
CPSU	Communist Party of the Soviet Union
CUF	Companhia União Fabril
DGS	Directorate General of Security (1969–74)
EEC	European Economic Community
FICO	Front for the Integrity of Western Civilisation (1974–75)
FIM	Military Intervention Force (1975)
FLA	Azorean Liberation Front (1975–)
FNLA	National Front for the Liberation of Angola (1961–75)
FP25	Popular Front of 25 April (1980–)
Frelimo	Mozambique Liberation Front
Fretilin	Revolutionary Front of Independent East Timor
FRS	Republican Socialist Front (1980)
FUR	United Revolutionary Front (1975)
GNR	National Republican Guard
IMF	International Monetary Fund
JSN	Junta of National Salvation
LP	Portuguese Legion (1936–74)
LUAR	United League of Revolutionary Action
MDLP	Democratic Movement for the Liberation of Portugal (1975–76)
MDP	Portuguese Democratic Movement (1974–)
MES	Movement of the Socialist Left
MFA	Armed Forces Movement (1973–75)
MIRN/PDP	Movement of Independent National Reconstruction/Party of the Portuguese Right (1977–)
MP	Portuguese Youth (1936–74)
MPLA	Popular Movement for the Liberation of Angola (1960–)
MUD	United Democratic Movement
NATO	North Atlantic Treaty Organisation

PAIGC	Guine and Cape Verde Africa Independence Party (1959–)
PCE	Spanish Communist Party
PCI	Italian Communist Party
PCP	Portuguese Communist Party (1921–)
PIDE	International Police for the Defence of the State (1945–69)
PPD	Popular Democratic Party (1974–76)
PPM	Popular Monarchist Party (1974–)
PREC	Revolutionary Process on Course
PRP	Portuguese Republican Party (1871–1935?)
PRP-BR	Revolutionary Party of the Proletariat/Revolutionary Brigades
PS	Socialist Party (1973–)
PSD	Social Democratic Party (1976–)
PVDE	Police of Vigilance and State Defence
SEDES	Social and Economic Development Study Group (1970–)
SUV	Soldiers United Will Win (1975)
UDP	Popular Democratic Union
UEDS	Union of the Democratic Socialist Left (1978–)
UEI	Union of Economic Interests (1925– ?)
UN	National Union (1930–69)

To my mother

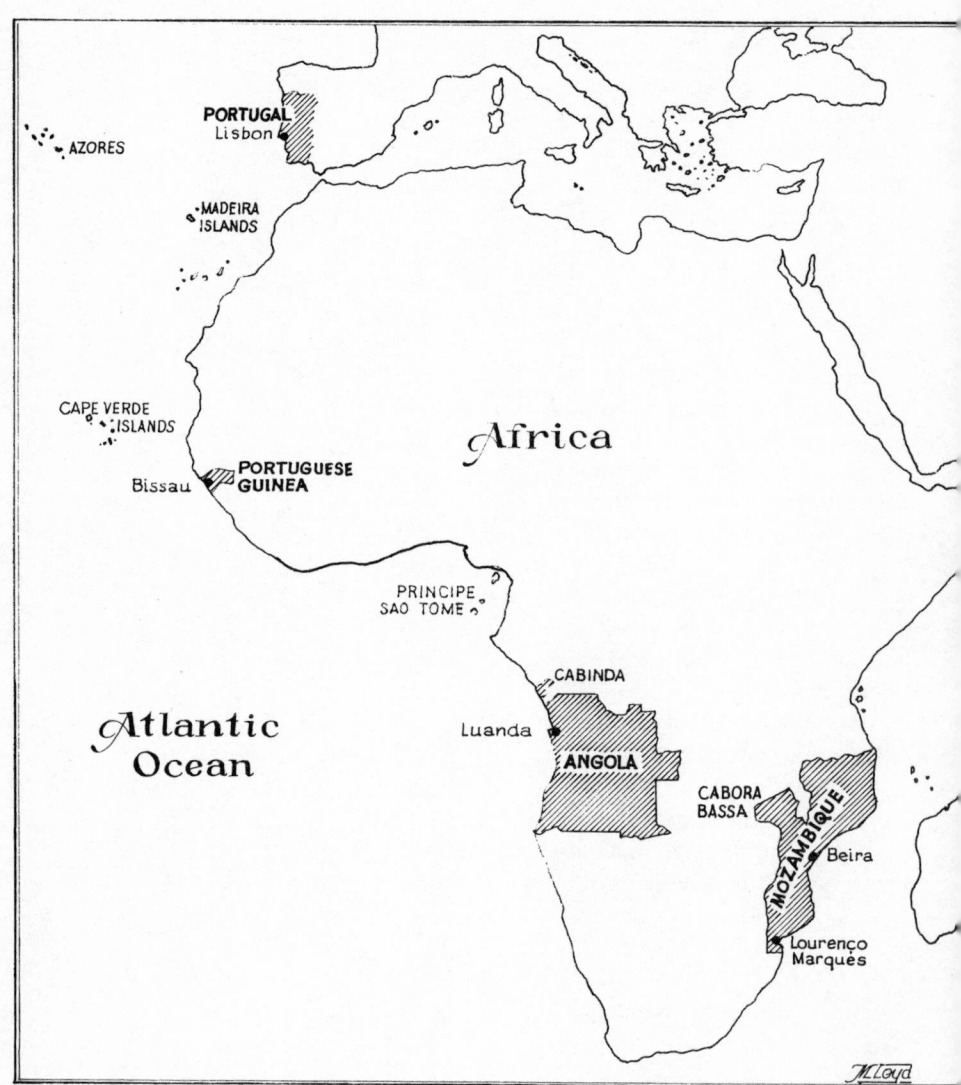

Portugal's African territories, 1974

Historical evolution

The birth of Portugal

Portugal today is the oldest and geographically most stable nation in Europe. In the 800-year history of the Iberian state a relatively impressive degree of cultural unity has been achieved. No linguistic, racial or religious minorities of any note exist. Indeed, the national boundaries have remained practically unaltered since the thirteenth century, giving Portugal perhaps the world's most stable continental frontier. Naturally, its geographical location at the westernmost edge of the European land mass has been a vital factor in the survival of this small and often ill-defended country. However, it would be wrong to ascribe complete isolation and remoteness from the rest of Europe.

No major physical barriers underwrite the political frontier between Portugal and Spain. In soil, climate and agricultural systems Portugal is an integral part of the Iberian peninsula. To the Spanish writer Salvador de Madariaga 'the Portuguese is a Spaniard with his back to Castile and his face towards the Atlantic'. Even the two great nineteenth-century Portuguese historians, Alexandre Herculano and Oliveira Martins, considered Portuguese independence somewhat accidental, the result of fortuitous political developments rather than any underlying geographical or cultural unity of western Iberia.[2] This does not make the separate development of Portugal an absolute fluke. Elsewhere in Europe geography and history often contradict one another. The unity of the north European plains was broken by frontiers which seem as arbitrary as those of Portugal, while the same can be said with even more certainty of many areas of post-colonial Africa and Asia.

Racially, the Portuguese emerged in the wake of recurring settlements and invasions carried out by a diverse range of peoples who included Celts, Iberians, Romans, Swabians and Moors. The first recorded arrivals in Portugal were the Iberians, who appeared sometime in the third millennium B.C. A branch of the Iberians, the Lusitanians, gradually populated the western edge of the peninsula, bringing with them a rather rudimentary tribal-based culture. The first inhabitant of the area to gain a place in history was Viriatus, a Lusitanian chieftain of the second century B.C. who is reputed to have held up the Roman occupation of the peninsula for a number of decades. Viriatus is one of Portugal's folk heroes and he has also been described as the first of the Hispanic world's *caudillos* or national military leaders.[3] However, over the long term, the Lusitanians were unable to resist the Roman advance. Lusitania became one of the provinces of the Roman empire but it was not coterminous with modern Portugal, since it did not include part of the north but did incorporate part of what was later south-western Spain.[4] Towns were built and Christianity was introduced during the second century A.D. On the dissolution of the Roman empire in the fifth century, the Swabians, a Germanic tribe, set up an independent kingdom in the western part of the peninsula. Here some sort of separate polity endured until the Moslem invasion of the pensinsula in 711. Within four years an army of Arabs and Berbers had conquered the entire peninsula with the exception of the mountainous region of Asturias in the extreme north. Soon a flourishing civilisation developed in Moslem Spain which, in the European Dark Ages, was unsurpassed in wealth, culture and power. However, later in the eighth century the petty chiefs in the northern Christian redoubt were able to organise resistance against the Moors. This fight-back marked the beginning of the Christian Reconquest, which would take almost eight centuries to complete, leaving in its wake an expansionist and militantly Catholic culture.

The first major inroads against the Moors took place in the north-west of the peninsula. By the middle of the tenth century, present-day Galicia in Spain and the northernmost provinces of Portugal had been taken from the Moors. Here an administrative fiefdom called Portucale emerged about 938. It was then part of the kingdom of Leon and appears to have derived its name from the Latin term *Portucalense*, which designated the county surrounding the old Roman town Portus Cale (the modern-day city of Oporto). As the local rulers of Portucale extended their territory southwards their autonomy increased, finally enabling a separate kingdom, Portugal, to emerge in the twelfth century.

Historians recognise Afonso Henriques as Portugal's first king. He ruled from 1128 to 1185, and by the end of his reign he had pushed the Moors farther south than any other contemporary Iberian ruler had succeeded in doing. A decisive victory was claimed over them at Ourique in 1139, a battle which is considered crucial for the consolidation of Portuguese independence even though its site has become lost and even its exact date is uncertain. Later, in 1147, Lisbon was captured with the help of foreign crusaders. This was deemed another milestone in the war of attrition against the Moors because of the town's strategic location on the shores of the river Tagus. Not until 1298 would Lisbon become Portugal's political capital, but by then it had already grown into her economic and cultural centre.

In the intervening period a series of strong kings had established

Portuguese sovereignty both against the Moors and against other Christian Iberian states. With one exception, Portugal's early rulers were long-lived and energetic men, each of whom reigned on average for over thirty years. Afonso Henriques, fifty-seven years on the throne, a stupendous reign in terms of the Middle Ages, provided firm leadership and created a vital national infrastructure of roads, laws, towns and agriculture. In 1149, during his reign, Portugal achieved her present boundaries, having expelled or conquered the Moorish rulers, a full 240 years before the same process was completed by neighbouring Castile, later known as Spain. Under King Dinis, who reigned from 1279 to 1325, the vernacular rather than Latin became the official language. As well as fostering an interest in Portuguese culture, especially poetry, Dinis appears to have shown unusually keen interest in land and farming. *O Rei Lavrador* (the Farmer King) considered agriculture to be the true source of national wealth, and for much of his reign he tried to persuade the feudal nobility and other privileged classes of the importance of rural development – ultimately, however, to no avail. A warlike and parasitical feudal class was ill-disposed to show enduring interest in the soil. One baleful outcome of the Reconquest was an inbred resistance on the part of a militaristic elite to engaging in economic and profit-oriented pursuits such as trade or agriculture. The poor regard which national leaders displayed towards economic occupations upon which the nation's prosperity depended was a grave handicap that blighted Portugal's development long after the end of the feudal age. However, there were countervailing trends which indicate a more complex pattern of society.

After the founding dynasty died out in 1383 with King Fernando, Portugal experienced a national revolution of sorts in which the lesser nobility and townspeople rallied round João (John) of Aviz, an illegitimate son of a previous Portuguese king, who defeated a large Castilian invading force at the battle of Aljubarrota in 1385. Portugal had asserted herself over a larger and more powerful neighbour, one which would continue to find it hard to accept that two kingdoms should share the Iberian peninsula. English help had been vital in safeguarding Portuguese independence, and Aljubarrota represents one of the few occasions when the alliance which the two countries agreed in 1386 with the Treaty of Windsor has so strongly worked in Portugal's favour. The victorious João I cemented the relationship in the 1380s by taking as his queen Philippa of Lancaster, daughter of John of Gaunt. As ruler of the new Aviz dynasty João I (1384–1433) enjoyed a lengthy reign, but his victory marked not the triumph of the middle classes, as is sometimes believed, but a regrouping of the nobility and the elevation of new elements from the lower nobility and the middle classes.[5]

The discoveries

Under the new Aviz dynasty strong royal leadership continued, and
Portugal came to possess some of the hallmarks of the early modern state
ahead of larger and later more powerful European countries. By the
beginning of the fifteenth century she already enjoyed a keen sense of
national unity and a strongly institutionalised government. During
almost the whole of this century, at a time when the other countries of
Europe were either ravaged by foreign or civil wars or else were
preoccupied by the Turkish advance in the Balkans, she was a united
kingdom virtually free of civil strife. Historians consider this domestic
calm a major factor in enabling her rulers to promote the voyages of
exploration which were shortly to open up so much of the world to west
European penetration. Having established firm territorial boundaries in
Iberia, a militaristic aristocracy allied to a firm, calculating royal
leadership was eager to seek new fields of adventure. After the Moroccan
town of Ceuta was seized from the Moors in 1415, Portuguese ships began
to explore the uncharted Atlantic waters to the west and south. A boost to
Portuguese confidence came with the discovery of the island chains of the
Azores and Madeira before 1431. Settlers were sent to these unpopulated
isles and it was not long before they were providing a profitable return in
agriculture, producing sugar and other commodities difficult to cultivate
in more temperate climes. Early encouraging results spurred explorers
and their patrons on to further voyages. In strictly economic terms,
Portugal was motivated by a strong desire to discover gold and obtain
spices and luxury goods available only in the Orient. During the
fourteenth and fifteenth centuries a keen demand had developed among
the privileged elites of Europe for Indian cotton, China silk and spices such
as pepper, nutmeg and cloves.

Less material considerations also spurred the Portuguese on. Henry the
Navigator, the prince who sent out several important expeditions which
explored the north-west African coast in the mid-fifteenth century, was
motivated partly by religious and partly by strategic considerations.
Fearing the rise of Moslem power in the southern and eastern
Mediterranean, one of his ambitions was to contact the mythical
Christian potentate Prester John, whose kingdom was thought to be
somewhere in the vicinity of Ethiopia, and make him an ally in the
struggle against Islam. From his headquarters on the rocky promontory of
Sagres at the very south-western tip of Portugal, Prince Henry organised
expeditions which, by the time of his death in 1460, had penetrated as far
south as the coast of present-day Liberia. Medieval sailors and navigators
who feared the dangers these unknown waters held grew confident as the
blood-curdling tales about the sea monsters and whirlpools lurking in their

depths proved groundless. After 1474, when young Prince João, the future João II, was put in charge of the voyages, the pace of discovery quickened. If any one individual deserves the supreme accolade for Portugal's maritime achievements, it is this cool-headed Renaissance prince, whose endeavours, unlike Henry the Navigator's, have tended to be forgotten. It was João who drew up a comprehensive plan of discovery whose primary objective was to reach India by sea. On becoming king, in 1481, he mounted a major expedition under the command of Diogo Cão which discovered thirteen degrees of coast south of the equator and penetrated as far as present-day Namibia, almost reaching the Tropic of Capricorn.

Although voyagers were disappointed that the coast swung ever southwards, a sea passage to India was thought to be close, and in 1487 Bartolomeu Dias set out on a voyage which at last took him right round the coast of Africa. Just over two centuries later the Scots political economist, Adam Smith, would describe the discovery of a passage to the East by the Cape of Good Hope as one of the 'two greatest and most important events in the history of mankind'.[6] Looking back, the fifteenth-century achievements of a small country of under two million people (which were soon to include the building of an empire on three continents) appear staggering, especially in the light of Portugal's later historical role. However, as the Portuguese historian, A. H. de Oliveira Marques, has commented, 'the relationship between great undertakings and the physical dimensions of a nation was not necessarily a direct one in those days'.[7] Venice, Genoa and Aragon had already built up economic empires (in the Mediterranean) of considerable size from a core area smaller than Portugal's, while tiny seventeenth-century Holland would go on to rule a great part of the world from an area half the size of Portugal.

One factor which enabled the Portuguese to embark on long-range expeditionary voyages was their expertise in maritime technology. The fifteenth century was a period of major innovation in ship design and navigational technology, and Portugal was undoubtedly in the forefront of developments. The creation of the long-voyage caravel, new types of sail rigging, and more reliable navigational devices now enabled the Atlantic maritime powers to contemplate long expeditions far from their home shores. In Portugal, Dias's rounding of the Cape of Good Hope was followed by Vasco da Gama's departure for India in 1479.

The main purpose in setting out to traverse 10,000 miles of ocean was to obtain Indian spices and other profitable merchandise. When they reached the port of Calicut in May 1498 the filthy and bedraggled Portuguese did not impress the local Asians. Nevertheless, Vasco da Gama was able to return in triumph to Lisbon laden with spices, having made a profit of 600 per cent.[8] Soon the king of Portugal was being proclaimed as the richest monarch in all Christendom. However, the

Portuguese were faced with the problem that the rich Indian cities were unwilling to trade with them, owing to Moslem domination of the area and to the fact that they were unimpressed by the goods brought by the Europeans. As a result, it did not take long for the Portuguese Crown to conclude that only force could create a profitable commercial position for it in India. In 1502 Vasco da Gama took the first major military expedition to India, which blasted its way into the spice trade a year later by winning a pitched sea battle against Arab naval forces. The next step was to build fortresses at strategic points along the northern littoral of the Indian Ocean in order to safeguard Portuguese trade. Garrisons were built from Mozambique to Viêtnam, and a territorial empire began to be established after the appointment of Afonso de Albuquerque as Portuguese viceroy in the East in 1509.

Albuquerque, more than any other individual, confirmed Portuguese power in Asia. In only six years he established Portuguese naval superiority in waters thousands of miles from Europe, destroying Moslem power in the Indian ocean and establishing a capital at Goa on the south-west coast of India in 1510. This nobleman has been described as the outstanding strategic planner of the sixteenth century and perhaps the most extraordinary of all the Hispanic conquerors.[9] In establishing a vast trade network and securing a line of communication with Portugal he fought Turks, Arabs, Moslems and the Moghul empire. Before his death in battle in 1515, he destroyed an Egyptian fleet in the Red Sea, planned an assault on Mecca, which he intended to hold as ransom for the delivery of Jerusalem, and even contemplated diverting the source of the Nile so as to ruin Egypt. Death was to prevent him using Portuguese naval superiority in a full-scale crusade against the heartlands of the Islamic world. Whether this would have worked is, of course, unknown, but the small Portuguese armies on the other side of the world, cut off from reinforcements in a hostile environment, did possess clear military advantages over their foes. Portuguese ships were swifter, more manoeuvrable and usually better constructed than those of the Asian powers. For a long time the Portuguese possessed another advantage in being the only force in the East to mount long-range artillery on their ships. By the mid-sixteenth century Portugal dominated more areas of the world than any other power, thanks to the freebooting imperialism so boldly practised by her military commanders in Asia and also the New World. Brazil had been discovered by Pedro Álvares Cabral in 1500 and settlements were built along this coast as well as on the African and Indian coasts. As early as the reign of Manuel I (1495–1521), Portugal was acclaimed as the richest land in Christendom thanks to the wealth she had acquired through her conquests. Precious stones, gold, spices and, increasingly, slaves were the basis of her prosperity. Manuel I, 'the

Fortunate', was also known as the grocer king. Lisbon became the commercial entrepot for much of Europe but it was not long before the drawbacks as well as the advantages of such new-found wealth for a small and, in many ways, still backward country began to manifest themselves.

Imperial decline

Discovery and conquest overseas may have brought Portugal international prominence but her social structure was not greatly altered by the wealth which flowed back to the *metrópole*.[10] The middle class and commercial sectors remained small and politically marginal. In fact, from the outset, private initiative had played a very limited role in Portuguese expansion. The discoveries had been a state enterprise which initially may have been beneficial, since 'it permitted a much quicker search for goals and a much better organisation of the necessary means'.[11] However, as the empire quickly became a commercial rather than a merely territorial one the absence of independent initiative began to produce detrimental effects. Profits were absorbed primarily by the court, the Church and the aristocracy, institutions which preferred to invest their wealth in land, building activities (churches and palaces) and in luxuries rather than in new commercial enterprises. The royal monopoly acquired the most lucrative commerce, with the result that the strong middle class which proved the backbone of the Dutch and Venetian commercial empires never emerged. The persecution and expulsion of the Jews in the early 1500s proved a debilitating measure over the long term. Since many were to be found in the professions, this affirmation of Catholic orthodoxy (in Spain as well as in Portugal) sapped economic resources and enhanced the feudal character of Iberian society; Lisbon did grow in size to become, by 1620, the third largest city in Europe after Paris and Naples.[12] However, much of this growth was gained at the expense of the smaller coastal cities. Soon Lisbon grew too large for the hinterland to support, and little wealth was siphoned back into the country. Unlike London or Amsterdam, the Portuguese empire's major metropolis failed to develop its own industry. Instead, foreign entrepreneurs benefited enormously from the Portuguese elite's preference for more efficiently produced commodities and wares from northern Europe. Much of Portugal's new-found wealth left the country as rapidly as it had entered it, and by mid-century the Crown was facing a severe liquidity crisis.

Despite its apparent wealth, the Crown found it increasingly difficult to obtain enough cash for the upkeep and defence of a sprawling maritime empire. As early as 1522 Vasco da Gama had urged a policy of contraction. His advice was not taken, nor were any reforms introduced which could have enabled Portugal to adapt to the increasingly complex task of running a seaborne empire from a tiny home base. The dominance of the aristocracy increased as profit margins fell and loans became increasingly difficult to obtain. The rigid caste system of Iberian society continued to require that leadership and authority in national affairs be given to men of noble blood rather than to better-qualified professionals.

In a centralised country like Portugal the calibre of the royal incumbents was also important. No ruler of equivalent merit succeeded João II, who, by the time of his premature death in 1495, had been recognised as one of the ablest European rulers of the century. But it was only in the latter half of the sixteenth century that the decline of royal leadership became of critical importance. In 1557 João III died, leaving as heir to the throne a three-year-old child, Sebastian. Sickly and poorly educated, he was mentally unstable and as he reached adulthood developed a burning obsession about launching a grand crusade against Islam. In 1578 Sebastian took a large army to Morocco in pursuit of this goal, a force which was almost entirely wiped out at the battle of Alcácer-Quibir. It was the most disastrous battle in Portuguese history, the king and 7,000 nobles and men-at-arms being numbered among the casualties. Sebastian was succeeded by his aged uncle, Cardinal Henrique of Lisbon, a past head of the Inquisition. On his death in 1580 the royal line died out, leaving Philip II of Spain one of the strongest claimants to the throne. Philip was not long in enforcing what he saw as his hereditary right to succeed the Aviz dynasty, thus uniting the Iberian peninsula under one king for the first time. Before 1580 had ended, Spanish armies occupied Portugal, with resistance coming only from the common people, who bitterly resented the annexation.

Iberian union

The nobility and clergy, on the whole, supported union with Spain. Castilian influence had been present at court and in the cultural tastes of the intelligentsia for several generations and, to begin with, Philip provided Portugal with better government than she had experienced during the last uncertain years of the Aviz dynasty. Indeed, the country retained a great deal of autonomy after 1580, a year which saw the formal end of independence but not total absorption by Spain.

The overseas empire continued to be ruled exclusively by the Portuguese, and Philip swore not to interfere in the laws, customs or government of the country. Portuguese businessmen were able to trade with Spain's vast empire in the New World, and for two years, between 1581 and 1583, Philip even established his capital in Lisbon, which was then the peninsula's leading city. Such even-handed treatment continued to be extended to Portugal for about the first thirty years of the union. But after 1610 Spain began to levy increasingly heavy taxes on Portugal, and the system of administration declined along with the amount of autonomy granted to the Portuguese. The overseas empires of Spain and Portugal also began to come under heavy attack from the Dutch around this time. Major losses were incurred by the Portuguese, especially in Asia, where they found it difficult to protect their far-flung coastal settlements. Gradually, hostility towards Spanish domination spread from the common people (never reconciled to the 1580 union) to the ruling class. Popular nationalism was kept alive by the appearance of several imposters claiming to be Sebastian, who, after his death, was known as the 'desired' or 'hidden' king. Sebastianism, really a messianic belief that a saviour would restore Portugal to independence and greatness, remained a potent folk myth up to, and perhaps beyond, the nineteenth century. In the short term, peasant millenarianism prepared the ground for the restoration of Portuguese independence in 1640. With Spain involved in foreign wars and facing a serious revolt in Catalonia, the Duke of Braganza, the leading Portuguese noble, declared independence in December 1640, all of Portugal and most of the empire quickly rallying to his cause.

Pombal and the Restoration period

Before the twentieth century Portugal was practically the only small nation in Europe to have regained its independence after once losing it to a larger power. However, Portugal's freedom was not really assured until the 1670s, by which time the Spanish finally abandoned attempts to restore their western neighbour to Madrid's territorial orbit. In the intervening thirty years of struggle in the peninsula, the Portuguese Crown had been forced to yield much of her far-flung overseas empire to the Dutch. In the colonial war between Holland and Portugal which raged intermittently during the first half of the seventeenth century Lisbon lost most of her Asian possessions while retaining control of Brazil and its sugar trade, as well as a large part of the West African slave trade.[13]

The revenue from Portugal's remaining territories enabled the new Braganza dynasty to rule in the style of its predecessors, but (as before) little royal interest was displayed for developing European Portugal. For a time, between 1675 and 1690, the Count of Ericeira, a domestic reformer placed in charge of national finances, did attempt to stimulate local manufactures through a policy of tariff protection, but after his suicide in 1690 little remained of his work. British merchants came increasingly to dominate Portuguese commerce, until Portugal's staunchest ally had virtually gained a stranglehold over the economy. The Methuen Treaty of 1703 revealed the kind of neo-colonial relationship that was emerging. Under it, Britain agreed to buy Portuguese wines (in preference to French ones) in return for Portugal throwing open its market to English textiles. These were of far greater value than Portuguese wines, and it is estimated that the revenue, mainly in the form of Brazilian gold, which was drained from Lisbon played no small part in creating the conditions for England's industrial revolution.

The bullion which remained in Portugal financed the extravagant life style of a royal court which modelled itself on that of Louis XIV of France. During the reign of João V (1706–50), the productivity of the Brazilian mines enabled the court nobility to display its wealth as never before. Magnificent churches, palaces and mansions were erected in rich baroque style. In an age of debauchery as well as opulence, the king and many nobles begot children from nuns of various convents which had become brothels of the aristocracy rather than religious houses.[14] In the midst of the gaiety the Inquisition continued to regulate social behaviour, winking at court peccadilloes and ruthlessly pursuing any trace of religious heresy. Until its curtailment in 1769 this institution passed a heavy number of death sentences, causing Portugal to be despised in more enlightened parts of Europe. Voltaire described how the monks and nuns who swarmed in the streets of Lisbon seemed often more numerous than ordinary citizens. Half an hour would not elapse without a religious procession, before which one had to kneel or risk arrest by agents of the Inquisition.[15]

Portugal would eventually experience the changes identified with the Age of the Enlightenment with the rise to power after 1750 of Sebastião José de Carvalho e Melo, better known as the Marquis of Pombal. Pombal was a petty noble who managed to surmount the rigid caste system of Portuguese society thanks to a combination of uncommon intelligence, fine looks and a shrewd marriage with a Hapsburg duchess. Time spent abroad as Portuguese ambassador in London and Vienna brought him into contact with the men and ideas of the Enlightenment and made him realise just how backward Portugal was. When he was appointed chief minister in 1750 by José I (1750–1777), an indolent king who displayed little interest in affairs of state, the governmental machinery was almost paralysed and trade revenues were in serious decline. Pombal was able to halt the immediate rot, but his gravest challenge came in 1755 when, on All Souls' Day, Lisbon was devastated by a major earthquake in which thousands were killed. This calamity severely dented the optimism of rationalist thought in western Europe. However, a breakdown of rule was averted by the presence of mind displayed by Pombal in the aftermath of the disaster. When an hysterical king yelled, 'What can be done? What can be done to meet this infliction of Divine Justice?' Pombal is said to have replied, 'Sire, bury the dead and feed the living.'[16] Opposing the king and clergy, who wanted the capital transferred to Oporto or Coimbra, Pombal rebuilt Lisbon, creating a splendid, modern city at one of the great moments of western architecture: the mid-eighteenth century.

Pombal was able to establish himself as the strong man of Portugal in the aftermath of the earthquake. His economic policies were designed to encourage the rise of a commercial middle class on British lines. One of his decrees gave the merchants the right to share with the aristocracy the jealously guarded privilege of wearing a sword, a policy which the nobility took great exception to. In 1758, when a noble plot was discovered to assassinate the king and overthrow him, Pombal seized the opportunity he had been waiting for: many top aristocrats were arrested and imprisoned. Those numbered in the conspiracy against the king were, after a hasty trial, placed on the scaffold in the centre of Lisbon, where their limbs and ribs were smashed with hammers, after which they were garrotted or beheaded. The Alveira and Távora families, two of the noblest in Europe, were decimated in this way, the aged Marquesa of Távora witnessing her sons undergoing their gory torments before herself being decapitated.

Next Pombal turned to deal with the powerful Jesuit order, who had reacted with ill-disguised hostility towards a modernising reformer for acquiring the kind of influence at court they had always exercised. In 1759 he suppressed the Jesuits, confiscating their property and publicly garrotting the head of the order. In a country where the Church had wielded more power than perhaps anywhere else in Europe, this was an incredibly bold move, but one that was soon emulated by the rulers of France and Spain. Pombal's policy of anticlerical nationalism which brought him fame abroad was generally popular at home, but the ruthless police state methods he used to carry out his policies made him a dreaded figure. Only by acting as a ruthless dictator did Pombal feel that his enlightened policies might succeed in what was still a medieval, backward country, scarcely out of feudalism. Until then, Britain had been fond of deriding Portugal's backwardness while being very unwilling to see any serious effort made to throw this off, since her own vested interests were bound to suffer.[17] Pombal assessed the power of Britain in his own writings: 'the system of Great Britain is to weaken the power of other nations in order to increase her own. Portugal is powerless and without vigour and all her movements are regulated by the desires of England.'[18]

The economic policies of this nationalist dictator helped to restore Portugal's commercial independence, but the unequal nature of the relationship between Portugal and Britain was not radically altered. Perhaps only by severing the commercial and political alliance between the two countries could Pombal have hoped to put Portugal back on her feet. As it was, new commercial enterprises were, more often than not, started by the state rather than by individual entrepreneurs, and Pombal's dictatorship failed to witness the emergence of a strong middle class. But elsewhere his record was not without positive achievement.

Slavery was abolished in Portugal in 1773 and major educational reforms were introduced during the same decade. After the expulsion of the Jesuits, many of the religious houses were turned into hospitals and almshouses, while the Papal Index was replaced by a censorship board which licensed many banned works (Rousseau, Voltaire, the Encyclopedists). Pombal even treated the court theatre to an unprecedented performance of Molière's *Tartuffe* in which the central figure was dressed as a Jesuit priest.[19] However, Pombal's power was secure only as long as José I lived. With his death in 1777 the Pombaline era came to a close. On being crowned queen, his devout daughter, Maria II, quickly banished Pombal to his estates, and much of the old order was restored. Portugal reverted to her slumber, being unaffected by the French revolution of 1789. For a long time it was hoped that her geographical remoteness might save her also from Napoleon's armies, but it was not to be. Portugal's alliance with Britain led to growing French hostility, and in 1807 Napoleon's forces invaded and quickly occupied the whole country.

Liberalism and revolution, 1820–51

Until the nineteenth century the social and political structure had been exceptionally stable in European terms. Popular revolts and challenges to the established order had always been conspicuous by their absence. No Portuguese monarch had been assassinated. Nor had prosperous and educated groups from outside the ruling elite ever pressed for admittance, or for a new political system. This had not even happened during the Pombaline era, which saw aristocratic and clerical rule replaced by a personal dictatorship, not by middle-class liberalism. However, in a very conservative country Pombalism, and then the French revolution, did provide dramatic examples of how the traditional fabric of rule could be undermined. Afterwards, liberalism became established through French and British influences. Freemasonry, introduced by foreign merchants, spread among a small section of the middle class at the beginning of the nineteenth century. Authors like Jeremy Bentham and Adam Smith began to be quoted and praised.[20] After the French invasion of 1807, radical ideas continued to make headway. The officer corps, which gained esteem in the Peninsular War when local and British forces were pitted against the French, came to demand a larger role in national life. The self-assertion of traditionally passive groups was possible because of a crisis in royal leadership.

After 1807 the royal family and much of the aristocracy had fled to Brazil, where it found conditions so congenial that it was unwilling to return after the French had been driven from Portuguese soil. While King João VI sojourned in Rio de Janeiro, a regency was established in his absence, at the head of which was a British general, William Beresford. Along with other post-Napoleonic rulers, Beresford set out to restore the *ancien régime* and wage strenuous resistance against progressive ideas. However, he quickly faced opposition from the intelligentsia, the army and middle-class elements influenced, to some degree, by the concepts of democracy, equality and popular sovereignty. Beresford's rule was severe, as the execution in 1817 of the head of the Freemasons, General Gomes Freire, demonstrated. The credibility of the regime was, from then on, increasingly undermined because it was foreign as well as reactionary. Liberals able to justify their opposition on patriotic, as well as on specific ideological, grounds received wide-ranging support. In 1820 a successful revolution occurred which drove out Beresford and – far more important – was to mark the beginning of Portugal's modern political evolution. With the 1820 revolution, middle- and upper middle-class civilian elites – and the Portuguese military – first came to the political foreground. They have been there ever since, the dominant elements in Portuguese national politics from the 1820s to the 1980s.[21]

Reformers were sufficiently influential after 1820 to ensure that the revolution would have important consequences over and above the curtailment of foreign domination. The most far-reaching was the constitution of 1822. A written document enacted after strong liberal pressure, it severely limited the power of the Crown, finally abolished the Inquisition and gave the vote to all, except women, illiterates and friars, in biennial elections for a single-chamber parliament independent of the Crown. When the drafters of Portugal's first written constitution declared that 'sovereignty resides essentially in the nation',[22] they were serving notice on the monarchy that it could reign but not rule.

However, Portugal's model constitution appeared at an inauspicious moment in history. Europe in the decade or so following the Congress of Vienna (1815) witnessed determined attempts to restore royal absolutism wherever it was threatened. Externally isolated, the liberal reformers faced daunting internal problems. First of all, their social base was a tiny one. Only approximately 9 per cent of the population could be classified as middle-class in the 1820s.[23] Secondly, excepting Lisbon and Oporto, few populated centres existed. Thirdly, domestic commerce was still held in check by the flood of British imports entering the country. Thus the conditions did not exist for the rise of the class of 'economically independent, prosperous townsmen' who, claimed one observer, acted as the seedbed of democracy in the world's first advanced pluralist state – the United States of America.[24] Instead Portugal closely resembled other parts of the Luso-Hispanic world, such as Spain or her former American possessions, where advanced constitutions proclaiming liberty, fraternity and equality were proclaimed in the midst of poverty, slavery and economic backwardness.

Early disputes inside the new political elite brought about a revival in fortune for traditional interests. Brazil's declaration of independence (1822) damaged liberal credibility. The 1822 constitution was not long in being scrapped after aristocratic and clerical attacks on it. Conservative and firmly royalist public figures came to rival the diverse exponents of radical jacobinism and liberalism. However, in their turn, more right-wing elements were unable to establish absolute political dominance for a long period.

Between 1820 and 1851, years of political strife in Portugal, liberalism was never totally eclipsed as a viable force. Traditionalist interests were unable to rely on a reactionary Crown as a matter of course. Nor, in times of trouble, were they able to fall back on a *regional* power base such as that possessed by the Carlists in north-east Spain. Moreover, for much of the nineteenth century, the military was a relatively liberal force: Portugal did not witness an extended period of personalist military rule at any stage after 1820. It is true that army *pronunciamentos* (pronouncements)[25] were launched against this or that ruling faction in the kaleidoscopic years following Beresford's expulsion. However, the military could often be just as confused and conflict-ridden as the multifarious political groupings fighting for power. Army divisions also tended to reflect civilian divisions, it being a long time before a corporate military identity emerged.

The 1832–34 civil war between absolutists and liberals was the decisive struggle for power in the post-1820 period, one that would determine the political orientation of the country for the following ninety years. In this conflict, Prince Miguel, the champion of Portuguese conservatism, received the support of the clergy, the provincial nobility and much of the peasantry, especially in the north, while his elder brother, Pedro, had the support of liberal interests. He could also rely on British sympathy and military backing which, in the end, proved decisive for his cause. Even before the 'War of Brothers' ended in 1834, the victorious liberals were able to launch an assault on the main stronghold of conservative power: the traditional structure of landowning. José Mouzinho da Silveira, an energetic reformer from the Alentejo, seized the property and estates of the Church and the Miguelite nobility in a lightning series of decrees enacted during 1832–33. His hope was to effect a far-reaching land reform and enrich the state by taking control of land that would have represented an invaluable source of wealth against the public debt. Instead a new class of wealthy landowners emerged who were drawn from the ranks of the liberal middle class. With the social status of land ownership conferred on it, this group had a dominant interest in political life for the rest of the century. As for the peasantry, they found it hard to believe that there had been anything approaching reform: the new legislation took away much common land while still requiring the payment of feudal dues, and inevitably their conditions tended to worsen. The Maria da Fonte uprising (1846–48), which paralysed much of the north, was a desperate affirmation of their plight. Only with some difficulty was Lisbon able to control this confused eruption of the rural underprivileged. Eventually, law and order were restored in the countryside, while, nationally, a convergence of moderate liberal and conservative opinion enabled Portugal to enter a politically far more settled phase after 1851.

Rotativismo and republicanism

1851 saw the final adjustment to the new conditions which had arisen with the collapse of the old order and the loss of Brazil. Politics and government came to be dominated by financial and agrarian oligarchs and their clients from the upper class and the upper middle class.[26] Two parties, the Regenerators and the Historicals (later known as the Progressives), alternated in power. Both were loose coalitions based on personal loyalties and local interests. Liberal and conservative labels were worn lightly. Ideological differences were of far less importance than personal or factional ones. When a party in government found it difficult to discharge its offices, the monarch offered power to the other. This dual arrangement became known as *rotativismo*.[27] On forming an administration, the incoming party usually organised elections in order to provide it with a parliamentary majority. Only one per cent of the population could vote, and no more than 4,500 people were eligible to sit in parliament. Inevitably discontent with the oligarchic political system was not long in making itself felt. In the 1860s urban intellectuals were already railing against the 'putrid peace' of Regenerationism. By the 1880s republicanism was becoming the ideal of many of the educated, politically aware, and lower middle-class elements whose status did not grant them membership of the political elite.

Nevertheless, the elitist form of liberalism which dominated politics after 1851 had not turned its back completely on a more radical past. Portugal was now a constitutional monarchy in which a few pioneering social reforms, such as the abolition of the death penalty for all civil offences (1859), were introduced. The army was still sufficiently liberal to allow someone like General Sousa Brandão, a republican and socialist, to hold important commissions.[28] Some opposition to the left of the main parties was permitted. Under a more traditional and regulatory political system, the Republican party could not have functioned so openly and the types of opposition generated would probably have been quite different.

Without overemphasising their value, the *rotativismo* era also witnessed a controlled programme of economic reforms. From the 1870s onwards the gradual accumulation of capital enabled large firms to emerge, producing textiles and manufacturing tobacco. By the 1890s the first important Portuguese industrialists and millionaires were already visible.[29] Their entrepreneurial efforts were aided by a well conceived policy of public works, aiming to produce an efficient infrastructure in which trade and industry could grow. The great damage which Portugal's transport and communications system had suffered in the upheavals of the early nineteenth century made a comprehensive public works policy a *sine non qua* for economic progress. António Fontes Pereira de Melo, the most successful politician of the *rotativismo* period, was closely associated with the modernising trend, to which he lent his name: *Fontismo*. Fontismo reacted against protectionism so that by the end of the nineteenth century Portugal was importing (mainly from Britain) twice as much as she was exporting.

The country still lacked the domestic capital, skilled labour and raw materials that were necessary for the economy to be industrialised. Just as seriously, the backward agricultural scene continued to be a burden. After 1851 crushing poverty, the absence of irrigation and proper fertilisers, emigration, primitive farm tools and frightfully low yields continued to be the hallmarks of the rural economy. While land tended to be over-exploited in northern districts, where a smallholding system later known as *minifundia* was often the dominant pattern of cultivation, huge, badly run estates dominated southern Portugal. Here the *latifundist* system of land ownership, where labourers tended the estates of local oligarchs, was very common, especially in the Alentejo province. The political power which the landed gentry wielded prevented agrarian reform far beyond the *rotativismo* era. Sometimes government intervention could be positively harmful, as in the case of the land law of 1863 which provided for *equal* division of property among heirs, thereby increasing the number of small and uneconomic farming units.[30] On other occasions the political elite deliberately killed legislation designed to alleviate rural conditions. The liberal polemicist Oliveira Martins's historic project, the Bill of Rural Development, presented to the chamber of deputies in 1887, was not even debated. Along with Alexandre Herculano, another noted man of letters in the nineteenth century, he saw the overall neglect of agriculture and predeliction for colonial adventures as the major factor in the national eclipse. However, like other thinkers who have decried the neglect of rural Portugal, Oliveira Martins and Herculano were prophets almost without a hearing in their own country.

Renewed colonial activity brought the first major crisis for the post-1851 regime. In 1890, when the Portuguese seemed to be on the verge of uniting their large African colonies of Mozambique and Angola by taking control of present-day Zimbabwe, Britain threatened war unless Portugal dropped her claim to that territory. The humiliation of what is known as the English Ultimatum badly stung the Portuguese. Many felt exceedingly proud about the empire which their late nineteenth-century explorers and soldiers were carving out in southern Africa. A credibility gap, not visible before 1890, grew up between the ruling circles of notables and the generally politicised elements in the country. By the Ultimatum, social and cultural changes had increased the politically aware to between 15 and 20 per cent of the population.[31] Teachers, journalists, small businessmen, clerks and artisans were among the new elements attracted to Portuguese republicanism and its proposals for full suffrage, separation of Church and state and, of course, the abolition of the monarchy. Perhaps the republicans' strongest appeal was to nationalism. Propagandists raised fears of Portugal becoming a British colony or a province of Spain and certainly in the towns were able to gain acceptance for the view that genuine patriotism was not synonomous with royalism.[32]

Solidarity within the elite began to erode in the 1890s, making the *rotativismo* system more difficult to operate. This was a boost for lower middle-class radicals, as was the establishment of republican rule in the two countries which enjoyed the closest cultural links with Portugal: France and Brazil. The consolidation of the third French republic in 1876 and the overthrow of the Brazilian monarchy in 1889 gave the Republican party (founded in 1880), encouragement and some degree of national respectability. Official circles in Lisbon reacted with concern particularly to the news from Brazil. Already two Portuguese generals made no secret of the fact that they were republicans. Lesser officers destined for active public careers after the disappearance of the monarchy, relate that the 1890 Ultimatum pushed many of them into the republican camp. In the Oporto military garrison feelings ran high enough for a republican revolution to be attempted in January 1891. One source reckons that 'had the movement been better organised, it could have spread to other centres and swept the monarchy away there and then'.[33] This is a doubtful assertion, especially with the higher echelons of the army (linked as they were by business and family ties with the civilian oligarchy) still mainly loyal to royal institutions. What, however, the 1891 uprising did signify was the end of a long period of settled politics.

Inevitably the Republican party benefited from the quickening pace of political life. But until the very eve of the 1910 revolution which overthrew the monarchy, it would still remain a rather small-scale force, addressing a mainly urban clientele and sometimes encountering serious downturns in activity.[34] Through some difficult years, what ultimately kept it afloat was *rotativismo*'s growing inability to provide stable government. Between 1896 and 1906 the system ceased to function as before. Differences within and between the Regenerationist and Progressive parties, formerly settled behind closed doors, were brought into the open. Both parties gave birth to dissident movements, so that by 1906 it was impossible for either to piece together a parliamentary majority. The lifetime of governments, previously fairly long, was shortened appreciably in these conditions. Finally, in May 1907, with makeshift arrangements proving only temporary expedients, a situation of absolute deadlock made the king decide to close parliament and appoint a royal dictator.

King Carlos I was not a popular monarch. His appointee, João Franco, was able but controversial. Sanctioning a dictatorship in 1907 alienated many royalists and made some Republicans decide upon extreme action: on 31 January 1908 Carlos and his eldest son, Crown Prince Lúis Filipe, were gunned down by two of them: Manuel Buiça, a teacher, and Alfredo Costa, a clerk. This was the first regicide to occur in Portugal's 800-year monarchical history. Ironically, aggrieved monarchists were implicated in the deed. In Lisbon a crowd estimated at 200,000 people turned out for the funeral of the assassins, while the king's interment was a much quieter affair.[35]

Why (in the light of past and future behaviour) did the army remain on the political sidelines during this time of protracted civilian crisis? It was not that men with political ambition did not exist within the military hierarchy. They did. Eyes were kept in particular on those officers who had won acclaim by their valorous deeds in Angola and Mozambique, where Portugal was engaged in stamping out African resistance to her rule. At home, the reputation of these colonial fighters (known as *Africanistas*), eclipsed those of querulous party bosses. One officer, Colonel Joaquim Mouzinho de Albuquerque, was a particularly renowned *Africanista* with strong authoritarian and monarchist views. However, the civilian elite was able to isolate a rogue-elephant like Mouzinho, who took his own life in 1902.

Even when alternatives to their narrow political system were being canvassed, politicians did not go in much fear of incurring the wrath of military men. In preceding generations the army had been steadily integrated into the political system. The upper ranks were generally unreceptive to republicanism as well as unswayed by authoritarian solutions. Another pillar of the establishment, the landed classes, was rendered quiescent by the fact that land reform was not a republican goal. Approaching change in the rural power structure is probably the one thing that could have led to a reactionary mobilisation during the last years of the monarchy. However, the Portuguese Republican Party was more in the tradition of the nineteenth century Iberian jacobin parties than of the left-wing republican parties which emerged in Spain during the 1930s.

After 1908 the monarchy found itself isolated and unable to counteract the republican challenge. João Franco resigned and the new king, eighteen-year-old Manuel II, was proving nervous and unsure of himself. No royalist politician was able to provide effective leadership, and the oligarchy as a whole remained exhausted and doubt-ridden, a wave of suicides having occurred among notables in the first decade of the century. By now the republicans enjoyed the solid backing of the urban intelligentsia and the lower middle class. Within the navy, many officers were impressed by republican propaganda slamming monarchical failure to win Portugal a proper place overseas. Against this backcloth, it was appropriately a naval revolt, on 3 October 1910, which initiated the first serious republican bid for power. The enfeebled royal government was in no position to offer stout resistance. The dowager queen Amélia had failed to gain any promise of Spanish help in the event of a republican uprising, while Republican representatives had already been unofficially informed during a visit to the Foreign Office in London that the alliance was between nations, not regimes, and that British intervention was out of the question. However, it is unwise to believe that the rebels' victory, which came on 5 October, was a foregone conclusion. For throughout the course of the revolution, Republican forces were outnumbered. Counting monarchist units and the civil police, the government had 3,500 troops to fight 450 republicans.[36] However, within many so-called loyalist regiments, offensive military activity was severely restricted by junior officers and sergeants refusing to obey instructions from their superiors.

Notes

1 Salvador de Madariaga, *Spain*, Jonathan Cape, London, 1946, p. 240.
2 Stanley G. Payne, *A History of Spain and Portugal*, Vol. I, University of Wisconsin Press, Madison, Wis., 1973, p. 113.
3 Eugene K. Keefe, *Area Handbook for Portugal*, Foreign Area Studies, American University, Washington, DC, 1977, p. 16.
4 Payne, *op. cit.*, p. 113.
5 *Ibid.*, p. 129.
6 J. H. Plumb, introduction to C. R. Boxer, *The Portuguese Seaborne Empire, 1415–1825*, Hutchinson, London, 1969, p. xxiv.
7 A. H. de Oliveira Marques, *História de Portugal*, Vol. I, *Das origens às revoluções liberais*, Palas Editores, Lisbon, 1976 (6th edition), p. 359.
8 Payne, *op. cit.*, p. 198.
9 *Ibid.*, p. 200.
10 *Metrópole:* European or mainland Portugal, excluding the Atlantic islands and former colonies.
11 Oliveira Marques, *op. cit.*, p. 361.
12 Payne, *op. cit.*, pp. 238–9.
13 Boxer, *op. cit.*, p. 110.
14 Oliveira Marques, *op. cit.*, p. 570.
15 Anthony Rhodes, 'The Marquis of Pombal, a dictator of Portugal'. *Encounter* (London), July 1976, p. 18.

16 *Ibid.*, p. 21.
17 V. G. Kiernan, 'The Old Alliance: England and Portugal', *Socialist Register 1973*, Merlin Press, London, 1974, p. 267.
18 Rhodes, *op. cit.*, p. 20.
19 *Ibid.*, p. 22–3.
20 A. H. de Oliveira Marques, *História de Portugal*, Vol. II, *Das revoluções liberais aos nossos dias*, Palas Editores, Lisbon, 1976 (3rd edition), p. 61.
21 Tom Gallagher, 'The Theory and Practice of Portuguese Authoritarianism: Salazar, the Right, and the Portuguese Military, 1926–1968', Ph.D. Thesis, University of Manchester, 1978, p. 2.
22 Stanley G. Payne, *A History of Spain and Portugal*, Vol. II, University of Wisconsin Press, Madison, Wis., 1973, p. 518.
23 *Ibid.*, p. 558.
24 Stanislav Andreski, *Parasitism and Subversion. The Case of Latin America*, Weidenfeld & Nicolson, London, 1966, p. 125.
25 A *pronunciamento* is a significant military uprising, and the term came into increasingly common use in the Luso-Hispanic world after 1820.
26 Douglas L. Wheeler, *Republican Portugal. A Political History, 1910–1926*, University of Wisconsin Press, Madison, Wis., 1978, p. 26.
27 *Rotativismo:* literally a system whereby two major parties rotate in office.
28 David Ferreira, 'General Sousa Brandão', in Joel Serrão (ed.), *Dicionário de História de Portugal*, Vol. IV, Iniciativas Editorais, Lisbon, 1971, p. 380.
29 Oliveira Marques, *op. cit.*, p. 13.
30 Tom Gallagher, 'O salazarismo e a agricultura: prudência ou negligência', *Diário de Notícias*, Lisbon, 17 July 1979, p. 7.
31 Payne, *op. cit.*, p. 552.
32 In a polemical burst V. G. Kiernan argues that Portugal had more to gain from occupation by Spain, which would have been burdensome but would have brought useful anti-feudal, anti-liberal reforms, than from occupation by Wellington, which was burdensome without holding out any chance of progress. He also quotes favourably a nineteenth-century Spaniard who believed that Portugal would have fared less badly at the hands of her long-time ally if actually incorporated into the British empire. See Kiernan, *op. cit.*, pp. 268 and 270.
33 Charles E. Nowell, *Portugal*, Prentice-Hall, Englewood Cliffs, N.J., 1973, p. 126.
34 Vasco Pulido Valente, *O poder e o povo. A revolução de 1910*, Publicações Dom Quixote, Lisbon, 1974, p. 63.
35 António Viana Martins, *Da I República ão Estado Novo*, Iniciativas Editorais, Lisbon, 1976, p. 14.
36 Douglas L. Wheeler, 'The Portuguese revolution of 1910', *Journal of Modern History*, 44, 2, June 1972, p. 181.

2

Portugal at the crossroads
The parliamentary republic, 1910–26

Republican Portugal, 1910–17

In 1910 Portugal became the third European republic after France and Switzerland. During 1976 a government publication described the Republican regime in Lisbon as Europe's first left-wing administration this century.[1] Certainly it was radical for its day, when all but three European states were under various forms of monarchical rule. However, the privileged sectors of the community were not noticeably alarmed by the 1910 upheaval: by now a great many notables had concluded that the monarchy was simply not worth preserving, since it was signally failing to provide stability. Republican spokesmen were also careful to emphasise that the constitutional upheaval was not the opening shot of a social revolution. The alliance with Britain was reaffirmed. Foreign and home investors were assured that the new government would honour its obligations. Many monarchists were even able to transfer their loyalties to new Republican groups in the hope that they could continue to play a role in national decision-making.

Acute governmental instability rapidly emerged as another hangover from the royalist era. In its thirty years of existence before 1910, no single individual had emerged to take overall charge of the Republican party and provide it with sound leadership. This was rather unusual for a land where *personalismo*, or the allegiance to persons over ideas and institutions, has been recognised as a major feature of national political culture. More predictably, the doctrine of republicanism was too vague and ephemeral to prevent serious differences breaking out among Republican politicians once the party's primary goal had been achieved in October 1910. In the space of just over a year the Republican party split asunder and three new formations emerged, the Evolutionist party, led by António José de Almeida, the Unionists, whose leader was Brito Camacho, and the Democratic party, which kept the PRP initials of the old party body as well as capturing its political machine.

Violent disagreement about what the Republic's attitude should be to the conservative, pro-royalist Catholic Church was a major cause of the split as well as an indication that the new political elite would be unable to avoid the internal cleavages which had ravaged its predecessor. Social radicals, grouped in the new PRP, had singled out the religious world for early attack, viewing the clergy (especially the religious orders) as the principal enemies of liberal individualist thought. Afonso Costa, a leader of the PRP, who hailed from a village in clerical Beira Baixa province, actually forecast an end to Catholicism in several generations when speaking in Braga, the religious seat of Portugal, during 1911.[2] As minister of justice Costa directed a vociferous anticlerical campaign culminating in the formal separation of Church and state during that year. Religious orders were suppressed, it became illegal to wear clerical garb in public, religious instruction in schools was curtailed, and clergy who quit the priesthood were offered governmental jobs. Over ten per cent left the priesthood during the republic's first years, but ultimately the Church was to survive the official vendetta against organised religion: while religion continued to decline in social importance in the towns, the Catholic faith would continue to hold its own in the northern countryside, where the bulk of the population was to be found.

Meanwhile, national elections were held eight months after the revolution which, it was hoped, would usher in a less disruptive phase in political life. In the new parliament, certain professions and institutions were heavily represented. The medical profession, followed by the military, returned the largest bloc of deputies. Lawyers came closely behind, followed by the academic and teaching professions.[3] The intelligentsia as a whole had many more elected members than its size warranted. Businessmen, workers and farmers' representatives were little in evidence. Very few deputies had sat in parliament before, monarchists having boycotted the elections.

The enactment of a new republican constitution had preceded elections. The 1911 constitution rejected presidentialism or decentralised power and vested major power in the legislative branch of government, leaving a feeble executive. In a situation where party discipline was already proving weak, this was a recipe for short-lived government and long-term political instability. If Portugal had been economically and socially more developed, the pitfalls of competitive democracy which this constitutional arrangement exposed might have been avoided. In 1910 one Republican leader, Basílio Teles, was already aware of the dangers involved in proceeding immediately from oligarchical rule to multi-party democracy. He argued that 'the Republican party would have to instal a revolutionary dictatorship of sufficient length . . . to remove the wreckage accumulated by the folly of constitutional monarchy'.[4] When his views went unheeded, Teles (influential in Republican circles before 1910) thereafter refused to involve himself in party politics. Other Republican politicians would follow his example in later years, but initially some stability was provided by the emergence of Costa's new PRP as the strongest party in parliament. The PRP was a paradoxical radical party which pursued a vendetta against the Church and hosted an international conference of freethinkers in Lisbon while leaving women disenfranchised and the working class underprivileged. Its socially radical but economically conservative stance was carefully pitched to suit the tastes of the urban lower middle class, which provided the backbone of its support. Perhaps the most popular PRP government was the one Afonso Costa headed between January 1913 and February 1914. This government is memorable for being the only one in the Republican era to balance the budget, a feat which Costa achieved for two years in succession through careful costing and a refusal to grant economic concessions to the working class. Generally, the middle-class republican regime could afford to spurn proletarian demands, since the working class was small and dispersed in many small-scale factories and workshops. Collective industrial action, rare before 1910, would increase during the Republic but the radical left would never be able to achieve a major political breakthrough, since workers had come under the sway of anti-political anarcho-syndicalist leaders.

Besides, with a new electoral law, Costa was able to disenfranchise much of the working class by reducing the electorate by more than half from 850,000 to 400,000, restricting the vote to literate males only. From the PRP's point of view, the enfranchisement of women (allegedly susceptible to clerical influence), the urban working class (allegedly prey to demagogy) and the rural peasantry (allegedly manipulable by reaction) was undesireable.[5] Portuguese republicanism was proving itself in practice to be a petty-bourgeois movement intent on carrying out reforms from which the lower middle class would mainly benefit. Some urban-oriented reforms were introduced by a somewhat broader ruling elite. However, when downtrodden farm labourers launched a series of rural strikes in the Alentejo in 1911–12, republican ministers reacted with almost as much hostility towards those peasant demands for social justice as the Salazar dictatorship did later on.

In the rural north, the bulk of the population was treated just as disdainfully by the PRP. Political instability, an acute shortage of funds, and the urban representative's disinclination to turn his gaze to the other Portugal which lay beyond Lisbon and Oporto, effectively prevented all change.[6] The framers of the 1911 constitution went back on a Republican promise to introduce a genuine system of municipal government which could have fostered political awareness in small-town and rural Portugal. Since the rural masses were disfranchised in national elections, there was no chance of a fairly progressive peasant party springing up as happened before 1930 in countries like Romania and Bulgaria which had even steeper levels of illiteracy than Portugal. Whether rural Portugal could have taken such a positive direction before 1926 is frankly doubtful.

Nevertheless, the Republican leaders deserve black marks for not letting some light into the peasants' enclosed and superstitious world, their inaction later helping rather than hindering the traditionalist enemies of the liberal republic.

However, in the short term it was the political system which exposed the weakness of the new regime. The excessive weight of parliament in national life accounted for much instability, parliament sitting for seven to ten months during most years. Often governments entirely dependent on parliamentary majorities fell because of petty disputes, personal quarrels or whimsical actions.[7] Even when the PRP had a majority the turnover of governments was rapid, since it functioned as a coalition of different factions, which was headed by a directory rather than an elected leader; Costa's government collapsed in 1914 after one year in office, it having alienated diverse interests including the military. Officers had been annoyed by his July 1913 electoral law which debarred all active military personnel from standing for parliament. The army had already reacted unfavourably towards PRP efforts to weaken the military hierarchy by granting privileges to sergeants and noncommissioned officers, groupings which then strongly supported the party. More senior elements tended to side with the conservative Evolutionist and Unionist parties and were drawn into increasingly bitter quarrels between these two and the PRP over the spoils of office and other contentious issues. In 1914 military opinion was deeply angered when a general was set upon and beaten severely by a vigilante group. This happened to several other officers, and inevitably civil–military relations grew tense. Although no attempt was being made to redefine corporate military interests, officers now cast increasing doubt upon the validity of civilian dominance in political life.

With competitive politics occurring in the absence of consensus or mutually agreed ground rules between the parties, the chance of a serious rift with the military increased. In January 1915 conservative elements in the Portuguese military finally crossed the Rubicon and imposed a period of military rule at the request of Manuel de Arriaga, president since 1911. A veteran republican politician, he was keen to reduce the influence of the PRP even if it meant acting unconstitutionally. Thus the accession to power of military officers reflected as badly on the Republican political family as it did on the military. Continued political in-fighting would ensure the repetition of such maverick behaviour. However, some time was to elapse before republican failures would cement military opinion against the parliamentary regime. During May 1915 pro-republican junior army officers, sergeants and naval officers were able to overthrow the conservative *ditablanda* (mild dictatorship) of the elderly General Joaquim Pimenta de Castro.

The first abortive attempt of some officers to dispense with party politicians would not ultimately weaken military determination to intervene forcefully in politics. Back in power after 1915, the civilian parties were unable to endow parliamentary rule with enough national legitimacy to hope to offset praetorian incursions. In 1916 Portugal's decision to enter the First World War on the side of the Allies was to cause escalating discontent within the top reaches of the army. In terms of training, equipment and numbers the Portuguese army was ill-designed to participate in a continental war of such dimensions. Fears that Portugal's colonies would be bargaining pawns in negotiations between the major combatants seem to have been the chief reason Afonso Costa (premier again in 1916–17) had for intervening.[8] Over a period of two and a half years more than 200,000 men were called up, a major mobilisation for a poor country of then less than six million people; the majority were illiterate peasants from the land who resignedly accepted conscription. In city and town, however, anti-war sentiment drastically reduced government support. Food shortages, soaring prices and reports of heavy casualties robbed the PRP of much of its urban following and paved the way for a fresh military assault on civilian political power. The bid, on 5 December 1917, took the form of a more broadly based military *coup* under the leadership of Bernardino Sidónio Pais, Portugal's last ambassador to Germany.

Sidónio Pais and the New Republic

Because of its brief life span, few people now remember that the Pais regime was Europe's first modern *republican* dictatorship. The collapse of central and east European monarchy and the ineffectiveness of inter-war democracy would help to throw up numerous examples of this form of secular authoritarianism in the 1920–45 period. But, before the Treaty of Versailles, it was Portugal which offered the first trial example of authoritarian rule in the full republican context, a form of government hitherto confined to Latin America.

The rule of Sidónio Pais was in the best personalist tradition. Capitalising on a youthful public image and a charismatic personality, he sought to construct as wide a popular following as possible. Inside the army, his power base was located among young officers who had received their commissions after the 1910 revolution. Too young to have directly known of the failings of *rotativismo*, their formative years of military preparation were spent in an atmosphere of national political confusion which made many of these young upper-class soldiers impatient with the new republican *status quo*. Slightly older officers, educated before the revolution, knew that a good deal of Portugal's problems antedated the

Republic, but many of them, embittered by the national conduct of the war, proved in no state of mind to rally to the defence of the civilian regime.

Tapping the discontent to be found at various levels of the army, Pais, an army major (who had been minister of finance for seven months in 1911–12), found himself able to seize power. In so far as he had a defined programme, the new president's main goal seems to have been the creation of a semi-authoritarian political system where the legislature would be firmly subordinate to the executive. One of his first acts was to proscribe the PRP and give important latitude to monarchist and Catholic groups. Unlike other political phases of the 1910–26 period, businessmen held major portfolios.[9] Moderate republicans also came within the umbrella of the *sidonista* regime, which was labelled the New Republic; Basílio Teles and the physician Egas Moniz (who in 1949 became the first Portuguese to win a Nobel prize) were the two most prominent Republican collaborators. Conservative certainly, this experiment was not avowedly counter-revolutionary, since Pais was anxious to retain most of the non-contentious trappings of the republican system. His immediate background was also hardly that of an out-and-out traditionalist. He had been a republican activist before 1910 and, for a brief while in 1918, revolutionary syndicalists were even prepared to co-operate with him. In May 1918, under a system of universal manhood suffrage, an electoral majority backed Pais although a great many of the opposition parties had abstained. Until internal difficulties began to plague the regime Sidónio Pais probably had a greater impact on the public than any other politician in the pre-1926 period.

Pais's hopes for a moderate political consensus around his presidency may have begun to come unstuck when moderate republicans, suspecting him of Bonapartist intentions, went over to the opposition. He became known as the Consul-King and his ambitions may have extended to a semi-monarchical form of rule akin to the plebiscatory empire of Napoleon III. Like the French emperor, Sidónio had a republican past and had participated in a major anti-royalist revolution before succeeding to power. Like him, Sidónio can be characterised as a modern political dictator somewhat ahead of his time. In the second half of 1918 Portugal was briefly a laboratory for the kind of politics that would follow after the final collapse of republicanism in 1926. Abandoned by his republican allies, Pais came to rely increasingly on upper-class youths, mainly army officers, students and sons of landowners, whose political philosophy was Integralism, a traditionalist creed perhaps best summed up by what it opposed: liberalism, individualism, socialism and any other doctrine thought to deny God, the family and traditionalist conservative precepts. Founded in 1914, the Lusitanian Integralist movement was the first sign that the unhappy republican experiment was producing a nationalist right-wing backlash. Though Pais never publicly embraced the ideals of his right-wing helpers, his regime, with its increasingly far-rightist orientation, deserves to be regarded as one of the chief forerunners of the corporative state eventually established by Dr Salazar in the 1930s. Foreign models, principally Mussolini's Italy, have nearly always been designated as the chief prototypes of Salazar's rule. However, the New Republic's senate, designed by Integralist leaders, is a clear forerunner of Salazar's *câmara corporativa* (corporative chamber). So perhaps it is time the New Republic's brief life ceased to obscure the fact that limited corporativist drives were a feature of political life in Portugal not only after but before 1926.

The New Republic had an acknowledged leader, but without a strong administrative base Pais was ultimately unable to consolidate his rule. Even talented right-wingers proved wary of accepting office. In August 1918 António de Oliveira Salazar, still an obscure young economics professor, refused an offer to become minister of finance, pleading lack of experience.[10] More galling was the fact that most of the army was in France and the military-oriented regime was thus denied ready back-up support from the organism best able to provide an authoritarian regime with well trained cadres. The navy was much closer at hand, but this was hardly a reassuring fact, since the sea arm had offered the greatest resistance to Pais's coup and had subsequently not been won over by the regime. Lacking an effective governmental system, the New Republic floundered and was thrust into deep crisis by the Allied victory of November 1918. Sidónio had been gambling on German success and, firm in this belief, he had scaled down Portuguese commitment to the war effort. On this decision critics placed much of the blame for the devastating losses suffered by the remaining Portuguese continent when the final German offensive occurred in the spring of 1918.

On 14 December 1918 Sidónio Pais was assassinated in Lisbon while about to board a train. His killer, José Júlio da Costa, was a radical corporal in the army returned from the war, and his deed signalled the end of the *sidonista* regime.[11] Like the earlier dictatorship of João Franco (1907–08), Sidónio's rule was unable to endure in a polarised political atmosphere. Personal attributes proved only temporary expedients, although *Sidonismo* would remain a potent memory for the right in the years ahead.

The politics of chaos, 1918–26

Political stability eluded the Republican regime in its second eight-year phase to an even greater extent than before. Within weeks of Pais's murder, civil war swept northern Portugal as monarchists, led by Henrique Paiva Couceiro, made an abortive attempt to restore the Crown. Four governments then held office in 1919, and nine in 1920. In October 1921 these most strife-torn years of the entire parliamentary era were climaxed by the murder of several leading republican personalities who included António Machado Santos, the chief hero of the 1910 revolution, and António Granjó, the current prime minister. Both men were opponents of the PRP, which was then in opposition, and for a long time their murderers were thought to belong to the vigilante societies which, like the well known Carbonaria, provided strong-arm support for the party. Soon the PRP was back in office, having no liking for opposition politics for however short a spell. By now the party derived most of its strength from being able to dispense patronage and control the public exchequer. However, 1921 had undoubtedly been a turning-point in its history. Witnessing the party's reluctance to abandon office, increasing numbers of opponents resolved not to modify or revamp the PRP but to destroy it altogether.

An ailing economy exacerbated the political troubles of the republican era. Thanks to the political confusion of 1910–26 and the absence of a properly worked out development strategy, the economy virtually ground to a halt and in some years the statistical indicators showed negative readings. At no time was the Republic able to gain the support of the rich or prevent the export of capital. As before, the economic structure continued to be based on the land. Primary products such as wine, cork and fruit were the chief exports, while the main imports were iron, steel and paper. After World War I, imports were still generally twice the value of exports. Nevertheless, some signs of greater industrial expansion were shown by the increased importation of raw cotton, coal and various types of machinery. In Barreiro, which sits opposite Lisbon on the southern bank of the river Tagus, the entrepreneur Alfredo da Silva was able to create a major industrial complex which would become the largest in the Iberian peninsula.[12] Farther north, at Maceira in the district of Leiria, the industrialist Henrique Sommer built up a large cement empire during the 1920s. However, these were isolated cases, not an indication of more general economic development.

Not a lot ought to be read, either, into the expansion of Lisbon during the parliamentary era. Between 1911 and 1930 the city's population increased by 22 per cent, against 13 per cent for the country as a whole.[13] Until 1926 the PRP built up Lisbon, its political power base, at the expense of the rest of the country. New jobs were created in the bureaucracy for party supporters but resources were too scarce to allocate between squabbling factions. The republican system was unable to satisfy the material demands of newly politicised urban citizens in the absence of real economic growth. As a result, agreement on basic values and willingness to compromise – criteria necessary for the maintenance of a stable democracy – failed to emerge. Instead Portugal experienced a period of government which, one observer believes, easily qualifies as 'the most politically chaotic of any single European (and probably Luso-Hispanic) state in the twentieth century'.[14]

By the early 1920s even the urban professional and middle-class sectors were beginning to abandon the parliamentary system. Beforehand, most committed supporters of the Republic had been found in this social sector. Lawyers, teachers, civil servants, small businessmen and artisans had originally backed the Republic, hoping to claim new political rights, better economic benefits and possibly even improved social status. When their most optimistic hopes were dashed and the regime began to exhibit the drawbacks of its monarchical predecessor as well as faults that were peculiar to itself, disappointment set in. But pluralist sentiments were still strong enough among the urban middle classes to enable the PRP to make two come-backs in 1915 and 1918 after brief authoritarian interludes. Only when a decade of insipid parliamentary rule failed to provide public order and, more important, protect living standards, did a strong reaction against the regime set in among previously keen supporters. After 1920 national and local elections were characterised by massive abstentionism. Few middle-class voters felt that betterment could be provided by a parliamentary system so closely identified with political deadlock and extra-parliamentary violence.

The stranglehold the PRP maintained in elections prevented the rise of a reform movement on the left, right or middle of the political spectrum. The Seara Nova (New Harvest) movement, founded in 1921 by progressive intellectuals, failed to make a major political impact, while later defectors from the PRP were unable to erode its electoral hegemony when they set up new parties. By the beginning of the 1920s disenchantment with what had become a dangerous as well as a frustrating calling had led to the early retirement of leading Republican politicians in all parties. The controversial Afonso Costa, who had proved himself a talented and energetic administrator, went into Parisian exile after 1919, disregarding many calls from his own party to return, although he continued to be elected to parliament for a Lisbon seat. High office fell increasingly to inexperienced and mediocre talents, many of whom were attracted to politics by material considerations. These were important. A large share of the national income passed through governmental hands and was open to interception. Lucrative fortunes were made by some politicians, while inflation, downward financial returns and the general climate of uncertainty caused businessmen acute difficulties. Many would go to the wall, according to figures which show service employment increasing from

22 to 27 per cent of the total between 1911 and 1930 and industrial employment falling from 21 to 17 per cent during the same period.[15]

What political options lay open for those urban middle-class elements fast abandoning liberal politics? Elsewhere, a middle class in flight from pluralist values would shortly fuel the rise of a right-wing mass movement in Italy and Germany. In Portugal, although the scale of middle-class discontent was no less intense, a parallel scenario would fail to unfold. Here the middle class was too small and economically marginal to give rise to an authoritarian mass movement along mid-European fascist lines. Already bourgeois political weakness had been highlighted by the failure, after 1910, of middle-class interests to underwrite a stable political system. It would be naive to ascribe this failure entirely to the folly and baseness of the major politicians. Party divisions, though miscroscopic, often mirrored larger economic rivalries in Portuguese society. One observer considers the mid-1920s to have been a time when 'several groups with contradictory economic interests were fighting each other in the political field'.[16] Agrarian capital, the professions, banking, commerce and industrial capital were the leading protagonists, each in pursuit of different sectional interests. None had been able to exercise power alone but, viewing the mounting cost of political in-fighting, each was gradually coming round to acceptance of a united supra-factional solution.

The middle class began to embrace traditional values rather than look to radical solutions to Portugal's political impasse. Even clericalism lost much of its stigma in the 1920s. When Guerra Junqueiro, the anticlerical republican poet, returned to the practice of Catholicism before his death, his conversion made a considerable impression[17] but it was merely one of many indications that the spirit of the age in Portugal was ceasing to be liberal and secular.

The end of liberalism

As liberal democratic values became increasingly discredited, the appeal of anti-parliamentary groups grew steadily. Lusitanian Integralism, founded in 1914, had been one of the first overtly counter-revolutionary movements to emerge. Beforehand, in 1900, Jacinto Cândido, leader of the Portuguese Nationalist Party, had unfurled a programme for a conservative, right-wing government which included provisions for administrative decentralisation and a corporative system of political representation in which the *rotativismo* parties would have no place.[18] However, it was only after the republic began to exhibit grave failings that right-wing ideas came to acquire a sizeable following. The group of intellectuals behind Lusitanian Integralism, notably António Sardinha, Luís de Almeida Braga, Pequito Rebelo and Hipólito Raposo, set out to convert the elite, particularly the young, to their traditionalist, illiberal and ultra-nationalist cause. Many of their ideas were derived from the French right, particularly Charles Maurras, the leader of Action Française. Like Maurras, they believed that a monarchy was a vital prerequisite for a regenerated land. However, the exiled Manuel II, remaining basically loyal to liberal constitutional ideals, did not fit the part they wrote for him[19] and, increasingly, the royal question produced divisions and finally schism within the Integralist ranks. The death of the movement's most original thinker, António Sardinha, in 1925 was a blow from which it did not recover. However, Integralism had already played a vital role in radicalising much of the post-1910 generation of upper bourgeois youth in an authoritarian direction. Its political values also penetrated the military world, where several hundred Integralist-inspired officers were to be found by the close of the republic.

Another small but increasingly influential right-wing pressure group was the Academic Centre for Christian Democracy (CADC). Founded in 1901, it was revived in 1912 after a long period of inactivity, by right-wing Catholic intellectuals, including the two men who were destined to be the twin pillars of Church and state in dictatorial Portugal: António de Oliveira Salazar and Manuel Gonçalves Cerejeira. 'Piety, study and action' was its motto, and it stimulated the development of a politically involved Catholic intelligentsia when anticlericalism was at its height in the new republic. Later the Church as a whole was able to make a strong come-back following the miracle of Fátima, which is reputed to have occurred in this small Portuguese hamlet on 13 May 1917. Between May and October that year the Virgin Mary is supposed to have appeared six times to three children, Lúcia de Jesus, aged ten, and Francisco and Jacinta Marto, both somewhat younger. She disclosed prophecies to the older one and soon throngs of peasants from all over central and northern Portugal were visiting the site of the apparition, Fátima becoming a means whereby a greatly weakened Church could mobilise the laity and launch a spiritual revival.

In the political realm, a Catholic party, the Centro Católico Português (founded in 1917) won seats at every parliamentary election held after 1918. In 1921 José Maria Braga da Cruz, a notable lay Catholic who was to hold important offices in the dictatorial era, was elected deputy for Braga, receiving more votes than any other candidate in the country.[20] António Lino Neto, the Centro's leader, was an energetic and moderate politician who condemned dictatorship and right-wing *coup* attempts and refused to back the monarchy against the republic. The CADC, too, wisely chose to remain neutral on this issue while showing itself increasingly hostile to parliamentary and electoral struggle. In the mid-1920s António de Oliveira Salazar confidently predicted that 'we are drawing near to that moment in political and social evolution in which a political party based on the individual, the citizen, or the elector will no longer have sufficient reason for existence'.[21] Two more right-wing movements had by now emerged to complete the quartet of civilian groupings massed against the liberal republic. In the early 1920s the conservative, authoritarian National Crusade of Nun' Álvares Pereira came into being while, more important, businessmen and landowners were able to bury previous differences in 1925 and form a Union of Economic Interests, which was soon dabbling in *coup* attempts.[22]

A major spur for this employers' alliance was provided by a series of progressive governments in office between December 1923 and July 1925 which decided to implement a set of relatively advanced policies. Led by politicians who defied the PRP machine and angered conservative urban and rural opinion, four short-lived governments discussed fundamental reforms in agriculture and education and put into effect important banking, taxation and social welfare reforms. The 1923–24 government of Álvaro de Castro was particularly energetic, and the efforts of him and his colleagues in the Seara Nova group, and also the Left Democratic Party, provide clear evidence that by no means every Republican politician was motivated by petty, personal considerations. However, lacking a parliamentary majority, the reformist ministries of 1923–25 were unable to survive and the spectre of social revolution which they had raised helped unite the forces of counter-revolution when previously these had been somewhat fragmented.

Hitherto the monarchist question had badly divided the right, exacerbating tensions which, in 1918, had helped bring about the collapse of the *sidonista* dictatorship. The monarchist cleavage in fact weakened the right during the greater part of the parliamentary republic's lifetime and helps to explain how the storm-tossed regime was able to last as long as sixteen years in power. Eventually, in the 1920s, a serious rethink over tactics seems to have led to the conclusion that dogged adherence to the monarchy was hampering the anti-liberal cause by making it too particularist. Thereafter, many doctrinaire rightists quietly abandoned monarchist restoration as a public objective. This move made the traditionalist right acceptable to many middle-class urban elements forsaking liberal political values out of political frustration or as a result of a decline in their living standards. As the young failed to embrace their parents' values, their idealism instead finding an outlet in nationalism, the membership of parties declined sharply. Among literate republicans there was a massive swing to the right in the 1920s. The concept of liberal democracy was assailed in the press and favourable coverage was given to authoritarian governments newly installed in Italy (1922), Spain (1923) and Greece (1925). Ominously for the professional politicians, calls for a military dictatorship began to emanate not just from the right but from other points along the political spectrum. The cry of 'The army to power' was, of course, heard at its loudest within the armed forces themselves. The experience of the officer corps during the First World War in Africa and Europe (the two theatres where Portugal had fought on the Allied side) had sown the seeds for a new eruption of militarism in the upper echelons of the army. Casting aside memories of previous unsuccessful forays into politics, many officers came to believe that the conduct of politicians had made them unfit to remain in charge of the nation and that only the army could save Portugal from impending national disaster. Naturally, altruistic and patriotic motives were not alone responsible for turning the army completely against the Republican regime. Inside the army, professional grievances helped to alienate full-time soldiers who might not normally have taken much interest in politics, thereby greatly widening the scope for outright military disaffection.

The poor state of military equipment, a shortage of uniforms for recruits, and the fact that the army was so run-down that it could not undergo manoeuvres, even less take to the field in real battle, were particularly wounding to professional military pride. Among senior ranks there was much bitterness over the fact that salaries for junior officers and sergeants had risen at a much faster rate than for colonels and generals. Between 1911 and 1922 noncommissioned officers and junior officers received pay increases which ranged between 420 and 1,200 per cent while officers from major to general had been granted rises which only ranged from 144 to 306 per cent.[23] By 1926 the purchasing power of top salaries was reduced to half what it had been in 1910, a state of affairs much commented upon by the increasingly reactionary Lisbon press. One newspaper, *A Época*, revealed that some generals were ashamed to send their children to school because they lacked proper footwear.[24] Other senior officers, in order to augment their income, had to suffer the humiliation of doing part-time work in offices where their superiors were sometimes lieutenants and sergeants. This was a situation calculated to inflame top military opinion against the ruling PRP politicians. By the mid-1920s the largest republican party was the object of intense hatred among conservative officers, who accused it of having tried to do away with the army on a number of occasions, of having callously sent it to Flanders to serve as fodder for German guns, and of having undermined internal discipline by boosting the authority of sergeants and corporals.

By 1925 between 300 and 500 out of 2,000 regular officers were fully agreed on the need to destroy the existing regime. The depth of military alienation was shown after two abortive *coups* on 18 April and 19 July 1925. Soldiers not implicated in the rebellion volunteered to become defendants as an act of solidarity with the officers in the dock, while the military prosecutor trying the conspirators (General Óscar Carmona) refused to discharge his responsibilities and recommended that they be acquitted. This sensational trial publicly revealed the contempt in which civilian politicians were held by the army. In January 1926, not long after the defendants had been acquitted by a military jury, a new military conspiracy was hatched to overthrow the parliamentary republic. By now, the prestige of the regime had sunk to a further low ebb owing to a bank scandal (the Angola & Metropole: one of the largest financial scandals there had been in Europe) as well as to state attempts to create a government monopoly in the tobacco trade.

Against this backcloth junior officers, with the support of higher-ranking soldiers, drew up their plans for a new revolt in the winter of 1925 and spring of 1926. The first revolutionary *junta* (committee) had been formed in the northern city of Braga on 10 January 1926 by Lieutenant João Pereira de Carvalho.[25] This young officer, like most of the 'captains and lieutenants of 1926', would not play a major role in politics during the lifetime of the dictatorship. However, the painstaking preparations of young right-wing officers ensured that the 1926 revolt would be a massive military movement against which organised opposition would hardly be feasible. So many garrisons were drawn into the *conjura* (conspiracy) that sectors of the public were quickly made aware that officers were planning to strike against the government 'weeks before the conspiracy moved into the streets'.[26]

Undoubtedly the 1926 revolt easily qualifies as being the biggest and most publicised conspiracy in the history of the First Republic. Yet the government of António Maria da Silva, in office since November 1925, appeared unable to save itself even though it knew of the unfolding conspiracy by spring 1926. As the cabinet insisted that calm reigned and the army would remain loyal the conspirators finalised their plans and looked around for a senior military figure who could take charge of the movement during the course of the *coup*. Military prestige, a non-royalist background and a relatively neutral political past were regarded as vital in order to win over as much of the army as possible during the actual period of the take-over. General João Sinel de Cordes, perhaps the most senior figure in the conspiracy, was disqualified from overall command because he still remained a self-confessed royalist. Among a heterogeneous band of several hundred plotters who included members of the Integralist movement, non-aligned republicans, and military supporters of various opposition parties, none carried sufficient personal weight to win the approval of their colleagues. After the merits and demerits of various outside candidates had been considered, an invitation was finally extended to General Manuel Gomes da Costa, a sixty-three-year-old war hero who had been in the public gaze since at least 1918.

Gomes da Costa consented to lead the military movement on 25 May 1926. Three days later, at 8 a.m. on 28 May, backed by the local garrison in Braga, he declared his intention of overthrowing the Lisbon government and winning support from all army regiments. Braga, the religious capital of Portugal, was an unusual place from which to launch a *coup*. Each of the successful power bids of twentieth-century Portuguese politics in which force was employed (the 1910 revolution, Sidónio Pais's *coup* of 1917, and the 25 April 1974 *coup*) had been centred on Lisbon, the capital. However, in 1926 the rebels deeply distrusted Lisbon, the main stronghold of the PRP, and preferred to strike out from provincial Portugal, where disenchantment with the Republican regime was far stronger.

In other ways the 28 May movement was also distinctive. At least until the consummation of the uprising, it was clear that no single officer or personality was bidding for power through the efforts of junior conspirators. The 1926 revolt was a collective military effort, unlike earlier *coup* attempts in the Republican era, which in several instances were motivated by the powerful ambition of a given officer. May 28 was also noteworthy owing to the almost complete absence of civilian participation. Previous *conjuras* (and conspiracies in the Salazar era), were often joint civil–military enterprises. In the spring of 1926 junior officers went out of their way to prevent major civilian involvement, largely because many of them distrusted civilian politicians *per se*. At the same time the organisers excluded lower ranks, such as sergeants and corporals, from the *coup*. Given the authoritarian elitist perspective of many of the military rebels, it was perhaps natural that they would wish to confine the conspiracy to the officer corps. There were also practical reasons for doing so. Residual support for the Republican regime was still strongest among sergeants and NCOs. If these groups had been made privy to the plot, then it might have been betrayed in such a way that the government could have tried to organise some effective resistance.

The *coup* was in fact bloodless and resistance was minimal. Learning that the military movement was spreading rapidly in every direction, Premier da Silva resigned with the cabinet on 29 May. The last premier of the liberal republic, da Silva had been head of government longer and more often (six times in all) than any other figure in the parliamentary era. However, the total length of time he spent as prime minister was no more than twenty-nine months all told. It is perhaps singularly appropriate that the parliamentary republic went out with a man whose own political career epitomised the profoundly unsettled nature of political life in Portugal from 1910 to 1926.

Nevertheless, in the wake of the *coup*, it was not readily apparent that a major watershed in Portuguese politics had been crossed with the success of this particular military revolt. Seeing the manner in which the PRP government collapsed in the face of the military's challenge, members of the public were persuaded that the power and influence of the party had been broken perhaps irretrievably. But, at least in the short term, there was no general feeling that the republic was being dismantled or that nearly a century of liberally inclined government was drawing to a close. Within the conspiratorial ranks, officers, including those who were nominal monarchists, were reluctant to discuss the possibility of abandoning the Republic, both before and after the *coup*. Few Portuguese, except for diehard rightists, believed that the existence of the monarchy could have made any notable difference to the course of national life after 1910. Among the conspirators few, except for the Integralists, set their sights on a thoroughgoing counter-revolution. In staging a symbolic march on Lisbon after 28 May, Gomes da Costa knew that he was emulating a similar dramatic gesture made by Mussolini in 1922, but the programme of this politically naive high officer was one of national salvation and unity, not Luso-fascism. The Portuguese Communist Party, which was in conference during the *coup*, was actually able to carry on its deliberations without any hindrance from the military,[27] for in essence the upheaval of 1926 was a violent reaction against the excesses of a middle-class civilian regime, not a pre-emptive strike against encroaching red revolution. Even supporters of the Left Democratic Party joyfully demonstrated in the Chiado, Lisbon's main shopping throughfare, in the aftermath of the *coup*, unaware that the action which had extinguished one tyranny would shortly give rise to a far more ruthless and lasting one.

Notes

1   *Portugal Informação*, October–November 1976, Ministry of Social Communications, Lisbon, 1976, pp. 38–9.
2   Wheeler, *Republican Portugal*, p. 69.
3   Payne, *Spain and Portugal*, p. 560.
4   Carlos Ferrão, *História da Ia República*, Terre Livre, Lisbon, 1976, p. 32.
5   Richard Robinson, *Contemporary Portugal. A History*, Allen & Unwin, London, 1979, p. 36.
6   Tom Gallagher, 'Peasant conservatism in an Agrarian setting: Portugal, 1900–1975', *Iberian Studies*, 6, 2, autumn 1977, p. 61.
7   Oliveira Marques, *História de Portugal*, I, p. 261.
8   Carlos Ferrão states that during the Anglo-German naval talks of 1912–13 the Asquith government had already offered a large swathe of Portugal's colonial empire to Germany in return for a halt in the construction of the German naval fleets deemed a threat to the hegemony of Great Britain on the high seas. See Ferrão, *op. cit.*, p. 95.
9   José Freire Antunes, *A desgraça da República na ponte das baionetes*, Livraria Bertrand, Lisbon, 1978, p. 66.
10 Wheeler, *op. cit.*, p. 140.
11 João Medina, 'O homen que matou Sidónio Pais', *História*, 10, August 1979, p.

44.
12 Oliveira Marques, *op. cit.*, p. 195.
13 *Ibid.*, p. 186.
14 Stanley G. Payne, in Graham and Makler (eds.), *Contemporary Portugal. The Revolution and its Antecedents*, University of Texas Press, Austin and London, 1979, p. 345.
15 Stanley G. Payne, *History of Spain and Portugal*, Vol. II, 1973, p. 574.
16 Bruno da Ponte, *The Last to Leave. Portuguese Colonialism in Africa: an Introductory Outline*, International Defence and Aid Fund, London, 1974, p. 11.
17 Edgar Prestage, 'Reminiscences of Portugal', in H. V. Livermore (ed.), *Portugal and Brazil. An Introduction*, Clarendon Press, Oxford, 1953, p. 6.
18 Wheeler, *op. cit.*, p. 12.
19 Robinson, *op. cit.*, p. 40.
20 Manuel Braga da Cruz, *As origens da democracia cristã e salazarismo*, Editorial Presença/Gabinete de Investigações Sociais, Lisbon, 1980, p. 282.
21 Philippe C. Schmitter, 'The impact and meaning of "non-competitive, non-free and insignificant" elections in authoritarian Portugal, 1933–1974', in Guy Hermet (ed.), *Elections without Choice*, Macmillan, London, 1978, p. 150.
22 Nun' Álvares Pereira was a brilliant military leader who played a major part in the revolution of 1383 and later joined the Carmelite Order.
23 Wheeler, *op. cit.*, pp. 189–90.
24 José António Saraiva, '28 de Maio: as verdades e os mitos', *Expresso (review section)*, Lisbon, 28 May 1979, p. 6.
25 Arnaldo Madureira, *O 28 de Maio. Elementos para a sua compreensão*, I. *Na génese do Estado Novo*, Editorial Presença, Lisbon, 1978, p. 47.
26 Wheeler, *op. cit.*, pp. 189–90.
27 Romeu Costa Reis and Manuel Rendeiro Júnior, 'Documento 28 de Maio 1926: como começou meio século da ditadura', *O Jornal*, Lisbon, 28 May 1976, p. 17.

3

Dictatorial rule
The military phase

The consequences of 28 May

As in Portugal's two other modern political watersheds – the revolution of 1910 and the later one in 1974 – the 1926 rebellion was a relatively bloodless armed uprising which triumphed over little or no opposition thanks to the existence of a political vacuum at the heart of the state. There are other interesting similarities between 1910, 1926 and 1974. A broad coalition of interests participated in each event, receiving general popular acclaim, only to dissolve in conflict once it was clear that no chance remained of the old order making a come-back. In 1926 the victorious coalition went almost the whole length of the Portuguese political spectrum. Republicans, Monarchists, Integralists, Catholics and Nationalists each had a role in the seizure of power. One of the first acts of the successful rebels was to order the closure of parliament along with the imposition of censorship; other arbitrary measures to follow would make it abundantly clear that the majority tendency in the new military regime had no residual faith in the efficacy of liberal democratic forms and democratic practice. Soldiers and politicians who could not keep up the fierce pace maintained by hard-liners at the centre of the stage after 28 May found themselves banished to limbo, their participation in the *coup* notwithstanding. But despite the initial purges and closing down of civilian institutions authorised by Portugal's military rulers, the *coup* and the consequent establishment of a dictatorship did not signify the triumph of authoritarianism over democracy: for, contrary to the claim of opposition politicians during the Salazar dictatorship, Portugal was not a freely functioning democracy in the run-up to 1926.

Civilian political primacy, rather than democracy, perished at the hands of Portuguese officers. Nevertheless, the regime that emerged from the debris of the corrupt parliamentary republic was more oppressive than anything Portugal had witnessed in the recent past. The oligarchical politicians in power for sixty years up to 1910 had never clamped down on opposition to the extent Portugal's military rulers would do after 1926. Unlike any of their predecessors, the leading figures of the regime would not even bother to pay lip service to democracy: they were determined to rule the country by force, since it appeared the only possible way to achieve orderly government and economic stability.

The tough uncompromising attitude of the new regime initially won it public support. Weary citizens felt that if an authoritarian government could provide the conditions for stability and economic recovery, it was more deserving of support than an outwardly democratic one that could ensure none of these things; a period of political quiet was widely desired. However, there was little general longing for a reactionary revolutionary, something which the 28 May *coup* prepared the way for. Defined by one observer as 'an overthrow of the legal order with the aim of re-establishing the privileges of the upper class which are disappearing or are being undermined', such a revolution by its very nature would directly benefit only a small proportion of the fairly broad cross-section of people that hailed the original seizure of power.[1] The middle sectors which, by their defection from the system, played a pivotal role in bringing the military to power stood to lose if the onslaught against liberalism went too far and produced an ultra-traditionalist authoritarian state. Throughout the previous century, much of political life had been shaped by the conflicts of upper-class and middle-class sectors, all with varying programmes. Usually, the less traditional elements had managed to ward off reaction and produce a situation of equilibrium. But by 1926 the moderate centre was dangerously compromised by its deep association with the outgoing regime, however frayed the association had become towards the end. Conservative upper-class elements were, by contrast, in a much stronger position; they also had social and family ties with the Portuguese military which the lower middle class lacked. Given the militaristic nature of post-1926 politics, this was an advantage from which conservatives would profit in their effort to decide the outcome of the revolution in their own sectional interest.

The power struggles of 1926

In the first instance, it was a member of the minority 'liberal' wing of the 28 May movement who attempted to fill the political vacuum left by the PRP. On 30 May 1926 the retiring head of state, Bernardino Machado, appointed Commander José Mendes Cabeçadas, a naval officer, as provisional president. The seventy-five-year-old Machado was a conciliatory figure, the nearest approximation in the doomed republic to a respected elder statesman, and his decision was not immediately challenged by any of the rebels. Cabeçadas, his appointee, was a long-standing republican and a member of the Liberal Republican Union, a party which was the vehicle of the civilian political chieftain Francisco Cunha Leal. One source has claimed that, through Cabeçadas, Leal intended to form a regime largely based on the Italian model in which he would be the strong man.[2] Leal was then perhaps the most prestigious

figure active in Lisbon politics on the eve of 28 May. As a fierce opponent of
the PRP, he was popular with the army, and if hostility to the idea of a
civilian emerging as the new leader had been less marked among military
conspirators, he could have realised some of his ambitions. However,
Leal's behind-the-scenes manoeuvres failed to secure his claim to the
political succession. His sponsor, Commander Cabeçadas, was a relatively
isolated figure within the 28 May movement whose republican
background and still relatively liberal outlook did not correspond to the
experience or opinions of the majority of the conspiratorial activists. His
status was further reduced in their eyes by the fact that he was a naval
officer. Without extensive links in the army, Cabeçadas was unable to
prevent Integralist officers deploying themselves in strategic positions
around Lisbon and within the war ministry.

On 17 June 1926 Cabeçadas and his aides were eliminated from the
provisional government by Gomes da Costa. The new head of state was in
control of the country until 9 July, when he too was ousted in an internal
coup d' état. Responsibility for this series of purges did not lie with any
ambitious officer behind the scenes. Rather, the outcome of the post-*coup*
power struggles seems to have been heavily influenced by younger officers,
many of whom were Integralists. Perhaps about three-hundred in number,
located in key positions within the military command structure and in the
lower rungs of the provisional government, they acted largely in concert to
back those officers within the military government with the most
authoritarian aims. No other military faction seems to have possessed the
same degree of organisational and conspiratorial zeal: during June and
July 1926 the 'young turks' made up a cohesive bloc in votes for regimental
leadership.[3] They were also responsible for enforcing press censorship and
for suggesting the names of likely cabinet ministers. That of Dr Salazar,
the future dictator, may have been one of them. He was briefly finance
minister between 3 and 19 June, having become a known and admired
figure among officers in the important garrison of Coimbra, Portugal's
university town.

Gomes da Costa's accession to the presidency had been a victory for the
right-wing tendency within the army. Nevertheless, the general quickly
managed to alienate military hard-liners by his clumsiness and by his
reluctance to press ahead with a full-blooded conservative programme. 'I
do not want a military dictatorship. Whoever says that lies like a cur,' had
been one of his off-the-cuff statements after 28 May.[4] Very naive and
totally lacking in political subtlety, he rapidly antagonised the men who
had emerged as the power brokers within the army and was replaced, after
twenty-two days in the presidential São Bento palace, by General Óscar
Carmona, the military prosecutor of the 1925 rebels.

The militant young turks in the army showed no desire to elevate one of their own number. Most preferred to promote the cause of a superior officer who could be relied upon to plot a steady conservative course. Junior activists were also careful not to overreach themselves by demanding the implementation of a full-blooded Integralist programme. Despite their deployment in key posts, they were but a small section of the officer corps as a whole. To go all-out for an ultra right-wing solution might only have panicked moderate conservatives into taking preventive action. By emasculating the liberal wing of the military movement and by knitting together a strong pressure group of young officers, the youthful hard-liners perhaps achieved the maximum they could have hoped for, considering the numbers they could muster: it would, in retrospect, be their greatest victory.

The 9 July palace revolution rather than the 28 May *golpe d' estado* (broad-based military *coup*) marked the triumph of the right, the emergence of Carmona confirming the victory of the most orthodox conservative sectors of the army. Once a clear-cut verdict had been reached, the prolonged in-fighting of the early summer subsided. *De facto* prime minister after July 1926, Carmona became acting president on 26 November 1926, two years prior to his elevation as formal head of state. However, within the more homogeneous and compact leadership line-up, no ready-made consensus existed about what sort of political system should take the place of the parliamentary regime. Although more intelligent and discreet, Carmona was as bereft of a political programme as Gomes da Costa. Beyond promising to uphold law and order and establish honesty and efficiency in government, no plan for national recovery was canvassed. However, the new president was able to rely on the army's allegiance because of his more marked ability to balance the factions within the military establishment. This was a vital requirement, since disagreement between monarchist- and republican-minded officers could have torn the regime apart; Carmona was a republican, a Catholic and a Freemason, an unusual breadth of experience which made him acceptable to a diverse range of military opinion. He was able to ensure that violent factional struggles did not occur by arranging informal compromises: no monarchist general became prime minister during the military dictatorship, but other key posts were given in compensation to members of this faction. In similar fashion, lesser differences between pro- and anticlerical officers, and between the two services, were smoothed over and prevented from rocking the foundations of the regime.

Externally, the military leaders drew confidence from the fact that another military government had been in power in neighbouring Spain since 1923. The circumstances leading up to military intervention in Madrid were not unlike those in Portugal. However, General Miguel Primo de Rivera's personalist style of rule did not produce an echoing response in Portugal. There the regime became known as 'a dictatorship without a dictator'.[5] This was not meant as a slur on Carmona, since it was actually the president who coined the phrase: it signified a low profile and a reluctance to allow a mystique to be built around his person. Such reserve was understandable. Firstly, Carmona was an uncharismatic staff officer who had spent most of his military career in administrative posts. Secondly, the military dictatorship (especially in its first two years), was a coalition of top officers in which Carmona was little more than *primus inter pares*.[6]

1926–28: rebellion and schism

The anonymity of Portugal's military leaders prompted one observer to describe the six-year span of the military dictatorship as 'that vague period about which we know very little but which is crucially important for an understanding of later Portuguese development'.[7] Naturally, the immediate imposition of censorship in 1926 and the consequent lack of contemporary newspaper accounts of internal political developments gave the era an aura of mystery. Confronted by major gaps in our knowledge of the evolution of Portuguese authoritarianism, it is tempting to assume that the regime led a relatively peaceful existence except for the occasional opposition outburst. After all, the military dictatorship would enjoy six years of continuous rule after years of quarterly cabinet crises. This could be a strong pointer to internal cohesion: observers have generally agreed. But the image of unbroken calm above and below the surface is an erroneous one which the regime advanced for all phases of its existence until the *coup* of 1974. By piecing together the various fragmentary reports of unrest with the new information which has emerged since 1974, it is now possible to argue that the regime was plagued by internal troubles almost from the outset.

The first hint of real division within the government camp came in September 1926 with the detention of Colonel João de Almeida on a charge of plotting against the state. This hard-line officer and colonial veteran would appear to have been caught in the act of attempting to unseat Carmona. However, the musical-chair phase of politics, which had marked the summer of 1926, had given way to a calmer period by the time of Almeida's *coup* attempt; six months of relative quiet followed during which the authorities were able to neutralise many of the secret societies and jacobin groups which had flourished under the liberal republic; during this time Afonso Costa paid two final visits to Portugal in September and November 1926. He may have been engaged in plotting, for on 3 February 1927 an opposition revolt flared up in Oporto, led by General Adalberto Sousa e Dias, one of the few really senior officers to back the PRP. This was *the* decisive power struggle between liberal republicanism and the reactionary right. Its fierceness dispels the view that the 1926 revolution sounded the death knell of constitutional republicanism: the rebels were able to deploy sizeable forces, and if Lisbon had risen at the same time as Oporto (instead of almost a week later), the seven-month government might have been hard pressed to contain the rebels. But (whatever its overall chances) poor co-ordination doomed the revolt to failure. After some days General Sousa e Dias and the troops loyal to him surrendered so 'as to avoid the complete destruction of Oporto' by government artillery.[8] By coming out on top against the rebels the regime had been enormously strengthened: however, the 3 February rising was the bloodiest Portugal had known in nearly a century.

Surviving a major attempt to unseat it enabled the government to embark on the crackdown which it had not felt strong enough to launch in 1926. Rebel army units were dissolved, as were political parties implicated in the *coup*. Mass arrests led to 600 people being deported to Portuguese Africa. The right to strike was withheld; interestingly, the dictatorship had not clamped down on strikes immediately. Not to have done so was evidence of caution on its part as well as of initial uncertainty. The caution remained even after February 1927: officers dismissed from the services were not completely beyond the pale, being allowed to draw half-pay. By contrast, conscripts and ordinary soldiers were more harshly punished.

Tough, resolute action in February 1927 consolidated the military dictatorship at the expense of the republican opposition, which grew increasingly feeble. The weakness of the opposition – as first revealed by the February rising – probably then encouraged schism, since government ranks were not required to be so rightly closed once the enemy had been routed. By far the greatest source of discord was the economy, which had not recovered under the dictatorship. Despite the promises made to the nation by top officers, this is hardly surprising. Portugal's soldiery came to lead the government and run its ministries without any prior training or experience in political and economic management. Exclusively military governments had not been seen in Portugal for nearly a century. Moreover, career officers had been unable to run their own services without much inefficiency, graft and needless expenditure.

The economy could have been helped, either, by the fact that government ministers and officials of the regime were very often not master in their own house. Until 1928 junior-ranking officers had a very direct influence on government affairs. George Guyomard, a French journalist who wrote the only contemporary foreign account of the military dictatorship, commented in 1927 that:

Lieutenants' soviets make the decisions for the generals. In regimental barracks,

each officers' mess is a parliament where those with the greatest authority are
not the officers with the most stripes. From time to time, groups of subalterns are
seen making their way to government ministries. This is a Lieutenants'
Commission in the process of delivering orders; this is the true dictatorship in
action.[9]

That lower-ranking officers possessed important political leverage is
one of the least known aspects of a little studied period. Given the survival
of the dictatorship, it is not particularly surprising that this episode has
not emerged into clearer light. Senior military personnel would not have
had any major desire to dwell on a time when they were forced to obey
orders emanating from the barracks. Carmona, above all, would not relish
memories of the 1926–27 period. António Sérgio, a noted Portuguese
scholar and oppositionist, comments that on occasions when the cabinet
was reshuffled the president had to send questionnaires to the various key
regiments asking:

1. Should the cabinet remain as it is or does it need to be remodelled?
2. If it ought to be changed, who are the ministers who should step down?
3. Who should replace those who have left?[10]

These questions were discussed in regimental halls by full officer
assemblies. After a debating session, votes were taken and the decision
was conveyed to the government. 'Anarchic barrack-room
parliamentarism', Sérgio called it.[11] Ultimately the regime would be able
to contain its impetuous lower-ranking supporters. Their ascendancy
proved only a temporary phenomenon, for several reasons. Firstly, co-
ordination between politically active subalterns from different regimental
barracks seems to have been limited; a young officers' *movement* failed to
emerge from among politically active junior rankers. Occasionally
ministers were confronted by a group of lieutenants offering conflicting
advice: the demand for an official's dismissal could be followed by a call
for his reinstatement. Junior officers also made the error of allowing
themselves to be used by ambitious ones intent on political advancement;
these tended to be firmly right-wing. Moderate officers favouring a
strongly based presidential republic as opposed to a more ideologically
defined authoritarian state were those whom junior-rankers sought to
discredit: these regimental factions knew what they were against –
'corrupt demo-liberalism' – but in most cases had no idea what political
forms might take the place of the old system.

Inability to set out aims in a politically defined way was perhaps the
central weakness of military radicals. Significantly, few of these
impressionable younger officers appear to have treated Integralism as a
serious doctrine which could have become the ideological basis of a new
authoritarian state: perhaps also significantly, no openly Integralist *coup*

attempts occurred between 1928 and 1932. Instead, many, including younger Integralist officers, pinned their hopes on the emergence of a charismatic military figure, perhaps a second Sidónio Pais.

In a situation of dual power where sometimes nobody was sure where ultimate authority lay, it was perhaps inevitable that one day a serious clash would occur between members of the government and a section of the assertive corps of junior officers. A confrontation of serious proportions involving these two parties did eventually occur in August 1927. The failure of an Integralist candidate to secure the newly created post of vice-president was one cause, but the main bone of contention was the stewardship of the finance minister, General João Sinel de Cordes; he was by now regarded as a political disaster by officers who wanted him replaced by somebody more competent in the financial realm. When the government, supported by business elements profiting from the finance minister's liberal distribution of credit, rejected calls for his dismissal, a crisis broke of sufficient melodrama to eclipse many of the tangled episodes of the First Republic.

On 12 August 1927 a pair of vociferous younger officers stormed into a cabinet session with an ultimatum. When the government persisted in refusing to drop its finance minister, gunfire was directed at cabinet ministers and Carmona was physically assaulted. After several hours the government regained control of the situation. The disaffected officers' badly planned and incoherent protest was quelled.[12] One sympathetic army unit was dissolved, and from the outcome of this affair one can perhaps date the restoration of hierarchical discipline within the military.

The regime emerged shaken and embarrassed, its authority having been so obviously flouted by junior-ranking activists blindly groping for a political alternative. A measure of the regime's weakness and uncertainty was the way in which it dealt with the August challengers. Despite the fact that the minister of justice, Manuel Rodrigues Júnior, narrowly missed being killed by one of them, no serious action was taken against any of the rebels. Instead the worst malcontents were posted to Angola, where they would remain at liberty – holding down important commissions.

By placing internal challengers where it was hoped they would cause the least trouble, instead of subjecting them to exemplary discipline, the regime remained in power beyond 1927 perhaps because no other faction of the military was prepared to shoulder the burden of the economy; even after the August 1927 uproar, no viable alternative to Sinel de Cordes's financial strategy emerged from any other branch of the military. The absence of any significant attempt to dislodge the regime from within before 1928 suggests, that despite their frustrations and rivalries, soldiers in the political wings were not sure if they could be fitter statesmen than the military incumbents in government.

Few officers quarrelled with a government appeal to the League of Nations late in 1927 for a loan of £12 million. Previously it had tried to raise cash from foreign banks. But in Paris, Republican opponents stymied this effort by warning that they would not acknowledge any loans to the military regime, if returned to power.[13] Eventually the League of Nations sent a mission to Lisbon to review the economic situation. On its recommendation the world body informed the Portuguese government that a loan would be forthcoming only if it accepted a tough series of prior conditions.[14] To one observer these amounted to 'international control of Portugal's finances'.[15] Lisbon summarily rejected the League's terms. Supporters and opponents of the government alike found them unacceptable; for the government they constituted a virtual loss of national sovereignty as well as spelling an end to the loose spending policies of Sinel de Cordes. One sure outcome of the episode was his political downfall. Regarded initially as the strong man of the regime, the monarchist general, by his incompetent handling of the economy, effectively destroyed his political career and may have gravely harmed the monarchical cause in the process. So poorly was the economy handled during the first two years of the dictatorship that the last years of the republic have been compared favourably with them. In fact, talented individuals like Ezequiel de Campos and Armando Marques Guedes did display flair in several economic portfolios, but the political rot was so deep that even the modest economic upturn experienced in 1925–26 could not have rescued the republic.

In its purely military phase, the dictatorship steadily lost public support. Evidence of discontent emerged in March 1928 when an army parade along the Avenida da Liberdade, Lisbon's main thoroughfare, was heckled by crowds who shouted slogans in favour of the navy, whose role in the Carmona government was a minor one. After being elected head of state for a five-year term by means of a dubious plebiscite on 25 March 1928, Carmona decided substantially to alter the regime in light of mounting dissatisfaction. In April 1928 he abandoned his executive duties and appointed a prime minister, Colonel José Vicente de Freitas, who replaced several lacklustre military men by civilian technocrats and 'experts'. In the critical finance ministry, Sinel de Cordes surrendered control to a lecturer in political economy from Coimbra university: António de Oliveira Salazar.

In April 1928 few of Salazar's immediate superiors could have foreseen that within five years he would be the political dictator of Portugal. Certainly nothing in his background pointed to his assuming such power. Most of his adult life had been spent studying and teaching at Coimbra, and even in earlier days he had the reputation of being a scholarly recluse. However, this had not prevented members of the Portuguese right beating a path to his door with several offers of political preferment: as a member of the Academic Centre for Christian Democracy (CADC) he had built up a reputation as a sound lay conservative. Several times between 1926 and 1928 he was to turn down the finance ministry. He pleaded ill-health, devotion to his aged parents, and a preference for the academic cloisters. More likely, he was unwilling to play the role of technical adviser in a none too stable government. Certainly he would ensure that this was not his position in the Carmona regime after 1928. From Carmona he secured a categorical assurance that, as finance minister, he would have a free hand to veto expenditure in all government departments, not just his own. If the regime had not accepted these conditions, one authoritative source believes, Premier de Freitas would have turned to republican politicians instead.[16] In the event his terms were met, no other European finance minister possessing such sweeping powers. Armed with considerable fiscal authority, he was financial dictator of the country virtually from the day he took office – 27 April 1928, a day before his thirty-ninth birthday.

1928–30: the regime civilianised

Thanks to the efforts of regime propagandists, Salazar has come down in history as a latter-day Cincinnatus who materialised to rescue the Portuguese nation at one of its most difficult periods. Like his predecessor in Roman times, he acted out of the deepest altruism, oblivious to personal considerations, moved principally by love of country and by concern at its decline in strength. An outwardly modest demeanour and Salazar's previous refusal of various public appointments lent conviction to such a portrait. However, there were deep scratches on the canvas. These would become evident after years of one-man rule had served to demonstrate that humility was not, after all, one of Salazar's strong points; the conditions he laid down for accepting high office were already, perhaps, one sign of overwheening ambition. Beforehand, during the winter of 1927, he had published a long series of articles in the Catholic newspaper *Novidades* which amounted to a sustained indictment of Sinel de Cordes's financial stewardship. These journalistic forays brought him into conflict with the finance minister and made his name widely known in political circles. On occasion the censor blotted out the most offending copy, Salazar ironically being an early victim of the suppression of information that he and his aides would shortly practice on a much grander scale; in the light of the *Novidades* articles, to continue to describe Salazar as not being an accomplice in his own rise is to do less than justice to the facts. Events *before*, as well as after, his ascent to power indicate that he was not the apolitical idealist his supporters have usually depicted.[17]

On eventually being sworn in as finance minister in April 1928, Salazar declared:

> I know quite well what I want and where I am going, but let it not be insisted that I shall reach the goal in a few months. For the rest, let the country study, let it suggest, let it object, and let it discuss but when the time comes for me to give orders I shall expect it to obey.[18]

From a ministerial novice this was a speech of exceptional bluntness and authority. Few of the soldier politicians had ever addressed the nation in such terms. Salazar was able to speak with confidence, aware that the army had little alternative but to accept his prognosis. Members of the dictatorship longed for a financial upturn and were prepared to suffer an assertive civilian expert if, in the long run, the reputation of the military regime could be rescued from the mire. But their patience could have reached breaking point if Salazar had persisted in treating the army in a cavalier manner: the Portuguese army is traditionally sensitive to civilian jibes. Salazar quickly changed his tack, did not repeat his abrasive 1928 speech, and began energetically to court the military world. Wisely, the armed forces were exempted from his sweeping economy drive even though much could have been saved by pruning their overgrown bureaucracy. Financial savings were got instead at the expense of the lower and middle income groups. During 1928–29 no less than 23·42 per cent of the budget (as compared with 10·43 per cent in Great Britain) continued to go on defence.[19]

Within the space of one year, armed with his special powers, Salazar balanced the budget and stabilised Portugal's currency, the *escudo*. Ruthless centralisation of control, improved collecting and accounting methods and cuts in expenditure for the navy and education, plus some internal borrowings, made the books balance.[20] Dramatic reductions in public expenditure gave him the first of many surpluses: in 1921, at a convention of commercial and industrial associations, he had developed a theory of cheap public management by cutting social services.[21] However, Cunha Leal claims that financial equilibrium was brought about not so much by reducing costs as by increasing the public contribution to the exchequer.[22] In exile, Afonso Costa fulminated about the 'equilibrium that kills' but Salazar was impervious to criticism even from right-wingers alarmed that regulation of the public purse, not expansion of the economy, was his priority. Then as later, Salazar's methods were those of a careful accountant, not an economic innovator. Perhaps to describe him as an economist is not quite correct. Two writers have found that the curriculum of Coimbra University shows that the subject he lectured on 'corresponded rather to chartered accountancy than to what we understand by economics'.[23]

The head of state had to intervene on his minister's behalf several times: without the success of Salazar's policies, Carmona's future would have been highly problematical. He backed him against opposition to certain of Salazar's views and policies emanating from inside the cabinet. Though right-wing, the cabinet was not politically homogeneous. Salazar's opinions on politics and finance were not shared by all his cabinet colleagues in 1928. Premier de Freitas was a relatively moderate figure in the camp of the dictatorship. So were several members of his incoming government. However, with power divided between himself, Carmona and Salazar, de Freitas was unable to make his authority felt in a generally unsuccessful premiership. The first blow to his position came in November 1928 when Salazar was joined in government by several political confederates sharing his right-wing Catholic perspective. One of the newcomers, the justice minister, Mário de Figueiredo, had trained for the priesthood with him in a seminary in northern Portugal. Both of them also hailed from this relatively conservative part of the country. At Coimbra the two kept up their friendship and formed an academic peer group with another seminarian, Manuel Gonçalves Cerejeira. Unlike them, the latter took his final vows, to become in 1929 at the age of forty-one Archbishop of Lisbon and the youngest cardinal in Europe.

The Portuguese Church was promoting a priest who might be able to restore the position of a national Church whose vigour had been sapped by years of Church–state conflict. So urgent was the task at hand that Cerejeira's fellow bishops were prepared to cast tradition aside and elevate the youngest of their number (Cerejeira was Archbishop of Mitilene before 1929) to the highest religious post in the land. This was not all. In quick succession, three northerners had stepped into important ecclesiastical and political posts at a comparatively youthful age. Their rapid rise (and connections with one another in the CADC) fuelled speculation that the Catholic lobby was making a bid for pre-eminence in national politics.

In June 1929 a governmental dispute enabled some Portuguese not left completely in the dark by censorship to discern that the religious issue was indeed a source of conflict within the cabinet. In the dispute, civilian and military ministers largely found themselves ranged on different sides. One view was destined to prevail over the other, making the outcome an interesting indicator of the relative strengths of the civilian and military tendencies within the *ditadura*.

An obscure quarrel between the Catholic Bishop of Évora and the army officer acting as the town's civil governor was the catalyst that prised open divisions within the government. The quarrel was over what the soldier viewed as the excessive use of church bells in the town. When eventually the government found itself adjudicating in the matter, the prime minister and the minister of war backed their brother officer while

Figueiredo and Salazar endorsed the bishop's stand. Deadlock ensued. Although in more junior positions, the two civilian ministers refused to fall in line with the prime minister. Instead they handed in their resignation to President Carmona.

Carmona had already shown partiality towards the Catholic lobby by ordering an assault on the Lisbon headquarters of the Freemasons in April 1929. All Masons apprehended in the raid were arrested and jailed, with the exception of army officers.[24] Three months later Carmona refused to accept the resignation of his Catholic ministers. Was Salazar banking on such a reaction to what was an act of brinkmanship? Certainly he must have been aware of the high esteem Carmona held him in: and this would not be the only time that the minister of finance would submit his resignation over what seemed a relatively trivial matter, only to emerge later greatly strengthened.

With neither the prime minister nor the finance minister prepared to back off or compromise, Carmona finally broke the political log-jam by accepting the collective resignation of his military colleague's government. The last meeting of the government had, at Carmona's request, convened in a Lisbon hospital, out of deference to Salazar, who was briefly a patient there in the course of the crisis. In the new administration that took over on 8 July 1929 Salazar was the only member of the outgoing government to stay on. Just as symbolically, the clerical line in the Évora controversy was upheld by the incoming administration headed by General Artur Ivens Ferraz.

The clear civilian victory in the trial of strength with mildly anticlerical officers during 1929 bolstered Salazar's position. The progressive civilianisation of the dictatorship henceforth appeared a much more likely possibility. Salazar would no longer have to rely so much on Carmona's protection in order to stay in office. In the finance ministry he began to construct his own personal power base. Future key ministers in his government like Armindo Monteiro, Marcelo Caetano and João da Costa Leite embarked upon their political careers as assistants to him. Other dedicated young right-wingers could be found at various levels of the regime, and as Salazar built up his own independent base he encountered less resistance from his military colleagues. Those sceptics who were unhappy with the fiscal powers he wielded often found themselves outmanoeuvred if they attempted to cross swords with him. Others (perhaps a majority of officers in the politico-military hierarchy), evinced growing satisfaction that his economic measures were removing the strong political pressure on the regime that threatened its stability, certainly until 1928. This stratum of officers also reacted favourably to the praise which Salazar lavished on the army in public addresses. Sir Frederick Lindley of the British embassy in Lisbon also found that 'when publishing accounts of his latest achievements and intentions, he is not wanting in self-advertisement'.[25] However, Salazar's expanding influence was not reflected in the Ivens Ferraz government, where the ministers of education and war identified themselves as political adversaries. Its moderate appearance, in parts, belied the strength of ultra-right-wing elements within the dictatorship as a whole. Because the cabinet was not representative it was weak and isolated, an easy target for hard-liners who desired an unambiguous exposition of right-wing views at all levels of the regime. Pressure for its replacement quickly grew, especially after reports began to circulate about Ivens Ferraz being in favour of the rehabilitation of civilian politicians identified with the fallen regime. Some conservative republicans whose ideological standpoint was not incompatible with that of the military leadership of the country between 1926 and 1930 already held middle-ranking positions in the administration. Their executive experience and political acceptability enabled many of them to survive the purges directed against other republicans. However, once Salazar began to place his protégés in middle-ranking administrative positions the few survivors of the previous regime found themselves in mounting difficulty.

In January 1930 the most prominent republican survivor holding a top public appointment, Francisco Cunha Leal, was ousted from his job as governor of the Bank of Angola after he had got into a dispute with Salazar. The point at issue was the banking system in Angola. Both men had conflicting views and refused to agree on a compromise. Informing the cabinet of the situation, Salazar announced that he planned to resign, unless the recalcitrant bank chief was dismissed. Once more this gambit worked and a Salazar appointee replaced Cunha Leal. A majority of the cabinet (including the premier), had not supported Salazar but this ceased to matter when it too fell within days. Ivens Ferraz's replacement was another senior officer, General Domingos Oliveira. This time Portugal had as prime minister a 57-year-old soldier who was altogether compliant to the minister of finance's views not just on the economy but also concerning the future political orientation of the regime.

1930–32: the emergence of the New State

Restoration of law and order and financial stability had largely been achieved by the fourth anniversary of the 1926 revolution: these had been the two principal goals of the military officers responsible for seizing power. With the 'original minimum programme' of the regime realised, the question that now loomed increasingly large was the long-term direction of the regime. In the uncertain years after 1926 the question was an awkward one to raise, given the heterogeneous nature of the dictatorship in its early stages. Until the 'financial dictatorship' it was largely shelved. However, once the more reactionary elements came to assert their political authority over moderate voices there was markedly greater willingness to discuss plans for the institutionalisation of the regime.

Many people within it and around it recognised that the military dictatorship was merely a temporary expedient. The armed forces, though in power, had yet to produce a recognised political leader. The mainstay of the regime was instead a civilian financial expert. Not unnaturally, he was the individual who took the initiative in mapping out the country's future political course. In two widely advertised speeches delivered on 28 May and 30 July 1930 he went far beyond his financial brief and discoursed at length on the desirability of a strong authoritarian state. Democracy was assailed and placed squarely in the dock as being responsible for the chaos and disorder of the 1910–26 period; the Portuguese, by temperament and experience, required a more ordered political system. The 'New State' was the name Salazar coined for the emergent political order he envisaged. Nineteen-thirty was the year in which the political term was first heard. Salazar and his collaborators may only have partly worked out their political ideas by then: corporativism would not be adopted as the regime's official creed until 1933. However, some of the steps that would bring the corporative state to reality were already being advocated: the abolition of political parties and trade unions; the implementation of total censorship; the vesting of political power in a narrow executive; the inculcation of the values of *Deus, Pátria e Família*.[26]

Salazar's advocacy of an ultra-right-wing political solution was a relatively sudden development. Right up to 1930, matters pertaining to his department had usually figured uppermost in his major speeches. In 1929, when he first pointedly spoke on non-financial matters, A. H. de Oliveira Marques finds that his message was one of 'solid, prudent, and conciliatory nationalism'.[27] Praise for the army was interspersed with frequent references to the importance of the family unit in national life. Emphasis was also placed on the lay role of the Catholic Church, but never to the extent that he would advocate any form of theocratic society. It would, of course, not have been politic for Salazar to reveal all that was in his mind at this juncture. Until 1930 he sat alongside ministers in government who would not have shared his virulently right-wing aspirations. Two of them occupied the premiership between 1928 and 1930. Both these senior officers preferred an authoritarian presidential regime to an ideological political dictatorship. Until their removal from office, Salazar was probably not free to give a complete rendition of his political philosophy.

Officially, Salazar's ministry ranked fifth in overall importance: even after 1930 he was technically in a position junior to four of his cabinet colleagues. However, ministerial grading did not do justice to the facts. Salazar completely overshadowed the military premier, Domingos Oliveira; in the eyes of Franco Nogueira, a prominent New State politician, this military figure was 'an apt administrator of the routine but an inadequate conductor of the revolution';[28] to a senior British embassy official in Lisbon the premier was described as 'rather a weak man and a supporter of Salazar'.[29] This was in 1930. In May 1931 the British ambassador reported to London that 'Dr Salazar is easily Portugal's outstanding figure'.[30] And in June the Foreign Office was told:

> For some time past, he [Salazar] has been taking a leading part in every debate in the Cabinet and I am told that his voice has generally been decisive. A change of Prime Minister would therefore be a recognition of what is, in fact, the position in the Cabinet today.[31]

Salazar's pre-eminence was highlighted in various ways. It was he, and not the premier, who on 30 July 1930 proclaimed the birth of the regime's official mouthpiece, the União Nacional (National Union), the first political body created after 1926. The UN furthered Salazar's rise by acting as a vehicle of personal support wherever branches were founded. Another indication of his immense personal authority two years before he became prime minister himself was given in March 1930, when he was instrumental in crushing a murky rebellion in the colony of Angola. The rebellion was directed against Captain Morais Sarmento, assistant to the military governor, Commander Filomeno de Câmara. These were two of the officers who had attempted to force political changes on President Carmona in August 1927. Since then they had run the local military administration in Angola, in the process of doing which they had alienated local business interests. Rebellion eventually broke out and Morais Sarmento was killed. When news of the affair reached Lisbon the government declined to aid Governor Câmara, ordering him instead to return to Portugal. Another officer was posted to Angola to restore peace.

The unorthodox handling of what developed into a largely military dispute was Salazar's doing: for some months in 1930 he was interim minister of the colonies and it was therefore his job to deal with the emergency when it arose. Military pride was understandably hurt by his decision not to support the senior military officer in Angola. However, this controversial action did not rebound on him or sully relations with the armed services; that he was able to intervene in a largely military matter like the Angolan rebellion and arrive at an independent decision without being challenged by members of the officer corps is yet another indication of the political weight he carried by 1930.

Which groups and interests were most receptive to the ideas that

Salazar was disseminating? Foreign admirers of the New State argued that support for the regime was widespread and could be found at all levels of society. In Britain, for instance, Salazar's Portugal was depicted as a popular dictatorship with discordant voices coming only from a handful of communists and what remained of the liberal opposition.[32] This was the view that the government was naturally advancing in its own propaganda. Hampered by censorship, and with little opportunity to observe people's attitudes at close quarters, most foreign observers did not question official claims about the regime's popularity. So thorough a job was done to convince the world that Salazar and his predecessors ruled with the consent of the people that post-1945 oppositionists were even prepared to concede that the New State was popular in its initial stages.

Did the regime's European press image in the early 1930s reflect Portuguese reality? Until the writer carried out an examination of British embassy reports conveyed to Lisbon he was prepared to accept that Salazar's work in the ministry of finance enjoyed some preliminary acclaim. Most of the contemporary published sources came to that conclusion. However, the Lisbon embassy gave a starkly different impression of the mood of the Portuguese people.

Three excerpts from reports communicated to London during 1930–31 show how completely the confidential findings of the Lisbon embassy diverged from the assessment of British and Continental authors and commentators. In January 1930 Sir Frederick Lindley was reporting to Arthur Henderson, then Foreign Secretary, that 'the Ivens Ferraz administration was the third government brought down by Salazar for apparently trivial reasons and it looked as though his reputation must suffer severely in the country'.[33]

Later, on 18 April 1931, Sir Frederick wrote to the Foreign Secretary that:

Outside the army, I gather that the feeling against the all-powerful finance minister has increased to quite a remarkable degree during the last few months. Portuguese friends of mine, *themselves adherents of Dr Salazar*,[34] tell me that in the provinces they can find no one with a good word to say for him. He is accused of being the ultimate cause of all the bank failures and scandals and of the unemployment from which Portugal is at present suffering; and there is a general demand that he should make way for a successor who will employ on the body politic of Portugal less drastic remedial measures than have been administered during the past few years. Amongst the general public, the feeling against the dictatorship has also, I am assured, been growing rapidly during the past few months. There is, as General Ivens Ferraz said in February, no longer any 'atmosphere' for a Dictatorship. People are getting tired of the restraints on their personal freedom which the Dictatorship entails, and complain more and more of the flow of dictatorial decrees which interfere with the conduct of their business.[35]

One month later, on 15 May 1931, Sir Frederick Lindley's superior, ambassador Sir Claud Russell, informed London that:

If free elections were held under manhood suffrage, no one doubts that the government would be turned out by an enormous majority.[36]

Being self-supporting and geared to reporting factual information that would enable the Foreign Office to keep abreast of the internal situation, the British embassy in Lisbon is one of the few reliably independent sources of information after 1930. If one is to believe this embassy, rather than Salazar's hagiographers, then the regime was unpopular even in its infancy. Popular disillusion was a feature of late 1920s and early 1930s as well as of later periods.

What support Salazar enjoyed, during the final phase of the military dictatorship, came from those sections of the population that were among the first to become alienated with the parliamentary republic. The Catholic Church ecstatically welcomed his rise: it was depicted as a victory for Catholic ideals over 'demo-liberal atheism'. Fulsome support also came from wealthier upper-class Portuguese: landowners, bankers, businessmen and managers. Salazar had put the economy on a more stable footing without hurting them, the rich and well placed. Though there were major exceptions, from much of the Portuguese intelligentsia – already permeated by right-wing thinking – Salazar's philosophy of government got rapt praise. A supporter of the counter-revolution was Fernando Pessoa, who came to rank as one of Europe's finest modern poets, and who is also recognised as the major figure in twentieth-century Portuguese literature. Pessoa was a believer in the occult, and during his lifetime he endorsed the military dictatorship in print, believing that Portugal was destined to play a major role in a new cosmic world order.

As for members of the officer corps, they could readily identify with the doctrine of the strong state expounded by the minister of finance. Some of the more abstruse aspects of his political thinking may have been above their heads, but officers saw much in Salazar's speeches that fitted in with their conservative, hierarchically structured view of the world. Since he showed few signs of wanting to tamper with their privileges, members of the military caste gave their minister of finance less cause to worry after 1930 than they had beforehand. By then, many officers were chastened and exhausted by their previous stint of single-handedly running the country, and were not opposed to the reins of power being transferred to more imaginative and capable hands.

Broad military approval for Salazar's plan to institutionalise the dictatorship was reflected in the Domingos Oliveira government (1930–32). In its two-and-a-half-year existence it avoided the rifts and disagreements that had plagued both of its shorter-lived predecessors. Its appearance of stability and internal unity was largely due to the fact that it was the most compact government Portugal had witnessed since 1926.

However, discontent increased among whichever elements of the population were feeling the sting of Salazar's austere deflationary measures. Worst affected were the ordinary classes. However, numbers of middle-class businessmen were restive also, since an important effect of government policy was to raise the cost of some staples and to discourage new production and expansion.[37] Another source of middle-class anger was Salazar's reorganisation of the Bank of Portugal in 1931: bond holders lost 20 per cent of their investment as a result.[38] Outside the working class, the only other active dissenters were liberally inclined members of the bourgeoisie, reluctant to completely denounce the parliamentary republic before 1926 and among the first to be alarmed by the implications for Portugal of the rise of Salazar and his new brand of authoritarian politics.

On 28 May 1932 the minister of finance was presented with the Tower and Sword, Portugal's highest decoration, usually only conferred on a civilian who had been prime minister for at least three years.[39] Only rarely have exceptions been made to this rule, and usually for a significant political reason: it was in Salazar's case. On 5 July 1932 his mastery of government became official when he formed his own government in place of Domingos Oliveira.[40] However, his elevation to the premiership did not pass off without violent opposition in some military quarters. One Lisbon regiment, as well as the secret police, was strongly opposed to Salazar's appointment.[41] However, military men suspicious of his political motives, or simply jealous of the civilian's swift political rise, were unable to deflect key units within the army from supporting him. Ex-premier Ivens Ferraz had attempted this in 1931. But he was thwarted by another army faction led by Colonel Raul Esteves and composed of younger officers who were partisans of the regime.

Each of the factions active in military politics had rendered themselves ineligible to dominate the new regime. The monarchists were badly discredited by the Sinel de Cordes episode. The conservative republicans were indirectly tarnished by the 1910–26 era. The extreme-right military faction was too weak and poorly led, while Carmona was not hankering after supreme power. So a civilian was able to assume the mantle of power and bring to an end a period of inchoate authoritarian rule by the military. After 1930, for the first time in a quarter of a century, Portugal enjoyed a stable administration. Salazar, the man given the leading credit for the regime's cohesion, was one of the few economic specialists to crown his administrative efforts with enormous personal success in the political field. Calvo Sotelo in the Spain of the 1920s, Hjalamar Schacht in Nazi Germany, and Roberto Campos and Delfim Neto after the Brazilian military *coup* of 1964, were other economists who made political capital out of policies they devised as members of right-wing authoritarian regimes. However, each would have to be content to remain in an auxiliary political capacity despite high visibility within his respective government. None was able to emulate Salazar's rise from a subordinate governmental position to one of commanding and overwhelming importance; even today, the minister of finance's ability to supplant military officers in a country where praetorianism has been a major, if not all-pervasive, feature of national political culture is striking. Perhaps Salazar's meteoric rise is less awe-inspiring if one recalls that Portugal has been plagued with economic troubles throughout most of her 800-year history as a nation-state: in the 1930s the particularly acute nature of Portugal's economic maladies placed an alleged miracle-worker in a very strong position, causing one observer to remark that in the kingdom of the blind the one-eyed man had become king.[42]

Counter-revolution in Portugal and Spain

In 1926 the first of the peninsula's two major counter-revolutions saw the Portuguese military come to power in an almost bloodless *coup* carried out against very little opposition. The take-over was effected in a matter of days, and government ministers simply abandoned their posts without making any show of resistance. If circumstances had been different and a longer, more arduous struggle for power had ensued, it is quite possible, as a result of the trouble it had gone to, that the army would not have been willing to gravitate back to the political sidelines. In Spain this was very much the collective attitude of the army once General Franco, its commander-in-chief, had established control of the country in 1939. Power had passed into his hands only after Spain had witnessed a three-year civil war of exceptional ferocity. During this exceedingly bitter conflict, civilian politicians on the conservative right dropped out of sight, not to re-emerge afterwards: José María Gil Robles, the major conservative spokesman in Spain before 1936 (who might well be depicted as Salazar's *alter ego* on account of his Catholic traditionalist views), disappeared altogether from the forefront of politics to plunge into virtual obscurity after 1939. Power instead passed into the hands of victorious army leaders, monarchists and Falange party chiefs, the subject of great admiration in right-wing quarters for having extirpated 'bolshevism' and 'degenerate liberalism' from Spanish soil.

The political stakes in Portugal had not been so high as in Spain, and consequently endorsement of the army's governmental role would not be as total or prolonged even from main-line supporters. For the Portuguese army had intervened not to avert revolution but to put the country on its feet economically and politically. When it was seen to be failing in this task, support diminished; after two years in control of the country, the Portuguese army leadership found itself worse off than its Spanish counterpart in terms of popular backing. Perhaps the *dénouement* in the case of Portugal is not altogether surprising, since armies, by their very nature, are more at home dealing with military as opposed to governmental problems. In Spain military problems were chiefly the ones that had to be overcome before the counter-revolution could succeed completely. This was far from being so in Portugal. Because the future prospects of an authoritarian government were inextricably linked up with the economy, the army found itself in an anomolous position: it had engineered the reactionary revolution but lacked the judgement and specialist economic skills to consolidate it. Just as bereft of a working knowledge of economics and the profession of government were Spanish officers. But after 1939 this was not of overriding importance, since even civilian economists were hard pressed to know how and where to begin the process of reconstruction, so severe was the damage done to the national economy. Also, by that time, Spain did not have any major external commitments that could have been put in jeopardy by a perilous economic situation at home. She was more insular and self-contained than Portugal in this respect, since the latter had retained a large colonial empire, mainly in Africa. This, since the 1880s, had been the object of envious glances from greedy or frustrated European colonial powers. At several points in time Portugal's small size, backward economy and far from formidable army had tempted larger powers to intervene in Africa against her. If the home economy had gone completely to rack and ruin this could have been a natural corollary. Aware of the disastrous external repercussions which could stem from internal economic collapse, the military government was unable to allow the country to stagnate as Franco did in Spain.

More was expected sooner from Portugal's military regime. While Franco would wait two decades before giving policy roles to civilians not connected with his seizure of power, Carmona and his colleagues were obliged by the exigencies of the Portuguese situation to do this in two, not twenty, years. The amount of power they delegated was also more substantial than Franco would bestow upon technocratic ministers at the end of the 1950s. Salazar, the chief civilian drafted into power during the late 1920s, was able to steal the thunder of the military leadership by the success of his economic policies. Moreover, he was able to benefit from the fact that there was no residual anti-intellectual feeling to be found in Portuguese military circles.[43] As a result, official hagiographers were able to deem his role in the finance ministry to have been more crucial for the success of the Portuguese 'revolution' than the actual military take-over itself. Such a reversal of roles would not take place in Spain. The economic advances of the 1960s did not vie in importance with victory in the civil war in the eyes of regime supporters. No event after 1939 downgrades the significance of the 'Nationalist' victory in the bitterly contested civil war. This was incalculably a more potent political symbol than the formality which was the May 1926 *coup* in Portugal; to establish its permanence in government, the regime there required more clear-cut and tangible successes to be chalked up over and above the actual seizure of power. The success of the counter-revolution would not hinge on the circumstances of its birth as in Spain but was to depend on how its mentors faced up to their responsibilities in government.

Notes

1 Andreski, *Parasitism and Subversion*, p. 235.
2 Saraiva, '28 de Maio', p. 6.
3 The use of the ballot as a means of promoting officers was not, of course, normal practice within the military. However, the need to replace certain unreliable regimental commanders with sympathetic officers, and the revolutionary atmosphere of the times, made a form of barrack-room 'democracy' acceptable in the summer of 1926.
4 Romeu Costa Reis and Manuel Rendeiro Júnior, 'A contra-revolução naçional', *História*, 9, July 1979, p. 14.
5 William Leon Smyser, 'Dictatorship without a dictator in Portugal', *Contemporary Review*, September 1930, p. 328.
6 However, Carmona, of all the post—1926 leaders, was the only one to have had prior governmental experience, the head of state having been war minister in a short-lived republican administration during 1923; thus there was little overlap in the membership of pre- and post-1926 elites. For a biographical study of Carmona see Leopoldo Nunes, *Carmona. Estudo biográfico*, Editorial Império, Lisbon, 1942.
7 Howard J. Wiarda, *Corporatism and Development. The Portuguese Experience*, University of Massachusetts Press, Amherst, Mass., 1977, p. 95.
8 Viana Martins, *Da I República*, p. 158.
9 George Guyomard, *La Dictature militaire au Portugal. Impressions d'un retour de Lisbonne*, Presses Universitaires de France, Paris, 1927, p. 93.
10 António Sérgio, 'Cartas de António Sérgio ao Capitão Sarmento Pimentel', *Diário Popular* (Lisbon), 24 March 1977.
11 *Ibid.*
12 Perhaps the most graphic description of what has become known as the 'Golpe de Fifis' is contained in Horácio Assis Gonçalves, *Intimidades de Salazar. O homen e a sua época*, Livraria Bertrand, Lisbon, 1971, pp. 69–75.
13 See A. H. de Oliveira Marques, *A Liga de Paris e a ditadura militar, 1927–1928 (Documentos)*, Publicações Europa–America, Lisbon, 1974.
14 Oliveira Marques, *História de Portugal*, II, p. 210.
15 Luis Araquistáin, 'Dictatorship in Portugal', *Foreign Affairs*, October 1928, pp. 48–50.
16 Cardinal Cerejeira, quoted in Christine Garnier, *Salazar. An Intimate Portrait*, Farrar Strauss & Young, New York, 1954, p. 87.
17 Gallagher, 'The Theory and Practice of Portuguese Authoritarianism', thesis,

p. 76.

18 António de Oliveira Salazar, *Doctrine and Action. Internal and Foreign Policy of the New Portugal* (trans. Edgar Broughton), Faber & Faber, London, 1939, p. 45.

19 Araquistain, *op. cit.*, p. 45.

20 Philippe C. Schmitter, 'The "régime d'exception" that became the rule: forty-eight years of authoritarian domination in Portugal', in Graham and Makler (eds.), *Contemporary Portugal*, p. 33.

21 M. Harsgor, *Portugal in Revolution*, Sage Publications, London and Beverly Hills, Cal., 1976, p. 4.

22 J. Cândido de Azevedo, 'O orçamento e o "milagre financeiro" de Salazar', *História*, 6, April 1979, p. 10.

23 Peter Fryer and Patricia Pinheiro McGowan, *Oldest Ally. A Portrait of Salazar's Portugal*, Dennis Dobson, London, 1961, p. 114.

24 Douglas L. Wheeler, 'The military and the Portuguese dictatorship, 1926–1974: "the honor of the army"', in Graham and Makler (eds.), *op. cit.*, p. 199.

25 Public Record Office (hereafter PRO), London, FO 371 W2325/2325/36, 1930, Annual Report on Portugal.

26 *Deus, Patria e Familia:* God, Patria and Family. This became one of the principal slogans of the regime.

27 Oliveira Marques, *História de Portugal*, II, p. 180.

28 Franco Nogueira, *Salazar*, Vol. II, *Os tempos aureos, 1928–1936*, Atlântida Editora, Coimbra, 1977, p. 145.

29 PRO, FO 371 15755 W796/796/36, 1930, Sir Frederick Lindley to Arthur Henderson.

30 PRO, FO 371 15755/W796/796/36, 15 May 1931, Sir Claud Russell to Arthur Henderson.

31 PRO, FO 371 15741 W7467/801/36, 25 June 1931, Frederick Adams to Arthur Henderson.

32 See Michael Derrick, *The Portugal of Salazar*, Sands, London, 1938.

33 PRO, FO 371 15026,W296/796/36, 1930, Annual Report for Portugal.

34 My emphasis.

35 PRO, FO 371 15758, W801/801/36, 18 April 1931.

36 PRO, FO 371 15758, W2907/801/36, 15 May 1931.

37 Payne, *History of Spain and Portugal*, II, p. 666.

38 PRO, FO 371 15755, W7467/89/36, 1931, Frederick Adam to Arthur Henderson.

39 Nogueira, *op. cit.*, p. 145 n.

40 In an intriguing report to the Foreign Secretary, Sir John Simon, beforehand on 14 April 1932 Ambassador Sir Claud Russell had stated that 'Dr Salazar, the minister of finance, is suffering from a nervous breakdown'. Naturally, this was not confirmed by the authorities and has never appeared anywhere else in print. Later, during the 1940s, there were other British embassy reports about 'a distinct deterioration in his nervous health': PRO, 7 November 1946, Owen O'Malley to Ernest Bevin, 29588. In two memoirs of Salazar published in 1977 two ex-ministers, Franco Nogueira and Marcelo Caetano, also refer to the dictator suffering frequent bouts of mental depression.

41 Marcelo Caetano, *Minhas memórias de Salazar*, Editorial Verbo, Lisbon, 1977, p. 47.

42 Kiernan, 'Old Alliance', p. 276.

43 Many army officers liked to describe themselves as 'intellectuals' and it was not unknown for an officer to pursue an academic and a military career simultaneously: Sidónio Pais is perhaps the best-known example of the academic soldier. Undoubtedly the prestige of learning would have worn thin if Portuguese intellectuals had begun to attack elite values and to champion lower-class struggles. However, this phenomenon, if common in other countries, had not yet occurred in Portugal by the time of the counter-revolution. In a country profoundly affected by French cultural tastes, army officers, like other members of the elite, continued to value intellectual distinction.

4

Salazar and the corporative 'revolution'

Salazar

In April 1926, when discussing the manner in which a future dictator would emerge in Portugal, Martinho Nobre de Mello, an Integralist spokesman, predicted that 'none of us will propose him. Our leader will impose himself.'[1] This was prophetic insight. However, Salazar hardly emerged from nowhere after 1926; he was no *deus ex machina*. For over a decade he had been a leading member of the CADC as well as a parliamentary candidate on at least three occasions.

The membership of the CADC tended to be less elitist and patrician than that of the Integralist movement, since the most devout Catholics did not always come from the wealthiest families. Salazar was a case in point. He grew up on a rural smallholding in the northern province of Beira Alta. His birthplace was the village of Vimieiro, not far from the small town of Santa Comba Dão in the valley of Beira Alta, and mid-way between the conservative provincial town of Viseu and Portugal's Oxford, the university town of Coimbra, in its own way just as conservative. In this picturesque wine-producing area (the Serra da Estrela mountains and Caramulo, the highest peak in Portugal are near by), the land holdings were often tiny, and although, in economic terms, many of the inhabitants were virtually proletarian, their social status was that of modest proprietors. Conservative, deferential and pious, this landowning peasant class would give major support to the Estado Novo during the first half of its existence. Salazar's own parents were not untypical products of a rural society where the absence of extremes of wealth and poverty encouraged a certain social cohesion. His father, António de Oliveira, who lived to be ninety-three and died in 1932, cultivated a smallholding and was an estate manager for one of the few big landowners in the district. His mother, Maria do Resgate Salazar, was both extremely devout and practical, exercising more influence over her only son than the father. Maria was already forty-three when Salazar was born on 28 April 1889 (eight days after the birth of Adolf Hitler). Both parents had been born in the first half of the nineteenth century so that the home atmosphere which he grew up in was even more conservative than might have been expected. Shy, delicate and intelligent, the young Salazar went to local schools and, at the age of eleven, entered the religious seminary at Viseu, the district capital.

For the rest of his adolescence he was educated in the only institution which, at that time, allowed a certain degree of upward mobility for ordinary Portuguese children. In the north especially, the Church used to provide a few poorer infants with a seminary education in the hope of turning them into priests. Salazar himself began theological studies in 1905, showing keen interest in the writings of Thomas Aquinas. He took minor orders in 1908 and, for a short time, preached in a parish church. However, he drew back from being ordained a priest, feeling, according to one source, that he could be of better service to the Church as a layman.[2] Others have speculated that it was the onset of the anticlerical Republic in 1910 which caused Salazar to abandon his priestly vocation. Shortly after the overthrow of Manuel II, he entered Coimbra university to study law, matriculating in November 1914 with a bachelor's degree. Quiet and studious, his only recreation during these years seems to have been his membership of the CADC.

Salazar helped to revive this lay Catholic body and after 1915 sharec digs in Coimbra on the Rua dos Grilos with two other Catholic activists, Father Gonçalves Cerejeira and Mário de Figueiredo. Using the pen name Alves da Silva, he wrote articles for the CADC journal while working on a doctoral thesis which was submitted to the university in 1918. By now he was already a lecturer there, two theses on the problems of wheat production and the commodity crisis having firmly established his reputation as an up-and-coming academic. Without ever declaring himself a republican, he accepted the republic as the established form of government. However, his known conservative sympathies got him suspended from the university in 1919 after Paiva Couceiro's monarchist uprising, although he was quickly exonerated in the subsequent inquiry. Shortly afterwards he stood as a parliamentary candidate for the CCP, the Catholic party, in Viana do Castelo. He was unsuccessful on that occasion but, two years later, he was elected for Guimarães. Taking his seat in Lisbon on 2 September 1921, he renounced his mandate that very evening and went back to Coimbra. Seeing how parliamentary politics was conducted from close up, he found the whole exercise very distasteful and some date this experience as the crucial one which turned him completely against liberal democracy.[3] However, 1921 was not the last year in which he put his hat into the electoral ring. One historian has recently discovered that he was a CCP candidate again in the 1925 election for the town of Arganil.[4] He failed to be elected, but in less than six months the republic was toppled and Salazar was invited to become finance minister by the first military dictator, General Gomes da Costa.[5] His writings on religious and financial matters as well as his presence at Coimbra, the clearing-house for the educated elite and for a long time the sole university, had brought him to prominence in conservative quarters. Although he would only be finance minister for sixteen days, owing to the acute turmoil of the post-*coup* period, he remained a name to be reckoned with, since there were so few trained economists in Portugal who had the political qualifications for membership of the conservative dictatorship.

After 1926 Salazar knew he was a valuable commodity, and he turned down several offers of the finance ministry before finally taking the post in 1928. The year before he had made his only visit outside the Iberian peninsula when he travelled to France and Belgium with a Catholic delegation. Thereafter he buried himself in duties of state which left him very little time for relaxation or socialising. This was undoubtedly the way Salazar preferred to have things. Although he enjoyed some female company and there were some old rumours of romantic attachments, he showed a fastidious disinterest in sex (possibly like other lonely authoritarian figures holding down important public jobs, such as J. Edgar Hoover, head of the United States FBI from 1924 to 1973, he was asexual).

Probably the person who was closer to Salazar than any other was Maria de Jesus Caetano, his no-nonsense housekeeper, who had been with him since his days at the Rua dos Grilos in Coimbra. Dona Maria, as she was known, brought up two children Salazar adopted, Micas and Maria António, one of them being a niece of hers. A brother-in-law of Salazar's, Mário Pais de Sousa, was already a member of the cabinet in 1931, which shows just how much Salazar was in practical control of the nation even before he became prime minister in July 1932. If a date had to be set on the start of his political hegemony it would probably be July 1929, the month President Carmona made it clear that he would not form a government which did not have Salazar in it. Thereafter Salazar ceased to be backward about his plans and intentions and quickly revealed himself to be a man with real dictatorial ambitions. No challenger emerged to thwart his bid for power in the years before he became prime minister. In fact the right possessed few nationally known personalities able to rival him. Until the closing years of liberalism, doctrinaire rightists had refused to take part in normal political life or form parties, so there were no major leaders ready to take advantage of the counter-revolution. Certainly, Salazar did not have to eclipse any figures of the stature of Spain's Calvo Sotelo or Gil Robles as his confederate General Franco had to do on his road to power in the 1930s.

The institutions of the *Estado Novo*

Most of the legislation which established the New State reached the statute books in the eighteen months after António de Oliveira Salazar became prime minister. No other period of the regime's history would witness such a concentrated phase of innovation and law-making. By far the most important initiative was the unveiling of a new constitution. An early draft had been published on 28 May 1932 which declared that the Portuguese state adopted the representative and democratic republic as its form of government. However, after Salazar became prime minister this clause was deleted and in article five of the final version the Portuguese state was declared a corporative and unitary republic.[6]

Some confusion exists about who was the principal author of the constitution. Pro-regime writers and spokesmen habitually described Salazar as the main author. However, until his death in 1935 the conservative lawyer and writer Avelino Quirino de Jesus insisted that he had largely drawn up the document. This elderly Madeiran, who had certainly worked closely with Salazar in the years immediately after 1928, quietly accused the prime minister of deceit in taking all the credit for the programme of juridical changes announced after 1932. Another former associate, General Vicente de Freitas, was more openly critical. In February 1933 he issued a counter-document that, while authoritarian in some respects, favoured a freely elected parliament and came out against a single-party state. This gesture had minimal effect. The government was able to dismiss Freitas from his job as civil governor of Lisbon just before a plebiscite was held on 19 March 1933 to ratify the constitution. In a population of just over six million, only 1,200,000 people were eligible to vote. Officially, 719,364 of them approved the constitution while 5,955 voted against. However, as many as 488,840 voters (about 30 per cent of the registered electorate) abstained but were counted as having voted yes.

The 1933 constitution proclaimed Portugal:

> a unitary and corporative republic founded upon the equality of all its citizens in the eyes of the law, upon the free access of all citizens to the benefits of civilisation, and upon the participation of all the constituent forces of the nation in its administrative life and in the making of laws.[7]

As if to reinforce this idealistic preamble, a long list of individual rights (freedom of speech, of assembly, of the press) were inserted in the constitution. However, they were effectively nullified by a clause which gave the government power to limit civil liberties 'for the common good'. Similarly undermined was the passage that recognised the importance of public opinion: another section declared that the government was obliged to perfect public opinion.

The powers allotted to the administration were far broader than under any previous constitution. Consciously reversing the 1911 document, the 1933 constitution gave almost supreme authority to the executive and only marginal powers to the legislature. In keeping with the *de facto* post-1926 situation, provision was made for both a presidential head of state and a prime minister. Theoretically, the former had major authority. To be elected by popular vote at seven-yearly intervals, he had the power to appoint and dismiss the prime minister at will and dissolve the parliamentary assembly at a time of his choosing. However, this authority was more apparent than real: not once during the whole of the *Estado Novo* period would it be exercised independently, despite the fact that in the following four decades fundamental disagreement between the head of state and premier was not unknown.

Actual key authority rested with the prime minister, usually known in Portugal as the President of the Council of Ministers. The type of arrangement which existed in reality was aptly described by Marcelo Caetano as 'the presidentialism of the prime minister'.[8] While the head of state's function was in practice to perform largely ceremonial duties, the prime minister had complete charge of the day-to-day running of the country. The authority to issue decree-laws without parliamentary approval was his. Government ministers were hired and fired on *his* recommendation to the president, which the head of state invariably acted upon. The prime minister could work with his ministers on an individual basis without convening the full ministerial unit: the constitution did not require the cabinet to meet in session. After 1933 Salazar fully exploited this constitutional provision. For forty years he seldom called the full cabinet together. It was not uncommon for months to go by without a minister coming into contact with him, either personally, by letter or by telephone, according to a cabinet minister in the democratic era.[9] For Salazar the best method of government consisted of the President of the Council of Ministers working individually with one of his colleagues. Rarely meeting as a whole, the cabinet had slight opportunity to exercise the limited authority it theoretically possessed. As a result, the prime minister was in a totally commanding position over his ministerial colleagues.

After November 1932 Salazar was president of the central committee of the União Nacional. This was the government party, but supporters described it as a civic association, since political parties were officially depicted as the source of Portugal's ills ever since the monarchy. Founded in 1930, a shadowy forerunner, the League of 28 May, had already existed since October 1927. It dutifully merged with the UN, and in 1932 Salazar made it plain that other parties would do the same. Next year the constitution formally outlawed political parties. Even Salazar's own Centro Católico was not exempted from this *Diktat*, and it was a chagrined Lino Neto who finally wound up the party in 1934.

Quite a number of right-wing politicians re-emerged as members of the National Assembly, the lower house of Portugal's new bicameral parliament. It met for the first time in 1935 but was a rubber-stamp affair with little independent power. Only meeting for three months of the year, usually from November to February, it was more a deliberative than a legislative body, its right to initiate legislation being subject to the proviso that no law or amendment might be proposed which would prejudice the national revenue. The government, for its part, could legislate by decree-law at any time without reference to the assembly when that body was not in session. During the months when it was, Salazar had the power to suspend its sittings should such action seem desirable.[10] As for his ministers, they were not required to belong to parliament, nor were they accountable to it to any major extent. In other words, then, the concept of parliamentary sovereignty hardly had any meaning under the 1933 constitution. From the outset the legislature played a very minor role in the decision-making process. It was never intended to be a separate or co-equal branch of government and was really a mere talking-shop of ninety deputies, a number raised to 120 in 1945, 130 in 1959 and 150 in 1971.[11] Every four years elections were held to choose the membership of the National Assembly, but only a tiny proportion of the population could vote (7·8 per cent of the total in the 1934–45 period). Illiterates (31·6 per cent of the population in 1960) were barred from voting, as, until 1968, were women, unless they could prove they were heads of families and/or had paid a certain amount of real estate tax.[12] Opposition candidates only stood after the Second World War, but none ever won a single seat, since the officially compiled lists were shamelessly manipulated.

The upper house of parliament, the Corporative Chamber, consisted of regime supporters chosen by major functional and corporative interests: agriculture, commerce, industry, the military, the Church, the universities, various ministries and municipal authorities. The task of the chamber was to debate and advise upon issues that concerned the elements represented within it. Its architects had hoped that the existence of a group-oriented body at the heart of the state might 'remove interest-group lobbying and influence-peddling from the dark cloakrooms of power'.[13] Meeting for only a few months of the year, and with its powers circumscribed by the state, it would hardly fulfil this function. In an environment where open politics had been outlawed, intrigue, conflict and power struggles involving sectional interests probably increased rather than dimished.

Having looked at the central features of the constitution, there is the philosophy of 'corporativism' itself to examine.[14] Since it attempted to rival socialism, liberalism and communism during only a relatively brief phase in modern European history (1922–45), this doctrinal phenomenon has not been the subject of consistent or sustained inquiry. However, even during its heyday, committed zealots could not fully agree about the doctrinal properties of corporativism.

In theory, corporativism saw the interests of various social classes as essentially harmonious. It promised the abolition of strife between worker and employer and the end of capitalist exploitation. The body which would theoretically realise this aspiration was the *corporation*. Sectional interests would be transcended in this new forum, since managers and foremen, owners and workers would be fairly represented. Grouped in the corporations, all could work together for the national good, and the public would benefit by increased production and the end of class conflict. Through the corporations the ordinary citizen could have more of a say in decision-making than was possible in the days of 'fraudulent' electoral democracy, and eventually the corporations would take over the essential running of the country.

The corporative ideal stretches back to medieval times when guild associations, operating under similar principles, brought master and artisan together. In the nineteenth century it was refurbished by various thinkers out of joint with the capitalist world for fragmenting society and breaking it into mutually hostile units or else alarmed by the rise of class-based political parties challenging the existing order. From both right and left, spokesmen emerged decrying capitalist individualism and the rise of the materialist state. A historic breakthrough for corporativism eventually came with the emergence of Italian fascism in 1922.

Benito Mussolini, the fascist leader, amalgamated the old corporative ideal with the concept of the all-powerful state. In fascist Italy corporations were depicted as the agents of state policy and national advancement. In the Italian corporate state, it was planned to unite the corporations in a single chamber which would replace the old parliament and administer the country's economy in accordance with Italian fascist principles. However, reality fell short of expectations. The Italian corporate state involved a mixture of party control and capitalist economy. Policy and administration came from an autocratic centre and not from 'the organic unity of all producers'. Mussolini retained state control in his own hands during the introduction of the corporative institutions. By 1939, when a corporative chamber finally replaced the old parliamentary system, he had made enough concessions to business and industry to nullify the egalitarianism of the corporations, which were, in reality, little more than bureaucratic sinecures for fascist chiefs and their followers.

Though paying occasional homage to Mussolini, Salazar never let it be said that the Portuguese corporative system was based on the Italian model. Features of the Italian system disturbed him, such as its populist character and Mussolini's 'pagan caesarism'. Salazar preferred to argue that Portuguese corporativism sprang from Portugal's 'special and distinct tradition'. Howard J. Wiarda, an American student of Portuguese corporativism, has given backing to this view. However, Portugal's corporative tradition does not seem to have been any more special than that of other European countries where the guild system had been a feature of late medieval society. Indeed, the last guilds had certainly disappeared by the mid-nineteenth century (something which supporters of the regime have themselves acknowledged), thus rendering unlikely any direct link between the medieval tradition and twentieth century corporativism.

The only external influence readily acknowledged by Salazar was that of the papacy. Two encyclicals in particular seem to have guided his thought, Leo XIII's *Rerum Novarum* (1891) and Pius XI's *Quadragesimo Anno* (1931). Both stressed the desirability of labour and capital collaborating for the common good. In Portugal the law that sought to institutionalise this tenet of corporativist thought was the National Labour Statute. Enacted on 23 September 1933, it outlined the state's economic and social thinking in much greater detail than the constitution. Under this statute, property, labour and capital were each viewed as having a social function. Strikes by workers and lock-outs by employers were expressly forbidden. Henceforth disputes were to be settled through compromise and arbitration rather than by violence or strife. Called by its architects 'the Magna Carta' of the Portuguese working class, the National Labour Statute was hardly that. For independent working-class activity was destroyed. Penalties for going on strike and continuing with genuine trade unions were imprisonment and, after 1936, captivity in the Tarrafal concentration camp, situated on one of the barren, tropical Cape Verde islands. Dozens of proletarian militants were incarcerated there. Few, if any, employers were singled out for such treatment.

On the same day that the National Labour Statute was enacted, another decree established a national system of *grémios* or guilds. The *grémios* were employer associations which supposedly repudiated both class warfare and untrammelled capitalism and were paralleled by a network of labour syndicates known as *sindicatos*. The *sindicatos* were animated by similar harmonious principles, and it was envisaged that both they and the *grémios* would work in unison. But it was hardly a marriage of equals. The *sindicatos* only really existed at district level, and even within the corporativist framework action on a national basis was very difficult. A *sindicato* required at least 100 members: this condition greatly restricted their scope, since most Portuguese factories were small family-run concerns. Only in the larger industries and commercial enterprises were the state *sindicatos* organised; this was no coincidence. Before 1926 the main industrial unrest had occurred in these larger concerns. By concentrating *sindicato* activity at industrial stress points, and by ignoring small-scale manufacturing firms, the regime demonstrated that it was more concerned with social control than working-class social justice.

Certainly, as a priority, regulating working-class activity was regarded as far more important than supervising the actions of private employers. Philippe Schmitter has stated that the 1933 legislation included 'a provision which recognised and tolerated the continuation of class associations already in existence'.[15] Now, Portuguese trade unions had been all but obliterated by then. But there is no evidence that any of the previous existing employer associations (285 in all) had suffered the same fate, although many subsequently dissolved themselves voluntarily. This information makes it fairly apparent that, as regards business employers, state compulsion was decidedly less in evidence.

The legislation referred to so far was mainly urban-oriented. On the same 'fateful' day, 23 September 1933, a law was passed establishing a nation-wide system of *casas do povo* or people's community centres. Low-level organs of corporativist activity, the *casas* were depicted by the regime as units of rural social co-operation. One was authorised for each parish in the country – controlled invariably by the most powerful local landowner or notable. Fishermen's centres known as *casas dos pescadores* were also planned along the same lines as *casas do povo*. Both agencies were designed to fulfil the social assistance function that in other European countries was the prerogative of the state. Branded by one source as 'glorified benevolent centres',[16] only about 20 per cent of the rural population had been enrolled in the *casas do povo* by 1959, the twenty-sixth year of the corporativist era.

The body responsible for co-ordinating the corporative system was the sub-secretariat of state for corporations and social affairs. Founded on 14 April 1933, it drew up and finalised the wide-ranging legislation passed in the autumn of that year. The individual at its head was a thirty-one-year-old former Integralist leader from an upper-class background, Pedro Teotónio Pereira. He joined the ranks of the governing elite, having carved out a reputation as a committed New State ideologue. Some of his colleagues were disappointed that corporations had not been made a full ministry with cabinet status. A few even argued that it should be a super-ministry towering over other portfolios. Pereira took a more moderate stance, hoping that corporations might be located within the premier's office, 'which would have given his agency better access to Salazar and presumably more influence in the governmental system as a whole'.[17] However, Salazar demurred, and corporations started out with a rank inferior to other established ministries even though, in all important spheres, national policy-making was being shaped according to corporativist principles.

Salazar at this time was being depicted abroad as the guiding apostle of Portugal's corporative 'revolution'. However, he was far from being the most committed advocate of the New State philosophy. Young ideologues, many grouped around Teotónio Pereira, campaigned for a more thoroughgoing adaptation of corporativist principles at all levels of the state. They clashed with more orthodox right-wingers, many of whom lacked the Integralist background of the leading exponents of corporativism. The first major disagreement occurred as early as 1934, when Salazar pushed through a decree-law giving larger businesses important autonomy in relation to the corporativist agencies. Through the *grémio* structure the regime continued to regulate small-scale concerns in much the same way as it controlled the *sindicatos*. However, to the great annoyance of some of the architects of the 1933 legislation, major private entrepreneurs were given important latitude.[18]

Salazar may have gone for compromise with the most powerful business interests out of an awareness that unbridled corporativism might destabilise the economy. The premier knew that not every propertied group appreciated having its prices, quotas and credits fixed by external agencies; it appears unlikely that he would have pushed through a full-scale corporativist revolution in the face of massive employer resistance. Too much would have been at stake politically. So, instead, strategic compromises were reached in areas where economic performance was thought more important than doctrinal purity. After 1936, to the relief of many businessmen, a marked slow-down occurred in the pace of corporativist development. No major innovations on the scale of the 1933–34 period occurred during the later 1930s. After the first phase of legislation the various component parts of the corporative state were not by any means all in place. However, the sense of urgency that seemed to pervade the Portuguese scene in the first years of the *Estado Novo* was not carried over into subsequent ones. The most obvious explanation was the eruption of civil war in neighbouring Spain in 1936. For three years the Salazar government was preoccupied with this emergency. However, events in Spain do not wholly explain why the corporativist drive came to a halt.

Perhaps the most serious blow to the corporativist experiment was the removal of Teotónio Pereira as corporations sub-secretary. Pereira had failed to persuade Salazar to speed up the corporativist programme and establish it as first among the regime's priorities. Ministers were prepared to go only so far in 'corporatising' their departments. Increasingly frustrated, Pereira appears to have quarrelled with Salazar during 1935–36, and in January of the latter year he was switched to the ministry of commerce. Later in 1936 he was removed altogether from home politics on being appointed head of a special mission to Franco's Spain. Thus Salazar got rid of an independent colleague and a possible rival. That Pereira had his own ambitions in the 1930s was shown when he arranged a demonstration of the Portuguese youth movement in his favour at every train stop on his departure route to Spain. However, an 'obstruction' on the tracks forced his train to take another route and the demonstration was not able to take place.[19] This curious incident highlights the fact that internal dissension occurred in highest ranks of the New State in the 1930s, supposedly an era of maximum conformity and unchallenged obedience to Salazar.

Given the existence of private political rivalry within the regime, could personalist factors have been partly responsible for the relegation of corporativism after 1936? Certainly it would not necessarily be correct to attribute the switch in priorities to economic, ideological or external factors alone. Salazar may have feared a reduction in his own authority if an inordinate amount of power was devolved upon 'unknown institutions'.[20] The bald decision to exclude the rural population from involvement in the socio-economic machinery designed to regulate national life perhaps reflected such a concern. Previously the rural population had been depoliticised, perhaps representing a model of social tranquillity that Salazar wished to extend over the whole of Portugal. Fears that some layers of the peasantry could have become self-assertive as a result of too literally swallowing the corporativist doctrine may have influenced his decision to leave the countryside undisturbed. The last thing he desired was major social change in rural Portugal. The admittedly crude form of social partnership fostered by the regime could, if fully translated to the countryside, have produced significant ripples in a previously stagnant pool. Weighing up the political risks may have put Salazar off the idea of expanding the corporativist programme in an area of society where nothing like it had previously been seen.

When everything is considered, Salazar's behaviour from 1936 onwards points to his being motivated 'more by the desire for personal power and the wish to remain in office than by corporatist ideology'.[21] Cabinet reshuffles ensured that none of his immediate contemporaries had time to build up a major power base. Loyal followers might retain one job for a relatively long period. But talented, ambitious figures who liked to preserve a certain independence were rapidly switched about. Teotónio Pereira is one illustration. Another was Armindo Sttau Monteiro: Salazar's deputy in the finance ministry until 1931, this bright technician served the next twelve years as colonial minister, foreign minister and ambassador to London before being dropped altogether in 1943. Unlike Monteiro, Pereira stayed on in regime politics, holding down various ambassadorial posts. However, he never regained the corporations portfolio. After 1936 Salazar saw to it that the holders of this job were dependable political allies or technicians and not ideologues impatient for change.

On Pereira's exit in 1936, much still remained to be accomplished in the corporativist realm. Perhaps the most glaring omissions were the corporations themselves. They were to be the focal point around which the entire corporative system revolved. One was set aside for each area of production – agriculture, fishing, commerce, industry, transport, etc. The corporations were the top-level organisations wherein the *grémios* and *sindicatos* were expected to settle their differences and arrive at the mutual agreement on which the cross-class corporative system was based. Overall, their function was to co-ordinate the activities of the lesser corporative agencies and generally see to the smooth running of the whole system. In theory the corporations were to be autonomous bodies, independent of government and free from domination by any single class. But, until their creation, state-run agencies known as Organisations of Economic Co-ordination discharged their responsibilities. Initially, these were viewed as only stop-gap agencies, stepping into the breach until the corporative programme was fully mapped out. However, these bureaucratic arms of government failed to wither away. The corporations were subject to various postponements. The Second World War put paid to plans to launch the corporations either in September 1939 or May 1940.

Ultimately, the legislation drawn up in the late 1930s stayed 'in mothballs' until 1956, the year in which the corporations were finally set up by the state. By then almost all the impetus had gone out of the corporative revolution. In the intervening years the state had centralised control of the economy and labour relations in its own hands. The existing corporative agencies had lost what little autonomy they had once possessed. In the mid-1950s the sudden appearance of corporations did not change matters. Decisions that mattered continued to be made by the state. The 1956 'corporative drive' had every appearance of a propaganda exercise designed to give a regime hardening at the arteries a surface appearance of vigour and ideological consistency.

Perhaps the entire post-1933 corporative episode smacks of a propaganda exercise. There are several compelling reasons for suggesting so. First of all, Salazar appears to have been little influenced by corporativist philosophy up to the point when he came to power. His views were more traditional and restrained than those of radical right-wingers. Yet the regime borrowed much of their corporativist vocabulary after 1933. Awareness of the threadbare quality of Catholic conservative propaganda (in a country whose secular tradition stretches back to the Marquis of Pombal in the eighteenth century) was perhaps what prompted Salazar to adopt the rhetoric and institutional hallmarks of corporativism. There were major advantages in this. Battening on to a still novel political creed would have enabled him to forge a clear identity for his political system in the initial formative period. Corporativism made the New State appear as different as possible from the pre-1926 regime while still enabling him to argue that he was not a pocket-sized emulator of Hitler or Mussolini. Above all, he was able to make use of the social justice aspects of corporativism to cloak anti-working-class economic measures in idealistic garb.

By appearing outwardly loyal to the style of corporativism while surreptitiously forsaking its substance Salazar stood to gain much. His governing system acquired the reputation of being a significant political innovation and not just another Latin *régime personnel*. Salazar himself was the hero of the conservative European right, which was profoundly impressed by the way he had seemingly produced order from chaos without resorting to totalitarianism. For ten years, between 1935 and 1945, the Portuguese leader enjoyed the same celebrity status among intellectual conservatives which was bestowed upon Alexander Solzhenitsyn in the 1970s. He was depicted as a compassionate if authoritarian idealist and not a mere seeker after power.

Perhaps in the long term there was never a systematic propagation of corporativism in Portugal because the traditional nature of society made a developed right-wing ideology unnecessary. The country had experienced neither reformation nor industrial revolution. With over half the population illiterate in the 1930s, traditional society had remained more or less intact as compared with Italy or Germany, where the social and political order had broken down in many spheres prior to the emergence of fascism or nazism. One observer, Perry Anderson, argues that it was the weakening to the point of collapse of traditional authority in these two countries that accounts for the virulence of the authoritarian backlash. He describes mid-European fascism as:

> an emergency operation: a last desperate attempt to prolong or resurrect by force a social order which once functioned as if naturally and 'automatically' without the open intervention of violence, but which is now irretrievably broken.[22]

Matters had not reached such a critical pass in Portugal. Hence this may be one of the overriding reasons why corporativism remained a somewhat 'half-hearted affair', with the regime never making any real attempt to propagate and build up the theory systematically. Instead token steps were taken in the corporative direction. New bodies were created that ultimately served only to expand the official bureaucracy in a country already administratively overladen. Hollow structures such as the corporative chamber acted as sounding boards for official propagandists. To describe Portugal as a corporative state even in the 1930s is perhaps a misnomer. Ultimately, the two primary elements that corporativists claim as the basis of their political philosophy were to be absent from the Portuguese scene. Decision-making was not devolved to self-governing corporations. Nor was 'a natural organic harmony' created based on voluntary mutual consent between capital and labour.[23] Instead, behind a facade of corporative power, a centralising state concentrated absolute authority in its own hands. Portugal, to paraphrase Marcelo Caetano, was a corporative state in intention, not in fact. Perhaps if one had the ability to probe into Salazar's mind, one would have found that it was not even that.

Economic policies

During the first years of the dictatorship the most important economic initiative from the government was in the field of agriculture. Henrique Linhares Lima, minister of agriculture from 1929 to 1932, launched the *campanha do trigo* (the wheat campaign) in an effort to expand wheat production and reduce costly imports. This was really an attempt to emulate fascist Italy, where a similar initiative had been attempted, and, initially, short-term surpluses were achieved once relatively poor land had been ploughed up. However, much of the new land had become exhausted by the late 1930s and thereafter nothing more was heard of the *campanha do trigo*. Nor was there any effort to improve yields in fertile areas by introducing or expanding irrigation and crop fertilisation. With a large and cheap rural labour force at their disposal, southern latifundists were content to derive their profits from traditional, if not archaic, methods. Few major landowners could be bothered to speed up the natural process of soil renewal by using fertilisers or introducing modern irrigation methods.

For the first two decades of the *Estado Novo* the latifundist sector had important influence within the power structure and it was able to determine the shape of new agricultural policies, something which commercial and industrial interests were not able to do. However, the New State was not the national steering committee of the latifundists or of any other economic lobby. The regime's determination to control areas of economic life which had previously been the province of private enterprise ought to indicate that. Salazar actually possessed major autonomy *vis-à-vis* economic interest groups. State policies sometimes antagonised quite major concerns. Low-key opposition, for instance, greeted the rise of the corporative state in the 1930s. Employers then hailed the destruction of trade unionism but were less happy about state interference in the running of firms. Perhaps the latifundists enjoyed such political leeway because their blind traditionalism and conservatism coincided with Salazar's desire to proceed with economic development at a cautious pace. He even introduced a law in the 1930s which enabled established concerns to veto the setting up of rival enterprises. Powerful economic monopolies were encouraged to grow in this way, and, not surprisingly, the rate of industrial growth was sluggish in the 1930s and beyond. While still a minister, Teotónio Pereira summed up the conservative and mercantilist viewpoint of the new elite when he candidly declared that 'economic efficiency is not everything and the introduction of machinery sometimes runs counter to human interests'.[24] This was the attitude of the political oligarchy for a long time to come. Speaking in the National Assembly in January 1945, João Antunes Guimarães (a former minister of commerce), spoke out against making provision for new industrial development zones in Oporto. He argued that 'industrial concentrations are flagrant anachronisms condemned in peacetime for destroying family life, weakening morality, and being a breeding ground for strikes and other forms of subversion, as in war, for being easy targets for new weapons of combat and destruction'.[25]

Not surprisingly, in the light of this mentality, the percentage of the workforce engaged in industrial occupations increased by only 1 to 2 per cent between 1920 and 1940.[26] In vain did the pragmatic ex-minister Ezequiel de Campos plead for a policy of industrialisation based on electricity. He published articles in the press and even wrote to Salazar, but to no effect. Salazar seemed content that Portugal had escaped the depression with minimal damage. Her burdens were eased after 1929 not so much because of the finance minister's economic wizardry, more because foreign capital had not entered Portugal to any major degree, nor had the state got itself into debt by incurring any major foreign loans.

The functioning of the corporative system was perhaps the main economic bugbear Salazar had to contend with in the 1930s. In 1939 Mário de Figueiredo, a leading New State politician, candidly admitted that 'from north to south, there is great clamour about the functioning of the corporative system. The clamour is general . . .'[27] Many landowners and industrialists recognised the corporative agencies for what they were, networks of state surveillance, through which the government sought to 'dilute any real interest group or class-based action'.[28]

Friendship and patronage networks, the cement of Portuguese society before and after Salazar appeared on the scene, enabled most landowners and businessmen to surmount the difficulties which corporativist red tape presented. Latifundists, for instance, were able to exert more effective pressure on a personal level than through the guilds. One Portuguese scholar, José Cutileiro, saw this at first hand when doing research in an Alentejo parish in the 1960s. When the minister of the economy paid a visit to the area to discuss the agricultural situation, he met the latifundists privately but did not consult the guild. This and similar observations led Cutileiro to conclude that 'the relevant exchanges preceding government measures relating to agriculture may not take place in parliament or in the appropriate government departments, but over dining tables or in the course of the shooting parties given by latifundists'.[29]

The political elite

The new national establishment which emerged as the *Estado Novo* gradually consolidated itself was very hierarchical and exclusive as ruling elites go in the western world. Plebeian and socially marginal elements tended not to gain access to the upper reaches of the political elite, although there were some exceptions, like Adriano Moreira and Franco Nogueira, ministers in the 1960s and sons, respectively, of a shepherd and a policeman.[30] Manuel Rodrigues, minister of justice from 1932 to 1940, also emerged from a relatively humble background, as indeed did Salazar himself. However, he was not marginal in the way that other major European leaders like De Valera, Hitler and Atatürk were, having been born in the middle of the country, of Portuguese parents, destined to spend all his formative years and the rest of his life in Portugal. Members of the upper class and, by extension, the political world were drawn from a narrow range of institutions and occupations. Basically the men with power in the *Estado Novo* were the largest landowners, the directors or owners of major industries, high-ranking civil servants, leading financiers, senior military officers, the Catholic hierarchy, university professors, and the elite of the medical and legal professions.[31] Not all the leading representatives in these occupations were politically active, and time would show that not all were slavish adherents of the *Estado Novo* either. However, it was men (rarely women) from these civil, military, ecclesiastical and professional backgrounds who staffed, or helped to appoint, members to the regime's political agencies; the most important official structures were the National Assembly, the Corporative Chamber, the União Nacional, the paramilitary Portuguese Legion and, of course, the cabinet. Eighty-seven men served as ministers under Salazar, the majority coming from four sources, the military establishment, academia, the industrial world and the legal profession. Many ministers had varied career backgrounds. Harry Makler, a US sociologist who has analysed the composition of the economic elite, found that in the 1960s 'the typical career pattern to a large modern corporation started with an assistant professorship at university ... movement into an undersecretarial [deputy ministerial] position and then either from there to a top industrial post or continuation in the government, moving into a ministerial position, and then into industry'.[32]

This was above all true of the 1960–74 period, when technocrats occupied a majority of government posts in some years, both under Salazar and under Caetano. Before then, the military and academic professions had been the dominant elements in the cabinet. The number of scholars in government fluctuated but there was high academic visibility in all phases of the New State period, something which has given rise to the term *catedradocracia* (the aristocracy of dons). Academics provided the great bulk of ministers as well as the two dictatorial executives: Caetano and Salazar. In the 1960s, when its influence was beginning to decline, businessmen still ranked the academic elite as the most prestigious profession.[33] No counterpart existed anywhere else in the world for this donnish monopoly of political posts. In 1936 professors from the law faculty of Coimbra University alone made up 23 per cent of Salazar's cabinet. The location of this university, over a hundred miles north of Lisbon, meant that a relatively high percentage of provincials were to be found in the regime's hard core. This being the case, one political scientist has argued that 'its rise to power involved the mobilisation of relatively privileged groups in the geographic, cultural and developmental periphery of society against the more sophisticated, cosmopolitan and 'progressive' elements of its metropolitan centre'.[34] Certainly the urban-based intelligentsia from south central Portugal did less well under the *Estado Novo* than under the 1910–26 republic, when indeed it was overrepresented in national political life. However, it would be unwise to see the 1926 revolution and its aftermath as representing the triumph of the traditional, clerical and 'provincial' north over the liberal, secular and 'advanced' south. In Oporto, the largest northern city and the industrial hub of the country until the 1960s, the business elite somewhat kept its distance from the regime and showed itself less caste-ridden and more prone to republican affiliation. The southern-based latifundists, on the other hand, enjoyed far more intimate links with the regime. The major latifundia families had important personal connections with the aristocracy, the monarchy, the officer corps and the bureaucracy, and were able to transfer their conservative values to these sectors.[35] Wealthy groups with foreign interests or economic connections abroad were not at all conspicuous within the ranks of the New State, which underscores the provincial and introverted character of the economic groupings influential in politics.

In terms of political affiliation, the political elite is also relatively easy to classify. Republicans, monarchists and Catholics were the three main political viewpoints that could be recognised in the *Estado Novo*. Since Salazar did not give major secular power to the Church, aware of the latent anticlericalism to be found in Portuguese society, politicians who were first and foremost representing Catholic interests were relatively uncontentious. However, relations between republicans and monarchists were cool and sometimes problematic, especially in the latter half of the *Estado Novo*, during times when there were rumours about Salazar's retirement. Aware of the tensions that existed between these two factions at ministerial level, Salazar carefully balanced his cabinet, giving a majority of seats to republicans, who represented a majority viewpoint within the political elite and the country at large.[36] In the initial phase, conservative and nationalist republicans, who had been active under the previous regime, were co-opted by the New State. In this way Salazar avoided creating potential opponents to his emergent authoritarian state among conservatives who, nevertheless, had some experience of parliamentary politics. Perhaps the most prominent old-guard republican in the *Estado Novo* was Albino Soares dos Reis. Although he only spent a year in the cabinet (as minister of the interior in 1932–33), this northern lawyer was one of the key *barões* (barons) of the *Estado Novo*, who had a domint role in both the UN and the National Assembly for four decades. Albino dos Reis was one of the intimate circle of advisers whom Salazar consulted on the eve of making important policy decisions or before cabinet reshuffles. Certain monarchists were on even closer terms with Salazar. Two in particular, João da Costa Leite and Mário de Figueiredo, were long-standing cronies. Salazar was himself a monarchist.[37] However, unlike these two friends, he always believed that a royalist restoration might jeopardise the *Estado Novo* by splitting the *situacionistas* (partisans of the *status quo*) and by heightening the political tensions which he had been so concerned to banish. It may not, either, have escaped his shrewd mind that to re-establish the monarchy would have meant losing Carmona, who, as president, was content to act as a retiring figurehead. A monarchical head of state might have been less pliable, and the premier could have had no guarantee that he would not develop political ideas at variance with his own.

Only after Carmona's death in 1951 did Salazar, prodded by Costa Leite and Figueiredo, appear to have looked seriously at restoring the monarchy. In reality the chances of this happening had been almost fatally dashed by the death, in England, of ex-King Manuel in July 1932. News of his death reached Lisbon on the day that Salazar had been asked to form a government. Leaving no heir, Manuel was also the last male member of the Braganza line, and his death prompted many monarchists to abandon their hopes for a royal restoration and become reconciled to serving under a republican New State. If they had remained unassimilated, Salazar could have been presented with a significant headache which might have prevented his achieving the long-term stability which came to characterise the New State. Nevertheless, in the event, monarchists like Fezas Vital and Fernando Santos Costa accepted senior political jobs and only occasionally troubled Salazar with the request that Dom Duarte Nuno, the descendant of nineteenth-century Prince Miguel, be groomed for kingship. The veteran conspirator Henrique Paiva Couceiro did make trouble for the authorities briefly after

1932, but this gnarled colonial veteran was very much an anachronism by the time of his death in 1944; most monarchists had taken to heart Salazar's admonition that 'what I ask of our Royalists – or, perhaps I should put it, what I advise them to do – is that, if and when they enter our public life, they shall put aside any false or even dangerous notion that their coalition in the present government is any step towards realisation of their aspirations'.[38]

The least troublesome section of Salazar's support, the lay Catholic element, passively accepted the disbandment of its political voice, the *Centro Católico* in May 1934. Party members joined the UN while many members of the CADC (the Catholic student association) actually graduated to the cabinet and were 'elected' to the National Assembly. No fewer than ten cabinet members were drawn from the CADC, despite its very small size, something which indicates the narrow elite base Salazar was drawing support from. Before 1926 the Integralist movement was larger (in its heyday) than the CADC and had more influence among the Portuguese right. However, relatively few Integralists cropped up in leading government posts, with the exception of younger ones. Some were, admittedly, to be found in the National Assembly, whose honorific function has already been described.

To argue, as Salazar did in 1932, that the UN's aim was 'to organise the nation' was inaccurate. From the first day of its existence, back in 1930, it had possessed little power. Membership was insignificant. Government ministers did not need to belong. Between 'elections' and occasional national conferences there were often long periods of total inactivity. For most of its lengthy existence it was a skeletal organisation, a cross between a club for partisans of the regime and a propaganda organ for official government views. This latter function was performed by the UN's own newspaper, the daily *Diário da Manhã*. This was a typical right-wing tabloid edited for many years by Manuel Múrias, a devoted partisan of the New State. *O Século, A Voz* and *Novidades* were competitors which reflected a republican, Catholic monarchist and Catholic republican standpoint in their editorials and choice of contributors.[39]

Behind closed doors, quite removed from the glare of publicity, monarchists, Catholics and republicans usually locked horns when the time came to draw up a list of candidates for the national assembly elections. The *barões* who headed the various factions busily worked to ensure that as many of their co-religionists and supporters as possible were placed on the UN slate. Generally, it was the president of the UN executive (for many years Albino dos Reis) who was responsible, along with the minister of the interior, for drawing up lists of eligible people. The minister liaised with civil governors of the leading towns, local notables and other worthies to reach a consensus about who or who was not 'deputable'. A valuable description of this selection process has been left by the right-wing author Jaime Nogueira Pinto, who relates that, once a list of government deputies had been drawn up, Salazar (in his capacity as president of the central commission of the UN) 'scrutinised it with pencil in hand, in the presence of its proponents . . ., requesting an explanation here, making a comment there, questioning an absence or inquiring about an entry, crossing out a name, adding another (rarely, though). He scrutinised the list of future fathers of the nation without giving it much importance.'[40]

Nogueira Pinto mentions that Salazar was reluctant to get involved in the nitty gritty of politics, 'that humble but necessary chore of choosing and nominating individuals for administrative or political posts'.[41] This may have been the case in his later years but it certainly was not an accurate picture of the first fifteen years of his premiership. In those years, especially before 1939, there was a high turnover of ministers, Salazar hiring and firing a succession of incumbents and taking over more and more ministries himself, until by 1936 he was not only prime minister but also minister of finance, foreign minister and minister of war.[42] One year before he had prepared the nation for such personal aggrandisement by publishing an official note which declared that 'unfortunately there are a lot of things that seemingly only I can do'.[43] During these years ministers only knew of their dismissal on the morning of the government's resignation. But later Salazar mellowed, and he even appointed individuals like Júlio Botelho Moniz (1958–61: minister of defence) and Adriano Moreira (1961–62: minister of the *ultramar*), who were very quickly conspiring against him.

Thirty years before, in 1932, when Salazar had first become prime minister, the average age of his cabinet was the same as his own: forty-three. Gradually the cabinet aged, Salazar invariably being the oldest member after 1950. Most, but not all, of his ministers were colourless retainers. Several – Marcelo Caetano, Fernando dos Santos Costa, Franco Nogueira, Teotónio Pereira and Duarte Pacheco – were able to establish their own imprint as politicians. Until his death in a car crash in 1943, aged only forty-four, Duarte Pacheco, the minister of public works had been particularly influential. In a report filed to London on 26 November 1943 the British embassy commented that 'Dr Salazar has lost the one man in his cabinet with character and initiative comparable to his own'.[44] Salazar 'consulted him on many matters far outside the already wide sphere of Senhor Pacheco's activities' and increasingly he had come to be 'a kind of minor dictator in his own right'.[45] If Pacheco had not disappeared suddenly, he might have emerged as the heir apparent who would be so signally absent in the years to come. An indication of the authority he wielded came in 1941, when Salazar decided to transfer all matters relating to electrical power from his ministry to that of the minister for the economy. Pacheco resisted the proposal, something few other ministers would have been able to do.

After the war Salazar was less close to his ministers, who were more employees than confidantes. When Manuel Cavaleiro Ferreira, justice minister from 1944 to 1954, one day told him that he would not permit him to interfere with the judiciary, it was very much an isolated action. Rivalry between ministers (such as the famous one involving Marcelo Caetano and Santos Costa) ultimately weakened their hand and redounded to Salazar's benefit. His cronies were now found outside the cabinet and tended to be men like Bissaia Barreto, a progressive student leader in his youth who became his personal physician, Albino dos Reis, long-standing president of the National Assembly, and José Nosolini, his minister to the Vatican. On the whole Salazar received far less trouble from the right-wing members of his entourage than from more modern and liberal-minded ministers such as Teotónio Pereira (in his later years), Caetano, Armindo Monteiro and Moreira. Within the spectrum of *Estado Novo* politics, Salazar himself belonged to the right rather than to the centre or left. Former *situacionistas* who became estranged from the regime were, usually, the less reactionary types. However, it is a tribute to Salazar's statecraft that only a handful of the scores of ministers to serve under him between 1932 and 1968 moved into the opposition camp, none of them *publicly* joining forces with his enemies.

Notes

1   João Medina, 'O Estado Novo: un "fascismo" cauteloso', *O Jornal* (Lisbon), 25 April 1980, p. 20.
2   Nowell, *Portugal*, p. 148.
3   In 1914 Salazar had made a speech in Oporto in which he declared, in the words of Hugh Kay, that 'democracy was a historical phenomenon and was now irrestistible'. See Hugh Kay, *Salazar and Modern Portugal*, Eyre & Spottiswoode, London, 1970, p. 24.
4   Braga da Cruz, *As origens*, p. 16.
5   Gomes da Costa had no idea who he was appointing. On 8 June 1926 he spoke to journalists: 'The new government is just the best we can find at a moment like this. The minister of finance is to be a certain Salazar from Coimbra. Everyone speaks very highly of him. Do you happen to know him?' António Ferro, *Salazar, Portugal and her Leader*, Faber & Faber, London, 1939, p. 112.
6   Robinson, *Contemporary Portugal*, p. 9.
7   Kay, *op. cit.*, p. 54.
8   Wiarda, *Corporatism and Development*, p. 101.
9   Jorge Campinos, *O presidencialismo do Estado Novo*, Perspectivas & Realidades, Lisbon, 1978, p. 79.
10 William C. Atkinson, 'Institutions and law', in Livermore (ed.), *Portugal and Brazil*, p. 81.

11 Salazar gave his own unflattering description of parliament to António Ferro when he interviewed him in 1938: 'there are three months of the year when you've got to listen to parliamentary debates. Of course, there are occasional ideas of value, but it is mostly just fine phrases, just words! The present Council of Ministers is good enough for me; it's a small Parliament in a way, and it's also useful and does something.' Ferro, *op. cit.*, p. 244.

12 Schmitter, 'The impact and meaning of "non-competitive, non-free and insignificant" elections', p. 146.

13 Wiarda, *op. cit.*, p. 101.

14 In some sources the corporative state is dubbed the *corporate* state, the ideological title Mussolini gave to his regime. However, Salazar preferred the Portuguese system to be known as *corporativism* so that it would, hopefully, be regarded as a political philosophy formulated to cope with specific Portuguese conditions. His wish not to appear derivative was interesting and prescient, given the manner in which Italian fascism had become thoroughly discredited by 1945.

15 Philippe C. Schmitter, *Corporatism and Public Policy in Authoritarian Portugal*, Contemporary Political Sociology series, Sage Publications, London, 1975, p. 22.

16 Fryer and McGowan, *Oldest Ally*, p. 124.

17 Wiarda, *op. cit.*, p. 10.

18 See Schmitter, *op. cit.*, pp. 21–5.

19 Wiarda, *op. cit.*, p. 183.

20 *Ibid.*, p. 115.

21 *Ibid.*, p. 147.

22 Perry Anderson, 'Portugal and the end of ultra-colonialism', *New Left Review*, No. 15, London, 1962, p. 13.

23 Schmitter, *Corporation and Public Policy*, pp. 24–5.

24 Christian Rudel, *Le Portugal et Salazar*, Editions Ouvrières, Paris, 1968, p. 229.

25 Romeu Costa Reis and Manuel Rendeiro Júnior, 'O Estado Novo e o "caminho da indústria" ', *História*, 10, August 1979, p. 66.

26 *Ibid.*

27 Cansado Gonçalves, *A traição de Salazar*, Iniciativas Editorais, Lisbon, 1975, pp. 54–5.

28 Keefe, *Area Handbook for Portugal*, p. 129.

29 Quoted in Keefe, *op. cit.*, p. 130.

30 Sarah Bradford, *Portugal*, Thames & Hudson, London, 1973, p. 143.

31 Keefe, *op. cit.*, p. 121.

32 *Ibid.*, p. 122.

33 Hermínio Martins, 'Portugal', in M. S. Archer and Salvador Giner (eds.), *Contemporary Europe. Class, Status and Power*, Weidenfeld & Nicolson, London, 1971, p. 70.

34 Schmitter, 'The "régime d'exception" ', p. 20.

35 The Portuguese aristocracy in the first half of the twentieth century lacked prestige and economic wealth, to a greater extent than any other former ruling caste in western and southern Europe. Portuguese nobles had lost out badly in the various power struggles which destroyed absolutism between 1820 and 1851, and they were in no fit state to mount a rearguard action in defence of the monarchy before its collapse or in the unstable republican aftermath. The weakness of the native aristocracy perhaps explains why the royal house

collapsed so remarkably quickly. Later, in the Salazar era, a few of the dwindling bands of aristocrats did enjoy a modest political comeback, João da Costa Leite, for instance, the Count of Lumbralles, being Salazar's deputy minister of finance from 1929 to 1936, his minister of finance from 1940 to 1950, and minister to the presidency (a new cabinet post) from 1950 to 1955. In his youth he had also been Salazar's doctoral student at Coimbra University.

36 Jaime Nogueira Pinto tells a story which illustrates the difficulty some republicans had in serving under Salazar as well as underlining Salazar's pragmatism in his choice of collaborators. 'Once a university professor of liberal democratic convictions, invited to head the under-ministry of the treasury objected to the prime minister: "Mr President, I am a republican." Salazar took from his pocket a one-escudo coin with the effigy of the Republic and retorted, "All I am asking you to do is administer this".' See Jaime Nogueira Pinto, *Portugal. Os anos do fim*, Vol. II, Sociedade de Publicações Economia e Finança, Lisbon, 1977, p. 87.

37 Salazar's monarchist affiliations are revealed by Franco Nogueira, minister of foreign affairs from 1961 to 1969 and a stalwart defender of the *ancien régime* after 1974. See Franco Nogueira, *Salazar*, IV, *O ataque*, Atlântida Editora, Coimbra, 1980, p. 233.

38 Ferro, *op. cit.*, p. 129.

39 *Novidades* was founded in 1923, a time when there was a fierce public disagreement between monarchists and Catholics about what tactics to employ against the republic.

40 Nogueira Pinto, *op. cit.*, I, pp. 64–5.

41 *Ibid.*, p. 64.

42 Salazar was minister of finance from 1928 to 1940, minister of foreign affairs from 1936 to 1947, minister of war from 1936 to 1944 and of national defence from April 1961 to December 1962.

43 Oliveira Marques, *História de Portugal*, II, p. 346.

44 PRO, FO 371 34645, 26 November 1943.

45 *Ibid.*

5

The Estado Novo
Philosophy and methods

Portugal and the Spanish Civil War

Despite the quiescence of the opposition, the *Estado Novo* lurched in a strongly authoritarian direction during and after 1936. The Spanish Civil War, which began in July 1936, was the ostensible reason for the radicalisation of what had been one of the blander European dictatorships. However, even before the eruption of this internecine conflict next door in Spain, there was already evidence that some of the more extreme *situacionistas* were intent on following in the footsteps of the developed fascist states in central Europe. After 1934 many members of the pro-Nazi Blueshirt movement had joined the *Estado Novo* after finding that they were not strong enough singlehandedly to divert the 'national revolution' in the direction they wanted it to go. The same year saw the launching of the Acção Escolar Vanguarda (AEV), a militantly right-wing youth movement, one of whose early leaders was António Eça de Queiroz, descendant of the great nineteenth-century Portuguese novelist. (Almeida Garrett was another great liberal writer whose descendants played a role in *Estado Novo* politics, a namesake being elected to the National Assembly.)

By 1936 the AEV was beginning to stagnate, owing to the lack of enthusiasm, on the part of most Portuguese youth, for fascist paraphernalia and rhetoric as well as to the strength of the clandestine Portuguese Communist Party in certain student quarters. Eventually, on 19 May 1936, the government itself explicitly intervened in youth affairs with the launching of the Mocidade Portuguesa (Portuguese Youth). Membership was compulsory for boys aged ten and upwards. However, only a small number showed conspicuous enthusiasm for wearing the green shirt and khaki trousers of the Mocidade. The fascist salute was also obligatory, and there was compulsory drill at weekends as well as weapons training for older members. Four months later, in September 1936, a complementary adult militia, the Portuguese Legion, appeared on the scene. The most dedicated supporters of the New State filled its ranks, along with public employees who were basically conscripted into the organisation and forced to swell its membership on pain of losing their jobs. In its heyday the Legion had 20,000 members and, as well as spending time combating the 'bolshevik' menace at home, it was able to send volunteers to fight for General Franco's insurgent army in Spain.[1]

Salazar had no doubts about what to do once the Spanish left and right began to square up for a confrontation in 1936. Hermínio Martins writes:

> Almost as soon as the civil war started, the Portuguese government more or less cast in its lot with the rebel forces and decided to support them by all means short of actual participation in the war. This decision . . . seems to have been based on the calculation that, whether by Spanish intervention or contagion, the new state would not survive a republican victory: thus aid to the rebels would not create risk of retribution since the regime would be lost anyway if the rebels were defeated.[2]

Aware that the *Estado Novo*'s fate hung in the balance as long as there was a chance of the Republican government staving off Franco's challenge, Salazar worked might and main to assist his co-religionists in Spain. German arms destined for Franco arrived in Lisbon and were speedily transported to Spain, despite Portugal having signed an agreement with Britain and France which committed her to refrain from assisting any of the combatants. A special volunteer force, the Viriatos, was recruited to go and fight for Franco. Eighteen thousand Portuguese volunteers joined up, according to a government announcement at the end of the civil war, and there were more than 8,000 casualties,[3] though others have questioned this high figure. Spanish refugees hoping to find sanctuary in Portugal got no help if they were Republican. Claude Bowers, then US ambassador to Spain, has described the horrible slaughter which occurred in the bullring of the frontier town of Badajoz, when large numbers of people who had escaped to Portugal were driven back to their deaths at the hands of Franco's Moorish troops.[4]

Portuguese anti-fascists did their best to help the Spanish republican cause. In September 1936 the crew of two Portuguese warships moored in the river Tagus mutinied and attempted to sail their vessels to Republican Spain. They were thwarted, but three months before, in July 1936, a Portuguese anarchist had killed General Sanjurjo, the initial leader of the military revolt in Spain, by placing a bomb in his plane before it took off from a Lisbon airfield.[5] Other bomb explosions occurred in Lisbon in 1937, culminating on 4 July in the only known attempt on Salazar's life. As he was stepping out of his car to go to Mass in a friend's private chapel in a residential suburb of Lisbon a massive explosive charge placed in an underground sewer was detonated, deafening his chauffeur but leaving the premier unhurt.

Gradually the emergency brought about by the Spanish Civil War receded as Franco's victory became increasingly certain. In 1938 Portugal officially recognised his government, based in the Castilian city of Burgos. This was the prelude to a treaty of friendship and non-aggression signed between the two leaders on 17 March 1939 and known as the Iberian Pact.

Both parties pledged themselves to protect each other's territory and frontiers and not to enter into any pact or alliance involving aggression against the other.

This alliance did not affect Anglo-Portuguese relations, but there was considerable British unease in the late 1930s about the growth of foreign, particularly German, influence in Portugal. In 1938 a British military mission was despatched to pave the way for the sale of heavy armaments to the poorly equipped Portuguese army. In reports to the British Foreign Office around this time, diplomats based in Lisbon showed alarm about the fact that Germans were helping to train the Mocidade, an organisation which regime apologists compared to the Boy Scout movement but which, in the eyes of the British embassy, was more akin to the German Jugend or Italian fascist Balila movement. The view still remained in some British circles that Salazar would not be strong enough to resist the hawks within his political entourage and that he might be unseated in a palace revolution. The Foreign Secretary, Lord Halifax, himself became so alarmed by the Portuguese situation that on March 31 1939, he took time off from more pressing matters to draft a long memorandum setting out his anxieties.[6]

Salazarism and fascism

Once the civil war ended in victory for the Spanish rebels during the spring of 1939, the Portuguese government did not relax its vigilance or lighten its rule. The repressive features of the *Estado Novo* introduced after 1936 took on institutional form and were retained even after the defeat of the major fascist powers at the end of World War II. Thirty years later, when authoritarian rule in Lisbon itself came to an end, most observers commented that one of the last bastions of fascism had been toppled. In democratic Portugal most of the population, when referring to the pre-1974 era, talked about the years of 'fascism'. One can see why. The *Estado Novo* emerged at the same historic moment as the larger mid-European dictatorships, encouraging the tendency to group them together. In a broad political sense, Hitler, Mussolini and Salazar shared many features in common: authoritarian political views, hatred of communism, a belief in hierarchy, and racialism. However, the ideology, structures and practices of the Portuguese regime differed markedly from those of the two major European dictatorships. The *Estado Novo* possibly bears more resemblance to the successful Third World dictatorships, such as Nasser's Egypt, Sukarno's Indonesia or Nkrumah's Ghana. Despite their progressive Third World 'socialist' reputation, these regimes were essentially non-communist, authoritarian and intensely nationalist political systems, dominated, as in Portugal, by a single leader. Nasser

indeed turned to Salazar's *Estado Novo* in the 1950s when he was searching
for an ideology suitable for newly republican Egypt and called his political
movement the National Union. However, regimes like Nasser's, Colonel
Gadaffi's in Libya or Saddem Hussein's in Iraq are considered too
'progressive' to merit comparison with 'fascist' Portugal even if the levels
of internal repression and violence, in the case of the Iraqi and Libyan
regimes for instance, are of a higher order than anything ever witnessed in
Portugal.

Even at the height of fascism, between 1933 and 1945, Salazar's rule
came across as much less violent and capricious than that of the 'great'
dictators. Though the harshest government Portugal had ever witnessed
in modern times, the New State often seemed positively benign in relation
to other contemporary systems. Salazar wielded power without resorting
to indiscriminate mass terror or systematic persecution of social
minorities.[7] Lisbon's main thoroughfare continued to be named the
Avenida da Liberdade, the Avenue of Liberty. Events occurred that have
no parallel in fascist Italy or Germany. In 1932 a statue of Pombal was
erected in central Lisbon on which was set out his achievements, the
'Expulsion of the Jesuits' being at the head of the list. Later, another
statue was erected in Luanda, the capital of Angola, in honour of General
José Norton de Matos, the opposition candidate in the 1949 presidential
elections who had been a governor-general of the territory before 1926.
Protest and real opposition were, of course, proscribed. It would be foolish
and deceitful to try and argue otherwise. However, oppositionists could
continue to reside in Portugal provided they forswore political activity and
lived as private citizens. Harsh penalties awaited persistent infringers of
the 'no politics' rule, especially if they were communists. However, the
death penalty was never restored and, compared to other inter-war
dictatorships, Portugal's security apparatus was small and far from all-
encompassing in scope.

In terms of personal freedom and civilising attributes, the *Estado Novo*
looks good by comparison with Hitlerian Germany or fascist Italy: so
would most of the ruling systems that have come and gone during the last
150 years. While possibly in some ways just as authoritarian in
temperament as the mid-European fascists, Salazar functioned in a
political environment which did not require such drastic regulation or
control; Portugal in the second quarter of the twentieth century was very
much in a pre-industrial and pastoral age. Mass parties, elsewhere a
phenomenon of European politics from the late nineteenth century
onwards, would not emerge until the 1970s. Proletarian revolution, the
spectre which in Germany, Italy and Spain drove conservatives into the
camp of the extreme right, did not preoccupy the establishment even
during the most desperate days of the parliamentary republic. In early

twentieth-century Portugal the urban working class was perhaps as numerically significant as the domestic serving class then was in Britain. Most Portuguese were Catholic peasants, politically unaware, socially quiescent, and conformist in their general cultural view. This was much more pliable material than the more powerful dictators had to contend with in Germany and Italy. Portugal had remained relatively static and unchanging, so that in his effort to foster national uniformity in politics the dictator may not have had a very daunting task.

A closer glance at the national political scene should indicate why. By the time of the 1926 revolution, active involvement in partisan politics was still confined to the elite sectors of society. The lower social orders were still largely outside the political process. Thus (except in the world of industrial labour relations), large-scale coercion did not need to be employed against them. Unenfranchised in most cases, the Portuguese masses had not founded major communist or radical parties by the 1920s. Nor had workers or peasants been involved in politics except when they were co-opted by one or two of the pre-1926 parties. In Portugal, a rural country, these parties were largely city-oriented, something which made Salazar's task of eradicating their national influence a relatively easy one. Also redounding to his benefit in this respect was the fact that only two political centres really mattered in Portugal: Lisbon and Oporto. As major centres, they were small by European standards. Their respective corps of activists and campaigners came from a relatively narrow circle of families and professions. Endeavouring to subordinate a political class as flimsy in size as the pre-1926 one hardly constituted an insuperable task. When (as in Portugal's case), this older elite was already discredited, one is drawn to conclude that Salazar had a lot going for him in his attempt to monopolise power points in society. He benefited from the fact that many of the individuals fuelling the unrest of the 1910–26 period joined the new power formation after the 1926 revolution, to become part of the emergent conservative elite.

Given the absence of major threats to the fabric of traditional society, Portugal's successful counter-revolution came to be characterised by relatively low-key authoritarian rule. The state did not seek to intervene at all levels of society. Its violence was restrained, predictable and limited in comparison with German Nazism and Italian fascism – at least in the metropole. In other significant respects, it is possible to set Portuguese authoritarianism apart from larger police states.

Conspicuous by its absence was a mass-based fascist party; at no time did such a party seek to exercise control over the functions of the New State: Salazar, in fact, declared himself antipathetic to the whole party concept. When he formed the UN in 1930 he was at pains to emphasise that it was an 'association' or 'non-party', something that came as a disappointment to radical right-wingers.

Their doyen in the 1930s was Francisco Rolão Preto, one of the founders of Lusitanian Integalism and an ambitious ideologue who regarded Salazar as a *parvenu*. With wider experience in right-wing politics than Salazar, Preto sought, in 1932, to boost his own authority by launching a personalist right-wing movement known as the Camisas Azuis (the Blueshirts). This movement's main weapon was a daily newspaper named *Revolução Nacional*. Edited by Rolão Preto himself, it evinced support for Salazar until his elevation to the premiership in July 1932. Then its tone gradually changed. By February 1933 Preto was daring to write a series of articles that were openly sceptical about Salazar's political philosophy. Nazi Germany, then in its advent, was viewed much more favourably. In January 1933 Hitler's appointment as German chancellor was the subject of several lengthy front-page articles applauding the Nazi rise to power. Similarly praised was the Portuguese military.

While Salazar was ignored or indirectly disparaged in the pages of *Revolução Nacional*, various foreign strong men were given enthusiastic treatment. Around Rolão Preto himself a cult of personality developed. The 'leader' toured the country on well publicised speaking campaigns and, according to one source, his movement, with a claimed 50,000 members, may have constituted a major political mobilisation for Portugal. Certainly the Blueshirts (they were also known as the National Syndicalists) came to be regarded as a serious political force in a relatively short period. In August 1932 Rolão Preto was received by the British ambassador in Lisbon, and in July the following year the president himself even granted him an interview at the Belém palace.

As a transitory but significant force National Syndicalism differed from the Salazarist New State in several key respects. Firstly, it was a more socially radical brand of right-wing authoritarianism; some members employed anti-capitalist rhetoric; there was a generally stronger emphasis on social questions than in New State propaganda. Secondly, the movement stands out for its advocacy and use of mobilisation and its preference for charismatic leadership based on mass popular appeal. Aggressive nationalism is a third important feature that sets Preto's movement apart from the *Estado Novo*: on several occasions Preto laid claim to the Spanish province of Galicia, and, battening on to its geographical, ethnic and historical ties with Portugal, he went as far as to say on 28 March 1932 that 'Portugal without Galicia is an amputated nation. Galicia without Portugal is a body without a head';[8] rather surprisingly, considering the major role British capital then played in some sectors of the Portuguese economy, anti-British sentiment did not loom large in Blueshirt propaganda.

It was towards Salazar that Preto's movement posed its principal threat. He eventually came to realise this fully. Official pressure was then brought to bear on the movement, especially on its upper ranks. Restrictions were placed on propaganda. In the summer of 1934 a showdown finally occurred between National Syndicalism and the government. After a particularly bold call for a political overhaul, Rolão Preto was deported to Spain. On 29 July 1934 an official note announced the dissolution of the National Syndicalist movement and its merger with the União Nacional; Salazar had been spurred into action some days after the assassination of the Austrian dictator, Dollfuss. His corporativist Catholic regime presents close parallels with Salazar. Noting the fate of Dollfuss and the ruthlessness of the Austrian Nazis, Salazar may have acted to forestall a similar power bid by ideologically extreme elements within Portugal. Some militant rightists were indeed sufficiently disenchanted to take up arms against the regime. However, they were politically isolated, as was demonstrated in September 1935 when an attempted *coup* in Lisbon, involving hard-core Blueshirts and anarcho-syndicalists (and some army officers), collapsed within hours.

The Blueshirts were perhaps five or six years too late in arriving on the Portuguese scene. By 1932–33 there was no longer a vacuum in right-wing politics. A conservative and non-revolutionary brand of authoritarianism was in the ascendant. Salazar, though retiring and uncharismatic (a dictator of the sacristy rather than of the balcony), was unwilling to share his authority with a movement that was already more dynamic than the UN. A Blueshirt-style movement would probably have fared better during the purely military phase of the dictatorship. If National Syndicalism had been a strong force between 1926 and 1928, its militarism and ultra-nationalism might conceiveably have drawn sections of the army to its side. However, militant right-wing radicalism was not yet an important European movement. Rolão Preto modelled his Blueshirt vehicle on aspects of German Nazism and it was not until the very close of the 1920s that Hitler began to make an impact on Continental rightists.

Essentially derivative, National Syndicalism emerged when the political succession had already been worked out to the satisfaction of probably most Portuguese rightists. Traditional authoritarianism had won out over more modern secular brands. The lower middle class, who would have provided the focal point of Preto's support, was probably not in the mood for revolutionary adventures. Revolution was already a familiar experience; it should be remembered that Portugal has been one of the few countries to experience a pre- as opposed to a post-World War I revolution of sizeable dimensions. Lower middle-class support had been noteworthy. However, years of disorder blunted the social radicalism of petty-bourgeois groups. Order came to be preferred to political experimentation. When calmer times did eventually come, the chaos of the Republican era may have been too fresh in bourgeois minds for them to relish another leap into the political unknown. Whatever the exact reasons, the middle sectors remained unmoved before Preto's blandishments even though he did gather a certain following behind his movement. Ultimately the scenario in Portugal would be played out in other countries that witnessed transitory radical right-wing movements, such as Brazil, Spain, Rumania and Japan. None of them came to power, before 1939 at least. Most were purged or else were submerged in totalitarian or orthodox conservative regimes.

Radical right-wingers would perhaps have found Getúlio Vargas's Brazilian *Estado Novo* a suitable model for their aspirations at home. Although he suppressed a pro-Nazi movement known as the Integralistas (led by Plínio Salgado), there were increasing signs in Vargas's Brazil of a genuine partnership between some sections of capital and labour at a time when Salazar's Portugal was rapidly emerging as a mercantile dictatorship in favour of the privileged. Vargas was in power from 1930 to 1945, and his political record affords some proof that the corporativist ideal is not a wholly reactionary concept. In fact his regime is one of the few *direct* links between the authoritarian 'fascism' of the 1930s and the radical populist regimes of the Third World. In a second period as president from 1950 to 1954 Vargas successfully assumed the mantle of radical populist before his suicide in the face of a looming authoritarian *coup*.

The mass political campaigns which occurred in the larger built-up fascist states were likewise not a feature of Portuguese authoritarianism. After the success of the 1926 revolution Portugal did not experience a right-wing cultural revolution of the kind witnessed in Germany and, to a lesser extent, in Italy. The reason why seems pretty obvious. Salazar's political philosophy centred around a desire to resuscitate the old, resist the new, and group the class order along traditional lines. Internally, his plans were nowhere near as ambitious as those of the two fascist party-states. If Salazarism had been an innovatory political movement intent on carrying out major feats of social engineering within Portugal, then undoubtedly its mass character would have been much more to the fore. However, the Portuguese leader deliberately eschewed such a radical departure. There was no Portuguese equivalent of the draining of the Pontine marshes or the mass official campaign against the German Jews. Crypto-Jews, living in north Portuguese villages, whose ancestors had survived the persecutions of the fifteenth and sixteenth centuries by going to ground, were not persecuted or discriminated against. The regime gave no overt encouragement to the anti-semitism of *A Voz*, the right-wing Catholic daily which, in 1938, was inciting attacks on crypto-Jews in northern Portugal. The opening of a synagogue in Oporto as well as the return to full Judaism of a number of the crypto-Jews (who were known as *Marranos*), appears to have been the pretext for the antisemitic press campaign. The Marranos retained important elements of their old faith and still, for instance, celebrated the Passover. A champion had emerged at the beginning of the dictatorship when Captain Artur Barros Basto promoted their welfare. During the early Salazar years he was the object of a smear campaign launched by the Catholic Action movement. Eventually he was court-martialled for immorality because he had promoted circumcision.[9]

Besides Jews and Marranos, atheists and Protestants were left untouched (this was not the case in Franco's Spain).[10] Naturally, the regime did not attempt to undermine the influence of organised religion by promoting secular forms of worship. Nor was the militaristic flavour of civilian life in peacetime Italy and Germany reflected in Portugal. It was Salazar's dearest wish to keep politics behind closed doors and not to have the streets turned into an arena of open political activity. To have adopted the style and organisation of German and Italian fascism would have been to sacrifice this aspiration.

In the fascist party-state the political indoctrination of the masses is treated as a key priority. To implant a particular ideology in the minds of thousands of citizens renders a large *apparat* essential. In Portugal no such organisational structure emerged, since Salazar never appears to have considered mass indoctrination a vital feature of his rule. There was no Portuguese equivalent of Joseph Goebbels in the area of propaganda. Nor did the corporative state throw up a theorist as prominent as Maurras, Rosenberg or the Romanian, Manoilescu. Despite Salazar's reputation as a latter-day 'philosopher king', his contribution to the corpus of modern right-wing social thought was a meagre one. Neither he, nor any other regime figure for that matter, broke new ground in the realm of corporativist theory. Salazar was an 'intellectual' prime minister whose route to authorship lay through the publication of his speeches and interviews, six volumes of them known as *Os discursos* – turgid, oratorical tomes animated by Portuguese nationalist themes. The lack of intellectual debate around corporativism, during the regime's four decades in power, only adds to the atmosphere of 'unreality' surrounding the corporative state.

To justify his rule and embellish it with a philosophical veneer, Salazar was content to fall back on traditional, nationalist and religious themes. To inculcate these values in the population, especially at school age, did not require much expense or effort on the part of the state. In provincial Portugal the regime could rely on a sympathetic Church to socialise rural Portuguese in a conservative direction. The clergy had, of course, been exercising this role before 1926. However, after that year, with a counter-revolution in full swing, the scope of the Church's lay activities widened considerably. In some of the most devout areas, particularly in the north, the priest exercised the same role on behalf of the regime as did the party chief in more developed authoritarian regimes. Parish priests in provincial towns and country villages acted as dispensers of official propaganda and agents of social conformity and political vigilance. Just to give an example: in 1958 the authorities in Braga (the birthplace of the 'national revolution' twenty-two years before) got priests in every electoral ward to identify parishioners liable to support the opposition electoral candidate, General Delgado, so that they could then be removed from the voting lists.[11]

It is no coincidence that the only on-going manifestation approaching a mass propaganda effort in pre-1974 Portugal was the cult of Fátima. Making a great impact on the popular consciousness outside the main urban centres, it took off in the 1930s and represented a vigorous counter-attack on the part of a national Church confronted by urban rejection, a previously hostile state, and a social base already beginning to crumble in some rural parts.

A revival in mystical religious worship constituted a boon for a regime embarking on a process of national depoliticisation. There were other, more direct, benefits. Salazar was depicted by some of the clerical promoters of the Fátima cult as the 'messiah' that Our Lady during her miraculous visitation of 1917, had promised would soon come to rescue Portugal. Such a characterisation impressed superstitious rustics confronted with the knowledge that their national leader had been approved by heaven as well as by the *excelentíssimos senhores* (most excellent gentlemen) of Lisbon. In the rural Portuguese milieu such crude parallels may have been as effective as the mass propaganda employed by the more modern dictatorships; in a country where over half the population was illiterate in 1930, more sophisticated propaganda would probably not have registered so easily. In 1930 superstition was still rife, especially north of the river Tagus. Alleged appearances by Our Lady in the mountains, frequent infanticides, inexplicable stoning of trains and witchcraft were not uncommon phenomena. A woman, allegedly possessed by the devil, was burned alive as late as 1933.[12] The educated public, towards which Goebbels directed much of his propaganda in Germany, was hardly a major component in a country as rural and economically backward as Portugal. Of course, in centres like Lisbon, clerical propaganda was not very effective. Football and *fado* (Portuguese folk music) were more important depoliticising agents than Fátima. So confident was Salazar of his ability to tranquillise the population in general that he allowed the press to retain a little independence. The regime did not seek to own the press (though it was happy if its supporters did take over newspapers) and, in the 1930s, it was even possible for a new Portuguese daily, *República*, run mainly by oppositionists, to be relaunched. Instead, the regime depended on the censor to maintain standards of 'dignity' and 'decorum' and to act as a bulwark against the forces of chaos and revolution.

In a regime which lacks (or can only caricature) the abstract and organisational hallmarks of modern fascism such as a mass party, a formulated ideology and significant grassroots participation, the leader's personality comes into prominence. In the case of pre-war Portugal, Salazar was much more visible than the authoritarian rulers of other second-ranking European states. Within a few years of taking power he had become the best-known Portuguese leader since Pombal. Even before he officially became prime minister, he was politically the most important figure in the country. Much of the regime's propaganda concentrated on his work in the finance ministry for years to come. However, this said, Salazar was never the object of a cult of personality on the scale of Hitler's Mussolini's or those of populist Third World leaders such as Nasser or Sukarno. The Portuguese leader did not possess a charismatic image; nor did he have a synthetic one manufactured for him. Only late in his political career were bridges, towns and public buildings named after him. Salazar never appeared in gaudy uniforms, gave few interviews, and operated behind the scenes, preferring to see the limelight descend on the military head of state. Possessing as tenacious a grip on power as the Spanish and German dictators, he was oblivious to its trappings. As a result, a major cult of personality was one other feature of developed fascism that remained largely absent from the Portuguese scene.

A belligerent and nationalistic foreign policy is a distinctive aspect of fascist regimes. During the inter-war years the strongholds of fascism pursued warlike, expansionist policies against their weaker neighbours that ultimately led to general war. Emulating their mightier confederates, the authoritarian regimes of eastern Europe behaved in the same predatory manner towards one another. However, Portugal did not follow the Italian, German or east European lead even though she had territorial grievances against Spain and Britain; Spain, for instance, had seized the Olivença district of the Alentejo when in alliance with France during the short 'War of Oranges' in 1801. The Treaty of Paris of 1814 specifically laid down that Olivença should be returned to Portugal. The Spaniards ignored it, and this border difficulty has been a bone of contention between the two countries ever since, without their actually coming to blows.

In 1939, when Spain joined Italy, Germany and Japan in the Anti-Comintern Pact, Salazar held back, preferring continued alliance with Britain to membership of a volatile right-wing international. Fully stretched trying to maintain and develop the resources of her African empire, Portugal had little incentive to imitate the major dictatorships by pursuing warlike foreign policies. No country of similar size had as large a colonial empire. Unlike Italy or Germany, Portugal was not a young state but one of the longest established nations in Europe whose historical claims did not need to be confirmed in the 1930s by acts of bravado at home and abroad. Her people's sense of national identity was a secure one, and Salazar knew that political isolation was the best guarantee of survival for an authoritarian regime of his type.

Political isolationism was not accompanied by economic protectionism. Portugal was one of the few countries which did not resort to highly protective and autarkic measures during the depression. The external tariffs imposed by Salazar were relatively moderate and there was never any attempt to emulate Italy and Germany by slashing imports or expanding home production in widely differing fields. Autarky would have been difficult for a country like Portugal particularly dependent on exporting primary products and lacking the capital to finance domestic industry. While this situation lasted the home market would remain too small for her to dispose of her own output internally, and there was the continuing need to purchase capital equipment from abroad.

The European right-wing regime which the Portuguese New State probably most closely resembled was Austria, which, like it, evolved independently from the central fascist powers. Portugal and inter-war Austria were two small, agriculturally based nations overshadowed by a larger powerful neighbour and dominated by a single metropolitan centre: Lisbon in the one case, and Vienna in the other. Both had shed ancient monarchies within eight years of one another but parliamentary democracy was unable to heal deep internal divisions, and by 1933 two self-proclaimed Christian corporative regimes were operating from Lisbon and Vienna. Their leaders, Salazar and Dollfuss, were not right-wing adventurers but conventional professional men from smallholding peasant backgrounds. Devout Catholics, they studied at their national university and at one time seriously considered joining the priesthood. Later, having established themselves in civil life, they attached themselves to rightist organisations in opposition to left-wing movements preaching reform and change.

In Austria and Portugal regime philosophy stemmed from a belief in the organic unity of all classes and was heavily overladen with nationalist sentiment. Corporativism was the official creed. But Salazar and Dollfuss rejected the essentially secular writings and beliefs of Hitler and Mussolini in favour of the papal encyclicals. However, internally they had to contend with native supporters of the larger fascist powers. In 1934, within months of one another, Dollfuss and Salazar took action against extreme right-wing movements deemed to be flouting the authority of the state. More menacing for these two regimes of the Christian right was the physical threat posed by their larger neighbours. After the murder of Dollfuss in 1934 Austria faced a mounting challenge from Adolf Hitler in neighbouring Germany. It was one the Viennese authorities would be unable to withstand and, by the spring of 1938, Austria was a province of the Third Reich.

The brief life span of the Austrian corporative regime has blurred the connection between two very similar regimes. Both Austria and Portugal may have been geographically far removed from each other, but, in the 1930s at least, both countries exhibited strikingly similar political features and it is perhaps true to say that Austrian corporativism was a more telling mirror image of Portuguese authoritarianism than either German Nazism or Italian fascism.

In setting the *Estado Novo* apart from developed fascism, the intention is not to absolve or whitewash it. Rather a claim is being made for it to be considered a different political entity. The anti-fascist officers who brought the dictatorship down on 25 April 1974 recognised this much themselves. Instead of placing President Americo Tomás and Premier Marcelo Caetano before popular justice, they were allowed to fly into exile after brief detention. There was no Portuguese equivalent of the Nuremberg trials. In the military and business world, purges were far from wide-ranging. None at all occurred in the religious sphere. Individuals within the umbrella of the fallen regime but not tainted by any serious misdemeanours were able, as often as not, to remain in public life. Jóse Hermano Saraiva and José Veiga Simão, Caetano's two ministers of education, are a case in point, as are Maria de Lurdes Pintassilgo and Francisco Sá Carneiro, two successive prime ministers in the democratic era who were members (albeit dissenting ones) respectively of the Corporative Chamber and the National Assembly.

Brutality and arbitrariness were part of the *Estado Novo's* make-up but it displayed few totalitarian features and was never dynamic or mobilising in the German or Italian sense. Rather 'it was traditional, paternalistic and conservative, and corporative institutions were used not to promote but to minimise change and maximise stability'.[13]

Salazar saw politics as representing a cancer which, after a century of 'decrepit' parliamentarism, had corrupted the body and spirit of the nation. In 1934 he declared that his goal was to create 'a government without politics'.[14] On another occasion he declared that he did not 'believe in universal suffrage because the individual vote did not take into account human differentiation. I do not believe in equality but hierarchy. Men, in my opinion, should be equal before the law but I believe it is dangerous to attribute to all, the same political rights.'[15]

In conversation with the journalist António Ferro, Salazar enlarged upon his hierarchical philosophy of government: 'Our greatest problem is how to form elites, capable of educating and leading the nation. The absence and insufficiency of proper leaders is Portugal's greatest problem ... The great problems of the nation are not solved by the rank and file of the people but by trained staffs around which the masses can group themselves.'[16]

Frankly an out-and-out pessimist, Salazar believed that 'there are things that only I can do', and he had little trust in the independent capability of his own people, whom he summed up as follows:

> The Portuguese are excessively sentimental and have a horror of all discipline; they are individualists without noticing it and lack continuity and tenacity in their actions. The very ease with which they grasp ideas without any great effort induces them to deal superficially with all problems and to rely too much on the quickness of their apprehension. But subject to discipline and proper control, there is nothing they cannot do.[17]

God, *pátria*, authority, family and work were the essential values of his puritanical regime. Other Portuguese thinkers and statesmen had expounded these values before him, among them João Franco, and Ramalho Ortigão, a nineteenth-century conservative polemicist who decried the usefulness of politics and placed great faith in the technical aspects of administration. Another precursor, and possible influence on, Salazar was Jacinto Cândido, leader of the Portuguese Nationalist Party at the beginning of the century. He advocated a tight fiscal policy and a strong Catholic role in national life, and was neutral on the issue of monarchy or republic, while hoping for the onset of an authoritarian political order. Against this background New State ideology gradually emerged. However, foreign thinkers, among them the French sociologists Le Play and Le Bon, and Charles Maurras had a more formative influence on Salazar's thought. An eager reception awaited French conservative and reactionary tracts during the first half of this century. So attuned was the Portuguese elite to French cultural values and tastes that few of Maurras's writings were translated into Portuguese, the French text being accessible to most prospective readers. Portugal, in turn, became a place of pilgrimage for French reactionaries after the collapse of Vichy in 1944.

Obscurantism and censorship

Early on in the New State's history, obscurantism rapidly emerged as one of its central features. This was most apparent in the field of education, where rival strategies were advanced by different sections of the political elite. The fact that in 1930 seventy out of every hundred Portuguese could not read shocked some people and reassured others. The progressive sections of the intelligentsia were constantly ashamed by this statistic, viewing illiteracy as the principle obstacle to national development. However, some important figures inside the *Estado Novo* openly advocated the 'glories' of illiteracy for the poor, believing that if the lower orders were taught to read they would inevitably be contaminated by subversive literature. One reactionary deputy, Querubim Guimarães, pointed out that the nation's greatest achievements – the Reconquest, the Discoveries and the Restoration – had all been accomplished by illiterate men.[18] This was indeed a far cry from the days of the liberal republic, when progressive educators were proud to have substituted the ABC for God. If the poor were to be taught at all, the *Estado Novo* was determined to turn the clock back and provide a heavy dose of religious teaching in order to make sure that poor children would grow up to accept the recondite values of the state. This view gained precedence over that of the advocates of illiteracy. The more realistic political leaders knew that the school system could not be changed overnight, nor did they think it desirable to close all the schools for the poor as the cultural extremists were advocating.[19] The examples of England, France and Sweden were often quoted in order to prove that social peace could perfectly well coexist with mass literacy. However, no sustained effort was made to take Portugal up from the bottom of the European table for illiteracy. Salazar was being deceitful when he told António Ferro in 1938, 'I estimate that within five years every child in this country will have the opportunity to read and write.'[20] His true policy had been revealed six years earlier when he stated categorically, 'I consider more urgent the creation of elites than the necessity to teach people how to read.'[21]

Higher education likewise suffered thanks to Salazar's blinkered outlook towards the world of learning. The faculty of arts at Oporto University had been closed at the start of the dictatorship and would not reopen again for many years. Eminent liberal and humanist scholars like Jaime Cortesão and António Sérgio, who had had teaching posts before Salazar's time, were turned out of their jobs, as, later on, were many other distinguished educators, including António José Saraiva, Vitorino Magalhães Godinho and Mário de Azevedo Gomes. More often than not their places were taken by mediocrities and government placemen. Mário Soares described the situation obtaining in Coimbra University during the 1940s as follows:

Most of the professors I knew in the department were second-raters and uninterested in their jobs. There comes to mind a vegetarian named Délio Santos, who was more devoted to theosophy than theology and was always advising us to go to the circus, his great enthusiasm being for charlatans in telepathic acts. And there was Moreira de Sá, a man publicly and demonstrably accused of plagiarism, whom the Dean sought to exonerate by telling us, 'You all think he's stupid, but you are quite wrong. He just finds speaking and writing

rather difficult.' To be brief and to take one more name from the role, we had
Joseph Prud'homme personified in Mário de Albuquerque. His fatuities were
the delight of foreign students, whose summer courses would be enlivened by his
discourse on 'Parrots: Their Discovery and What it has Meant for the
Civilisation of Portugal'.[22]

Things do not seem to have progressed since the 1750s when, in *Candide*,
Voltaire wrote, only half jokingly, that 'the University of Coimbra had
pronounced that the sight of a few people ceremoniously burned before a
slow fire was an infallible prescription for preventing earthquakes'.[23]

Deep down, Salazar was a classical reactionary in whose eyes Keynes,
Galbraith and Adam Smith were possibly just as subversive as Lenin,
Marx and Che Guevara. The dictator can be compared with Francisco
Cunha Leal, his only serious rival after 1926, who wished to front an
authoritarian state, one that would probably have been a modernising
conservative one (possibly in the Brazilian *Estado Novo* vein), whereas
Salazar's was traditional and sterile. In the late 1950s Coca-Cola, the
leading standard-bearer of the American consumer society, was not
allowed to enter the country, for moral or aesthetic reasons.[24] Some years
before, Salazar himself displayed his obscurantism as well as a
misanthropic caste of mind when he declared to the French writer,
Christine Garnier:

> Women show such a need for freedom, such frenzy for the pleasures of life. They
> don't understand that happiness is reached through renunciation rather than
> enjoyment . . . The great nations should set an example by confining women to
> their homes . . . The law excludes married women from the nursing profession
> and from any work at our ministry of foreign affairs. I tried very hard to get this
> law broadened to cover all types of work. Alas, I failed. Both the facts and the
> theory of the case were against me, and even the Church disapproved. Catholics
> went so far as to argue that this law would encourage immorality. But I shouldn't
> concede defeat. Convinced as I am that a wife who has in mind the care of her
> home cannot do good work outside, I shall always fight against the independence
> of married women.[25]

Salazar's reclusive nature was virtually imposed on the people as a
model of political activity. Football, fado and Fátima came to be viewed as
the pastimes of a nation with little interest in politics. Ultimately,
Salazar's vision of a sanitised Portugal forswearing politics ('a happy
country with no history' as he once described it), would be an unrealised
dream. The explosion after 25 April 1974 showed just how much pent-up
political energy had been lying dormant for the previous forty-eight years.
However, Salazar was successful in preventing the growth of an aware and
enlightened public during his own lifetime. The key weapons he used to
enforce conformity and suppress information and values hostile to his
regime was censorship. In the long run it was probably far more effective
than the secret police or state terror in keeping the public apathetic and

politically docile.

Under Decree No. 22469 of 11 April 1933, censorship committees had been set up to operate a system of 'prior censorship' as a measure 'indispensable to a labour of reconstruction and moral cleansing'.[26] Under this important law, newspapers and books were examined by a panel of censors (composed largely of army officers) before they were published. Permanently installed in newspaper offices, these men turned the Portuguese press into practically the world's most boring. Towards the end of Salazar's rule the censor was even prohibiting horoscope columns in newspapers and magazines from publishing pessimistic forecasts for the sign of Taurus (Salazar's birth sign).[27] José Cardoso Pires, the Portuguese novelist, even relates that news of a plague of colorado beetles was suppressed by the censor. John Stuart Mill and President John F. Kennedy were among a long list of prohibited authors. Sometimes interviews with Salazar himself were censored, since, in the words of Mário Soares, 'what is suitable for readers abroad was not necessarily good for the public at home'.[28] To counteract the censor, journalists used code words or underground metaphors such as 'dawn' or 'daybreak' for socialism, 'spring' for revolution, 'comrade' for prisoner, 'vampire' for policeman and 'poppy' for popular victory.

The parochialism and ignorance which Salazar fostered obliged the opposition political culture to become clandestine and increasingly oral. Poets such as the Algarvian António Aleixo created a popular sub-culture that was in opposition to the values of the regime. Novelists such as Aquilino Ribeiro, Alves Redol, Ferreira de Castro and Castro Soromenho, whose books often dealt realistically and critically with life in contemporary Portugal, managed to get their works circulated to the reading public although official persecution and even imprisonment took their toll on the lives of many writers.

The Second World War

Like her oldest ally, the year 1940 was in many ways the finest hour of the Salazar dictatorship. Perched on the edge of the European land mass, Portugal had avoided being sucked into the vortex of war. While the curtain was opening on the second act of a dreadful European civil war, Portugal commemorated the 800th anniversary of her nationhood and the 300th anniversary of her recovery of independence with great ceremony and patriotic symbolism. Seeing the rest of Europe drowning in a horrible bloodbath, this may have been one of the most satisfying moments the regime ever enjoyed.[29]

Compared to the rest of Europe, Portugal enjoyed a quiet war, but it was far from uneventful. The dangers that menaced her were apparent to

Salazar even before general hostilities began in September 1939. During the previous year, in a vain attempt to direct Hitler's energies away from Europe, the British premier Neville Chamberlain had been contemplating the cession of Portuguese territory in Africa to Germany.[30] Salazar, through Armindo Monteiro, his ambassador in London, protested to the British government. But it was Hitler's contempt for the whole scheme, not Portuguese protests, that would cause it to be abandoned. That the idea was mooted at all is eloquent testimony that Portugal in the late 1930s was regarded in official British circles as more of a client state than a trusted ally. This overbearing attitude would be carried over into the Second World War. Early on, plans were drawn up for an assault on Mozambique and the Atlantic islands. Neither would be made immediately operational, since the Portuguese government adhered to a neutral line and the early fighting was never close to these locations. However, in the summer of 1943, with the battle of the Atlantic raging, the British government was seriously considering the invasion and occupation of the Azores, the archipelago a thousand miles west of Lisbon. Glyn A. Stone, a student of the Anglo-Portuguese alliance, has revealed that in 1943:

> Both Churchill and Roosevelt had received a formal statement from the Combined Chiefs of Staff which stressed the importance of acquiring the use of the Portuguese Atlantic Islands at the earliest possible moment. The British Prime Minister, while in Washington in May 1943, communicated to the War Cabinet his opposition to a diplomatic approach being made with the aim of requesting permission for the Allies to use the Azores and Cape Verde Islands. He believed the Portuguese government would turn down such a request and that in making the approach the Allies would have forewarned them of their interest in the islands and the element of surprise in military operations would be lost. Consequently, Churchill favoured military operations against the islands as soon as possible. The War Cabinet, meeting on 21 April 1943 in Churchill's absence, expressed the opinion that a diplomatic approach should be made first and that if they attacked the islands without warning 'such action would be badly received in the United Kingdom, would create a very unfavourable impression on the Allies, and would damage Britain's reputation after the war'.[31]

Eventually, moderate ministerial counsel prevailed over Churchill's preference for buccaneering action. The British government formally asked Portugal to be allowed to build a naval base on the Azores. In September 1943, after Salazar had agreed to the request, men and equipment began to be landed on the islands. Anglo-Portuguese relations were then normal for the rest of the war. But it is true to say that, during its whole course, Portugal's oldest ally would present a greater danger to her territorial sovereignty than Germany. The aggressor elsewhere in Europe, Nazi Germany steered clear of the Iberian peninsula, although Oliveira

Marques has argued that this was by accident rather than design: 'Mussolini's awkwardness in attacking Greece in the winter of 1940 . . . was the main factor which prevented Hitler from invading the Iberian peninsula and occupying Portugal.'[32]

General Franco's ability to stall and outmanoeuvre Hitler must also not be overlooked when appraising how and why Portugal retained her neutrality. Although the Spanish leader had signed the Anti-Comintern Pact six months before the start of war, he was not keen to be drawn into a new conflict so soon after the cessation of the one that had brought him to power. The only time when Franco's resolve to bide his time appears to have seriously weakened was in the summer of 1940, when, in the face of what seemed like an inevitable Axis victory, he seriously contemplated joining in at the finish to be eligible for some of the spoils of conquest in the Mediterranean and North Africa. However, in the end, Franco did not move. Salazar may have been instrumental in persuading him to remain neutral in the days and weeks after the fall of France. Even then, at the zenith of Hitler's success, Salazar, with strange percipience, was prophesying an Allied victory at the end of a long war, according to the American historian, Charles Nowell. According to Nowell, he came to this conclusion sooner than any other European statesman except Winston Churchill, being intuitively aware that the United States would enter the war long before most people thought.[33] This view is supported by Manuel de Lucena, the author of a hostile analysis of the Portuguese corporative system.[34]

If reactionary in domestic affairs, Lucena reckons Salazar to have been a 'lucid conservative' in his appraisal of wartime Europe and where it was going.[35] Salazar, in common with De Gaulle and Churchill, quickly realised that Hitler's territorial appetite was insatiable. To make lasting peace with such a man was impossible:

This was Chamberlain's pathetic dream and Pétain's necessary illusion . . . In the event of a Nazi victory, Mussolini would not have survived for long. Nor would Franco. Nor Salazar. Thus, the latter never entertained hopes for such a victory. A form of Nazism strong enough to restrain the Russians and perhaps to overthrow the Communists would have been convenient . . . But nothing more. In the Second World War, Salazar's neutrality was the genuine article.[36]

This is an *intuitive* assessment. Salazar was careful never to emphasise publicly the acute distrust he harboured for Hitler's political creed, and it is only in retrospect that his anti-totalitarian views have been appreciated. Ironically, he may have been most forthcoming about the more extreme European right at a time when Hitler and his associates were not yet regarded as dangers to the continental peace.

In May 1934, at a meeting of the UN, he declared:

We must resist the impulse tending to the formation of what might be called the Totalitarian State. The state which would subordinate everything without exception to the idea of nation or race, as represented by it morally, legally, politically, and economically, which would put itself forward as an omnipotent being, a beginning and end in itself . . . would involve an absolutism worse than that which the liberal regimes had succeeded to, for such a state would be essentially pagan, naturally incompatible with the temper of our Christian civilisation.[37]

Five years later, Pope Pius XII would authoritatively echo this statement, declaring totalitarianism to be an attempt to 'divorce civil authority from every kind of dependence upon the Supreme Being and from every restraint of a higher law derived from God'.[38]

These words were repeated in an Irish periodical during January 1940, when it asked in an article, 'Is Portugal Totalitarian?' The author, John J. Ryan, depicting totalitarianism as 'a form of idolatory and as such contrary to the First Commandment' had no such hesitation in clearing Salazar of this charge. Other Irish Catholic writers spoke up for Salazar's Portugal during this uncertain period. In 1942 the influential Catholic weekly *The Standard* had for its heading, 'Catholic Statesmen seek Peace and Order', and under this caption were portraits of the three statesmen referred to: Pétain, Franco and Salazar.[39] Two years later Dr Cornelius Lucey, the present Bishop of Cork, wrote in *The Irish Ecclesiastical Record* of March 1944:

Salazar is frankly a dictator. But he is a dictator with a difference. His regime is authoritarian not totalitarian; his outlook is Christian not materialist and pagan. . . . He acknowledges that the Government (of which he is the embodiment) is as subject to moral law in its conduct of affairs as the individual is in his private life. . . . He is the perfect dictator if ever there was one. . . .[40]

This is substantial praise. Coming from one of the leading Irish churchmen of his generation, it is a measure of the regard in which Salazar was held in overseas Catholic circles. For the Portuguese leader such support may have been quite important. It certainly helped to counteract left-wing claims on both sides of the Atlantic that he, and Franco, were Iberian fascists who warranted more or less the same treatment as the larger dictators. This was a fairly prevalent view in Allied circles during the early stages of the war. Newly arrived in Lisbon as British ambassador, Sir Ronald Campbell in March 1941 felt he had to refute it. Writing to Sir Anthony Eden in London, he declared that 'no greater mistake can be made than of classing Dr Salazar among the dictators'.[41] Churchill, by his pugnacious stance over the Azores two years later, showed that he was not entirely in agreement with this view. If anything, Roosevelt, his US colleague, was even more suspicious of the Iberian leaders. Indeed, in a volume of memoirs published in the late 1960s George Kennan, the senior

American diplomat, reveals that in some Washington circles Salazar was regarded as 'a dangerous fascist and in league with the enemy'.[42] Working on this premise, plans were actually drawn up to foment a popular revolt on the Azores against the Lisbon authorities. The Office of Strategic Services (OSS), the wartime forerunner of the Central Intelligence Agency, was responsible. Eventually the scheme was halted before it reached the operational stage, but only as a result of the vigorous intervention of the US legation in Lisbon.

During part of World War II it was Kennan who was the chief US representative in Portugal. That such a high-ranking official of the State Department should be despatched to what previously had always been regarded as something of a diplomatic backwater is indicative of how strategically important Portugal was during the war years. With the major European cities in the hands of the Nazis, Lisbon took on the appearance of a European Shanghai, used by the Allies as a listening post for news from a darkened continent. Many refugees and visitors passed through the city in the war years, one of them being the Duke of Windsor, the former Edward VIII, who stayed with the Portuguese banker Manuel Espírito Santo e Silva in July 1940, and who the British feared was in danger of being snatched by German agents during the course of his stay.[43]

Given the high wartime visibility of Lisbon, internal Portuguese politics came under closer scrutiny than before, especially from the Allies. On the British side it gradually became apparent that although Salazar, morally and temperamentally, did not favour the Axis, the same was not true of all of his cabinet ministers. According to information reaching Britain's Lisbon embassy in 1943, of the nine members of the government, six were 'known Germanophils'.[44] This was no cause for immediate concern, since Salazar held the key portfolios of war and foreign affairs and his domination of the government showed no sign of waning. However, there was occasional anxiety about the fact that his assistant in the war ministry (the man in daily charge of the army) was reputed to be a staunch Germanophile. This was Captain Fernando dos Santos Costa, whose relationship with Salazar was always a curious one.

While still a mere captain, Santos Costa became under-secretary for war in May 1936. As a lieutenant he had first met Salazar ten years before at Coimbra University, where the future dictator briefly taught him political economy in the faculty of law.[45] The 1926 revolution then intervened and Santos Costa, busy with plotting, was actually failed by Salazar. Contact was resumed in the mid-1930s when Santos Costa was pointed out to him as a hard-working and capable officer who knew far more about the army and the war ministry than the high officers who had been in the cabinet during previous years. Much later Santos Costa would claim that during 1936 President Carmona had been seriously considering the idea that only a foreigner could reorganise the topsy-turvy armed forces and place them on a proper footing.[46] In the past non-Portuguese like Schomberg, Lippe and Wellington had performed the task, and Carmona had an Englishman in mind for the job, but, not surprisingly, Salazar was completely against the idea. Salazar took the war ministry himself and left Santos Costa to run it. This he did with loyalty and skill. Salazar came to trust his judgment, and years later, when he became a full minister, he would be the only one whom Salazar addressed in the familiar vein of *voce* instead of the more formal *vossa excelencia*.[47]

Long after he had retired Santos Costa would claim to be largely responsible for the creation of the modern Portuguese army. In charge of the military for twenty-two years up to 1958, he probably has a greater claim than most people to say this. However, during his first years in command he was bitterly unpopular with military colleagues on account of his willingness to implement Salazar's austerity measures inside the army. After 1937 the salaries of officers were particularly poor, and even the uniform is said to have deteriorated in standard. In some quarters Santos Costa grew to be positively hated because, while still a captain, he had become virtual dictator of the army, something which appalled many people in an institution where rank and hierarchy were all-important. Enmity towards him was sharpened by the fact that he was not one of the upper-class soldiers who had traditionally held top military posts but came from a humble rural background (much like Salazar's).

Santos Costa's unpopularity with many of his colleagues may have encouraged the belief (which became rife after World War II) that he was a confirmed pro-Nazi. This stocky, grim-faced man was a monarchist who belonged to the right within the *Estado Novo*, so his detractors may have had something to go on. One of the claims made against him was that he had contemplated liquidating pro-Allied officers in 1941 and that a co-ordinated plan for this Lusitanian night of the long knives involved other military figures.[48] Captain Fernando Queiroga, an anti-Salazar officer, also alleged that in the spring of 1941 Santos Costa tried to engineer a confict with Britain in the Azores at a time when a German push in the Iberian peninsula was being considered.[49]

Santos Costa has admitted that in 1943 he was the only cabinet official to vote against the proposal that military facilities be ceded to the Allies on the Azores.[50] However, he insists that he was not anti-British but was primarily concerned with defending Portuguese interests. He made the point that both he and Salazar 'had been educated in a tradition of respect and admiration for Britain and the British people' and, in an interview, was not very complimentary about Germany.[51]

These may be the views of a man who has mellowed in retirement. One point in his favour is that he remained in Portugal (in Lisbon, of all places) during the revolution of 1974–75 while colleagues fled abroad. In his own words:

> I walked around during the revolution just like any other citizen. I was not a bit worried about being molested. Of course, I did hear that there were some people who, like bulls in the bullring, were pawing the ground waiting to charge. But they never did.[52]

This does not sound like the attitude of a man with a guilty past, although a lot more needs to be discovered about the political career of Fernando dos Santos Costa before any definite judgements can be expressed.

The pro-German faction within the *Estado Novo* grew more subdued as the war swung increasingly against Hitler. In 1944 Santos Costa was rewarded with the post of full minister of war by a dictator who may have been disturbed by his independence of his mind but who valued enormously his managerial skills and ability to control the army.

Meanwhile, many Portuguese hopefully awaited the collapse of the Salazar dictatorship in the wake of the international Allied victory. Before the end of the war this was not an unreasonable expectation. In neighbouring Spain the belief was widespread that Iberian authoritarianism could not survive in the face of a total military defeat for the Continental right. This view was even prevalent in some higher circles of the Franco regime. Several elite dignitaries were preparing, in the closing stages of the war, to flee to Latin America. Fearing an Allied invasion, General Adolfo Kindelan, former head of the insurgent air force in the civil war, sought at the end of the greater conflict to overthrow Franco and engineer a Bourbon restoration.[53]

There is little evidence of such rampant unease within the Portuguese power elite. Having been in power for over a dozen years, Salazar was in a much stronger position, internally, than his Spanish counterpart, who in 1945 had just established his hegemony over various civil war colleagues. In Salazar's case this process had been carried through fairly early in the previous decade, and, since the external pressures on Portugal were much less severe than those brought to bear on Spain, it is highly improbable that the 1944–45 period saw any attempt by Salazar's colleagues to ditch him. Then (as in the regime's later stages), individuals identified with the *Estado Novo* would be motivated by the ethos that they must hang together or hang separately. Undoubtedly Salazar knew how to play on his colleagues' fear of what might happen to the regime (and to them) when he was gone, and it was one of the chief reasons why alienated colleagues would never, ultimately, bring themselves to unseat him.

Despite the monolithic appearance of the regime in 1945, many citizens believed that, at last, the game was up for Salazar and his *barões*. In May 1945, on VE Day, an estimated 500,000 people marched up the Avenida da

Liberdade in Lisbon in commemoration of the defeat of fascism. However, no help was forthcoming from the Allies. There is no record of Stalin bringing active pressure on the western allies to move against either of the Iberian regimes. The West itself refrained from hostile acts against Franco and Salazar once the Cold War got under way. Territorial communist expansion rather than lingering fascism became the principal international bugbear in north American and west European eyes. To spearhead a drive against fascism in the Iberian peninsula might only be to see this strategic geo-political zone fall into communist hands. Had not the pre-war left been much stronger in Iberia than in the successor states of eastern Europe, by now satellites of the Soviet Union?[54]

Notes

1   The only good study of the Legion is Josué da Silva's *Legião Portuguesa, força repressiva do fascismo*, Diabril Editora, Lisbon, 1975.
2   Hermínio Martins, 'Portugal', in S. J. Woolf (ed.), *European Fascism*, Weidenfeld & Nicolson, London, 1968, pp. 322–3.
3   Payne, *History of Spain and Portugal*, II, p. 669.
4   See J. B. Trend, *Portugal*, Ernest Benn, London, 1957, p. 195.
5   Until 1980 it had been thought that Sanjurjo had met his death in an accident. However, at a conference on Portuguese fascism held at the Faculty of Letters of Lisbon University, it was revealed for the first time that he had been assassinated. See *História*, No. 18, April 1980, p. 84.
6   PRO, FO/371/W11368/160/36, 31 March 1939, Lord Halifax to Admiral Chatfield.
7   This was not the case, however, in Portuguese Africa, where the regime did not hesitate to use the most extreme methods to crush popular protest.
8   *Revolução Nacional*, 28 March 1932.
9   *Time Magazine*, 'Catholics who celebrate the Passover', 11 April 1977.
10 The persecution of Protestants and atheists in Franco's Spain is detailed in Paul Blanshard, *Freedom and Catholic Power in Spain and Portugal*, Beacon Press, Boston, Mass., 1962.
11 Siles Cerqueira, 'L'Église Catholique et la dictature corporatiste portugaise', *Revue Française de Science Politique*, Vol. XXIII, No. 3, June 1975, p. 496.
12 Maria Filomena Mónica, *Educação e sociedade no Portugal de Salazar*, Editorial Presença/Gabinete de Investigações Sociais, Lisbon, 1978, p. 98.
13 Ben Pimlott and Jean Seaton, 'Political power and the Portuguese media', in Lawrence Graham and Douglas Wheeler (eds.), *The Portuguese Revolution*, University of Wisconsin Press, Madison, Wis., 1982.
14 Mónica, *op. cit.*, p. 88.
15 Gallagher, 'The Theory and Practice of Portuguese Authoritarianism', thesis, p. 84.
16 Ferro, *Salazar*, p. 66.
17 *Ibid.*, p. 65.
18 Maria Filomena Mónica, 'Moulding the minds of the people: popular education in twentieth century Portugal', paper presented at the International Conference Group on Modern Portugal symposium at the

University of New Hampshire, USA, 22 June 1979, p. 10.
19 *Ibid.*, p. 16.
20 Ferro, *op. cit.*, p. 25.
21 Mónica, *Educação e sociedade*, p. 116.
22 Mário Soares, *Portugal's Struggle for Liberty*, Allen & Unwin, London, p. 28.
23 Voltaire, *Candide*, Penguin Classics series, Penguin, London, 1974 (latest ed.).
24 In reality Coca-Cola may not have been allowed in because the 'case was mishandled and pressure was applied too heavily and at the wrong spot'. See Mary McCarthy, 'Letter from Lisbon', *New Yorker*, 5 February 1955, p. 92.
25 Garnier, *Salazar*, pp. 6–8.
26 Robinson, *Contemporary Portugal*, p. 56.
27 José Cardoso Pires, 'Changing a nation's way of thinking', *Index on Censorship*, spring 1972, No. 1, p. 96.
28 Soares, *op. cit.*, p. 70.
29 M. Harsgor relates how in 1942–43 a priest turned to his flock at Guimarães in northern Portugal and remarked, 'God be praised, my children! Europe has been destroyed, the Christians are dying there under the bombs or of hunger, whilst we, mind well, we have calm and tranquillity and even our daily bread.' See M. Harsgor, *Naissance d'un nouveau Portugal*, Seuil, Paris, 1975, p. 41.
30 Keith Middlemas, *Carbora Bassa. Engineering and Politics in Southern Africa*, Weidenfeld & Nicolson, London, 1975, pp. 13–14.
31 Glyn A. Stone, 'The official attitude to the Anglo-Portuguese alliance', *Journal of Contemporary History*, Vol. 10, No. 4, 1975, p. 741.
32 Oliveira Marques, *História de Portugal*, II, pp. 215–16.
33 Nowell, *Portugal*, p. 160.
34 Manuel de Lucena, *A evolução do sistema corporativo português*, Vol. I, *O salazarismo*, Perspectivas e Realidades, Lisbon, 1976, p. 46.
35 *Ibid.*, p. 46.
36 *Ibid.*, pp. 45–6.
37 Rev. Richard Devane, SJ, 'The religious revival under Dr Salazar', *Irish Ecclesiastical Record* (Dublin), 1937, p. 491.
38 John J. Ryan, 'Is Portugal totalitarian?' *Irish Monthly*, January 1940, p. 5.
39 John Whyte, *Church and Society in Modern Ireland, 1923–1970*, Gill & Macmillan, Dublin, 1971, p. 71.
40 Quoted in Paul Blanshard, *The Irish and Catholic Power*, Verschoyle, London, 1954, p. 15.
41 PRO, FO 371 C2252/41/31, 7 March 1941.
42 George Kennan, *Memoirs*, Little Brown, Boston, Mass., 1967, p. 150.
43 The manner in which the war impinged on Portugal in the crucial year of 1940 is discussed by Douglas Wheeler in his 'O duplo centenário de 1940', *Diário de Notícias*, 10 June 1980.
44 PRO, FO 371 C692/66/36, 27 July 1943.
45 I was able to interview General Fernando dos Santos Costa in Lisbon during July 1981. Much of the information which I obtained is contained here, and some it it can be regarded as a corrective to the traditional view of him, represented, for instance, by my own 'Portugal's Beria: General Santos Costa and the 1926–74 dictatorship', *History Today*, February 1981, pp. 42–6.
46 Interview with General Santos Costa, Lisbon, 16 July 1981.
47 *Ibid*.
48 Rui Cartaxana, *A Luta*, 2 September 1976.

49 See Fernando Queiroga, *Portugal oprimido*, Seculo, Lisbon, 1974, p. 201.
50 Interview with General Santos Costa, Lisbon, 20 July 1981.
51 *Ibid.*
52 *Ibid.*
53 Eduard de Blaye, *Franco and the Politics of Spain*, Penguin, London, 1976, pp. 158–9.
54 Tom Gallagher, 'Controlled repression in Salazar's Portugal', *Journal of Contemporary History*, Vol. 14, No. 3, July 1979, pp. 392–3.

6
New tension and growing contradictions, 1945–51

Opposition revives

Salazar's ascent to power after 1928 was not hindered by any major opposition unrest. In the formative stages of his rule he always had more to fear from aggrieved right-wingers than from the liberal opposition, whose spirits had been effectively crushed perhaps even before the collapse of the parliamentary republic. Small-scale revolts took place in Lisbon on 20 June 1928 and 26 August 1931 which were easily suppressed by the authorities. The only substantial revolt after 1928 occurred in April 1931, when Madeira and the Azores were seized by Republicans exiled there. In the same month Spain had become a republic. However, the dictatorship was able to crush the islands revolt in a matter of weeks, the defeat marking the end of a clear phase in opposition activity. Thereafter armed opposition to the regime would cease to be civilian-inspired. Only feeble protest greeted the onslaught on the labour movement in 1933–34. Anarchists and communists, then vying for dominance among the politically aware sections of the working class, squabbled about what tactics to employ against the *Estado Novo*. Led by Bento Gonçalves, the PCP adopted a rather docile position in 1933, 'criticising illegal activities as being in the interests of the fascists' and even denouncing those who indulged in them to the authorities, according to one hostile source.[1] Eventually, in January 1934, the far-left realised the gravity of the threat posed to it and called for a general strike. But except in the glass-making town of Marinha Grande, which was briefly taken over by workers, the authorities had little trouble in quelling the unrest.

After 1934 the Communist Party gradually replaced the anarchists as the dominant movement among the working class. In the years to come, members would display great ingenuity and fortitude in their struggle against Salazar. However, the early history of the party was rather ignominious; founded in 1921, the PCP's first leader was Carlos Rates, a man who later defected to the right and became a journalist in the Salazar era. Under his leadership the party was little more than a narrow intellectual sect with almost no influence among the working class. Today Rates is chiefly remembered for putting forward the idea in the 1920s that the colonies be sold to the larger western powers so that the communists could get the money to finance socialism in Portugal.[2]

Eventually, in the 1930s, more dedicated people came to the fore in the PCP and it began to put down roots within the working class, which was now experiencing the harsh economic privations of the authoritarian period. By the 1960s decades of exploitation and unrelieved hardship had left the Portuguese working class the most downtrodden in Europe. Social distress and economic privations got worse for the humbler sections of the population from the late 1920s onwards. Salazar had publicly stated that, under the *Estado Novo*, the workers would not be a privileged class, and he was more than true to his word.[3] But the regime was to pay an increasingly high price for its stringency. Long years of PCP missionary activity helped to radicalise important groups of workers. Dockers, shipbuilders, transport workers and textile operatives were among the party's staunchest supporters after the Second World War. In Portugal's largest province, the Alentejo, the PCP developed a geographical power base among the landless peasants who tilled the large estates. However, it took years of clandestine activity on the part of tough and resourceful party cadres before the PCP was able to mould a working class that was strongly Marxist in its loyalties. For one thing, militants had to run the gauntlet of the secret police, which made the hunting of communists its top priority from the mid-1930s onwards. By the end of the dictatorship the then twenty-two-strong PCP central committee had served a total of 308 years in Salazarist jails, an average of fourteen years per individual.[4] Bento Gonçalves, the person who had reorganised the party in the 1930s, died in Tarrafal concentration camp in 1942. His eventual successor as general secretary was Álvaro Barreirinhas Cunhal. Both men came from markedly different backgrounds, Cunhal hailing from a wealthy liberal home and Gonçalves having been raised in the backward rural province of Trás-os-Montes. Strangely, Cunhal would never end up in Tarrafal, though the most wanted communist in Portugal from the 1940s onwards. There are tentative grounds for believing that the type of treatment meted out to PCP members depended on their social background. Married in later life to a member of the Rapazote family, which provided a hard-line minister of the interior from 1968 to 1974, Cunhal was able to sit his final law exams while in prison in 1938. The papers were marked by none other than Marcelo Caetano, who told Cunhal, 'You are very talented. What a pity you are a communist.'[5] Caetano (himself married into the opposition Barros family) awarded him his doctorate in law, and Cunhal walked out of prison in 1938 with some of the best marks ever given to any law student in Portugal. However, if the authorities were hoping to capture this brilliant mind by giving him preferential treatment they were to be disappointed.

Released from captivity in 1941, after serving another short sentence, Cunhal was able to organise an impressive series of protests against the regime during the Second World War, a time when the PCP emerged as the most important organised force in Portuguese opposition politics. A major wave of strikes occurred in July/August 1943 which was the most serious confrontation between the regime and the working class during the whole forty-eight-year history of the dictatorship. One source reckons that around 50,000 people (almost the entire industrial workforce in the Lisbon area), participated in strikes, demonstrations and hunger marches.[6] The spur, according to Sir Ronald Campbell, the British ambassador, was the fall of Mussolini, 'which stirred the imagination of the Portuguese and led them to hope that it would be followed by the fall of their dictator'.[7] More strikes in May 1944, in which farm labourers as well as workers participated, produced a savage wave of repression. Ultimately the labour unrest would not prove destabilising, since the Portuguese state apparatus was much better suited than Mussolini's to roll back the waves of protest.

The PCP was unable to mount anything like an equivalent industrial challenge until the final months of the dictatorship in 1974. Between 1949 and 1951 the PIDE mounted a concerted offensive against the party in which Cunhal and other leading members were detained. Cunhal then spent ten years in jail, seven of them in solitary confinement, and day-to-day control passed to Júlio Melo Fogaça, a talented organiser and a veteran of Tarrafal. Fogaça kept the party going, and in 1956 he made a visit to the Soviet Union, where he was deeply influenced by Khruschev's denunciation of Stalin and much of his work, at the famous 1956 party congress. Back in Portugal, he steered the PCP in a more liberal direction, backing the popular, ex-fascist General Delgado in his bid for the presidency in 1958 and even proposing the abolition of the hammer and sickle as the party's official symbol.[8] However, any possibility that the PCP might have become an early proponent of Euro-communism was dashed in 1960 when Fogaça was detained by the PIDE along with a male colleague who confessed that he had had sexual relations with him over several years. In a practice which was routine, the PIDE circulated this confession to the PCP, hoping to sow divisions in its ranks. Later a short note in a clandestine PCP newspaper announced that Fogaça had been expelled for moral reasons.

In the Hobbesian world which it inhabited before 1974 the PCP prized orthodoxy and austerity, and 'deviants' of whatever kind were given short shrift. Such exacting rigour was probably helpful in forestalling infiltrators (one central committee member, Manuel Domingos, had been executed as an informer in the 1950s) but many anti-fascists were quickly turned off by the harsh discipline and exacting duties required of members. Among younger members of the liberal elite who joined the party there was a high turnover of membership, especially after the defects and excesses of communist rule in the Soviet Union became clear in the post-Stalin era. In 1964 the party suffered a split as a result of the Sino-Soviet feud, a small pro-Peking group led by Francisco Martins Rodrigues advocating a policy of armed struggle. However, under Cunhal's leadership the PCP remained more or less in one piece during the difficult years of clandestinity and repression. The backbone of its support remained the alienated and dechristianised working class within which communism increasingly functioned as an alternative religion, complete with its own martyrs, gospel and demonology. The party was also able to infiltrate student and intellectual groups as well as the armed forces. A United States embassy report, dated 6 May 1962, revealed that the party (whose strength was put at 8,000 members), had also penetrated various government ministries and even the police.[9]

At various times (above all the 1940s and again in 1958) the PCP collaborated with the liberal opposition, forming a united front and backing opposition election candidates. The main pre-1926 parties had ceased to exist in organised form but individuals were able to stand against official candidates in a number of elections held between 1945 and 1958. The opposition never won a single seat, and candidates withdrew in despair on all but one occasion during the Salazar era. However, the fact that these 'elections' took place at all made the *Estado Novo* virtually unique among authoritarian regimes.

In the month or so officially given over for campaigning before a presidential or National Assembly election, censorship was technically lifted. This enabled opposition papers like *República* or the *Diário de Lisboa* to print opposition manifestoes and to report meetings and speeches. The degree of harassment which the authorities inflicted on them during campaigning usually indicated just how much leeway democrats could expect at the polls. At no time were candidates given a guarantee that there would be a fair contest. Salazar indignantly refused to allow any neutral international bodies to supervise elections. A recently published book consisting of official documents reveals in stark form the amount of fraud and impersonation which went on before and during every poll.[10] So why bother to hold elections? Several hypotheses have been put forward. One view is that 'elections' were tolerated so as to legitimise the regime in the eyes of foreigners. Alternatively, it is argued that a major function of elections was to find out just who the opposition was.

Whatever the reason, it is one of the ironies of our time that no country in Europe has had as many elections as Portugal had in the dictatorial era. From the establishment of the corporative state in 1933 onwards, it had no less than seventeen, six more than in Ireland, eight more than in France, and more than double the number than in Italy.[11] However, only a selected number of adults were able to vote, the electoral register encompassing only 7–8 per cent of the total population in the 1930s. Nevertheless, a very high percentage of this mini-electorate (83–86 per cent) turned out to vote during the initial stages of the regime, probably an indication of general approval on the part of strongly elitist voting groups for the policies of the regime. Abstentions thereafter increased, and by the 1960s Portugal was placed eighty-eighth out of ninety-two countries in the world in terms of voter turn-out, followed only by Sierra Leone, South Africa, South West Africa and Rhodesia.

Philippe Schmitter has argued that Portugal had a latent four-party system in the authoritarian era: (1) the regime-supporting party (measured as a percentage of the population voting for the UN); (2) the abstentionist party, measured as a percentage of registered voters not voting in a given election; (3) the disfranchised party, measured as the percentage of the eligible population not registered to vote; and (4) the opposition party or parties, measured as the percentage of the eligible population voting for any non-UN party.[12]

The first stage-managed election which had some degree of opposition participation took place in autumn 1945. Having recently begun to call his corporative state an 'organic democracy', Salazar brought forward the date of the parliamentary elections by a year and intimated that opponents could challenge regime nominees. Newsboys in Lisbon yelled at the top of their voices, 'Salazar on toast, Salazar on toast,' when the announcement was published in the press.[13] But, after years of enforced inactivity, the old-guard opposition was in no state to challenge the well oiled UN machine at the polls and after a while it withdrew, accusing Salazar of foul play for bringing the election date forward. Moreover, age and association with the unsuccessful parliamentary era made an active political role rather unrealistic for members of the elite opposition. As a result, standard-bearers at elections were often from outside this circle. Senior officers predominated. Every opposition candidate for the presidency between 1949 and 1958 was a general or an admiral; the regime's presidential nominees were also high officers. However, the type of military individual who belonged to the opposition was changing. Until just after the Second World War the great bulk of military oppositionists were liberal officers of pre-1926 vintage. Perhaps the most distinguished of their number, General José Norton de Matos, was the 1949 opposition presidential candidate. Two years later, when the death of President Carmona necessitated another contest, it was seventy-one-year-old Admiral Manuel Quintão Meireles, someone who had been an initial backer of the counter-revolution, who headed the ticket. Disillusioned partisans of the regime were thus now prepared to cross over to the opposition and join its military confraternity. The number of soldiers declaring their political independence in this way was small in the 1940s, but in the 1950s and early 1960s the numbers increased, it being true to say that each post-1926 military generation yielded up important opposition converts. Names like Captain Henrique Galvão, General Delgado, Admiral Meireles, General J. Botelho Moniz and Marshal Craveiro Lopes come to mind. The regime's civilian support agencies never displayed equivalent independence. Except for individual churchmen and monarchists like Francisco Vieira de Almeida, defections to the orthodox opposition were virtually non-existent.

Members of the liberal professional class dominated the non-communist opposition through all stages of the New State. At elections the government's list of candidates could often show a 'relatively balanced representation of local notables, prominent bourgeois, eminent professionals and "ordinary folk" ', while the opposition ticket was drawn from a narrower social range.[14] If the liberal opposition had succeeded in creating a geographical power base, or if abstention levels had changed significantly, then perhaps elections in Portugal might have taken on a different meaning before 1974. However, internecine opposition disputes as much as government harassment and fraud regularly sapped opposition strength. Personal feuds among old-guard republicans proved a serious obstacle to unity. Patricia McGowan Pinheiro was being only too accurate when she wrote:

> It is often hard to get unity even for manifestoes and open letters. Dr X in Coimbra is only prepared to sign if he knows that Professor Y in Lisbon is in agreement and neither of them will sign if Colonel Z's name is to be included.[15]

Ideological schism likewise did great damage to the opposition cause. The PCP and liberals quarrelled at the height of the Cold War in the 1950s and again in 1969 after the Soviet invasion of Czechoslovakia. A particular bone of contention was the future of Portugal's African empire. While the communists demanded complete self-determination for the people of Angola, Mozambique and Guinea-Bissau, some old-guard oppositionists backed Portuguese colonialism, albeit not the highly repressive kind practised under Salazar. Cunha Leal in 1946 addressed an open letter to Salazar asking for the creation of a United States of Portugal with its capital in Luanda, Angola, an idea that was being seriously contemplated in *official* circles at the beginning of the 1960s. Later, in the mid-1960s, a left-wing united front, created in Algeria, whose government provided a variety of facilities to the Portuguese, was wrecked by disagreements over cash and the rather high-handed behaviour of its leaders, Fernando Piteira Santos and Tito de Morais. Controversy about their stormy relations with the opposition hero, General Delgado, was still raging fifteen years later.[16]

Some moderate oppositionists, on the other hand, were unhappy in principle about having any dealings with the PCP. But Salazar himself does not seem to have been greatly perturbed by the party's prominence in opposition ranks. Despite his genuine terror of communism, a more centre-oriented opposition would have presented clear problems. Firstly, there would probably have been a much higher defection rate on the part of alientated Estado Novo politicians. Less important, it would have been more difficult to blacken the opposition with hostile propaganda if it had presented a more moderate and less ideological image. As it was, the liberal–communist alliance was a dubious coalition, representing as it did, on the one hand, a discredited liberal parliamentary 'past' and, on the other, a doubtful communist 'future'. One observer has written that a Catholic–socialist convergence (which many were forecasting in the 1960s) would have been more fruitful for the opposition.[17]

Realistically perhaps, the opposition backed away from direct physical confrontation with the *Estado Novo*. The PCP did not think that armed struggle was feasible in Portugal as long as the regime had a secure grip on the country, and it was only anarchists who would attempt to eliminate Salazar physically. Violent confrontation did occur in the universities during the early 1960s between police and students. Portugal was actually the first European country to be affected by the student troubles which later in the same decade got more publicity when they occurred elsewhere. However, Salazar dealt cleverly with student protest and made sure that he would not be brought down by it as happened in one authoritarian country, Greece, where a massacre of protesting students was a prelude to the overthrow of the Colonels' regime in 1974.

Despite its defects, the opposition camp was characterised by indomitability and consistency as well as by failure and isolation. Amazingly few individuals abandoned the job of opposition to make their peace with the regime. Some dramatic escape *coups* were pulled off by imprisoned activists such as Henrique Galvão and the less well known Hermínio Palma Inácio, Portugal's Scarlet Pimpernel. Once, on being asked by a judge whether he wished to say anything in his defence, he replied that 'he wished nothing except a dark night and a storm'.[18] That very night he escaped from one of Portugal's top security prisons.

Repression

The one *Estado Novo* institution which gained undoubted fame beyond Portugal's borders was the PIDE, the name of the secret police between 1945 and 1969. Portugal, like other authoritarian regimes lacking a popular base, such as Iran and Chile, needed an efficient, ruthless and ubiquitous undercover police force. Back in December 1926 the military dictatorship set up one of the first comparable forerunners of the PIDE when it created a special information police in the capital under the control of the civil governor. Another was set up in Oporto during 1927, and in 1928 both were transformed into a national agency whose importance grew as the authoritarian regime tightened its grip on the country. Opposition was increasingly driven underground and, with the appearance of the PVDE (the Police of Vigilance and State Defence) in 1933, the secret police established itself as the most feared weapon of the state.

Torture was routinely practised on political suspects. Individuals who had been ministers or deputies before 1926 were arrested and beaten up if they challenged the *Estado Novo*. José Catela, an early director of the PVDE, is reported to have once spoken to a pre-1926 deputy, who was complaining about being arrested, in the following vein:

> Your rights! What rubbish! Here I arrest whoever I like and can keep him in prison for as long as I want to. There are only two people I cannot touch, the president of the republic and the prime minister ... but, as for the first, I sometimes have my doubts.[19]

To increase the secret police's professionalism, instructors were imported from Italy and Germany to provide training in the latest police state techniques of the 1930s. Fernando Gouveia and Henrique Seixas were two PVDE operatives who acquired particular notoriety, one as a talented hunter of communists, the other as a cruel sadist who, after being stationed in Tarrafal concentration camp, became Salazar's own personal bodyguard. Another name worthy of mention is José Gonçalves. He was an ex-anarchist who joined the secret police in the 1930s and became a top informer, around whom a special brigade was assembled. Eventually the PVDE and its successors built up a nationwide network of spies and informers who operated in cafés, railway stations, post offices, hospitals, factories, the universities and other public places. Several sources reckon that as many as 20,000 people were employed in this fashion altogether.[20] Known as *bufos*, these eavesdroppers were despised by their fellow citizens, who for nearly half a century hardly dared to discuss politics in the open.

Ironically, the regime enacted its most repressive legislation in 1945 after the defeat of fascism elsewhere in Europe. António de Figueiredo has written that 'after 1945 . . . the regime passed from the arbitrary but casual stage of repression to the development of a scientific system which, in its operative methods was tantamount to a neo-Inquisition'.[21] On 30 April 1945, nine days before the surrender of Nazi Germany, an ambiguous decree announced that 'preventative measures' against crime could be taken by a special court. Then, on 13 October 1945, the secret police was renamed the International Police for State Defence (PIDE), initials which it would retain for the rest of the Salazar era. With this change of acronym its powers were further extended. It now had the power to detain anyone suspected of hostile political activity for forty-five days without bringing a charge. The regulation was designed for use against plebeian offenders, and in 1956 another law enabled the PIDE to keep indefinitely under arrest all those who were believed to be dangerous to society.[22]

For use against more distinguished political opponents, a decree was introduced on 1 June 1947 which gave the government power to (1) dismiss officers of the armed forces who shirked their loyalty to institutions of the state; and (2) dismiss all those public functionaries who had taken part in acts of sedition . . . and who gave no guarantees of co-operation in carrying out the high aims of the state.[23] That Salazar had not previously directed such punitive measures against state employees and members of the armed forces is proof that he had not faced serious opposition from that quarter before. As a precaution, the regime now provided the PIDE with its own extensive armoury. The weapons it housed were quite sophisticated but it is unlikely that they would have enabled the PIDE to head off a serious attempt at a *coup*. Its primary function was to prevent rather than contain unrest.

Internationally, the PIDE was rather slow in acquiring the dark reputation which it enjoyed within Portugal itself. In the late 1940s Agostinho Lourenço, an early PIDE director, was even able to become head of Interpol in Paris without much of a Continental stir being caused. Later, in 1967, Pope Paul VI, on his visit to the shrine of Fátima, decorated several PIDE functionaries, including the director, Fernando Silva Pais. Some years before, the PIDE had been sufficiently confident about its bland overseas image to mount a prosecution in the British courts against the *New Statesman*.[24] However, later in the 1960s Portugal's secret police became much more internationally visible thanks to its prominent role in the colonial war being waged in Portuguese Africa against insurgent nationalist forces. Grouped in counter-terror squads known as *flechas*, PIDE agents operated behind enemy lines and farther afield in independent black Africa. This was made apparent in 1969 when a parcel bomb killed Eduardo Mondlane, the Mozambiquan nationalist leader, when he was in Dar-es-Salaam. Four years later Amílcar Cabral, the Guinea-Bissau liberation leader, met his death at the hands of PIDE agents in Sekou Touré's Guinea.

It was probably during the 1960s that the PIDE's influence reached its zenith. During Salazar's twilight years the last PIDE director, Silva Pais, exercised strong influence over the dictator. The two conferred often, and more than one source refers to the PIDE as being a grotesque state within a state at the regime's close.[25] There is evidence that the PIDE even placed cabinet ministers under surveillance. Rui Patrício, foreign minister between 1970 and 1974, was regularly tailed when abroad, according to one source.[26] It is also claimed that in 1961, at a time of university unrest, the rector of Lisbon University, Marcelo Caetano, was on the point of being arrested by the PIDE but for Salazar's final rejection of this move.[27]

Numerically, the PIDE increased in size during the 1960s. However, there is evidence that quality was not keeping pace with quantity. Individuals with lower educational standards were gaining admission to the force. The rate of expulsion for 'dereliction of duty' was also correspondingly higher than before. So were the number of jail break-outs involving political prisoners. These are the most serious blots on the PIDE's professional reputation.

Between 1958 and 1969 three of Portugal's leading anti-fascist personalities each managed to escape from incarceration. The most spectacular incident occurred on 4 January 1960 when Álvaro Cunhal escaped from the grim prison fortress of Peniche. A year earlier Henrique Galvão had freed himself from a Lisbon prison hospital, and eleven years later there took place Palma Inácio's sensational break-out from an Oporto jail.

Despite these blows to its prestige, the PIDE, operating from headquarters in the Rua António Maria Cardoso in downtown Lisbon, maintained its fearsome reputation in the minds of the public. This may have been because its operatives consistently displayed a high degree of rationality in the terror sphere. Without liquidating large numbers of people, the PIDE succeeded in suppressing the underlying population and paralysing the elite opposition for a long period. An optimum amount of terror rather than a crude maximum level was always its objective.[28] In this it succeeded. The *Estado Novo* was always successful in avoiding major public showdowns. Between 1933 and 1974 there were few disturbances involving loss of life. There was never any Salazarist equivalent inside Portugal of the killing of unarmed Swedish mineworkers at Adalen in 1931; of the shooting of six students at Kent State University, USA, in 1970; or of the Bloody Sunday killings in Northern Ireland on 30 January 1972. These incidents, involving the forces of the state, took place in perhaps the three most advanced of Western pluralist democracies.

Only several hundred people were actually eliminated in *metropolitan* Portugal during the forty-eight-year hold of the dictatorship. Nevertheless, the public was more or less completely subdued during this time. The widespread use of informers is perhaps one key secret of the PIDE's success. Another is the unchanging nature of repression. There was no wide fluctuation in PIDE behaviour of periodic liberalisations to encourage bolder spirits.

Civil–military relations

Although Salazar radically changed the nature of the authoritarian regime immediately on taking office, he encountered little overt opposition from the military. Most politically attuned officers accepted the corporative constitution, though with varying degrees of enthusiasm. If, in the full flush of enthusiasm, the *Estado Novo* had sought to corporatise the army (i.e. regulate its routine behaviour in the same manner as it was extending its control over the labour and business world), right-wing officers might have welcomed such a step but less committed soldiers and neutral professionals would probably have mounted resistance.

Actually, not until 1935 were there any indications of strain in the civil–military relationship. In the second half of the year the British embassy reported to London that:

> Lisbon has been full of rumours as to friction between the Prime Minister and the Army. ... The equipment and armaments of the Portuguese Army have been allowed to fall into a scandalous state, so that it is no longer capable of taking the field: its rifles are war ones which are now worn so smooth as to be unfit even for target practice, whilst the equipment is so old, worn-out and exiguous that not one of the four divisions of the army could be put on a war footing.[29]

The army had been in a materially deficient state for quite some time. What brought matters to a head in 1935 was the fact that the navy had recently been re-armed and provided with a new warship. The sea arm, with a large overseas empire to defend, was naturally almost as important as the land arm in strategic terms. But the army traditionally carried more political weight, and officers were aggrieved that it was being passed over in favour of the smaller service. Nevertheless, Salazar refused to make funds available for army modernisation until the substantial number of officers in purely sinecure jobs were got rid of. By 1935 the premier appears to have considered himself sufficiently powerful to crack down on over-staffing and wastage, even though the British embassy believed that 'Dr Salazar is playing with fire if his reforming zeal is indiscreet enough to offend the army'.[30]

Salazar gradually overcame his difficulties with sections of the army. On 11 May 1936 he appointed himself minister of war and became one of the few civilians to take charge of what had always been regarded as an exclusively military appointment. General Raul Esteves, one of the architects of the 1926 revolution, protested to President Carmona on hearing the news, believing that 'a grave and humiliating injustice had been inflicted on the army on the tenth anniversary of the 28 May revolution. Already we have reached a situation where there is no military chief who was a major architect of the revolution.'[31] This, of course, was a strong indication that civilian supremacy in the new authoritarian state was already far advanced. Fernando Queiroga, a former army officer, believes that Salazar planned his elevation to the war ministry well beforehand by appointing to the job, in rapid succession after 1932, a series of military men of doubtful ability. This made it easier, Queiroga writes, for him to then 'turn round to the nation and the army to say in effect that only he, Salazar, was capable of proceeding with the reorganisation of the army'.[32]

Towards the end of 1937 a series of decree-laws were published by the war ministry which showed the full extent of Salazar's reforming zeal. Pay scales were altered. The size of army units was alternatively lowered or raised. Large numbers of officers were pensioned off before retiring age, ostensibly to reduce costs and to make room on the promotional ladder for more dynamic officers. The army had not witnessed such thoroughgoing changes in perhaps a generation: governments before 1926 would have been extremely loath to tamper with military structures in so forceful a manner; the military dictatorship of 1926–32 would have been similarly constrained, aware of how precarious its authority was in many barracks, even at the best of times.

Nevertheless, Salazar's changes did not go completely unchallenged. Strong corporate pressures in defence of career interests were brought to bear on the Portuguese leader. General Luís Câmara Pina, a former army chief of staff in the 1960s, has admitted that the 1937 legislation nearly caused an open breach with sections of the army.[33] In January 1938 large angry meetings were staged in some Lisbon barracks on the publication of the full list of decrees. Fierce objections were raised to the changes governing pay and promotions. Ultimately the temperature was sufficiently heated for the military governor of Lisbon, General Domingos Oliveira, to intervene with the prime minister. Later a slightly conciliatory official note declared:

> The Military Governor of Lisbon was received by the Prime Minister, who was informed that objections were being raised to the recent military reforms. . . . The government is prepared to concede the possibility of deficiencies and anomalies being found in a document of this nature. It is intended that these will be ironed out and satisfacorily dealt with when the reform measures are put into effect.[34]

To a degree, Salazar's military reforms were a leap into the unknown. He may well have decided to go ahead with them aware that the military was unlikely to drop the pilot with war ranging next door in Spain. Already the army had reacted with equanimity to the setting up of the paramilitary Portuguese Legion in 1936. Actually, it was rapidly obvious that the Legion had not been set up in competition with the army as paramilitary Nazi agencies were in Germany during the same period. The Legion's cadres were mainly retired officers or active ones borrowed to drill Legion members. Regime propaganda never exalted the Legion above the army: the Legion was always subject to military discipline whenever it was required to collaborate with the orthodox defence forces.

The existence of a loyal paramilitary force may have decided the government against politically colonising the army. If Salazar had thought such a move expedient, he would probably have completely destroyed the forces' independence of action. However, he did not, and chose, instead, to bind the army closer to the regime by means of various informal regulations. The most irksome restriction, enacted in 1940, made it obligatory for army officers to marry in church. Civil marriage was forbidden to members of the officer corps, and so, in effect, was divorce, since church weddings could be annulled only in special circumstances. Fryer and McGowan Pinheiro reckon that the object of this rule was to eradicate the anticlerical element which had hitherto been influential in the army. Equally desirable was closer military liaison with the civilian upper classes. To this end, the regime laid down that no officer could marry a woman who was not a university graduate or the possessor of a large dowry; the officer's match was also subject to the prior approval of two senior officers.[35]

In these restrictions there was logic. If, through marriage, officers came to be linked with the wealthier sections of Portuguese society, Salazar would not have to worry about military pay. With officers finding other means of support, he could have a relatively low-cost army; and that is how it was. Officer rates of pay remained consistently low, so that serving officers without an alternative source of income lived in rather straitened circumstances. These officers grew discontented after Salazar ordered *cuts* in military pay during 1941.[36] For many, another job was an economic necessity. Some of the most senior officers grew very rich, like Manuel Ortins de Bettencourt, the navy minister between 1936 and 1944. Ultimately, Salazar's plan to tie layers of the officer corps to the moneyed classes (and give them a stake in the economic *status quo*) appears to have met with long-term success. By dint of subtle manoeuvring, he was able to rely on the passive loyalty of an army that was one of the most poorly paid in Europe.

Beyond the above regulations, Salazar did not penetrate much further into the military domain. The premier did fill top command posts below the rank of general from lists presented by a selection committee of general officers, but at no time do political witch-hunts seem to have been organised against politically suspect officers. Most who were thrown out of the service gave themselves away be being implicated in a *coup* attempt at one time or another. If a republican or mildly left-wing officer belonged to a quiet unit, he could still function, as long as he was not caught engaging in clandestine activity. When this happened the army usually took its own disciplinary measures. These do not appear to have been harsh, although the degree of retribution depended on the rank of the officer, the extent of his deviation, and the current political situation. General Norton de Matos managed to remain in the military command until the date of his official retirement in 1933 even though he had formed an *anti-ditadura* Republican–Socialist alliance in 1931. At the other end of the spectrum, two republican sergeants arrested in 1938 were handed over to the PVDE and badly beaten up. However, the PIDE did not involve itself in army affairs except on rare occasions. Even loyal officers might have resented its intervention, since it would have been casting doubt on the military's ability to keep its own house in order. One exceptional case was the Beja uprising of 1962, the only post-war attempt to unseat the government (before 1974) in which firearms were actually discharged. In the aftermath the *coup* leader, Captain João Varela Gomes, was handed over to the secret police and remained in custody until the 1974 revolution.

Discontent with military conditions, and the changing international scene, led to sporadic military unrest in the post-war era. When Salazar gave up the army portfolio in 1944 complaints about the forces' poor state were surfacing anew. The 1937 legislation had been a belated attempt to patch up some of the most glaring military deficiencies, and by the 1940s it was clear that there was no on-going programme of reform. In addition, the new minister of war, Santos Costa, proved unpopular with many officers for his brusque and authoritarian behaviour. Some hard-line officers adopted increasingly liberal views. The two most famous ones were Humberto Delgado and Captain Henrique Galvão.

After becoming high inspector of colonial administration in Angola during 1937, Galvão presented increasingly critical reports about native conditions without seeing any results. The reputation he had won as a defender of the revolution in 1926–27 put him in a strong position, but he became increasingly impatient with Salazar. Finally, in 1947, after being elected to parliament, he delivered a speech setting out the appalling conditions of the African population, the first time any major criticism of the regime had been publicly aired in the National Assembly. An investigation by a judge was then ordered, but its findings were never published, and in 1950, after completing his term as deputy, Galvão publicly joined the opposition.[37]

Often the *Estado Novo* could never predetermine the actions of the military or be absolutely sure of the political reliability of certain officers. This weakness may account for the sudden crises that blew up at different intervals and in which army figures were invariably the major participants. Attempted *coups* (albeit small-scale and often badly planned oned) took place in each decade between the 1930s and 1970s (Franco's Spain, interestingly enough, was spared these tremors). In their wake, the regime often tightened its control over the military, legislation passed in 1947 being the clearest example of this. However, the military never completely lost its freedom of action, as renewed unrest in the 1950s and early 1960s served to demonstrate. Inside the army, senior officers could express their views about the regime with remarkable frankness. In 1958 General Delgado wrote a letter to four senior generals which was scathing in its criticism of Salazar. Ten years later Colonel António de Spínola frankly told Salazar that the war in Guinea-Bissau was unwinnable. Spínola compared the local guerrillas with a flea continually biting a man trying to sleep in a haystack:

> The flea has carried out his mission [he told Salazar], which was by feeding off you to keep you from sleeping. But you cannot carry out yours, which is to find the flea. Imagine this happening for a whole week; you would die of exhaustion.[38]

Some commentators have used incidents like these to argue that Salazar was in power only on the suffrance of the army. The fact that the head of state was always a member of the armed forces may add weight to this argument.[39] However, it is an unrealistic one which does not take account of the fact that Salazar enjoyed complete dominance over the military world for long periods. It also overlooks the fact that the military was far from united in its attitude to the regime. A majority of officers were usually apathetic, neutral, or afraid of taking action against it. The minority liberal wing was complimented by a larger hard-line one which, in the 1960s, was known as the Centurion wing, and had its own newspaper, *Agora*. Rivalry between the army and the navy also diluted the power of the military *vis-à-vis* the civilian regime (some of the navy's liberal traditions seem actually to have survived the rise of Salazarism).

The religious establishment

It is hard to generalise about the Catholic Church in Portugal. Religious observance fluctuates greatly from north to south. The country which, in the eighteenth century, witnessed the first state-inspired anticlerical campaign in Catholic Europe was the only one in the western half of the continent where not a single sign of Protestant activism was reported in the Reformation period. But by the twentieth century the great days of the Portuguese Church were behind it. No latter-day churchmen have emerged to match Padre António Vieira, the renowned seventeenth-century preacher and missionary, or St Anthony of Padua, Lisbon-born although identified with his adopted Italy, or, for that matter, Pedro Julião, the only Portuguese ever to become pope (John XXI: 1276–77).

Despite the onset of a Catholic corporative dictatorship in the 1930s, this century has been a depressed period for the Church. Even Salazar, despite his complete identification with the Catholic lobby before coming to power, did 'nothing directly for religion' in the initial phase of his rule, even if one counts his ending of 'religious persecution so that the Church was granted liberty of life and action'.[40] Church and state remained apart. No attempt was made to establish a theocratic polity. Nor were relations between Salazar and Cardinal Cerejeira as close after 1932 as in previous years. Those who sometimes alluded to a 'Salazar–Cerejeira' dictatorship were widely off the mark.[41] Cerejeira was not Salazar's instrument or vice versa. Possibly relations between the two men were never the same again after Cerejeira made a written plea for a wide-ranging political amnesty in 1930.[42] In private Salazar reacted angrily to this clerical initiative, and, once it was made clear that the New State was all about creating an authoritarian order, Cerejeira never again repeated his call for liberalisation.

In dealing with the Church, Salazar was constrained by the fact that a section of the political elite was still anticlerical. He seems to have concluded that to advance politically and socially a Church with a tenuous hold over much of the population was just asking for trouble, and not just from the *Estado Novo's* traditional enemies. This caution was even noticeable in the wording of the Concordat which Portugal signed with the Vatican on 7 May 1940. After the disruptive liberal republican era, cordial relations between Portugal and the Holy See were re-established with the enactment of this document. The authorities now even showed themselves prepared to help the Church financially. For example, if the faithful provided 70 per cent of the cost of a new church, the government was prepared to make up the difference from a building fund which the state administered. After 1940 churches and seminaries were also exempt from taxation. However, the Concordat was not a one-way transaction. Article 10 stipulated that the Holy See must, before nominating a bishop, communicate the name of the person selected to the Portuguese government in order to determine whether there was any objection of a political nature.[43] Moreover, the legislation of the parliamentary republic was not fundamentally altered: religious teaching in schools remained voluntary; civil marriage and civil divorce were retained;[44] religious oaths were not re-established.

Although a shot in the arm for the Church, the Concordat did not stem falling attendances at Mass or revive the authority of the faith in secular fields. Indeed, in the second quarter of the century organised religion was already in a parlous state. This was most apparent in Lisbon, where, in the 1930s, a diocesan population of one and a half million was served by only 320 priests, many of them old and worn-out clergy.[45] On 8 December 1935 a pastoral issued by Cardinal Cerejeira painted an especially dismal picture:

Black Africa of the Pagans is at the very gates of Lisbon – the mother-church of so many Christian churches in Africa, Asia, Oceania. Should things continue thus, the time will not be long coming when our Christian land will be completely turned into a cemetery of glorious Catholic and apostolic tradition like those brilliant dead churches in north Africa that were once illuminated by the genius of St Augustine.[46]

An appeal for surplus Irish priests to come to Portugal was made in the 1930s, but one did not need to look as far as Ireland. In 1931 the northern city of Braga had three times as many priests as huge Lisbon, while a small rural diocese like Vila Real had almost as many again. On the whole, the position of the Church was far healthier in the north, where priests played a central role in the lives of many communities. An opinion poll published in 1972 revealed an acute divergence between the two parts of Portugal in terms of religious outlook. While between 15 and 35 per cent of all Roman Catholics regularly attended church on Sundays, there was over 90 per cent attendance in the north, less than 20 per cent in the centre, and only 5–10 per cent in the south.[47] In the north there were nearly two priests per 1,000 Catholics, in central Portugal one priest for approximately 4,500, while in the south a priest might theoretically have as many as 12,000 people to look after. One source also reported that in the two most populous districts (Lisbon and Oporto) only fifty-seven new priests were ordained between 1968 and 1970.[48]

Eighty-five per cent of people questioned in 1972 declared themselves Catholics, and 12 per cent stated that they were atheists or merely indifferent to religion.[49] The youngest groups in the sample and the best educated were most inclined to separate themselves from Catholicism. Huge areas, including the Alentejo and the Algarve, were by now classified as mission fields. Here parish priests sometimes tried to compensate for low attendances by erecting loudspeaker systems in the small villages so as to broadcast Mass to the whole community.

Indirect proselytising of this kind yielded few positive results. If the Church wished to revive its credibility with communities which had become virtually dechristianised it would have had to adopt a far more socially progressive outlook, one that would sooner or later have brought it into conflict with the state. This the religious hierarchy steadfastly refused to do during the forty-two years Cerejeira was Patriarch of Lisbon (1929–71). Officially, the Church claimed that it did not mix in politics at all. However, if (as happened) the PIDE was able to carry out surveillance in seminaries, this claim was a hollow one, and the Church was in fact enlisting itself under the regime's banner.[50] An examination of some of Cerejeira's actions shows this to be the case. Priests who raised their voice against the widespread poverty and oppression of the Salazar era were removed from their parishes and cloistered in religious institutions. In 1958, when the Bishop of Oporto, António Ferreira Gomes, publicly criticised the appalling conditions of life which he had witnessed in his diocese, he received no support from his fellow bishops. After being exiled, he was in fact ostracised by them at the Second Vatican Council meeting in Rome during 1963, and he was forced to seek lodgings with South American bishops.[51] Nevertheless, it was Oporto more than any other diocese which reflected the new, modern outlook of the Vatican II Catholic Church. Under its energetic bishop, who nevertheless spent ten years in exile (between 1959 and 1969), the diocese saw important innovations. A progressive weekly newspaper was founded, pastoral activities were organised, and a Council of Justice and Peace provided socio-political criticism up to 1974.

Ferreira Gomes also had several counterparts in Portuguese Africa. Monsignor Sebastião Resende, Bishop of Beira from 1943 to 1967, frequently denounced the excesses of the *Estado Novo* in the tropics, while, in the 1950s, it is true that other colonial bishops did take a stand against forced labour. Much later, Bishop Manuel Vieira Pinto of Beira declared in the early 1970s that 'we prefer a Church that is persecuted but alive to a Church that is generously subsidised but at the price of a damaging connivance at the behaviour of the temporal powers'.[52] Bishop Pinto openly favoured a political rather than a military solution to the wars in Africa, and he was expelled from Mozambique on the very eve of the 1974 revolution.

For a brief period, in the second half of the 1960s, it looked as if a strong dissenting wing might emerge within the Church in metropolitan Portugal. Seventy-eight priests wrote to Cardinal Cerejeira in December 1968 pointing out that the malaise of the clergy was great, indicating problems in religious education, in the lack of innovation in pastoral care, and referring openly to damaging clerical compromises with the state.[53] However, Cerejeira was unmoved, and from 1969 to 1974 there was little conflict inside the Church, since most of the dynamic elements either left or lapsed into silence.[54] Several followed in the footsteps of Joaquim Alves Correia, an eminent Portuguese theologian whose writings anticipated many of the changes brought about by the Second Vatican Council. He quit Portugal altogether in the middle years of Salazarism and ended his days teaching sociology at the University of Pittsburgh.

Strangely, religious progressives got little backing from the Holy See even in the wake of Vatican II. Conservative papal nuncios were sent to Lisbon, where they bolstered the position of the reactionary clerical establishment by nominating conservative bishops. In Madrid, during the late Franco era, the papal nuncio was vital in promoting reform in the Spanish Church, but Rome seemed to prefer a static Portuguese Church and made no effort to really aid Catholics who got into trouble under Salazar for attempting to implement the directives and encyclicals of

Vatican II. Cardinal Cerejeira was influential in Rome and there had been a persistent rumour 'that, in the event of his being seized by the Nazis, Pius XII had given precise directions and authority to Cardinal Cerejeira, Archbishop of Lisbon to take command of the Church'.[55]

Unchanging Portugal, 1945–51

Salazar was still only fifty-six when the Second World War ended in 1945. However, his physical appearance had altered dramatically over the previous fifteen years. The rather slim and youthful figure who had been attractive to many middle-class women aged rapidly during the years of peninsular and international war and he also put on weight. Salazar suffered from a number of ailments such as migraine, dizziness and eyestrain. Throughout his career he was periodically afflicted by insomnia, and there is no doubt from the photographs that he was a tired and exhausted man by the mid-1940s. Nevertheless, he still obstinantly refused to delegate authority and introduce a more collective form of decision-making. In 1950 a new cabinet post, minister to the presidency, was created but it did not presage a new departure. For the next eleven years, until it was abolished in 1961, three men, Costa Leite, Marcelo Caetano and Teotónio Pereira, held the job, but the *Estado Novo* remained as much as ever a centralising autocracy and Salazar gave no hint that any of the three incumbents was being groomed to succeed him.

The age gap between Salazar and all his ministers widened as he grew older and replaced contemporaries with increasingly younger men. In the longer term a greater diffusion of power would undoubtedly have enhanced the stability of the regime. Mexico provides a useful example where an authoritarian depersonalising polity has derived enormous long-term benefit from subsuming political individualism within a collective bureaucratic framework. Although corresponding much more closely than the *Estado Novo* to the corporativist ideal, Salazar rejected the Mexican political model as involving too many compromises with liberal democracy. Although, for reasons of expediency, post-war Portugal suddenly began to be termed an 'organic democracy', pluralist concepts were still anathema to the Portuguese leader after the fall of fascism. To liberalise the country was at best to suffer the return of squabbling politicians or at worst to allow the communists to slip into power. Democracy still held too many uncertainties. Until his death, Salazar remained convinced that universal suffrage meant the rule of the mob, except in countries like Switzerland and Britain where local conditions somehow made this system of government feasible. With these prejudices, he retained his dictatorial paternalism and does not appear to have considered modifying his regime by replacing the New State with a facade democracy or a 'strong' democratic state along the lines of Gaullist France. Despite the strong current of urban opposition to the New State controlled liberalisation might just have been feasible in a country where the majority of people were still illiterate or near-illiterate peasants. Perhaps aware that open elections might not spell the end of the regime but could rather cause it to enter a healthier phase, right-wing individuals within the official power structure occasionally pressed for change but ultimately to no avail. If the regime had been less insular and more aware of the range of political possibilities within existing democracies, it might perhaps have approached the prospect of partial liberalisation with less trepidation. Provincial 'despotisms' have flourished in outwardly robust democratic states without giving rise to concern. Countries of the English-speaking world (still the heartland of liberal democracy) have yielded noteworthy examples of local authoritarianism coexisting with representative democracy at national level (for instance, in Great Britain: Northern Ireland 1920–72; in the USA: the south 1875–*c.* 1965; and in Canada: Quebec 1936–59).

Internationally, little pressure was brought to bear on Salazar after the Second World War. In 1946 Norway made the request that Angola be turned into a Jewish homeland, but it was not taken up seriously. Portugal was refused entry into the United Nations, along with Ireland, another wartime neutral, but she was invited to join the North Atlantic Treaty Organisation in 1949 as a founder-member and by 1955 had also become a member of the United Nations.

For the first time in many years it was the domestic, not the foreign, situation which troubled Salazar when, in 1946, a few progressives in the army summoned enough confidence to launch a revolt against the *Estado Novo*. Known as the Mealhada revolt, it was the first uprising against the authorities in ten years. Setting out from Oporto and led by Captain Fernando Queiroga, the intention of the rebels was to march on Lisbon in the manner of the 28 May revolutionaries. However, with only one armoured column, the thirty-seven-year-old Queiroga did not get very far. Other centres failed to rise and loyal forces stopped the rebel column before it reached Coimbra.

The dismal collapse of the Mealhada revolt highlighted the continued weakness of the army 'left', really only a collection of individuals none of whom would display the temerity of Queiroga. The regime was also aware how isolated the 1946 rebels were, and it treated them rather leniently: Queiroga spent only three years in prison. However, the leaders of a conspiracy detected on 10 April 1947 would not escape so easily. High-ranking officers were involved who had hitherto shown no disloyalty to the regime. Some even owed their seniority to their past willingness to back the *Estado Novo* inside the army, and by no stretch of the imagination could all of them be described as 'liberals'. Hence this high-level conspiracy came as quite a shock to the regime, which, in June 1947, speedily enacted decrees providing much severer penalties for rebellious civil and military functionaries. The officers apprehended in April were drummed out of the service and put on trial. Suffering from a heart condition, General José Marques Godinho, the leader of the conspiracy, died in custody on 24 December 1947. The opposition claimed that he had been treated harshly by war minister Santos Costa because he had letters in his possession proving that the minister had been pro-Axis before 1945. For part of the war Godinho had been military governor of the Azores even though it was known then that he was not a staunch supporter of the *Estado Novo*. Much later, in 1981, Santos Costa broke a long silence with the publication of an article in which he denied having had any role in Godinho's death.[56]

In court next year, one of the defendants in the 1947 conspiracy claimed that the rebels had the tacit backing of no less a person than the head of state, General Carmona. Certainly, clear evidence exists to suggest that the president had become disillusioned with Salazar by the mid-1940s. By now he had little direct influence on national affairs. His role as puppet head of state evokes comparison with Italian fascism's figurehead, King Victor Emmanuel III. He eventually helped to topple Mussolini in 1943, and there were many people in Portugal who hoped that the same scenario would unfold there. Encouragement came in October 1945 when the president agreed to receive a delegation from the opposition United Democratic Movement (MUD). This was the first official audience anti-Salazarists had had with the president in many years. Thirty-five years later, in 1980, one of the delegates, José Magalhães Godinho (Portugal's first Ombudsman after 1974), recalled what happened. At the meeting Carmona sounded weary and vague, but he stated that if it became clear to him that the opposition had the support of the army, then he would have no hesitation in dismissing the government. However, he could do nothing without army backing.[57] Beyond that the aged Carmona would not be drawn, except that he kept repeating the same rather enigmatic phrase to his guests: 'If only you gentlemen knew, but you don't.'[58]

In January 1946 members of the democratic opposition handed the president a statement which spelled out their case against the government as well as their aspirations for a democratic regime. Incredibly, Carmona passed this manifesto on to the government, recommending 'that it be studied'.[59] Santos Costa and Colonel Júlio Botelho Moniz, the ministers of war and of the interior, described it as nonsense. However, interestingly enough, two others, the education and justice ministers, declared that 'there was substance in some of the MUD points', an indication that inside the government there was a Salazarist 'left' and 'right'.

In the end, Carmona's advice to the government went unheeded. Army officers who dropped in at the palace were soon hearing the president making bitter references to his isolation. If anything, Senhora Carmona was even more embittered. Her dislike of Salazar was proverbial, and in 1948 an opposition defendant revealed in court that when he mentioned news of an impending military plot to her she replied; 'Well, keep up the good work! I'll get on horseback and lead it if you want me to.'[60]

Although he had the power to dismiss Salazar at any time, Carmona did not act. For elucidation, Mário Soares has referred to the dictator having a hold over Carmona – an unexplained murder case that had been hushed up and was said to have involved one of the president's daughters.[61] By now Carmona was also a fast aging septuagenarian whom Soares described as 'a man of straw ... surrounded by equally ancient soldiers and retainers'.[62] In these circumstances (and despite the rumours) Salazar does not appear to have regarded him as a threat. In 1949, at the age of eighty, he was even re-elected for another seven-year term. However, opposition to this decision came from inside the political establishment. At a meeting of the UN executive a clear majority (nineteen to four) voted that Salazar be the next presidential candidate. He refused, but the issue was reopened on 18 April 1951 when Carmona died just as he was about to embark on the twenty-fifth year of his presidency.

Under the constitution, another election was required. By now Salazar was several years older than Carmona had been when he first became head of state in 1926 and, once more, there arose a demand that he assume the mantle of the presidency and hand over the reins of power to a younger man. The person really behind this idea was Marcelo Caetano, the president of the UN. At forty-five, he was definitely ambitious and somewhat less docile than other ministers. This may explain why a man of his talents served only six years as a minister between 1932 and 1968 even though he had been a drafter of the 1933 constitution and a leading activist in the counter-revolution almost from its inception.

In November 1951, at the third congress of the UN, Caetano set out fully his views on the succession:

> It is no secret that since 1947, I have been calling for Salazar's elevation to the Presidency of the Republic. ... The elevation of Salazar to the supreme office of the nation would enable him to be replaced in the premiership, and the nation could then grow accustomed to an ordinary man in the job, one nevertheless wise, experienced and devoted to the public good.[63]

This little-known declaration is perhaps the most outspoken public utterance made about the dictator by a senior member of the regime. When all is said and done, Caetano was pressing for Salazar to be kicked upstairs to a largely honorific post which the premier himself had deliberately made powerless in the 1930s. To avoid disgrace, Caetano had to choose his words carefully and give the impression that it was patriotic and statesmanlike reasons that motivated him to speak out. Certainly it was not merely ambition. Caetano, an anti-democratic right-winger, was clearly worried about the regime's prospects if it did not change:

> We are accustomed to seeing in Salazar the personification of the New State's authority, the chief who unites, arbitrates and guides us. How can we assure his succession in normal circumstances? Will what we consider to be the virtues of the New State be only a projection of Salazar's political talent? Will the New State be a genuine political system – that is, a system of properly instituted procedures for governing the country – or will it be nothing more than a conjunction of helpful circumstances, enabling a man of exceptional governmental capacity to exercise power?[64]

Caetano was endeavouring to replace Salazar in his own lifetime. However, Salazar had already expressed his unwillingness to become president in 1949, and two years later only Santos Costa echoed Caetano's views, which must have been depressing, since both men were rivals, the defence minister perhaps coveting the premiership as much as Caetano himself.[65] In the event, ministerial backing was forthcoming for neither. On 5 June 1951, when Salazar told his colleagues that he had decided to stay on as premier, nobody demurred.

The pomp and ceremony of the presidency were obviously not for him. However, before making up his mind, Salazar wrote to Charles Maurras (for almost half a century the principal spokesman of the French right and then serving a life sentence for treason) to seek his opinion. Maurras had always been a dominant external influence on the otherwise inward-looking Portuguese counter-revolutionary elite. Salazar maintained a fitful correspondence with him until his death in 1952.

In his reply (delivered at the end of May 1951) Maurras urged Salazar to remain in power. 'Restez. Tenez!' he instructed in a letter which Salazar read aloud to his cabinet a few days later. However, matters did not rest there. The monarchist faction within the dictatorship sought to exploit the Maurras letter for its own ends. The royal pretender, Dom Duarte Nuno, a passive figure, remained aloof from these partisan manoeuvres: 'I am a pretender but I don't pretend that I can be king,' is how he once realistically summed up his position.[66] Nothing came of an attempt towards the end of 1951 by a group of monarchist officers to persuade Salazar to restore the monarchy by passing a vote in the National Assembly to that effect. Probably the experiences of 1951 only strengthened his resolve to remain at the centre of national affairs. Salazar had never trusted the judgement of his entourage even in essentially minor matters, and the internal ructions of that year must have alerted him to the danger of major in-fighting in the event of his retirement.

The danger was a real one, as the turn of events following Salazar's retirement in 1968 would demonstrate. However, almost sole responsibility for long-term uncertainty about the regime's direction lay with the aging dictator-premier, who, in the 1940s and 1950s, was already demonstrating a singular incapacity for making rational long-term policy decisions.

Notes

1 Phil Mailer, *Portugal. The Impossible Revolution*, Spokesman Books, London, 1977, p. 72.
2 Patricia McGowan, *O Bando de Argel. Responsibilidades na descolonização*, Intervenção, Lisbon, 1979, p. 225.
3 *Opção*, No. 15, 5 August 1976 (Lisbon), p. 1.
4 Gallagher, 'Controlled repression', p. 393.
5 Profile of Álvaro Cunhal, *Current Biography 1975*, Wilson, New York, 1975.
6 José Dias Coelho, *A Resistência em Portugal*, Editorial Inova, Oporto, 1974, p. 17.
7 PRO, FO 371 34643, C8710/66/36, Sir Ronald Campbell to Sir Anthony Eden, 12 August 1943.
8 *Expresso* (review section), 2 February 1980, 'Júlio Fogaça: a história de um "expulso" do PCP', p. 9.
9 John F. Kennedy Library, Boston, Mass., box 54, file No. 1269/62, Central Intelligence Agency report, 6 May 1962.
10 *Eleições no regime fascista*, Commissão do Livro Negro Sobre o Fascismo, Gráfica Europa, Lisbon, 1979.
11 Schmitter, 'The impact and meaning', p. 146.
12 *Ibid.*, p. 161.
13 Soares, *Portugal's Struggle*, p. 60.
14 Schmitter, *op. cit.*, p. 158.
15 Fryer and McGowan, *Oldest Ally*, p. 202.
16 See McGowan, *op. cit.*
17 Hermínio Martins, 'Opposition in Portugal', *Government and Opposition*, Vol. 4, No. 2, spring 1969, p. 263.
18 Mailer, *op. cit.*, p. 51.
19 Alexandre Manuel *et al. PIDE. A história da repressão*, Jornal do Fundão, Lisbon, 1974, p. 20.
20 See Kenneth Maxwell, 'Portugal under pressure', *New York Review of Books*, 29 May 1975, p. 20; and 'Para a história do fascismo português: o PIDE', in *Portugal Informação*, No. 18–19, Lisbon, 1977, pp. 31–8.
21 António de Figueiredo, *Portugal. Fifty Years of Dictatorship*, Pelican, London, 1975, pp. 115–16.
22 Oliveira Marques, *História de Portugal*, II, p. 188.
23 Figueiredo, *op. cit.*, p. 122.
24 Gallagher, 'Controlled repression', p. 401 n.
25 Maxwell, *op. cit.*, p. 10; Oliveira Marques, *op. cit.*, p. 224.
26 Reporter Sombra, *Dossier PIDE. Os horrores e os crimes de uma 'policia'*, Lisbon, 1974, p. 162.
27 *Ibid.*
28 Martins, *op. cit.*, p. 263.
29 PRO, FO 371 20510, W9280/387/36, Sir Claud Wingfield to Sir Samuel Hoare,

14 October 1935.

30 PRO, FO 371 20511, W4056/933/36/W4427/403/36, Sir Claud Wingfield to Sir Samuel Hoare, 20 January 1936.

31 Nogueira, *Salazar*, II, p. 365.

32 Fernando Queiroga, *As forças armadas de Portugal* (pamphlet), Rio de Janeiro, 1958, p. 3.

33 Interview with General Luís Câmara Pina, Lisbon, 14 March 1977.

34 *Cinquenta anos da história do mundo*, o Século, Lisbon, n.d., pp. 1140–1.

35 Fryer and McGowan, *op. cit.*, p. 125.

36 PRO, FO 371 26793, C2257/2257/62, 2 February 1941.

37 *Times* obituary, 26 June 1970.

38 *Sunday Times* Insight Team, *Insight on Portugal. The Year of the Captains*, Andre Deutsch, London, 1975, p. 27.

39 Interestingly, the three heads of state who served under the dictatorship each came from different branches of the armed forces.

40 Devane, 'The religious revival', p. 480.

41 While deeply reactionary, Cerejeira was pro-Allied in World War II, as British embassy despatches to London make clear.

42 Nogueira, *Salazar*, II, pp. 93–7.

43 Thomas C. Bruneau, 'Church and state in Portugal: the crisis of cross and sword', *Journal of Church and State*, Vol. 18, No. 3, autumn 1976, p. 471.

44 Gallagher, 'The Theory and Practice of Portuguese Authoritarianism', thesis, p. 140.

45 Richard Devane, 'The plight of religion in the patriarchate of Lisbon', *Irish Ecclesiastical Record*, July 1937, p. 40.

46 *Ibid.*, p. 39.

47 Keefe, *Area Handbook*, p. 154.

48 *Ibid*, pp. 153–4.

49 Gerhard Grohs, 'The Church in Portugal after the *coup* of 1974', *Journal of Iberian Studies*, Vol. 5, No. I, spring 1976, p. 37.

50 Jean Nicholas, 'Portugal after Salazar – a view from France', *Studies*, spring 1969, p. 26.

51 Keefe, *op. cit.*, p. 52.

52 *Ibid.*

53 Bruneau, *op. cit.*, p. 21.

54 *Ibid.*

55 Carlo Falconi, *The Silence of Pius XII*, Faber, London, 1970, p. 86.

56 Seè Fernando Santos Costa, 'No rescaldo do 10 de Abril', *Diário de Notícias*, 26 May 1981, p. 8. Several leading *Estado Novo* figures were involved in this case besides Santos Costa. After the dead general's widow accused him of manslaughter, the minister of justice, Manuel Cavaleiro Ferreira, had her arrested, much to Santos Costa's annoyance. Her lawyer, Adriano Moreira, was also detained. He later became minister of the *ultramar* in 1961.

57 José Magalhães Godinho, 'Salazar, Franco Nogueira e o MUD, (2) O encontro com Carmona', *O Jornal*, 16 May 1980, p. 12.

58 Ibid.

59 Gallagher, thesis, p. 189.

60 Soares, *Portugal's Struggle*, pp. 78–9.

61 Franco Nogueira, the ex-foreign minister, does not believe that a rift developed between Salazar and Carmona after the Second World War. He claims that there was only one occasion when he might have been seriously

considering the replacement of Salazar, and that was in 1943 when Britain was putting pressure on Salazar to stop exporting wolfram to Germany. The British ambassador, Sir Ronald Campbell, was friendly with one of Carmona's daughters and both of them sowed seeds of doubt in Carmona's mind about the wisdom of the premier's policy. See Nogueira, *Salazar*, III, pp. 514–18.

62 Soares, *op. cit.*, p. 76.
63 Quoted in José António Saraiva, *Do Estado Novo à Segunda República. Crónica política de um tempo português*, Livraria Bertrand, Lisbon, 1974, pp. 46–47.
64 *Ibid.*, p. 49.
65 The war ministry had been broken up into two new portfolios, defence and the army, during 1950. Santos Costa took the most senior post and thereafter was known as minister of defence.
66 Interview with Franco Nogueira, London, 6 October 1979.

7

The end of Salazarism, 1951–68

Economic stagnation

By the middle years of the Salazar era Portugal had acquired some of the economic features which have enabled other countries to undergo a successful industrial revolution. The country had enjoyed many years of political peace and was one of the most stable in Europe. The national workforce was low-paid and generally quiescent. An efficient infrastructure of modern roads, railways and new port facilities had been created since the 1930s. In the African empire Salazar had a vast store of ores, minerals and raw materials which, although largely untapped or under-exploited, was a future source of supply for new industries and boosting exports. Finally, Portugal had managed in the 1940s to get over the shortage of capital which had dogged her economic prospects for centuries. During the Second World War alone, gold reserves rose from $93 million to $433 million thanks to the European combatants' demand for Portuguese products, especially her wolfram.[1]

Any attempt at major economic development would have been impeded by serious structural defects such as the stagnant rural economy, which in 1950 absorbed 50 per cent of Portugal's manpower but yielded only 25 per cent of the national income, or the low level of technical skills possessed by industrial workers. Nevertheless, by the third decade of the *Estado Novo* Portugal was possibly in a better position to transform her economy than at any other time in her recent history. However, no capitalist take-off occurred until the 1960s, when the country experienced a modest economic boomlet. In the post-war era Salazar set his face against rapid economic expansion. Beginning in 1953, three economic development plans were launched during the remainder of his premiership but no transformation of the sluggish Portuguese economy occurred. Instead, the husbanding of the vast gold reserves in the national treasury became a virtual fetish, and he would not have them invested in industrial development or in the revitalisation of agriculture. Some *Estado Novo* luminaries like Daniel Barbosa, minister of the economy in 1947–48, as well as the economist José Ferreira Dias Júnior, publicly voiced concern about the direction the economy was going in, but they were unable to deflect Salazar. This pre-Keynesian figure was even opposed to relying on credit to fuel the economy. Borrowing was next to being a sin, and it is true that one of Portugal's strengths was that she had virtually no foreign debts. However, the obsession with paying one's own way meant that the economic growth of a small country like Portugal would be limited. Salazar could live with this. Indeed, industrial growth was *opposed* where it might jeopardise the traditionalist goals of the state. Such economic retardation was a conscious goal in order to hold back trade unionism, secularism, mass politics, urbanisation, consumerism and other modernising trends. Salazar was not only anti-liberal but also anti-capitalist in several key respects. He was not eager to accept Marshall Aid when it was offered to Portugal by the United States in the late 1940s. Some years later, when it was reported to him that oil had been discovered in important quantities in Angola, his response to the excited official was 'Oh! What a pity!'[2]

Salazar himself was a university-trained financial 'specialist'. Why did he hold such extraordinary ideas about economic development? One view is that his fanatical orthodoxy stemmed from an assumed need to restore Portugal's reputation in the wake of a banknote scandal in 1925 which was another nail in the coffin of the floundering parliamentary republic. Artur Virgílio Reis, a financial adventurer, had attempted to take over the Bank of Portugal by privately printing millions of escudos' worth of new notes. His attempt only narrowly failed, and the shock engendered by news of the incredible scheme may have helped propel Salazar into power in 1928. There his ultra-cautious financial outlook became evident almost immediately, an undoubted legacy of the Portuguese leader's small-farming background, where frugality, thrift and strict management were necessary habits for the small peasant.

Initially, Salazar's antediluvian economic philosophy blended well with the prevailing international situation. The world depression placed fierce restrictions on credit, and even if he had wanted to borrow, it would have been very difficult. Later, however, economic conditions changed dramatically: after 1945 nations undertook large external loans to restore war-shattered economies. The era of Keynesian economics was at hand, the ground rules of which Salazar studiously ignored. Gradually the repercussions emanating from his stand-still economic philosophy were beginning to make themselves felt in the 1950s. While Portugal dozed, countries which had been ravaged in the Second World War were beginning to enjoy the first fruits of a startling economic recovery. In ten years small states like Austria and Greece (not incomparable with Portugal) had made up for crippling wartime losses and were beginning to outdistance her in terms of investment, consumption and growth. Expansion in north-west Europe was even more pronounced. However, it would be unrealistic to compare Portugal with such countries as the Netherlands or France, despite the levelling effects of war. Spain presents a closer approximation to the Portuguese norm, and here too Portugal would find herself easily outdistanced, though at a later date, since, until the late 1950s, the Franco regime pursued an autarkic and *dirigiste* course, not dissimilar to Salazar's own.

Failure to grasp economic opportunities naturally helped to thrust the structural defects of the economy into sharp relief. By far the most backward area was agriculture. Under Salazar rural Portugal stagnated to an even greater extent than under the city-oriented liberal republic. Although the balance of economic power was slowly shifting away from latifundists to industrialists, the former were still able to defeat all proposals for reform, no matter how modest. This is what the handful of regime functionaries who spoke out about the rural question soon found. António Castro Fernandes, minister of the economy from 1948 to 1950, had advocated change within the umbrella of the existing corporative structures (which smacked of an attempt at squaring the circle) and was still attacked by powerful rural interests.[3] Luís Texeira Pinto, who held the same job from 1962 to 1965, actually advocated land reform as well as major structural transformation of the agricultural sector. Not surprisingly, these ministers (hardly progressive figures) were never in any danger of being Salazar's longest-serving ministerial protégés. Thanks to latifundist pressure, very few of the findings reached by the Junta of Internal Colonisation (a state development agency in the rural zone), were ever implemented. When some technicians were actually bold enough to ask proprietors to give up land that had been lying fallow, one president of the corporation of agriculture actually threatened to use machine-gun bullets against any usurper intent on refashioning his estates.[4] And before 1974 there were occasional reports of arsenals and private armies assembled in the Alentejo with the intention of fighting 'communism', a label that encompassed a surprisingly broad sector of the political spectrum in the eyes of some diehard latifundists.

Some basic form of rural rationalisation was needed to curb the gross regional imbalance between north and south. North of the river Tagus, which divides the country at the centre, the rural population density was high, farms were small (mostly less than two and a half acres) and minifundia was accordingly widespread. Here land was often regarded as an heirloom rather than as a means of production. In the south landowners were wealthier and latifundia were very often the rule, especially in the province of the Alentejo. Here crop rotation and the use of agricultural machinery would have been feasible means of modernising the rural economy. However, the aristocratic families of the Alentejo set their face against change and clung to antiquated farming methods. They preferred to make their profits by exploiting a hard-pressed rural proletariat which began to flee from the land in the 1950s. This, in turn, aggravated existing problems by putting land out of production, so that in some years agricultural growth (never more than 2 per cent at the best of times), could actually go into reverse, thus necessitating extremely costly imports of food.

A dynamic ministry of agriculture, conscious of the scale of the rural crisis, could have conceivably embarked upon a recovery programme. But between 1936 and 1974 there was no ministry of agriculture. Instead, during this period, agriculture and fisheries was the concern of the minister of the economy – along with commerce and industry. This downgrading of the agrarian sector is amazing in view of the fact that Portugal was still overwhelmingly a rural country. Only in March 1974 was there an attempt to halt the rot by restoring a ministry of agriculture to the cabinet. But by then it may have been too late for a right-wing regime to do anything: OECD reports in the early 1970s had been warning that 'the economic base of agricultural production was being destroyed'.[5] Unbeknown to Caetano's minister of agriculture, his days were also numbered: six weeks after his appointment came the 25 April *coup* and the prospect of more drastic rural surgery.

Salazar's treatment of agriculture might serve to give the impression that immobility characterised national economic life at all levels. This was not strictly true. In the areas of communications, energy and public works, there was progress of sorts. From the 1930s onwards, an expensive programme of road-building and repair got under way, along with the expansion of the telephone system, port facilities and the building of bridges and dams. These improvements demonstrated that Portugal was on the move, according to Salazarist propaganda. Just how valid was this claim? Although the stress on public works undoubtedly did not harm the country in the way other policies did, it nevertheless had negative connotations. Often expenditure on public works 'was effected at the cost of savings in social assistance and education'.[6] Moreover, it was often only propaganda reasons which led to the creation of some projects. Lisbon, for instance, was beautified in order to make a good impression on tourists (home-owners were compelled by law to repaint their houses every five years), while Oporto remained a grimy, foggy, industrial city which received much less state patronage in relative terms.

One novel aspect of the post-1930 public works boom was the fact that contracts for a given undertaking were often issued to the same entrepreneurs over and over again. As a result, powerful private monopolies emerged which were reluctant to venture into new undertakings unless absolutely assured of security of profits. This was a practice the Portuguese government did not attempt to discourage. Instead, Salazar backed up the economic oligarchs by passing 'a law . . . peculiar to Portugal and fundamental to its particular form of development':[7] *A Lei do Condicionamento Industrial* (the Control of Industry Act).

What it did was to make government permission obligatory for the construction of any new factory, the start of any new industry, the change of location of a factory or even the extension of an existing one. Without government approval none of these ostensibly simple tasks could be carried out. Furthermore, any company which felt threatened by another's plans could argue for permission to be refused.

This law was nothing less than a recipe for economic petrification. It was deeply resented by small businessmen, whose avenues of expansion were effectively blocked. By the 1950s many of them were being badly squeezed by discriminatory legislation of this kind. Figures gathered by the Portuguese economist Ramiro da Costa show that large numbers of petty-bourgeois Portuguese were being 'proletarianised'. For instance, between 1950 and 1960 the number of *patrões* (commercial farmers) dropped from 136,000 to 76,000, a fall of 40 per cent.[8] It is a fair assumption that many of these casualties had been political supporters of Dr Salazar. However, in penury, they could not be expected to continue supporting the New State: at the 1958 presidential election many instead backed the opposition candidature of General Delgado. It was at last beginning to dawn on erstwhile supporters of the *Estado Novo* that its claim to have avoided the excesses of both liberal capitalism and socialism was in fact a sham. Instead, it had created an economic order which encapsulated the worst features of both systems: extreme inequality in the distribution of wealth and income and deep-seated class exploitation on the one hand; stultifying administrative control and reduced capacity for innovation and initiative on the other.[9] One villager said to a foreign scholar once that 'Portugal is the most advanced country in two things: licences and fines.'[10] To own a cigarette lighter, or repair a wall, one needed a licence. During fieldwork in the 1960s Joyce Riegelhaupt adopted a rule of thumb which laid down that 'anything that is not expressly permitted is probably prohibited. Or if a given act is not forbidden, one probably needs a licence to undertake it.'[11]

Many small businessmen were located in the area round Oporto. Having been the main industrial region of the whole country, it was gradually overtaken by the Lisbon–Setúbal conurbation, one into which the government channelled increasing resources. Even by the standards of other capitalist countries, economic wealth came to be concentrated among a small circle of people. To European bankers who dealt with them, these privileged entrepreneurs came to be known as 'palaeo-capitalists', individuals whose fortunes were not always matched by business acumen.

The deeply conservative and unadventurous outlook of Portugal's economic oligarchy cannot be underestimated. In the absence of natural competition, their combines were often badly run and inefficient. Indeed, the basis of much large-scale industry was artificial, as it was heavily dependent on forcibly depressed raw material prices in the colonies and drastically protected markets there and at home.

Economic magnates often preferred to cream off in personal profit what more rationally-minded industrialists would have reinvested. Salazar was aware of the oligarchy's habits. Nevertheless, he kept Portugal on the same monopolistic course. Though ruinous in the long term for the national economy, this strategy of mollycoddling big business paid dividends for the regime. Salazar was able to anticipate most eventualities in the economic sphere, given that the same handful of families (the Melos, the Champalimauds, the Espírito Santos and the Quinas) dominated the economy year after year. In the absence of sharp fluctuations (the budget was relentlessly balanced every year from the 1930s onwards), he also found it possible to familiarise himself with the working of the national economy and be on good terms with its leading figures. They, in turn, were grateful for his patronage and offered unswerving loyalty to the dictatorship. This proved of vital importance once the colonial wars got under way in the 1960s. A more heterogeneous business class would undoubtedly have been less of a bulwark for the regime.

Workers in Babylonian captivity

In a situation where power, freedom and wealth were commodities enjoyed by a tiny section of the community alone, the plight of lower-income groups was dire. When reviewing conditions for the Foreign Office in 1946, Sir Marcus Cheke, the biographer of Pombal, was moved to comment that 'the era of King John V when the courtiers were millionaires and the poor crowded for alms at the convent gates . . . seems to have been revived in Portugal'.[12] 'Nobody knows how the poor can live,' he went on to remark, which was no exaggeration. Even leaders of the *sindicatos* (the pseudo-unions under the supervision of employers, the state and the police) were moved to protest about the squalid reality of Portuguese class solidarity. As early as April 1942 *sindicato* representatives were frankly affirming to Salazar that 'the corporative regime in Portugal had not brought social justice'.[13] Three months later the government replied by conceding the need for wage revisions and by announcing the introduction of family allowances. However, these were paltry measures which failed to halt the downturn in workers' living standards. For many urban workers the parliamentary republic now seemed like a golden age compared to the dark political night that had descended upon them in the 1930s. In this decade one of the government's slogans had hypocritically proclaimed that 'as long as there is a worker without bread, the revolution continues'.[14] However, by then, Álvaro Cunhal reckons, the proletariat as a whole was earning a third less in wages than had been the case in 1914.[15] Figures from the OECD certainly lend credence to this claim. Whereas in the industrially advanced countries of the OECD trade unions, collective bargaining and pressures inherent in the consumer society enabled labour to take some 70 per cent of the national income, with capital earnings taking the remainder, the proportion in Portugal during the early 1960s was almost reversed: capital earnings were 53 per cent of the total and labour (including the managerial classes) less than 45 per cent.[16]

The resultant social misery was stark. In 1960 the rate of infant mortality was the highest in Europe (88·6 per 1,000 children born), and higher than in some colonial and ex-colonial territories (67·5 in Senegal).[17] Tuberculosis was also more prevalent than anywhere else on the Continent (51 deaths per 1,000 people in 1962), and Portugal had a minister of health only from 1958.[18] These dismal statistics are not unrelated to the fact that *per capita* income of $162 (1960) was also the lowest in Europe, Turkey's being $219 and the United States' $1,453.

The opulence of the Portuguese oligarchy represents an incredible backdrop to the misery barely hinted at in these figures. In 1961 two observers, Peter Fryer and Patricia McGowan, noted the surprise of a Portuguese sociologist on discovering that the five richest men in Britain had smaller fortunes than their Portuguese counterparts. In that case, the sociologist explained to the authors, 'Portugal had far more exceedingly rich men with far greater fortunes than Britain, a country with five times the population and far greater wealth.'[19] This indeed was true. When Alfredo da Silva, the wealthiest Portuguese oligarch, died in 1942 *Time* magazine reckoned him to be the owner of the world's sixth largest personal fortune. With another three decades of Salazarism still to come, the economic conditions were obviously ripe for other business leaders to emulate and surpass Silva. Eventually the appetite of members of the Portuguese oligarchy became so voracious that a special term, *tubaronismo*, derived from the Portuguese for shark, came to be applied to their behaviour.[20]

General Delgado and the 1958 election

For the elite as a whole the 1950–57 period was probably the most stable one in the *Estado Novo's* entire history. No internal or external crises troubled the regime. The cabinet met infrequently and Salazar spent long periods at his home in the village of Santa Comba Dão, north of Coimbra. While there, in 1950, he toured the north-west of Portugal and Spain with the Spanish leader, General Franco, the only occasion when the two

Iberian dictators really got together socially. On Sunday Cardinal Cerejeira sometimes said Mass for Salazar, who 'was retreating more and more into the solitariness of spirit that always characterised him'.[21] In the 1950s his inner council consisted of six people, the president of the National Assembly, the president of the Corporative Chamber, the ministers of the presidency and the interior, the president of the executive commission of the UN and the leader of the UN in the Assembly.[22] A frequent topic of discussion was Goa, Portugal's colonial enclave on the Indian subcontinent which the Delhi government was endeavouring to acquire. (It is interesting to see, in the fourth volume of Franco Nogueira's biography, how much of Salazar's time this issue and more trivial ones took up in the 1949–58 period.)

A more pressing problem was presented by Higino Craveiro Lopes, Carmona's successor as president. A stiff, punctilious figure, he alienated many members of the political establishment, not so much because of his personal demeanour, more because he also emerged as a partisan of moderate reform during his presidency. In 1951 Salazar could not have known that the man who had commanded the Portuguese forces which had fought alongside Franco in the Spanish Civil War would later gravitate in this direction. In fact Salazar was not instrumental in choosing Lopes for the presidency: it seems that his name was suggested by Augusto Cancela de Abreu, a former minister of the interior.

Another election was due in 1958, and by the beginning of the year Salazar had made up his mind not to reappoint Lopes. (He had been under pressure from the UN for some time, many members wanting a replacement figure.) However, the election would not be an uneventful one. Most regime and opposition figures were taken completely unawares when a serving general, Humberto Delgado, announced in April 1958 that he would be running against the official candidate. This was a political bombshell. Up till then the fifty-two-year-old air force officer had been thought of as a safe establishment man who (although personally mercurial) was unlikely to contemplate political rebellion. Until the eve of his defection, Delgado's career background would reinforce such a view.

Born into a lowly military family on 15 May 1906 (his father was a career sergeant), Delgado as a junior officer enthusiastically backed the counter-revolution and took up arms to defend it against the sporadic republican rebellions of the late 1920s. Then a member of the newly created Portuguese air force, the young officer was also the prolific author of political tracts and articles which heaped praise on the 'National Revolution'. In 1933 he published a book which was one of the most violent diatribes issued against the liberal republic after its overthrow.[23] About the same time he was quickly ascending the ladder of military promotion so that, by 1952, he had already become, at forty-six, the youngest general

8

Caetano and the 1974 revolution

Marcelo Caetano

None of the other European regimes commonly known as fascist survived the demise of their founder, be it Hitler's Germany, Franco's Spain or Mussolini's Italy. Portugal proved an exception, since the old order outlasted its chief architect by six years and could probably have been maintained even longer but for the escalating conflict in Portuguese Africa. Marcelo José das Neves Caetano, the man who ensured this period of continuity, resembled his predecessor in some ways but not in others. Like Salazar, he was an intellectual and an academic who was committed to the ideals of the corporative state (perhaps even more so than Salazar). Strongly anti-communist and ardently Catholic, Caetano was no believer in parliamentary democracy. His liberal reputation was acquired as a result of the impatience he displayed towards the rather bogus way the Portuguese corporative state had evolved under Salazar. Observers who took his show of political independence after 1958 as proof of his political liberalism were misguided, as his defence of Salazar's political record after 1974 makes abundantly clear.[1] Nevertheless, Caetano was far more outgoing and personally flexible. A family man with four children, he had been born and brought up in Lisbon and was to travel widely before and during his premiership. His more open political style is indicated by the fact the he was known as Marcelo even by political opponents. Salazar's colleagues would not have referred to him as António even in his absence.

The son of a primary schoolteacher, Caetano was born on 17 August 1906 and educated at the University of Lisbon, where he graduated in law. His adolescence and early manhood coincided with the most strife-torn years of the parliamentary republic, and by 1926 he was a militantly right-wing student leader. A prolific contributor to the right-wing press, he was the editor of *Ordem Novo* (*New Order*), which proclaimed in its first issue that it was 'anti-modern, anti-liberal, anti-democratic, anti-bourgeois and anti-bolshevik; counter-revolutionary and reactionary; Catholic, Apostolic and Roman; monarchist, intolerant and intransigent; showing no solidarity with writers, journalists, or any other professionals in the arts, letters and press.'[2]

Although he moderated some of these views after the downfall of the parliamentary republic, and renounced his monarchism, Caetano's rise in the armed forces. In between, he had also shown a marked anglophile stance in the Second World War, for which he was decorated with the MBE by King George VI in 1946.[24]

Delgado's rise was meteoric: normally a conscientious military officer could only hope to become a general at around the age of fifty-seven. However, there was a mysterious gap in his career which suggests early caution on the part of his political superiors. At no point was Delgado ever placed in personal command of troops. On friendly terms with Dr Salazar but always 'honest and forthright' with the premier at the same time, he may have struck the dictator as too independent to be wholly trusted.[25] Certainly his postings (major executive ones in the 1950s) were rather non-military (he was responsible for creating the national airline) and involved spending much time abroad. His lengthiest stay outside Portugal extended from 1953 to 1957, years when he served as air attaché in Washington.

While in North America Delgado apparently became steadily disenchanted with the political scene at home. Already, in the early 1950s, his daughter remembers him frequently remarking how 'Portugal is going down the drain'.[26] Delgado was angered by the realisation that dramatic material progress occurring in other Western countries was by-passing his country. Ultimately his experiences in non-authoritarian countries led him to reject the repressive political system at home. When recalled to Lisbon in 1957 he had become an *estrangeirado* (that is, a foreignised, modern-minded Portuguese whose struggle against the *castiços*, the traditional, counter-Reformation element in national life, has been identified as an enduring feature of post-seventeenth-century Portuguese history).

Delgado's friendship with Henrique Galvão, an earlier military heretic, probably hastened his passage to the opposition camp. He used to visit him in prison after his arrest in 1952. To do so was a bold gesture on the part of a serving general. However, Delgado never seems to have been warned off, an indication of the *Estado Novo's* flexible attitude towards the army, or perhaps of its faith in the general's innate trustworthiness. When such trust was seen to have been misplaced the official Salazarist reaction was bitter. Regime propagandists accused him of being motivated by blind ambition or of being psychologically unbalanced. These barbs were not entirely without foundation. Delgado was ambitious as well as undoubtedly eccentric.[27] But he was also a man of ability, strong personal charisma and honest ideals. At first unwilling to back Delgado, about whom they knew very little, most anti-fascists went over to his side when the new challenger proclaimed that, if elected, he would most certainly dismiss Salazar. The two other opposition challengers dropped their candidature in favour of Delgado's, and his act of defiance was greeted with mass demonstrations of support in Lisbon and, above all, Oporto, where hundreds of thousands turned out to greet him in May 1958. Peasants thronged many of his meetings and it was noticed that he had a strong charismatic appeal among the rural population, especially in the north (hirtherto regarded as a power base for the regime by some observers). This was an appeal the *Estado Novo* was unable to counter, despite its control of the media and of bountiful campaign funds. Salazar's candidate, the colourless admiral Américo Deus Rodrigues Tomás, minister of the navy from 1944 to 1958, made no popular impact whatsoever. His candidature angered moderate officers inside the army, who attacked Santos Costa, the defence minister, for having played such a prominent role in ousting Craveiro Lopes. Delgado tried to take advantage of this military friction by organising at least three different *coup* attempts in 1958, on 2 June, 2 July and 18 December. Each fell through at the last minute for lack of military support.[28] Disillusioned Salazarists like the outgoing President Lopes were 'ready to wound but afraid to strike'.[29] No disaffected senior officer would display the same degree of self-sacrifice as Delgado in what was turning out to be a vendetta against Salazar. This is indisputable. Nevertheless, within the military hierarchy 'the general without fear' was rather a marginal figure: unlike most other top officers, he did not have a stake in any major private business, nor, according to his daughter, was he interested in pecuniary spoils;[30] few fellow officers had spent as long abroad; and, coming from a modest social background, he did not share the oligarchic antecedents of his general command colleagues. Each of these badges of unorthodoxy set him apart from his peers and may well explain why his rebellion against the New State took such a dramatic form.

Delgado was also a case apart in relation to the liberal opposition. Previous electoral candidates had always withdrawn before polling day, claiming official malpractice. Delgado did not. Instead, he broke new political ground by pressing his challenge up to (and beyond) the count itself.

The result was unusual. For the first time ever, a large body of votes was cast against the regime. Official figures gave Delgado 236,528 votes as against 758,998 for Admiral Tomás: he had polled just under a quarter of the vote in a ballot restricted to property holders. Other restrictions excluded illiterates and low taxpayers, so that well over half the population was effectively disfranchised. But that was not all: the state could disqualify electors at will; each voter had to make a personal application to vote; opposition candidates had to be approved by the government; and there were frequent instances of opposition representatives being turned away from the count, their supporters being arrested, and ballot papers being seized by the police.

In the face of such obstacles, to receive almost a quarter of the vote was a creditable performance, especially taking into account the fact that most voters were middle or upper-class. However, Delgado would not rest content with this large protest vote. He claimed to be the real winner, a claim scornfully brushed aside by the regime press. But there is evidence that his protestations may have been valid. First of all, there *was* massive vote-rigging. In Oporto, where Delgado had received his greatest welcome, only 27,107 out of 400,000 citizens contrived to vote for him, according to government figures: in Lisbon the picture was much the same, with only 105,978 votes being recorded for him out of a population of 900,000. However, Delgado did win in some rural areas, where it seems the regime did not envisage strong support for the opposition candidate. These districts included the select Lisbon suburb of Sintra, Bragança (the capital of remote Trás-os-Montes), Rio Maior and Vila Franca de Xira, as well as many parts of Angola and Mozambique.

What is significant about places like Bragança and Rio Maior is that they emerged as strong centres of right-wing opposition during the 1974–75 revolution. If the opposition managed to win in such outwardly barren soil, the obvious inference is that Delgado's support must have been much greater in places like Lisbon and Oporto where Salazar could not politically afford to concede victory to the opposition. In private, government supporters conceded as much themselves. On 13 May 1961 the usually cautious London *Economist* revealed 'how some government supporters in their cups were saying that the vote split 70-30 *in favour* of General Delgado.'[31]

Salazar's outraged reaction to the 1958 election may also be a clue to the real as opposed to the official result. In a speech delivered in Lisbon in July 1958 he condemned the fact that too many people had shown themselves prepared to listen to and follow the first adventurer who came along, and bluntly threatened that if this was where elections led, then clearly elections must stop.[32]

Nine months later the electoral system was drastically altered. In what would be the most important constitutional change in the history of the *Estado Novo*, direct elections for the presidency were abolished and what passed for universal suffrage was replaced by an electoral college system. Henceforth the president would be chosen every seven years by a joint session of the National Assembly and the Corporative Chamber. In practice, the presidential electorate now consisted of 500 people, where before it had been approximately one-tenth of the population.

During the 1958 election it had been the defence minister, Santos Costa, who probably ensured that General Delgado's campaign did not turn into a popular revolt against the regime. While the interior minister, Trigo de Negreiros (in charge of the police and security), seems to have lost his nerve, Santos Costa kept his, and he took charge of the situation after Delgado's triumphant meeting in Oporto in May. Observers believed that if he was able to repeat the same triumph in Lisbon, then the Salazar regime would be finished. Santos Costa ensured that it did not happen by redirecting Delgado's train away from the station, where thousands waited, to another part of Lisbon. He showed such decisiveness that it now appeared there was some truth to opposition claims in the 1950s that, in reality, the regime was a Salazar–Santos Costa dictatorship.

What happened next took everyone by surprise. As was the custom when a new head of state took office, the collective resignation of the government was offered. As before, it was Salazar who was asked to form a new government. But incredibly, after twenty-two years, Santos Costa's name was not among his list of ministers. The new minister of defence was General Júlio Botelho Moniz, a republican officer who had been moving in a more liberal direction in recent times.

Various explanations for Santos Costa's exit from government have been given. He claims himself that he resigned voluntarily, being disillusioned with the number of sycophants and mediocrities who were increasingly to be found around Salazar.[33] There was nothing more, it seems, that he could do in government, and he was unhappy that more top-level attention was not being given to Portuguese Africa, where he expected trouble after making a military tour of inspection in 1957. Santos Costa recommended consulting the Portuguese people in a plebiscite about what role Portugal should play in Africa, but he did not get very far with Salazar: 'he had an in-built resistance to consulting ordinary people who tilled the soil. . . . He would never accept that men who tilled the soil had the same right to vote as an educated man.'[34]

Franco Nogueira, Salazar's biographer, concurs with the claim that he left voluntarily in 1958. However, few others can be found to back up the claim. One view is that Santos Costa fell victim to Salazar's abiding distrust of overmighty ministers, that when he acquitted himself so well in 1958 he was not bolstering his position but in fact jeopardising it. Another line stresses the fact that it was not just Santos Costa but Marcelo Caetano who was dropped in the reshuffle of 14 August 1958. This enabled Salazar's cabinet to become much more homogeneous, in the absence of two politicians who represented left- and right-wing groups within the umbrella of the *Estado Novo*. The opposition greeted Santos Costa's departure with acclaim, the communist newspaper *Avante* terming it a victory for the popular forces in the anti-fascist struggle. There was relief that the man who had controlled the army for so long, and had kept it loyal to Salazar, was gone. But criticism of Santos Costa's reactionary views continued because of opposition fears that his withdrawal from government might be only a sabbatical. In the 1958–60 period the campaign of vituperation against Santos Costa reached its height. Quite a strenuous one was launched to prevent him becoming general, a rank which he attained in 1961 after having taken the requisite exams. That he had not signed the papers authorising his promotion when he was in a position to do so is a sign that a lot of opposition attacks may have been far-fetched. Salazar too could have authorised his elevation long ago. That the suspicious dictator did not do so is interesting in itself.

On being asked why the opposition had hated him so much, Santos Costa replied simply that 'they know very well that if I had remained on the scene there would have been no revolution of 25 April 1974'.[35] Before leaving the defence ministry he revealed that on more than one occasion he had broached the question of the succession with Salazar. He tried and failed to arrange a meeting which could make contingency plans for the latter's eventual departure. 'Neither of us will last for ever,' he said to the premier.[36] Salazar retorted that the political system had a natural hierarchy and that it was up to the president as head of state to choose another premier, a decision no one else could interfere with. He was also against the idea of having an heir apparent, because, it seems, he would inevitably attract a court, which would leave the present ruler out in the cold.

Santos Costa believes that Salazar's faculties were failing even before his illness in 1968 and he thinks the best time for him to have retired from office would have been in 1965, when President Tomás was elected for a second term.[37] However, Salazar was evidently deeply pessimistic about what would happen after he was gone, and for this reason, at least, he hung on for as long as possible. His poor opinion of his own people did not make it any easier for him to step down. 'A cursed race, half of whom wouldn't do anything without a whip ... Thank God it is we who have the whip and that we are men of good Christian character. You will see what it would be like if ever there is a change and others have the whip.'[38]

Before the downfall of the regime in 1974, it was in the years after 1958 that power seemed most likely to fall into the 'wrong' hands. Initially Salazar sought to defuse the situation by offering General Delgado a lucrative diplomatic post in Canada in return for a promise to abandon opposition politics. Delgado rejected such blandishments and went on trying to stitch together a military movement against the regime. However, officers who would have been happy to see a restructuring of the *Estado Novo* in a liberal direction did not act. Some were alienated by Delgado's decision to enter into a pre-electoral alliance with the PCP.[39] This was purely a marriage of convenience on Delgado's part. Nevertheless, it would have been natural for liberal-conservative officers to view this pact with suspicion. Many were aware that the demise of authoritarian regimes elsewhere had led to social chaos or full-blooded revolution. This was not Delgado's goal; he was a militant liberal, not a fully fledged radical.

One final factor that may have deterred certain sections of the army from rallying behind him was the reaction of the neighbouring Spanish regime to a successful *coup* in Lisbon: it would undoubtedly have been negative. According to Benjamin Welles, the *New York Times* correspondent in the early 1960s, many Portuguese believed that Franco would send his army into Portugal in the event of Salazar's violent overthrow.[40] In 1962, after the abortive Beja uprising, there were reports that 'within six hours . . . Spanish army tanks were rumbling ominously towards the . . . city of Badajoz and the Portuguese border'.[41] Certainly, it is highly unlikely that there would have been serious high-ranking objections to direct Spanish intervention in Portugal from the non-communist world, since by the late 1950s Spain had become an important if unofficial member of the Western military alliance.

1958–62: a continuing crisis

The Portuguese opposition had few important friends abroads, as Delgado discovered on leaving Portugal in April 1959. From Brazil, then North Africa, and later west Europe, he made repeated attempts to infiltrate the armed forces (from which he had been dismissed by Salazar). On 21 March 1959 a *coup* attempt was foiled when the authoritarian government got advance warning. But two years later the Portuguese opposition drew unprecedented world publicity when, on 23 January 1961, Captain Henrique Galvão hi-jacked the 25,000 ton Portuguese liner, the *Santa Maria*. António de Figueiredo, a Portuguese anti-fascist, claimed that this act of 'piracy' had a significant impact on events in Angola, where a local African revolt erupted in February 1961.[42]

One frankly doubts whether the *Santa Maria* incident was that much of a catalyst. However, the revolt in Angola, which would represent the start of the thirteen-year war in Africa between African nationalist insurgents and the Portuguese, had an immediate impact in Lisbon. There, in March 1961, General Botelho Moniz and high-ranking military colleagues drew up a plan to oust Salazar at a top-level defence meeting on 8 April 1961. This was the most serious internal challenge the *Estado Novo* would ever face before 1974. Numbered among the conspirators was practically the entire top layer of Portugal's defence staff: the defence minister himself, Botelho Moniz; the minister of the army, Lieutenant Colonel Almeida Fernandes; the commander-in-chief of the air force, General Albuquerque de Freitas; the under-minister of the army, Colonel Costa Gomes; the chief of the defence staff, General Beleza Ferraz; the commander of the first military region, General Valadares Tavares; and the military governor of

Lisbon, General Silva Domingues.

The events of the troubled spring of 1961 provide conclusive evidence that Salazar had more to fear from apparent supporters than from manifest opponents.[43] How does one explain this? Certainly, many top-ranking dissidents were undoubtedly disillusioned by a close-up view of Salazar's executive style: it is no coincidence that the two most senior military rebels, Botelho Moniz and Craveiro Lopes, swung into opposition *after* being promoted to positions which gave them ready access to the dictator. Familiarity seems to have bred contempt as these men realised that the nub of many opposition salvoes was true: Salazar was not so much an altruistic statesman, more a scheming Machiavellian figure much obsessed with power.

Hermínio Martins has reckoned that by 1961 'such consensus of opinion within the top cadres of the armed forces could not have developed without a serious backlog of discontent'.[44] Certainly, Botelho Moniz had been critical of the government as early as March 1959, when he wrote a letter to Salazar denouncing 'the adulteration of the 28 May movement by spent and worthless politicians, in many cases ones bereft of moral sense'.[45] However, he held his peace until the Angolan crisis of 1961, several aspects of which deeply worried him. First of all, Salazar was not well when it broke, and as a result the government's reaction to the emergency was rather slow; to Botelho Moniz and his colleagues this was ample confirmation of the dangerous possibilities inherent in a situation where power was centralised in the hands of an elderly civilian. Salazar, by now, had not even the saving grace of efficiency. Perhaps equally disturbing was the reaction of Portugal's principal NATO allies to the 1961 crisis.

On 15 March 1961 the USA was one of the member states which roundly condemned Portuguese colonialism in the United Nations Security Council. To Portuguese officers who had come under growing North American influence as a result of the integration of the Portuguese forces into NATO, the American stance came as a profound shock. Without the support of the USA, Portugal was dangerously isolated. Under Salazar she had experienced long bouts of isolation in the past. However, these had been largely self-induced. Until the 1960s the state had never really faced the threat of ostracism, which, at this juncture, could not have come at a worse time. For defence reports reaching Lisbon even before the spring 1961 crisis cast doubt on the ability of the army to cope with large-scale colonial warfare. The Botelho Moniz faction appeared to accept this bleak conclusion: next door to Angola, in the Congo, the scenario which many Portuguese officers dreaded was already being played out. Here Belgium, a small European power, was embroiled in a bloody post-colonial civil war. Portuguese officers, pondering events in the future Zaire, recalled that it was only within recent living memory that many parts of Portuguese

Africa had been completely pacified.

Reviewing the balance sheet in Africa, Colonel Francisco Costa Gomes, a member of the opposition military faction, concluded that there could be no permanent military solution for Portugal. In the event of widespread guerrilla action breaking out the government 'would have to negotiate with the independence movement',[46] a view he advanced in a document prepared for the defence minister. Botelho Moniz, in turn, agreed with this perspective, and in March 1961 he relayed his thoughts to the American ambassador in Lisbon. He informed the envoy that a large section of the high command favoured a timetable of decolonisation phased over ten to twelve years.[47] He also raised the possibility of US moral and material help to bring about the realisation of his scheme.

To Salazar, Botelho Moniz's arguments were utter heresy. He was absolutely convinced that Portugal must remain in Africa 'to defend Western and Christian civilisation'.[48] Loyalist officers and ministers agreed with him. One of these *ultras*, Colonel Kaúlza de Arriaga, the under-secretary for the air force, succeeded in discovering the conspiracy at quite an early stage. His superior in fact kept him abreast of developments, unaware that Kaúlza's loyalties were firmly with the Salazarist camp. This incident highlights the lack of professionalism exhibited by conspirators belonging to a military organism which had not managed a successful *coup* in almost forty years. However, the regime was hardly better prepared for the crisis. In fact no action was taken when Kaúlza attempted to warn Salazar that a plot was afoot. Owing to the premier's ill-health, the upper levels of the state apparatus were practically immobilised. Perhaps it was only when Botelho Moniz wrote to President Tomás and Salazar to let them know of military opposition to fighting a colonial war that the dictator and his close entourage realised the gravity of the situation. This foolhardy move seems to indicate that the conspirators planned an informal palace revolution rather than a full-scale military *coup*. Whether or not this is so, the rebels must have been extremely confident to have behaved in such a nonchalant manner.

Their confidence was misplaced. Despite the galaxy of important officers who had come out against him, Salazar rallied his own forces and organised a counter-attack. His most loyal supporters were the cadre of monarchist officers which Santos Costa had built up inside the army, as well as the Portuguese Legion and the paramilitary National Republican Guard (GNR).

The nerve of the rebels quickly collapsed on hearing that they were being challenged. By 14 April 1961 the regime had regained the initiative. Realising that the *coup* could now probably succeed only after much bloodshed, the rebels abandoned their attempt to unseat Salazar and awaited events. Probably still not sure of himself, the prime minister merely sacked the dozen or so 'traitors' and took no further action. One of them, Colonel Costa Gomes, was even given a sinecure in the Alentejo and was able to publish a letter in the *Diário Popular* reiterating his view that a military solution in Africa was unlikely.

Given less faith in constitutional propriety, the army rebels would surely have been able to topple Salazar and, as was their intention, exile him to Switzerland. Instead, defeat was snatched from the jaws of victory and, against all the odds, the regime muddled through its most serious crisis. To celebrate his exceedingly narrow escape, Salazar carried out a drastic cabinet reshuffle on 3 May 1961. New ministers were installed in foreign affairs (Alberto Franco Nogueira), in the interior ministry, in education, in corporations and in the overseas provinces (the *ultramar*) ministry. Over the whole spring period, seven out of fourteen ministers were replaced; in June General Venâncio Deslandes was appointed governor-general of Angola and commander-in-chief of the armed forces. He thus possessed immense power, since these two posts were rarely combined. However, Salazar himself (at seventy-two) also expanded his authority by becoming minister of defence in place of the luckless Botelho Moniz.

Despite the neutralisation of the April plotters, foreign correspondents, who flocked to Lisbon in 1961, were expecting a fresh wave of unrest to swamp the regime. The *Sunday Times* of 7 January 1962 revealed how:

In the hot, poverty-stricken plains of the Alentejo . . . many have taken to the fields to avoid call-up. Recently, police and national guardsmen were called to the town of Évora to deal with incipient mutiny on a troop train. . . . There is now growing fear of an armed uprising in Portugal. . . . Portugal, it seems, now has its maquis. At present, this mainly consists of men who, fearing arrest for subversive activities, in some cases no more serious than incitement to strike, have sought refuge in the Serra d'estrella mountains of north-central Portugal. Many have secured arms.[49]

Efforts to whip up working-class chauvinism were proving useless in the face of general opposition to the military draft. Moreover, the regime appeared to be faring little better with the middle class, who, after July 1961, were penalised by increases in income tax and purchase tax on superfluous and luxury consumption. The need to find the revenue for Portugal's swollen military budget made such measures necessary. By the early 1960s it was clear even to Salazar's financial advisers that he would be unable to extract further resources from the working class, simply because 'there was nothing further to be drained' from the ordinary public.[50] In a situation where the financial exploitation of ordinary folk had reached saturation point, the *Estado Novo* had to risk antagonising its principal social mainstays by turning to them for new resources.

It was a risk that might not have come off. During 1961–62 important elite figures, who included former ministers and at least one serving member of the cabinet, continued to conspire against Salazar. Information contained in US State Department files housed in the John F. Kennedy Library, Boston, reveals that Marcelo Caetano, Salazar's successor in 1968, had aligned himself with the Botelho Moniz–Craveiro Lopes faction and 'was in complete agreement with the necessity for the removal of Salazar'.[51] This *camarilla* also received overtures from General Fernando dos Santos Costa, who expressed himself in the following terms in June 1962:

> Salazar is nearly hopeless as a leader by virtue of age and personality. However, it is best not to be openly hostile to the regime, some fundamental principles of which might be supported, but to avoid giving the impression of complete approval of Salazarism. While the regime procession is going down the street I will watch it and applaud, but if the paraders should call me to join them, I would answer that I could not, since I have important things I must attend to.[52]

Divisions among what was a very heterogeneous collection of opposition notables ultimately frustrated the efforts of any one faction to remove Salazar. Although seemingly estranged from the *Estado Novo*, Santos Costa was prepared to use force to prevent his enemy Adriano Moreira (minister of the *ultramar* in 1961–62) from coming to power. A brilliant academic who had also proved a dynamic minister when placed in charge of the administration of Portuguese Africa, Moreira definitely sought to replace Salazar during 1962. But according to an admiring colleague Franco Nogueira:

> Power went to his head. He made very outspoken statements which he thought Salazar did not get to hear. But he did. Salazar used to say 'Why is he doing this? He only has to wait.'[53]

Salazar decided to replace him as minister of the *ultramar* after he had got into a bitter quarrel with General Deslandes, the military supremo in Angola. Deslandes was sacked in September 1962 and Moreira departed three months later. According to Nogueira, Salazar offered to switch him to the ministry of education. However, Moreira rashly refused to accept this job unless he could also be 'special assistant' to the premier at the same time. Salazar flatly turned him down and, after a meteoric rise, Moreira found himself in the political wilderness, where he has remained since.

Salazar's Indian Summer

By the close of the Moreira episode the political crisis had largely abated. Salazar was to hang on for another six years, thanks largely to the disunity of his opponents and to his own skills as a political tactician, which were undimmed by age or ill-health. He had regained the political initiative, possibly as early as the summer of 1961, when the rebellion in Angola was finally put down. The morale of unpoliticised officers (i.e. the majority) was raised by the success of the operation mounted against the rebels from the Bakongo tribe who had seized much of the province's northern area in their sudden spring offensive. However, in terms of life, the cost of the Angolan uprising was a heavy one. Hundreds of white settlers were killed, many in brutal fashion. Utilising traditional methods of warfare, the rebel National Front for the Liberation of Angola (FNLA), led by Holden Roberto, suffered heavy casualties in the face of superior Portuguese arms. However, most of the African dead – estimated at around 20,000 by the British Baptist Missionary Society – had been non-combatants who were the victims of a pogrom unleashed by a hastily formed militia of Portuguese settlers. The main target of the white terror was the small educated African minority known as the *assimilados*, who had been granted certain citizens' rights down the years. Thousands of *assimilados* lost their lives not only in the north but in other parts of Angola where no fighting had occurred at all. Even the pro-Salazar *Daily Telegraph*, on 25 July 1961, could refer, through its correspondent Richard Beeston, to 'a widespread persecution of educated and semi-educated Africans ... ruthlessly carried out' by the PIDE as well as by white settlers. And according to the sister paper, *The Sunday Telegraph*, 'the reign of terror' was only stopped 'by fear of the authorities that the white militia was getting out of control'.[54]

Despite the snuffing out of the spring 1961 rebellion, insurgency continued in Angola and began in Mozambique and Guinea-Bissau during 1962 and 1963 respectively. Career officers, even those opposed to the war in its initial stages, were not prepared to raise too many awkward questions once it had got under way. To do so was to risk being branded a coward, one of the worst insults that can be made to an officer's *honra e dignidade* (honour and dignity). The sense of weary acquiescence with the war even survived the loss of Portugal's smallest and oldest colony, Goa, at the end of 1961, in what was 'one of the most humiliating incidents in the history of the Portuguese army'.[55]

Ever since Indian independence in 1947 the New Delhi government had sought peacefully to persuade the Portuguese to vacate this enclave on the western coast of the sub-continent. However, Salazar refused even to enter into talks over Goa. In 1954 he rejected an offer of negotiations with a characteristically chauvinist refrain:

> We would be giving or selling the Portuguese of India, the land of Afonso de Albuquerque and our epic achievements in the Orient, the saints of the Church, our country's martyrs. And for how much? For how much?[56]

Eventually Nehru, the Indian leader, made it clear that he was prepared to use force to secure Goa. The Portuguese garrison there consisted of just 3,000 men, mostly with obsolete equipment. Nevertheless, on the eve of the invasion, which took place on 18 December 1961, Salazar cabled the military commander, General Vassalo e Silva, to say:

> I contemplate no truce and I wish no Portuguese to be taken prisoner. No ship is to surrender. Our soldiers or sailors must conquer or die.[57]

Sensibly Vassalo e Silva and his troops rejected this medieval vapouring. Resistance did occur, but within thirty-six hours Goa was in Indian hands. To Salazar the loss was a devastating one which he would never come to terms with. From 1961 on, Goa was 'occupied territory' and until 1974 it continued to be represented in the National Assembly. As for General Vassalo e Silva, Salazar would have made an example of him but for the intervention of the military establishment, who succeeded in dropping court-martial proceedings against their unfortunate colleague. He quit the army in 1963 very much under a cloud but was reinstated after 1974, and in the spring of 1980 he paid a return visit to Goa which was reported in lavish detail by the Lisbon weekly *Expresso*.[58]

Appropriately, it had been armed insurrection in the *ultramar*, the most exploited theatre of Salazarist rule, which plunged the *Estado Novo* into its greatest crisis at the beginning of the 1960s. Incredibly, there were more high-level military opponents of the *Estado Novo* in April 1961 than in April 1974 when the dictatorship finally perished. How does one explain Salazar's survival? Familiarity in the ways of power after thirty-five years and the ability of the regime to derive some patriotic mileage from the war are explantory factors. Also, for the economic elite, the tax increases and austerity measures announced in 1961 proved tolerable. Nor would the 1960s witness further encroachments on the wealth and comforts of the higher bourgeoisie. To pay for the war Salazar swallowed a cardinal political principle and decided in the 1960s to allow much increased foreign investment into Portugal. Decree-law 46312 in April 1965 substantially reduced restrictions on the entry of foreign capital.[59] Inevitably, in a situation where foreign investment in industry rose from 1·5 per cent in 1960 to 27 per cent in 1970, the dictator premier's overall control of the economy was reduced.[60] Nevertheless, tensions within the power elite subsided as the upper classes found themselves materially benefiting from the spurt being given to the national economy by the injection of external capital. Lower-income groups benefited also, but to a much lesser extent. No dramatic increases in employment occurred, since many of the new plants being set up in the 1960s were labour-extensive. Instead the 1960s saw a massive exodus of workers and peasants to seek higher-paid jobs in France, West Germany and the Benelux countries.

There has been a long tradition of emigration in Portuguese history. But before 1960 emigration to other parts of Europe had been negligible, most preferring to settle in Brazil, North America or Portuguese Africa. The rapid expansion of the French and German economies in the 1960s and the demand for cheap migrant labour from southern Europe changed this pattern dramatically. From 1965 to 1969, 70 per cent of all departing Portuguese settled in countries of the EEC and, between 1970 and 1973, if the number of clandestine emigrants is included, 82 per cent of all emigrants went to European countries.[61] This exodus represented the greatest movement of population in Portugal's history. An estimated 1,033,030 people left during the 1960–70 period alone. Between 1961 and 1974 1,500,000 Portuguese found jobs abroad, leaving a labour force of only 3,100,000 in Portugal itself.[62] Northern districts like Vila Real, Viseu and Bragança consistently registered the highest rate of emigration. Many young men left to avoid the military draft, to seek higher wages, or because there was no other alternative, since, on many farms, excessive fragmentation of land dictated that the eldest son inherit the property to ensure its viability.

France was the destination of most emigrants, and by the 1970s Paris had become the second biggest Portuguese city in terms of population.[63] To counteract this drain the government tried to draw more settlers to Portuguese Africa. In particular, it sought to attract ex-soldiers who had served in Africa to front-line settlements in Mozambique and Angola. However, this programme met with little success. By the time of the 1974 revolution the government had small hope of reaching its earlier target of attracting half a million Portuguese to the Cabora Bassa district of Mozambique, where it was constructing a vast hydro-electric project designed to provide much of southern Africa with energy supplies.

Salazar himself never once set foot in any of the overseas territories. He once explained this away by arguing that 'to direct a battle does a general himself have to be on the battlefield? . . . Our empire is far-flung: only from a distance can one view it as a whole.'[64] Despite the existence of forced labour and other forms of disguised slavery well into the twentieth century, he also frequently referred to Portugal's civilising mission in Africa and to the historical aptitude of the Portuguese for getting on with people of different races. This rosy assumption has been supported by Gilberto Freyre, the Brazilian sociologist who, in studies published by the Portuguese government and others, claimed that with Portuguese expansion in the fifteenth century a new type of civilisation began in the tropics, one which developed a unique feeling of solidarity between coloniser and colonised based on the idea of belonging to a common Lusitanian community. Portugal's unsavoury reputation for exploitation and the centuries of African resistance to her rule are major historical nettles which Freyre prefers not to grasp. Most academic students of Portuguese Africa reject his pretentious defence of Portuguese policies, one writer, Gerald J. Bender, even concluding that black–white relations under the Portuguese were neither better nor worse than elsewhere on the continent.[65]

Though not unimportant, it would be unwise to explain Portuguese determination to remain in Africa entirely in terms of sentimentality or Lusitanian nationalism. First and foremost, it was compelling economic reasons that militated against decolonisation. Until 1974 the colonies acted as a vital captive market for Portugal, taking 25 per cent of her exports, many of which were not competitive on the world market. Many were made from raw materials imported from the *ultramar* at low cost, an unequal relationship that obviously would not last if Portuguese Africa succeeded in winning meaningful independence. Unlike France, Britain or Belgium, she was too economically underdeveloped to hope to have a major *post*-colonial role in Africa. Portugal lacked the technology and resources which enabled other colonial nations to maintain a substantial degree of hidden power in black African states formerly under their control. Accordingly, a policy of intransigence and military repression seemed the only one open to the Portuguese authorities. Ironically, Salazar had boxed Portugal into a corner through his economic policies at home. His curbs on domestic development stultified industrial progress and meant that Portugal was in no position to provide aid or large numbers of technicians in return for the maintenance of favourable trading relations with an independent Mozambique or Angola. The Guinea-Bissau nationalist Amílcar Cabral may well have been right when he claimed that:

> If Portugal was economically advanced, if Portugal could be classified as a developed country, we should surely not be at war with Portugal today.[66]

Nevertheless, economically and materially Portugal expanded in the 1960s far more rapidly than in any of the other three decades when Salazar was in charge of her destinies. However, it was with reluctance that the premier sacrificed a few of his stale economic nostrums, and the relatively slight progress which occurred did not nullify Walter Lippmann's 1962 view that 'Dr Salazar's policy is the same kind of menace to the public peace as was Marie Antoinette's inability to understand why the hungry people in Paris did not eat cake'.[67]

As before, more innovations and skill were possibly shown in foreign relations than in domestic affairs. In their determination to retain Portuguese Africa, Salazar and his foreign minister, Franco Nogueira (perhaps the most able member of the cabinet in the post-1945 era), managed to avoid total diplomatic isolation and encirclement. Relations with the Eastern bloc were non-existent except for an embassy which was maintained by Cuba in Lisbon even after Castro's rise to power. However, Soviet journalists officially visited the Portuguese colonies and Portuguese academics who were supporters of the regime even attended conferences in Moscow during the 1960s.[68] Soviet support for left-wing insurgents in what was now the world's largest remaining colonial empire was not as great as might have been expected, and pressure from Moscow and her allies in the United Nations slackened off perceptibly after the initial outbreak of fighting in Angola. Portugal was even able to play a prominent role in destroying the effects of British sanctions imposed on the rebel Ian Smith regime from 1965 onwards without suffering any adverse repercussions. The monarchist entrepreneur Jorge Jardim, Salazar's deputy minister of industry from 1948 to 1952, and a man of great influence in Mozambique up to 1974, played a vital role in the sanctions-busting operation.[69]

Against the United States, however, Portugal fared less well. Although pressure on Salazar (to mend his ways in Africa and think about leaving) declined after President Kennedy's assassination at the end of 1963, relations between Lisbon and Washington remained cool for a long time. Franco Nogueira believed that the USA would like to have replaced Portugal as the dominant power in Angola on account of the territory's vast mineral resources. His feelings were not mollified by a further brush with the USA in 1965, the year in which Portugal approached Brazil with the proposal that a Lusitanian federation of all the Portuguese-speaking lands in the northern and southern hemisphere be set up. Brazil considered the scheme but turned it down, according to Nogueira, because the US lobbied strongly against the idea. Franco Nogueira believes that the history of Portugal and her African territories would have been very different if a grand federation had been achieved, but obviously this is a matter of conjecture.

While armed opposition increased in each of Portugal's African territories, with the exception of the Cape Verde Islands, anti-Salazarist activity declined at home after 1962. The last open revolt before 1974 occurred on 1 January 1962 when Captain João Varela Gomes tried to seize the Beja military barracks in the Alentejo. The revolt failed, although Colonel Jaime de Fonseca, the under-secretary of the army, was killed in error by his own troops. A major blow to opposition hopes came in 1965 when General Delgado was murdered by the PIDE on 13 February, near the Spanish frontier town of Badajoz. Along with his Brazilian secretary and mistress, Arajaryr Campos, who also died, he seems to have been lured there by a traitor within the ranks of the opposition. The whole story of what happened has yet to be properly told, and one of the investigators of his disappearance and killing, Fernando Oneto, himself met a mysterious death in 1976. Few of the general's right-wing assassins have been brought to book, while Portuguese conservatives claim that the hands of the PCP and socialist politicians are not entirely clean, since Delgado had quarrelled with them before his assassination. Nevertheless, there is little doubt that it was PIDE agents who murdered Delgado. Salazar's role is less clear. He had aged greatly during the 1958–62 crisis and gave the secret police increasing latitude. He also showed favour to the monarchists, whose pretender, Duarte Nuno, had been living in Portugal since 1950. More significantly, the Causa Monárquica (Monarchist Cause) was, by the 1960s, officially recognised by the regime and allowed to exist openly.

One source reckons that there were 20,000 monarchists in Portugal by the 1960s. There was even a report in 1967 that 'the Portuguese military high command was expected to declare a monarchy on the death of Salazar'.[70] Pushing rather hard for this solution were some of the confidants who surrounded the premier in his declining years. Known as *eminências pardas* (grey eminences), these political oligarchs were increasingly consulted for political advice. Perhaps the best known *eminência parda* was Admiral Henrique Tenreiro, a right-wing naval officer who became enormously wealthy under the dictatorship. During 1958 he seems to have influenced Salazar when it came to choosing Admiral Tomás as president – his own brother-in-law and someone who reflected Tenreiro's reactionary political viewpoint.

Never popular, the circle around the aged Salazar was tarnished by the *Ballet Roses* scandal in late 1967, when several leading notables, including José Correia de Oliveira, the minister of the economy, were allegedly involved in a prostitution racket involving young girls. Confronted with what seemed like an example of gross personal licence, Salazar nevertheless did not act.[71] For all his puritanism, the seventy-eight-year-old leader was content to sweep the whole affair under the carpet. There were no sackings. Indeed, Correia de Oliveira was retained for another year when Marcelo Caetano took over as premier on 26 September 1968.

Salazar's health had been fairly good for most of that year. Although he was white-haired and looked frail in photographs, he was still quite vigorous in conversation face-to-face, according to Franco Nogueira.[72] Nogueira refutes the claim that he had begun to go senile, but admits that after Salazar was involved in an accident in August 1968 things began to go wrong. The premier injured his head when a deckchair collapsed under him while he was having his hair cut. Soon he was having memory blackouts and, at his last cabinet meeting, he went over a whole series of matters which had been settled the day before as if it was entirely fresh business.[73] At the end of the session he asked Nogueira what the lavish party had been like which Simon Patino, the tin baron, had held in Lisbon. Previously he had shown no interest in this ostentatious gathering and had urged people not to go. Franco Nogueira wondered why he had mentioned it and, looking more closely, realised that he was far from well: bent over, the premier shuffled slowly out of the room with his papers under his arm.

Some days later, on 6 September 1968, he collapsed with a clot on the brain. Gradually, over the coming month, it became clear that he would not recover, and a search for a successor got under way. This was a task which belonged to the Council of State, an honorary body composed of Salazarist notables. The candidates they considered included sixty-eight-year-old Santos Costa, the former justice minister, João Antunes Varela, Teotónio Pereira, Adriano Moreira and Marcelo Caetano – who emerged as the victor.

In some ways Caetano was a surprising choice: he had been out of politics for ten years. In 1961 he had resigned as rector of Lisbon University after clashing with the regime over university autonomy; why had he been chosen to succeed Salazar? Perhaps the reasons may become clearer if his career is put into somewhat broader perspective. First of all, Marcelo Caetano was, after Salazar, the most enduring figure in *Estado Novo* politics. He had helped create the conservative autocracy in the 1930s and, after thirty-six years, was still only sixty-two. If not always in cabinet, he was never far from the corridors of power and, despite flirtations with certain opposition circles, always showed himself to be a man of the right. In 1968 the Council of State was also advancing a statesman who was committed to maintaining Portugal's African presence in the face of nationalist opposition. A guarantee to this effect had been given by the incoming premier. Thus, for all his much-vaunted liberalism, Caetano was broadly prepared to uphold the policies of his predecessor.

Salazar recovered some of his physical powers after 1968 but was only a shadow of his former self. He died in Lisbon on 27 July 1970, still thinking he was head of government. For almost two years President Tomás could not summon the courage to break the tidings of dismissal to him. From time to time cabinet ministers even gathered round him to receive and pretend to take note of instructions. In his last interview, which he gave to the French *L'Aurore* on 6 September 1969, he said that he regarded himself as being in office as before.[74] Apparently he knew nothing of Caetano's accession.

Notes

1 Costa Reis and Rendeiro Júnior, 'A contra-revolução nacional', p. 67.
2 Neil Bruce, *Portugal. The Last Empire*, David & Charles, Newton Abbot, 1975, p. 41.
3 Franco Nogueira, *Salazar*, Vol. IV, *O ataque, 1945–1958*, Atlântida Editora, Coimbra, 1980, p. 174.
4 Nowell, *Portugal*, p. 15.

5   Kenneth Maxwell, 'Portugal: a neat revolution', *New York Review of Books*, 13 June 1974, p. 18.
6   António de Figueiredo, *Portugal and its Empire. The Truth*, Gollancz, London, 1961, p. 51.
7   *Sunday Times* Insight Team, *Insight on Portugal*, p. 57.
8   Ramiro da Costa, *O desenvolvimento do capitalismo em Portugal*, Cadernos Peninsulares, Lisbon, 1975, p. 93.
9   Schmitter, 'The "régime d'exception" ', p. 41.
10 Joyce Riegelhaupt, 'Peasants and politics in Salazar's Portugal: the corporate state and village "non-politics" ', in Graham and Makler (eds.), *Contemporary Portugal*, p. 182.
11 *Ibid.*
12 PRO, FO 371, 23389/1086/36, Sir Marcus Cheke, 9 April 1946.
13 W. C. Atkinson, 'Portugal, the war, and after', *Fortnightly Review*, July 1944, p. 21.
14 Nogueira, *op. cit.*, II, p. 265.
15 Mónica, 'Educação e sociedade', p. 232.
16 Anderson, 'Portugal and the end of ultra-colonialism', p. 87.
17 *Ibid.*
18 *Ibid.*
19 Fryer and McGowan, *Oldest Ally*, p. 143.
20 Figueiredo, *Portugal and its Empire*, p. 45.
21 Nogueira, *op. cit.*, IV, p. 147.
22 Caetano, *Minhas memórias*, p. 371.
23 Humberto Delgado, *Da pulhice do homo sapiens. Da monarquia de vigaristas pela república de bandidos. A ditadura de Papa*, Livraria Depositária, Lisbon, 1933.
24 Delgado's pro-Allied stance in wartime is discussed on p. 145.
25 Interview with Senhora Humberta Lourenço Delgado, Lisbon, 19 March 1977.
26 *Ibid.*
27 In the 1950s, before he joined the opposition, Delgado seriously considered seizing the disputed frontier region of Olivença as a gesture which, he hoped, would raise the Portuguese from their torpor. An RAF officer in the Second World War has also recalled how Delgado pleaded with him to get him on to a bomber raid over Germany 'so that . . . he might once again feel the "frisson of danger" '. See R. E. Vintras, *The Portuguese Connection*, London, 1975, p. 63.
28 David L. Raby, 'Populism and the Portuguese left: from Delgado to Otelo', in Graham and Wheeler (eds.), *The Portuguese Revolution*.
29 Anthony Verrier, 'Portugal on the brink', *New Statesman*, 19 October 1962, pp. 518–19.
30 Interview with Senhora H. L. Delgado.
31 My emphasis.
32 Fryer and McGowan, *op. cit.*, p. 123.
33 Interview with General Santos Costa, Lisbon, 20 July 1981.
34 *Ibid.*
35 Interview with Santos Costa, Lisbon, 16 July 1981.
36 Interview with Santos Costa, Lisbon, 27 July 1981.
37 *Ibid.*
38 *Ibid.*
39 Avelino Rodrigues *et al. O Movimento dos Capitães e o 25 de Abril*, Moraes Editores, Lisbon, 1974, p. 158.

40   Benjamin Welles, 'Salazar in trouble', *Atlantic Monthly*, July 1962, p. 58.
41   *Ibid.*, p. 57.
42   Figueiredo, *op. cit.*, p. 202.
43   For amplification of this view see Tom Gallagher, 'From hegemony to opposition: the Portuguese right before and after 1974', in Graham and Wheeler, *The Portuguese Revolution.*
44   Martins, 'Opposition in Portugal', p. 255.
45   Rodrigues *et al. op. cit.*, p. 154.
46   *Sunday Times* Insight Team, *op. cit.*, p. 23.
47   Jorge Lopes, 'O golpe Botelho Moniz', *Opção*, No. 31, 25 November 1976, p. 59.
48   *Sunday Times* Insight Team, *op. cit.*, p. 23.
49   *Sunday Times*, 7 January 1962, p. 2.
50   Anderson, *op. cit.*, p. 110.
51   John F. Kennedy Library, Boston, Mass., box 54, Portugal 6/16/62 – 7/17/72, Central Intelligence Agency report, June 1962.
52   *Ibid.*
53   Interview with Franco Nogueira, London, 6 October 1979.
54   *Sunday Telegraph*, 20 July 1961.
55   *Sunday Times* Insight Team, *op. cit.*, p. 12.
56   *Ibid.*, p. 13.
57   *Ibid.*, p. 14.
58   *Expresso*, 28 June 1980.
59   Romeu Costa Reis and Manuel Rendeiro Júnior, 'A industrialização em Portugal: de Salazar a Marcelo Caetano', *História*, No. 11, September 1979, p. 69.
60   Keefe, *Area Handbook*, p. 323.
61   *Ibid.*, p. 98.
62   *Ibid.*, p. 83.
63   By 1974 the minimum wage in France was more than that earned by 92 per cent of Portuguese people at home.
64   Garnier, *Salazar*, p. 130.
65   Gerald J. Bender, *Angola under the Portuguese. The Myth and the Reality*, Heinemann, London, 1978.
66   Ponte, *The Last to Leave*, p. 31.
67   *The Observer* (London), 21 January 1962.
68   McGowan, *O Bando de Argél*, p. 195.
69   See Jorge Jardim, *Rodesia. O escandalo das sanções*, Intervenção, Lisbon, 1978.
70   See Ronald C. Chilcote, 'Portugal', in *Britannia Book of the Year, 1967*, Britannia Books, London, 1968.
71   When the writer referred briefly to the Ballet Roses scandal in an article published in 1981, it elicited a reply from a member of the far right. Barradas de Oliveira published an article entitled 'Os oitenta e sete ministros de Salazar' in the August 1981 number of an obscure Portuguese journal called *Resistencia*. The title of his piece, 'The eighty-seven ministers of Salazar', was the same as the one I had used in the February 1981 issue of *História*. He endeavoured to refute some of my comments on the ministerial elite and, in particular, criticised me for linking Correia de Oliveira with the 1967 scandal. In the process he provided much new information about this episode, including the names of others linked with it.

72 Interview with Franco Nogueira, London, 6 October 1979.
73 *Ibid.*
74 Soares, *Portugal's Struggle*, p. 236.

was meteoric during the early years of the counter-revolution. In 1929, at the age of twenty-three, he became legal adviser to the minister of finance, an appointment which marked the start of his long political relationship with Salazar. The prime minister apart, probably no person was more responsible for the important legislation enacted in the early 1930s which gave juridical substance to the New State. Before he was thirty Caetano also emerged as Portugal's leading constitutional lawyer, and in 1933 he was appointed to the Chair of constitutional and administrative law at Lisbon University. In 1940 he became head of the Mocidade, the state youth movement, and from 1944 to 1947 he was minister of the colonies. There followed a period of two years spent trying to revitalise the stagnant União Nacional as well as a more rewarding spell as president of the Corporative Chamber from 1949 to 1955, before he was appointed minister to the presidency in 1955, a post which has been compared to that of deputy premier.[3] Caetano fell out with Salazar after 1958, the year in which he left the government, and four years later he resigned as rector of Lisbon University after the unauthorised entry of police into the University grounds during a period of student unrest. There were some who saw this as Caetano's final break with a regime whose political philosophy he still adhered to but whose sluggishness and long dominance by Salazar he found increasingly irksome. However, he remained in political contention during the final years of Salazarism. He was a member of the Council of State and he continued to move among the various important brokers and notables of the *Estado Novo*.

1968–71: liberal interlude

On taking office in September 1968, Premier Caetano adopted as his slogan 'Evolution within continuity', implying change within the broad framework of the Salazarist system.[4] In his first speech he added the rider that 'faithfulness to the doctrine brilliantly taught by Dr Salazar should not be confused with stubborn adherence to formulae or solutions that he, at some time, may have adopted'.[5] Initially, these were not empty words. Within a year of taking office he made a series of gestures to the opposition which seemed to indicate that thoroughgoing liberalisation was finally on the way. Mário Soares, the socialist politician, was allowed to leave his enforced exile on the Portuguese African island of São Tomé at the end of 1968, while in 1969 Dom António Ferreira Gomes, the outspoken Bishop of Oporto, returned to the diocese after a long period abroad. Censorship was also relaxed to the extent that Marxist literature was allowed to go on sale in the bookshops. Novels, plays and films previously deemed subversive could be seen and read, while in 1969 the feared PIDE was rechristened the DGS (General Directorate of Security) and some of its powers were curtailed. In the same year government approval ceased to be obligatory for elected representatives of the state trade unions (the *sindicatos*), something which enabled PCP militants significantly to expand their influence in the labour movement. But in other directions, changes were disappointingly slow. In November 1968 Portugal still claimed to have 187 political prisoners, most of them communists or members of far-left groups which had sprung up in the late 1960s. No attempt was made to disband fascistic hangovers like the Portuguese Legion of the Mocidade, even though it has been claimed that Caetano possessed enough authority to get rid of these anachronistic bodies. However, the official political movement of the *Estado Novo*, the União Nacional, *was* subjected to an important overhaul. During December 1968 José Guilherme de Melo e Castro, a progressive Catholic who belonged to the most liberal section of the political establishment, was appointed head of the party and was charged with revitalising it in readiness for National Assembly elections due in October 1969. Known to favour political pluralism and a free press, Melo e Castro brought young progressive elements into the UN and his appointment coincided with a new electoral law which enabled all Portuguese who could read or write, including literate women (hitherto mostly barred from voting), to take part in future contests.[6]

But just how free would elections under Caetano be? Though expressing scepticism, the non-communist opposition felt that it might make some impact and it was decided to stand against the UN in almost every constituency, the first time in forty-four years that the opposition went to the polls in such a concerted fashion. However, it was badly weakened by internecine strife which diminished its standing with sections of the electorate. Instead of presenting a united front, two rival slates offered candidates, the CDE, an alliance of progressive Catholics and left-wingers headed by an economist, Dr Francisco Pereira de Moura, and the CEUD, a more moderate coalition of socialists and liberals which made little impact (although among its leaders were men who would rise to great prominence in the democratic era).

One of the CDE candidates in the Atlantic islands was Ernesto Melo Antunes, a junior army officer, who would play an important role in the 1974–75 revolution. He was forbidden to return to the islands after the election was over, but it is interesting that this serving officer's act of defiance did not get him into any worse trouble. Only a few incidents marked the election campaign, one opposition candidate, Francisco Sousa Tavares, being beaten up in a Lisbon street by members of the Portuguese Legion. At the count, it was announced that the UN had polled 88 per cent of the vote, as against 10·5 per cent for the CDE and 1·6 per cent for the CEUD. Opposition spokesmen complained of ballot-rigging and general fraud, but it is probable that their own divisions and the fact that living standards had risen appreciably in the first year of Caetano's premiership also contributed largely to the result. The early years of the Caetano era was probably one of the only times when the authoritarian regime could rely on more than coercion, propaganda and superstition, something which its opponents would never acknowledge. Although the proletariat as a whole remained desperately poor, real wages improved for various groups of workers between 1968 and 1973, and opinion polls conducted in the late 1970s indicate that the Caetano years were rememberd by many with some nostalgia. However, it would be unwise to depict the October 1969 elections as a vote of confidence for Caetano's 'evolution in continuity'. Only about 18 per cent of Portugal's 9·5 million people were eligible to vote, and since there was an abstention rate of around 60 per cent, only 10 per cent of the population went anywhere near the voting booths.

After what was, in effect, a highly successful public relations exercise rather than a genuine test of public opinion, Caetano pressed ahead with more changes, some merely decorative, others quite thoroughgoing. Before the end of 1969 the *Estado Novo* had become the *Estado Social*, and soon the UN would be renamed Acção Nacional Popular (National Popular Action). Then, in January 1970, Caetano formed a new government consisting in the main of protégés who were loyal to his new policies. Baltasar Rebelo de Sousa, a highly talented politician, became minister of corporations, health and welfare, Rui Patrício, the premier's godson, became foreign minister, while Maria Teresa Lobo as under-secretary for health and welfare became the first woman to be appointed to a Portuguese government. Perhaps the most unusual appointment was that of the Cambridge-trained scientist Francisco Veiga Simão as minister of education. A progressive figure who would have been at home in the liberal republic and who some years later joined the Socialist Party, he drew up a programme for the expansion and democratisation of Portuguese education which, had it been fully implemented, would have made it among the most modern education systems of its kind in Europe. In the economic sphere, important innovators also emerged who advocated more dynamic industrial policies and closer links with the EEC. Technocrats who had been critical of the regime's economic performance in the past such as João Salgueiro, Rogério Martins and Xavier Pintado joined the government as secretaries of state for planning, industry and trade respectively. Rogério Martins, in particular, was seen as a coming man, and it is true that he did enjoy some success in breaking local monopolies and modifying the licensing laws which had previously encouraged them. However, the influence of these modern-minded economists was devalued by the fact that they were subject to the authority of the minister of the economy and were not members of the cabinet, where crucial political and economic questions naturally came to be debated.

Under General Franco in Spain, technocrats like Laureano López Rodó and Gregorio López Bravo enjoyed far greater influence and were in fact dominant figures in the government up to the last years of the dictatorship. Caetano was unable to extend the same latitude to his more enlightened conservative ministers because of the strength of the Salazarist old guard within the establishment. The diehards had not simply vanished with the retirement of the old prime minister. Instead, from President Tomás down, they continued to watch Caetano's every move and make criticisms whenever it was thought that he was straying too far from the path of *Estado Novo* orthodoxy. As early as February 1969, Foreign Minister Franco Nogueira was quoted as saying that 'dialogue between the government and the opposition could lead to generalised anarchy; contestation destroys authority and its final aim is the socialisation of chaos'.[7] Some months later, Nogueira quit the government to become a hard-line deputy in the National Assembly. However, António Gonçalves Rapazote, the tough minister of the interior appointed under Salazar, continued to defend traditional *Estado Novo* views right up to the close of the regime. A former Integralist and Blueshirt, and a convinced monarchist, Rapazote took a strong position on law and order and ruthlessly pursued far-left urban guerillas who, from the late 1960s onwards, were responsible for a number of incidents which included bank raids, bomb attacks on NATO installations in Portugal and the sabotage of military equipment destined for Africa. LUAR (the United League for Revolutionary Action) and ARA (Armed Revolutionary Action) were the main resistance groups who employed terror against the regime. In the summer of 1968, before Salazar's retirement, LUAR tried to seize the textile town of Covilhã, in the north, but was foiled in advance by the authorities. When insurgency continued, some hawkish figures concluded that Caetano was not being firm enough against terrorists. In June 1971 General António Malheiro Reymão Nogueira publicly attacked members of the regime whom he branded as 'well-wishers or indifferent spectators of disorder which was gaining ground throughout the nation'.[8] Caetano immediately dismissed this officer from his post as commander of the Coimbra military region. However, right-wing discontent continued to be expressed, particularly towards Veiga Simão's educational policies. These Caetano did not repudiate, but he was forced to carry out a delicate balancing act involving concessions to the right. Salazar's 'not an inch' policy over Portuguese Africa was not only maintained but incursions were allowed to take place into neighbouring African countries thought to be harbouring insurgent nationalists. In November 1970 a military invasion of Guinea-Conakry was briefly attempted when a company of commandos led by Captain Alpoim Calvão tried to seize the capital. The exact aims of the mission have never been explained, but according to Major Otelo de Carvalho, who was serving in Guinea-Bissau at the time, they may have included the assassination of Sekou Touré, the Guinea-Conakry leader, of Amílcar Cabral, head of the Guinea-Bissau insurgents, the destruction of their headquarters in Conakry, the destruction of planes at the local air base, and the liberation of Portuguese prisoners held in the city prison.[9] The raid failed, however, when the local armed forces mounted resistance against the Portuguese, who rapidly withdrew to Guinea-Bissau.

Here another mysterious incident which has never been fully explained had occurred earlier in 1970 when a helicopter crashed, killing three liberal deputies, Leonardo Coimbra, Jaime Pinto Bull and Pinto Leite. The crash was probably an accident, but some wonder whether it was not an all too convenient way to get rid of three members of the liberal faction which had been elected to the National Assembly in 1969 on the victorious UN ticket. Until they gave up any hope of reforming the dictatorship from within, the liberals in parliament comprised a vocal pressure group from which, in 1970, sprang a new quasi-political association known as SEDES (Social and Economic Development Study Group).

SEDES was the first body of its kind in forty years to be given legal status by the authorities. It took a lot of lobbying before they granted it recognition.[10] By 1972 this civic organisation comprised 588 members, most of whom were businessmen, economists, lawyers and other professional people, overwhelmingly drawn from Lisbon or Oporto. SEDES saw itself as a promoter of developmental change, and it organised various seminars and conferences whose papers were often sent to ministers and civil servants in a bid to influence public policy. SEDES's views on teaching reform, censorship and co-operatives were actually published in Portugal. It publicly endorsed Francisco Sá Carneiro, one of its members, in parliament when he called for the direct election of the president of the republic, a return to parliamentary democracy, freedom of religion, of the press and of assembly, and equality of opportunity. This was a clear sign that SEDES was becoming a 'tolerated centre of criticism of the government and regime rather than a second governmental support organisation'.[11] In parliament, members of the liberal wing of the UN's successor, the ANP, were even more outspoken about Caetano's policies, and occasionally only edited versions of their speeches were allowed to appear in the press. The actual size of the reformist group in parliament varied somewhat. During the 1969–71 period, when Caetano appeared set to liberalise the country, it comprised twenty to twenty-five deputies, but after 1971 the genuine liberals had dwindled to around six or seven, according to Francisco Pinto Balsemão (one of the progressives elected in 1969 who went on to found the influential weekly *Expresso* in 1973).[12]

The last Bourbon period, 1971–74

Around 1970–71 moderate reformers began to abandon their belief that the political system could be reformed from within. Before then, Caetano had been rather successful in his attempt to gain credibility with moderate opposition forces so as to broaden the basis of support for himself and his regime. However, by 1971 no major institutional changes had occurred that indicated a move towards genuine liberal democracy. The political atmosphere had certainly grown lighter, and Portugal was freer than at any time under Salazar, but Caetano was loath to dismantle any of the regime's authoritarian structures. This was not, according to the moderate conservative politician Adelino Amaro da Costa, because Caetano was a prisoner of the extreme right. 'One chooses one's own jailers', and the prime minister simply lacked the resolve to carry out genuine liberalisation.[13] He had too many links with the regime in its earlier phases and, unable to formulate a clear political strategy on the domestic front, he tended to vacillate.[14] His feelings oscillated from one day to the next, according to Amaro da Costa. Pinto Balsemão, echoing this view, has recalled that he used to get angry letters, sometimes ten pages long, from Caetano, attacking his liberal stance in parliament. The next day the prime minister would act as if nothing had happened. But when the ANP liberals waited in vain for constitutional changes anticipated in 1970, it was realised that the process of evolution through continuity was at a standstill. The disillusionment of Sá Carneiro, Balsemão, Miller Guerra and other ANP deputies was deepened in 1972 when the seventy-eight-year-old President Américo Tomás decided to have himself re-elected for another seven-year term. Tomás, dull, good-natured and very reactionary, was seen as the protector of the old order by the *duros* (hard-liners) of the regime. He was possibly the strongest of the three heads of state which the dictatorship witnessed, since, prodded by his reactionary friends, he began to use the presidential powers entrusted to him under the constitution which had previously lain dormant.

Six hundred and sixteen members of the 669-member electoral college voted for Tomás in 1972. Early next year, Sá-Carneiro resigned his seat in the National Assembly, being disinclined to continue taking part in what seemed increasingly like a political charade. Outside the chamber, state repression seemed to be on the way back after the relaxation of the 1968–71 period. Balsemão's very professional weekly, *Expresso*, was savagely censored and would have ceased publication altogether but for the onset of the 1974 revolution. The women's liberation movement acquired three Portuguese martyrs after the publication in 1972 of *New Portuguese Letters*, a book attacking the suppression of women's rights in Portugal which the authorities branded as an outrage to public decency. The authors, the 'Three Marias' (the poet Maria Teresa Horta, the novelist Maria Velho da Costa, and Maria Isabel Barreno) were arrested in 1973, their case attracting much sympathetic attention from abroad. Journalists who visited the country during the last years of the dictatorship found that the secret police (though less ubiquitous) could still arrest people and hold them without trial for up to six months. Moreover, the names of political prisoners were not made public, issues which the non-communist opposition emphasised when it met in conference at Aveiro during April 1973. A united broad-left front was in fact established in preparation for National Assembly elections which took place on 28 October. A month before, Caetano had enacted a pathetic decree designed to prevent candidates retiring before polling day. However, after using the campaign to mobilise opinion against the regime, every opposition candidate pulled out, nobody wanting to give Caetano's 'elections' any spurious legitimacy as had to some extent happened in 1969.

Industrial growth was stepped up during the first four years of Caetano's premiership as foreign companies opened new factories and the state encouraged domestic investment in industry. Foreign investment in Portuguese industry rose from 1·5 per cent of the total in 1960 to 27 per cent in 1970.[15] But there was no major growth in industrial employment, since most of the expansion occurred in capital-intensive industries; the estimated total employment in manufacturing in 1974 was 702,600, compared with 655,400 in 1960, an increase of only 7·5 per cent for the fourteen-year period.[16] Two areas, Lisbon–Setúbal in the south and the Oporto–Aveiro–Braga region in the north, are estimated to have accounted for about three-quarters of net manufacturing output in 1970. In 1974 the industrial labour force in continental Portugal totalled about one million people, slightly over 700,000 in manufacturing, 267,000 in construction and public works, 17,000 in public utilities and 12,000 in mining.[17] Given the massive emigration of workers and peasants to better-paid jobs in the EEC countries (which continued unabated after 1968), a labour shortage actually developed which was partially solved, at least in the building industry, by bringing around 20,000 Cape Verdeans to work mainly in the Lisbon area.

Industry grew at an average annual rate of 9 per cent in 1970–73, while the service sector expanded at around 7 per cent per annum, compared with 5·9 per cent in the previous decade.[18] This boomlet was fed by two sources of finance: remittances from emigrants and, more important, an easy credit, low-interest scheme devised by the Caetano government. In a *volte-face* which Salazar would hardly have tolerated, his successor encouraged banks to lend money more widely and companies to sell shares to individual investors so as to generate higher economic growth. However, more often than not, the banks lent the money to wealthy and familiar customers who bought existing shares and helped create a speculative boom in share prices during the early 1970s.[19] In April 1973 the secretary of state for finance, João da Costa André resigned from the government because of its unwillingness to bring the banks to heel. Next year he wrote an article attacking the big banks which was due to appear in *O Século* on 12 April 1974 but was suppressed by the authorities.

But by now the economy was in deepening trouble, especially as a result of the increase in world oil prices which came in the wake of the October 1973 Arab–Israeli war. More than most Western countries, Portugal depended on oil as a prime energy source, since she lacked indigeneous resources of her own, at least in the *metrópole*. To make matters worse, Arab countries reacted most unfavourably to the news that the government had allowed refuelling facilities to US aircraft airlifting supplies to Israel during the 1973 war when all the other NATO countries and Spain had refused to grant this facility. Increased fuel costs helped raise inflation to 20 per cent in 1973, a year which saw wages rise by only 12·5 per cent.[20] Ordinary people began to grow resentful, and in 1973–74 a rash of PCP-inspired strikes occurred as the boom in stock exchange prices continued unabated. The rich grew richer while inflation ate into the modest advances made by the poor. The growth in the Lisbon area of shanty towns known as *barracas* from the 1960s onwards indicated that no great transformation had occurred in proletarian living standards. As many Portuguese still died from tuberculosis in the Caetano era as from road accidents. Third World diseases like kwashiorkior and pellagra were common in certain parts of rural Portugal. Admittedly, state assistance for the poor expanded more quickly under Caetano than under his predecessor. But, the soaring costs of the war in Africa meant that the military took the lion's share of the budget, which was actually in deficit in 1972 and 1973 thanks largely to military overspending. In another act of heresy Caetano took to borrowing from abroad, one more development which made Portugal more vulnerable to downturns in the international economy than had been the case under Salazar.

The *Estado Novo* in Africa

One thing Salazar and Caetano had in common was the fact that they had both served as minister of the colonies before assuming the premiership. Although Salazar held the post for only a few months during 1930, he took the opportunity to pass the May 1930 Colonial Act, which abruptly curtailed the growth in colonial autonomy witnessed during the republican era and reimposed strongly centralised rule from Lisbon. Before 1926 strong governors-general such as General José Norton de

Matos in Angola from 1921 to 1923 and, less successfully, Manuel Brito Camacho in Mozambique during the same period, pursued development-oriented policies sometimes independent of Lisbon.

After 1930 the colonial ministry, situated in the Terreiro do Paço in Lisbon, reasserted its authority and subordinated local administration and interests to metropolitan dictates. Under the important 1930 legislation European settlers were given practically no say in how the colonies were to be run, while the position of local African inhabitants worsened appreciably. According to the *Estado Novo* legislation (as well as previous statutes), they enjoyed the status of *indigena* (natives) rather than citizens and were morally 'obliged' to work, a legal clause which enabled the authorities to employ forced labour on a massive scale. In Mozambique, where some of the worst effects of the forced labour scheme were seen, Africans were compelled to cultivate land for cotton, neglecting the growing of food, a policy which sometimes brought horrific results when harvests were poor. The large monopoly firms which became a feature of economic life during the latter stages of Salazar's rule derived much of their strength and profits from colonial operations involving native exploitation. Because Salazar had put his own domestic house in order, no outcry ensued from Britain (unlike the 1910–26 era), the League of Nations or any other international agency when word occasionally leaked out about the human costs of Salazar's 'civilising mission' in the Portuguese empire. Initially the dictator paid little attention to the colonies. Famine and drought ravaged the Cape Verde islands in the 1940s, a decade which saw the population drop by 18 per cent, without any conspicuous concern from Lisbon.

At least in the first decade of his premiership, Salazar appeared more concerned to see the colonies profitable, or at least not a financial drain, than with the fact that they represented four hundred years of Portuguese settlement and expansion. During and before World War II he ably prevented Portuguese Africa becoming a bargaining pawn or a sop to Nazi Germany to divert Hitler from pursuing expansionist goals in Europe; in 1930, however, his arch-rival Cunha Leal was speculating that, given the right opportunities, he might be happy to sell off Angola, the richest territory in the empire.[21]

Was Salazar the first sceptic about the empire spawned by the highest ranks of the *Estado Novo*? Certainly big cuts in government expenditure reduced immigration and seem to have caused an actual decline in the white population in Angola and Mozambique during the 1930s.[22] However, a politician as traditionally-minded and nationalistic as Salazar could not be expected to give a lead to the other European powers in the matter of decolonisation. While in some respects he proved quite prophetic in the 1930s and 1940s about the expansion of communism in areas where its prospects did not seem particularly rosy, he failed to anticipate the growth of anti-colonialism and black nationalism in the post-war era. In 1951 the African territories came to be known as 'overseas provinces' (and much later as 'states' within the Portuguese nation), a disingenuous public relations exercise which perhaps underlined how badly Portugal had read the changing mood in Africa and how far she was out of touch with thinking elsewhere in the West. In 1962–63 more substantial changes came about as a result of new laws which conferred citizenship on the previously 'non-civilised' African and made it no longer obligatory for Africans to work for Europeans.[23] By now, of course, Portugal was encountering serious opposition in its mainland African territories which would shortly give way to generalised warfare in parts of each one of them. Lisbon made plain its determination not to quit by pressing ahead with economic development schemes the like of which had not been seen before in Portuguese Africa.

During the final thirteen years of Portuguese rule Angola and Mozambique may have witnessed more economic expansion than in the previous hundred years. The reforms and changes of the 1960s have been commonly viewed as a shocked response to the Angolan revolt of 1961, although one historian has argued that they were already in the pipeline as part of the development Portugal herself underwent from the mid-1950s onwards.[24]

Another historian has described Salazar's intransigence over the African territories as a form of 'archaic fanaticism' in which he stubbornly refused to 'understand the profound movements of human history'.[25] This is the view of many other commentators, but ultra-nationalism was no monopoly of the conservative anti-democrats of the *Estado Novo*. Previous regimes, including the republican one, had invariably pursued stridently imperialistic policies in Africa which found a popular response. In some ways Salazar was able to turn the 1961–62 crisis to his advantage by tapping popular nationalism (although this has always been more readily expressed over threats to the sovereignty of the metropole than to the colonies).

Once the Angolan emergency had turned into a war of attrition, patriotic fervour quickly abated and apathy gave way to anti-war sentiments before many years had passed. Among the whites of Angola and Mozambique it was different. Here could be found the staunchest defenders of the thesis that Portugal stretched from Minho to Timor in east Asia. If Lisbon had been of a mind to, it might have tried to build up a strong political movement among the Europeans in Africa, to be used to thwart waverers in the elite or coerce domestic opponents of Portugal's presence in Africa. The *colons* of Algeria had mobilised themselves in just such a way during the latter stages of the 1954–62 Franco-Algerian war.

The white settlers of Rhodesia are an even more obvious example. However, most white settlers in Portuguese Africa were recent arrivals, unlike their Algerian or Rhodesian counterparts. In the political sphere, Lisbon had seen to it that they had never enjoyed any measure of power or responsibility which might have thrown up political leaders and sharpened local opinion. Finally, compared to pre-independence Algeria or Rhodesia, the Portuguese settlers in Angola were not greatly attached to the land or to farming. Thus the incentive to stay and fight which land and property instilled in many Europeans in other settings was lacking in Angola and Mozambique, where most Europeans ended up in the cities and towns.

So the far right was not mobilised in Africa during the 1960s: although the temper and mood of settlers grew more extreme, a far-right leader like the Mozambiquan-based Jorge Jardim (who had been deputy minister of industry from 1948 to 1952) was a relatively isolated and untypical figure. Nevertheless, despite the blinkered way Lisbon responded to its colonial crisis, the *Estado Novo* was perhaps seen at its most innovative and radical during its vain attempt to retain Portuguese Africa after 1961. In some ways Portuguese Africa witnessed the 'revolutionising of the counter-revolution', which, despite propaganda claims, had hitherto failed to happen in the metropole. The 'hearts and minds' campaign of civic action which local military commands launched during the latter half of the war and the harnessing of energies and skills to meet the war effort, demonstrated an urgency and dynamism which the *Estado Novo* had not previously exhibited. The new-found social awareness of the authorities, and their willingness to think in terms of psychological as well as military warfare, did not ultimately stem the insurgents' advance, not least because they were desperately belated measures rather than genuine attempts to transform the lives of exploited people. The same could be said of General António de Spínola's efforts in Guinea-Bissau, where he was governor-general from 1968 to 1973. He sought to transform Guinea-Bissau and stave off the threat from the nationalist PAIGC by operating on the premise that 'we must develop and propose an effective counter-revolution, thus combating ideas with ideas'.[26] His ambitious but doomed programme of civic–military action has invariably been viewed as an essential part of the final countdown to revolution at home and disengagement in Africa. Perhaps it should also be seen in the context of *Estado Novo* politics, where it presented a clear and radical departure from conservative norms. Ironically, it was the bush and swamps of Guinea-Bissau during the final years of the *Estado Novo* that may have seen the radical right finally given its head.

Throughout the war Lisbon was confronted with its most serious guerrilla challenge from Guinea-Bissau and Mozambique. The initial revolt had begun in Angola in 1961, but here the Portuguese were able to contain the level of guerrilla activity thanks mainly to the existence of rival insurgent movements. If guerrilla warfare on the scale of that waged by the PAIGC and Frelimo had been occurring in Portugal's richest territory, then it is quite likely that the collapse would have occurred some time before 1974.

Tribalism hampered the growth of one all-embracing nationalist movement in Angola, and this was a weapon the Portuguese sought to exploit throughout their empire in order to retain control. Ironically, Catholic Portugal found stauncher allies among Moslem tribes such as the Fula in Guinea-Bissau and the Makua in Mozambique than among mission-educated African groups, who were more likely to join the nationalists. The conservatism of their social structure made Moslem tribes better allies of the Portuguese, who flew pilgrims to Mecca and built mosques in Guinea-Bissau in return for the support of local chiefs.

Where co-operation failed, coercion was of course readily employed. Massacres, and the use of napalm when bombing insurgent strongholds, could not be concealed from the rest of the world. Terror campaigns were also directed against the leadership of the nationalist movements. They were spearheaded by the PIDE, which was formed in Portuguese Africa only in 1957 but which proved successful in controlling densely populated areas, making sure that African resistance to Portuguese rule would not be accompanied by urban guerrilla warfare. The towns and cities remained peaceful, and the PIDE was able to extend its activities into neighbouring countries, Eduardo Mondlane, the head of Frelimo, being assassinated in Tanzania in 1969 and Amilcar Cabral meeting the same fate in Guinea-Conakry in 1972. The PIDE was able to encourage internal dissension and splinter groups within nationalist ranks, and, significantly, it was African defectors from the PAIGC and Frelimo who actually carried out the killings of Cabral and Mondlane.[27]

These squalid killings made Portugal even more a pariah throughout much of the world and hastened recognition for the insurgent movements ranged against her. Beforehand she had sought, not without success, to intervene in African politics in other ways. Portugal was able to exert influence over states like Malawi, Zaire and even Zambia which were potential or actual sanctuaries for the guerrillas but which were also reliant on the communications network of Angola and Mozambique. Portugal helped to break the sanctions blockade against Ian Smith's Rhodesia and, less successfully, she intervened on behalf of the insurgent Biafrans in the 1966–69 Nigerian civil war. Farther afield, official US disapproval of her hard-line colonial stance was stilled after President Kennedy's death by the occasional reminder that military facilities on the strategic Azores islands had not been granted to the USA in perpetuity. In

1967 Pope Paul VI's visit to Portugal was hailed as a diplomatic triumph, but three years later it had turned sour when the same pontiff met the leaders of the liberation movements in the Vatican.

On the military front, the Portuguese found themselves fighting a war of stalemate or attrition. No major towns were lost or bases captured, even in Guinea-Bissau, where the PAIGC was in control of large areas of territory after the mid-1960s. The African guerrillas were not in a position to inflict a military defeat, with the possible exception of those operating in the smallest mainland African territory. As early as 1963 the defence ministry was openly admitting that 15 per cent of Guinea-Bissau lay in the hands of the nationalists. In 1965 the new military commander, General Arnaldo Schulz, publicly declared that the war would be over in six months. Instead the next three years witnessed major guerrilla successes, until, in 1968, Schulz was replaced by General Spínola. By then fears of a Portuguese Dien Bien Phu were beginning to pervade the army and even the sober London *Economist* could headline a piece on Portugal's most troublesome colony 'The War the Portuguese are Losing'.[28]

After more than a decade of warfare the guerrillas showed no sign of giving up or losing. In Mozambique, Frelimo was able to bounce back after General Kaúlza de Arriaga launched the most ambitious counter-offensive of the war (Operation Gordian Knot) against them in 1970. This hard-line officer was also prominently linked with the policy of grouping the population in large protected settlements called *aldeamentos*. These were a partial copy of the American strategic hamlets in Vietnam and were designed to seal the rural population off from the insurgents. By the early 1970s at least a million Angolans had been resettled in this way, and in 1973 Arriaga was claiming that the government intended to shift all rural Africans in Mozambique into *aldeamentos* within five to six years.[29] In its own way such a policy would have been as stark an admission of failure as any military defeat, but upheaval in an unexpected quarter would shortly extricate Portugal from the colonial morass she had got herself into.

The Portuguese army at war

Portuguese officers were markedly affected by participation in what would, after 1945, be the longest colonial war fought by any European or Atlantic power. The experience was all the more traumatic since the Portuguese army had not seen active service since World War I. Until the sudden onset of colonial war, military professionals and members of the wealthier classes had undergone much the same socialising experience. The fact that the military and civilian elite had an identical social outlook and shared values was a boon for Salazar which helped to minimise discontent within the military.

But from 1961 onwards the army began to draw apart from civilian society. No longer were full-time officers regularly mingling with upper and middle-class citizens from the same narrow social circles. In Africa, for year after year, officers would live and fight in a predominantly military society created by the exigencies of war. In time the experience would spawn new values, traditions and grievances that were not immediately those of civilian society. The regime seemed unaware of the subtle change that was coming over the military world, and it promoted the glorification of the army in a vain attempt to keep recruiting figures up. But by the mid-1960s war service in Africa offered little glamour for young Portuguese males. To meet its intake requirements, the government gradually lowered the conditions for entry into the officer corps.[30] Such a decision was forced upon it by the unwillingness of upper and upper-middle class youths to enter the service. Previously these scions of the Portuguese oligarchy had dominated the officer corps of the three services. With the onset of war the social balance in the army was drastically altered. As traditional officer types saw greater security in business, industry or the professions the officer corps came to be recruited increasingly from lower middle-class ranks.

Many of the new officers taking up a military career were from the provinces: few came from well-known Lisbon families. Not a few were from the colonies, motivated chiefly 'by the chance to travel and possibly establish a footing back in Portugal itself'.[31] In the absence of an army career such upward mobility would have been hard to achieve. The post-1961 generation of officers were the sons of shopkeepers, poor landowners and lowly bureaucrats in rural areas and provincial towns whose parents could not have afforded a university education for their sons. Neither would the possibility of satisfactory employment have been easy to realise in many cases. Hence, for this vulnerable social sector, the army seemed (even in the war conditions of the 1960s) a worthwhile career. It afforded an escape from the confines and limited opportunities of small-town Portugal and provided benefits (a smart uniform, entrance to the military academy, promotion, status, a regular officer's commission) that, at least in the beginning, would have outweighed the dangers and inconveniences of being a full-time soldier.

It is seldom appreciated that fundamental changes in the military world were taking place before the African wars. In 1958 the recruitment pattern to the officer corps began to alter drastically when Salazar waived tuition fees for the military academy. For the first time, modest salaries were offered to cadets, and many of the candidates who took advantage of the more flexible recruitment system came from families with no previous military connections and limited economic resources. For the first time a traditionalist Portuguese regime was educating and promoting officers from outside its own circle. (In pre-revolutionary Egypt a parallel development had occurred when, in 1936, the ruling Wafd party opened the military academy to lower-class recruits. Over the next sixteen years, broader recruitment encouraged growing military alienation from the unpopular Farouk monarchy, and in 1952 the Egyptian revolution was in great part led by non-elite officers. Sixteen years also lay between the Portuguese military reforms of 1958 and the *coup* of 25 April 1974.)

The integration of the armed forces with NATO when Portugal became a founder member of the Western alliance in 1949 is another important *ante-bellum* development. Salazar was able to purchase sophisticated weaponry which might not have been forthcoming if, like Franco's Spain, Portugal had remained in political isolation. Until March 1973, when the Guinea insurgents began shooting down Portuguese jet fighters with Sam-7 ground-to-air missiles, the Portuguese always enjoyed superiority in weapons over their nationalist opponents. But the defects of the military leadership failed to turn this into a decisive advantage.

No overall plan to defeat the nationalist forces had been worked out. Military policy remained haphazard and unco-ordinated. Strategy was usually defensive and *ad hoc*, owing more to the judgement of individual officers, be they in Lisbon or in Luanda, than to corporate military planning. Often local military policy was inexplicably changed on the arrival of a new commanding officer. Liaison between senior officers could be further affected by inter-service rivalry, seniority problems, and disputes between Lisbon generals and colonial governors. Rivalry between staff and combat officers has been remarked upon by several sources. Along with Venezuela, Portugal in the 1960s was the only country to retain a staff corps. According to Douglas Porch, 'most armies abandoned them in the mid-nineteenth century', modern military theorists increasingly reacted against the custom of placing a corps of officers in permanent desk jobs.[32] However, even in the midst of a vital war, the military establishment refused to see the sense in alternating officers between troop service and staff duty. The increase in numerical military strength was hardly matched by a qualitative leap in imagination or initiative. Combat officers resented the privileges enjoyed by their desk-bound colleagues, which included higher pay and quicker promotion. They were often angered by the lateness and inaccuracy of operational plans from Lisbon, a situation which the new defence minister, Professor J. M. Silva Cunha, sought to rectify in 1973 when he decreed that all staff officers report to work at 9 a.m. rather than their habitual 2 p.m.[33]

Business commitments and other extra-curricular activities often came between officers and their professional calling and can explain the dilatoriness of the staff; even at the height of the colonial wars, the most senior officers served simultaneously on the boards of large companies. In other Western countries such a practice has been frowned upon in peacetime as well as in war. However, in Portugal the regime deliberately encouraged the coupling of the military elite with the business elite, since it was thought that the enrichment of top-ranking officers would reinforce their loyalty towards the state. This was an accurate assessment. However, military conformity was gained at the expense of military effectiveness in Africa and soured relations between senior and lower-ranking officers; increasingly the junior ranks contrasted their poor pay with the opulent extra salaries being earned by their superiors whose life style was very much that of peacetime officers. By the close of the war the Portuguese army contained the most meagrely paid junior officers in Europe alongside some of the wealthiest generals and admirals. Ultimately, by its efforts to reduce the possibility of friction between the military and civil establishments by integrating the two, the regime had sown much greater discord within the army itself.

Another major error was the subordination of professionalism to political orthodoxy in the promotion of officers. Under Salazar, the cabinet filled higher command posts from lists presented by a selection committee of top generals; under Caetano this job passed from the cabinet to a Supreme Defence Council.[34] However, political reliability often remained the primary criterion in selecting officers for crucial military posts. In war as in peace, professional skill was of secondary importance. As a result, talented officers failed to reach the rank their abilities merited because they were unable to identify with the pro-Salazar military establishment or because they appeared politically too detached. Others were promoted far beyond their talents, having given ample proof of conformity if not of professional competence. In this way short-term political expediency was allowed to interfere with, and seriously retard, long-range military goals.

Military favouritism, bad leadership and profiteering by generals led the disadvantaged half of the army to seek retribution in 1974. Among the first victims of the *coup* were the ninety or so brigadiers and generals who made up the military gerontocracy. Within days, virtually all of them would be axed. However, lower-ranking alienation had been demonstrated much earlier in relation to the military *status quo*. Although outright indiscipline was rare, oral and written evidence from the 1960s and 1970s indicates that many officers were unwilling to confront and tackle the enemy. As early as 1962 a correspondent for *The New Statesman* pointed out how in Angola:

A force of 40,000 Portuguese plus some black units from Mozambique is concentrated in five main areas north and east of Luanda. They guard townships and lines of communications, thus containing revolutionary activity, but they are unwilling, unlike British troops in Malaya, to go into the jungle and bush to hunt for their opponents. The average conscript officer and his platoon can see no point in doing so.[35]

Because of censorship in Lisbon and relative international unconcern with Portugal's African wars, at least until the 1970s, similar contemporary reports are rare. However, in the aftermath of the 1974 *coup* the impression of military apathy conveyed by this quotation was borne out by the testimonies of officers who had served for long periods in Africa. In one interview with an ex-officer who had served four years in Angola (1961–65) the writer was told how officers ordered out on raids would deliberately take their men round in circles and then return to base, rather than attempt to flush the enemy out.[36] Conscript officers were naturally least willing to engage in combat; but the overall calibre of front-line officers was not high, and discipline was often lax. Though performance varied according to the unit, its commander and the scene of operations, as well as guerrilla strength, the army was run and led in a somewhat lethargic way. Although guerrilla numbers were relatively small until the mid-1960s, the military were unable to mop up their opponents either then or later. Given the superiority the Portuguese enjoyed over the nationalists in each major sphere of warfare (numbers, fire-power, communications), low-level military commitment appears a sound explanation for Portugal's African malaise. But with the military so central to national life, few have been willing to probe into a sensitive area of recent history. As a result, it is impossible to say for sure what casualties the Portuguese suffered in Africa, although it is safe to assume that official figures were an underestimate of the true figure.

According to the military attaché of a nation regularly invited to tour the African war zones, 1,500 men had died in action in Guinea-Bissau by the end of 1971. Another 2,000 had been killed in accidents, by tropical disease or from other causes, an amazing comment on Portuguese military efficiency.[37] The comparable figures for Angola, according to the same source, were in the region of 2,500 killed in eight years of fighting; the figure makes no allowance for those who died of other causes.

The rising total of war dead and wounded produced an increasing flow of draft dodgers and military deserters. An estimated 110,000 conscripts failed to report for military service between 1961 and 1974. Most emigrated to France rather than serve their turn, which in 1967 was increased to four years. To make up for this manpower loss the authorities increasingly relied upon black troops, who, by the end of the 1960s, made up over half Portugal's army overseas. In Guinea-Bissau black soldiers actually outnumbered white troops by a ratio of six to one. Only in Mozambique were whites in a majority inside the army.

In 1968, with Salazar gone, the contradictions inherent in Portugal's military role in Africa were not so obvious to full-time and conscript officers as to cause actual dissent inside the forces. Decades of nationalist propaganda and depoliticisation were still able to counter rising anti-war sentiment. Junior officers serving in Africa were not as war-weary or discontented as their American counterparts in Vietnam, fighting a similar jungle war but under much greater insurgent pressure. Day-to-day discipline was maintained. Narcotics were not in widespread use. Nevertheless, internal pressures were building up which in the early 1970s would lead to a parallel degree of alienation with national war aims and their political formulators. Casualty figures for the late 1960s pointed the way. According to one opposition estimate, the number of soldiers killed in Africa up to 1969 was proportionately more than equivalent to the American dead in Vietnam.[38] Per head of population, Portugal also had more men in uniform. With a population in the late 1960s of just over eight million, one in four men of military age was in the services. According to Kenneth Maxwell, the armed forces thus represented a proportion per thousand of the population (30·83) exceeded only by Israel (40·9) and North and South Vietnam (31·66 and 55·36): five times that of the USA, three times that of Britain or Spain.[39]

Figures such as these acted as a long-term catalyst, gradually altering the mood and consciousness of the army once they were translated into human terms. In the context of authoritarian Portugal, the army's involvement in a thankless jungle war was transforming it from a supine instrument of state will into a politically aware force whose thoughts were increasingly at variance with the antiquated ideas of its political masters back in Lisbon.

The *coup* of 25 April 1974

In 1968 it was with some percipience that Richard Bourne, correspondent of *The Guardian*, wrote that 'comparing the military and budgetary requirements today with three years ago, it is clear that if they continue to grow at this rate, something will snap long before another seven years are out'.[40] By the early 1970s divisions were already starting to appear in the civilian and military establishments, caused by the absence of any military breakthrough and the growing financial and social strains imposed by a war which entered its tenth year in 1971. Leading businessmen who had previously backed the government's uncompromising stand began to modify their view once it became apparent that the African colonies were a less important export market than western Europe. Between 1960 and 1969 the proportion of exports going to the colonies actually fell from 34 per cent to 25 per cent and by 1973 had declined to only 15 per cent.[41] The formation of the European Free Trade Association in 1958, with Portugal a founder member, and the entry of Britain (her main trading partner) into the EEC fifteen years later, helped to orientate the economy more closely towards that of other west European countries, which by 1973 accounted for fully two-thirds of both imports and exports.

As their economic priorities shifted away from Africa, some of the leading financial oligarchs began discreetly to lobby for a federal solution which would involve the creation of a United States of Portugal or a new Lusitanian commonwealth perhaps drawing in Brazil as well. Marcelo Caetano himself had expressed federalist views during his liberal phase in the early 1960s. In the early 1970s these were taken up by General António de Spínola, the only real war hero to emerge before 1974. As governor-general of Guinea-Bissau from 1968 to 1973 he sought to stem the advance of the PAIGC insurgents by launching ambitious welfare and community projects in a bid to win the hearts and minds of the local population. He used his troops as a sort of community service and made many public relations tours in Portugal's most troubled colony which he ensured were well covered by the media in Lisbon. While waging this propaganda offensive, Spínola still believed (as he had told Salazar himself in 1968) that the war in Guinea was militarily unwinnable. Nevertheless, his imaginative policies, allied to the latest counter-insurgency methods in the field, may have slowed down the PAIGC advance, a fact which was enough to earn Spínola a hero's welcome when he returned to Portugal in 1973. Emboldened by his reception, the general decided to set out his master plan for the colonies in a book, *Portugal e o futuro* (*Portugal and the Future*), which came out on 22 February 1974. The publisher was a subsidiary of CUF, the country's leading economic combine, and, despite his baroque literary style, *Portugal e o futuro* ran to three editions within a fortnight. Caetano had read it before publication and, although he preferred greater autonomy for the colonies to Spínola's scheme for a loose federation, he did not attempt to have it suppressed. His attitude hardened after the outraged reaction of military *ultras* like Generals Kaúlza de Arriaga, Henrique Troni and Joaquim Luz Cunha. Having actually suggested to President Tomás that power be transferred to Spínola and his like-minded military colleague General Francisco Costa Gomes, Caetano ended up sacking the pair after they had refused, on 14 March 1974, to make a speech of loyalty in favour of existing policies in Africa. The prime minister's erratic behaviour during the final months of his rule indicates just how bereft he was of a clear-sighted political strategy towards the war and its increasingly serious domestic repercussions.

Power slowly gravitated into the hands of diehard *situacionistas* who favoured internationally unacceptable solutions such as the total integration of Portugal and Africa or a hand-over of responsibility to white settlers. This was an idea increasingly promoted by Jorge Jardim, the influential settler leader in Mozambique, who was actually drawing up plans for a unilateral declaration of independence during the last months of the Caetano regime. A rapid deterioration in the military situation in the province during 1973 had convinced him that white settlers, along with moderate elements of the black population, would be as capable as the army of containing the Frelimo guerrillas. Hitherto confined to the northern Tete province, Frelimo had begun operations in central Mozambique, much to the dismay of white settlers, who stoned Portuguese troops on a number of occasions in 1973–74 for supposedly failing to provide adequate protection. Abroad, the Portuguese army in Mozambique was subject to widespread criticism but for a different reason. In July 1973, on the eve of Caetano's visit to Britain to commemorate the 600th anniversary of the Alliance, *The Times* revealed that 300 – 400 villagers had been massacred in the Wiriyamu district of Tete province by troops under DGS (i.e. secret police) command. News of the outrage brought deep discredit on the Portuguese government and encouraged international recognition for the liberation forces in Guinea who had declared their country independent in 1973, up to sixty countries recognising the PAIGC as the sovereign authority despite the Portuguese presence.

Back in Portugal in July 1973 after his unhappy visit to London, Caetano faced unrest among full-time officers, who bitterly resented the passage of a new Bill, decree law 353/73 (13 July 1973), which gave conscripted officers (*milicianos*) parity with full-timers. It was this internal military squabble over a professional grievance that led to the revolutionary upheaval the following year. Unwittingly the defence minister, J. M. Silva Cunha (a civilian), had passed the law to encourage conscript officers to stay on and so ease the acute shortage due to the reluctance of Portuguese males to join the colours. However, full-timers who had worked their way slowly through the military academy and spent years in the bush before reaching the rank of captain or major did not take kindly to this attempt at rationalisation. A radical soldier like Major Ernesto Melo Antunes dismissed their protests as emanating from 'a reactionary co-operative of privilege'. He and more politically aware soldiers had been influenced by the writings of Che Guevara, Mao-Tse-tung and Amílcar Cabral, which some of them first came across as recommended texts in the counter-insurgency classes in military school. In the course of time these Marxist tracts helped to turn several apolitical lower-ranking officers into prospective revolutionaries. Some of their colleagues had already come to Africa imbued with radical ideas. Most *milicianos*, for instance, had been conscripted as students, and under Caetano the universities remained a hotbed of unrest. By conscripting and

then promoting student officers Portugal was in effect importing shiploads
of Trojan horses into its creaking empire.[42] It did not take long for many of
them to develop considerable respect for the political beliefs and military
skills of their nationalist opponents, while reacting with increasing
cynicism to official propaganda which proclaimed that Portugal was one,
from Minho (on the Spanish frontier) to Timor in the East Indies. Even
captains and majors who were less politicised no longer believed in the
principles of Salazarist ideology that justified their presence in the three
rebellious colonies. The realisation that it was countries like the USA,
West Germany and South Africa that were really doing well out of the
African colonies, not underdeveloped Portugal, was another factor which
eroded military confidence in her African mission. Multinational firms
dominated the economy of mineral-rich Angola, as well as Mozambique,
to an even greater extent than in Portugal, and nationalist officers were
outraged to discover that they were being used as fodder to maintain the
flow of mineral wealth and profit not to Portugal but to Johannesburg,
New York and Dusseldorf.

Military discontent which had been latent before 1973 broke through to
the surface after the controversy over the 1973 decree-law. This
professional rumpus did not prevent the small core of uniformed political
activists and the larger mass of simply war-weary officers drawing closer
together. If the non-political professionals did not share the creed of the
Marxist fraction, they had many of the same grievances. Low salaries (the
pay of junior officers who risked death in Africa was at the level of an office
clerk's in Lisbon), long postings abroad and unpleasant living conditions
were among the principal complaints. When civilian reactionaries in the
Portuguese Legion tried to use the military by holding a Congress of Ex-
servicemen in the early summer of 1973, 400 military personnel signed a
public letter disassociating themselves from it. So deep was the anger of
junior officers exhausted by years in the field and determined not to be
made scapegoats for a military defeat that they showed little fear of
retribution from the authorities. However, army malcontents were more
discreet in preparing the first meeting of the military movement which
would become known as the Armed Forces Movement (MFA).

On 9 September 1973 about 140 junior officers met quietly at a
farmhouse near the Alentejan town of Évora which was owned by a cousin
of one of the participants, twenty-six-year-old Dinis de Almeida. The
discussion was lively and sometimes heated. Following a pattern common
to most modern armies, infantry officers were most rebellious, cavalry the
most conservative, while the engineers and artillery officers stood
somewhere between the two.[43] At future meetings, openly subversive
courses of action were discussed with increasing frequency, but it was not
until November 1973 that the proposal for *coup* actually arose. It came

from a high-ranking officer, Lieutenant-Colonel Luís Ataíde Banazol, and it was not well received. Younger officers were not impressed by Banazol's proposal to occupy the Evora garrison, and regarded it as an opportunist gesture by someone about to be posted to Guinea. But at least talk of a *coup* had cleared the air, and the subject resurfaced at the next general meeting of the MFA, which was held in Óbidos, a town north of Lisbon, on 1 December 1973. Eighty delegates turned up who claimed to represent several hundred officers. Moderate motions were passed in the main, advocating continued protests through official channels rather than anything more drastic. This disappointed left-wing soldiers who saw a military revolt as the only way to extricate themselves from their African Vietnam and so, at another meeting on 8 December at Costa da Caparica, across the Tagus from Lisbon, it was decided to set up an inner steering committee which would be able to plan activities in a more conspiratorial way. This development, a watershed in the evolution of the MFA, marked a switch away from the military trade-union format, where large bloc-votes were thrown on the side of caution, towards a more tightly knit conspiratorial force. The new steering committee comprised only three people, Captain Vasco Lourenço, Major Otelo de Carvalho, who was to take charge of military organisation, and Major Vítor Alves, who helped to draw up the MFA's political programme.

The revoking of the controversial July decree-law by the government on 21 December 1973 did not deter the MFA. However, around the same time it almost got embroiled in a right-wing plot devised by General Kaúlza de Arriaga in order to seize power from Caetano while the latter was on a visit to Spain. Kaúlza approached some MFA officers who proved receptive, but radical members of the MFA's co-ordinating committee foiled him by publicly revealing what he had in mind. The episode showed how rudimentary the political awareness of some of the MFA members was, and it alerted the authorities for the first time to the danger of a *coup* from the soldiers' new pressure group. Soon after, known radical officers like Carlos Fabião, Dinis de Almeida and Vasco Lourenço were switched to different postings, giving them an ideal opportunity to make new contacts and establish MFA cells over a whole number of new units.

In the middle of this proselytising by the MFA Spínola's book appeared, and it acted as a catalyst which accelerated events. Left-wingers who thought many of his views smacked of neo-colonialism were nevertheless glad to witness the emergence of a rebellious senior officer who stood a good chance of rallying his uncommitted colleagues in the event of a *coup*. Plans now went ahead for a full-scale assembly of the MFA which took place at Cascais on 5 March 1974. Two hundred officers attended, the majority convinced that the old regime had to be displaced by force. But the participants argued through the night about the draft programme for a post-dictatorial Portugal drawn up by Melo Antunes as well as over the respective merits of Spínola and General Costa Gomes as leaders of the revolution. The authorities rapidly found out about these deliberations, as they had about past meetings, but Caetano was paralysed by indecision and the DGS no longer had the ability to act on its own volition in the way that the PIDE could do in Salazar's last years. The government's disarray was highlighted when an abortive *coup* took place on 16 March 1974 in the wake of Spínola's dismissal from his top military job. Without the knowledge of the leading MFA conspirators, officers loyal to him decided to move their troops on Lisbon from Caldas da Rainha, fifty miles to the north. The rebels, Major Casanova Ferreira and Major Monje, along with 200 men of the 5th Infantry, were rapidly intercepted by loyalist forces. But the hard-core MFA conspirators were left at liberty unless sent to new postings, and the final agreed draft of the MFA's political programme was published on 24 March. The document set out, as its main aims, the overthrow of the Salazar–Caetano dictatorship, the decolonisation of the empire, the introduction of genuine democracy at home, and the redemption of military honour. In detail the programme was not revolutionary, but General Spínola took exception to several aspects of it, especially the clauses referring to the colonies. He nevertheless agreed to support the plotters in principle while keeping out of the operational planning of the *coup*. This was acceptable to most MFA officers (although the more radical ones had reservations about Spínola from the beginning), since soundings carried out after his dismissal revealed that a wide cross-section of the army would not now resist a *coup*.

In reality this crude exercise in psephology proved to be accurate. By 23 April 1974 arrangements for a *coup* had been finalised, the date chosen being 25 April. The signal for the plotters to move was to be *Grândola, Vila Morena*, a song by the folk singer José Afonso which was to be broadcast by a Lisbon radio station at twenty-five minutes past midnight. By 3 a.m. on the morning of 25 April the insurgents had already occupied the centre of the capital. No resistance was mounted by loyalist forces. The *Estado Novo* simply collapsed without a single shot fired in its defence. Caetano, who had taken refuge in the National Republican Guard headquarters in the Carmo district of Lisbon, handed over power to General Spínola, having earlier refused to surrender to Captain Salgueiro Maia of the MFA. In this way the outgoing premier sought to ensure that power did not end up 'in the hands of the mob'. Spínola's position *vis-à-vis* the MFA was strengthened as a result. But time would quickly show that the 25 April revolt had been not simply a *coup* but the opening salvo in a full-blooded revolution whose course nobody could with ease predict.

Notes

1 See Marcelo Caetano, *Depoimento*, Distribuidora Record, Rio de Janeiro, 1974, and *Minhas Memórias de Salazar*, Editorial Verbo, Lisbon, 1977.
2 Figueiredo, *Fifty Years*, p. 57.
3 Wiarda, *Corporatism and Development*, p. 255.
4 Bradford, *Portugal*, p. 91.
5 *Ibid.*
6 Granting women the vote probably had something to do with the publication of a survey shortly beforehand which found that, as in other countries, women were rather more conservative than men.
7 Lester A. Sobel (ed.), *The Portuguese Revolution, 1974–1976*, Facts on File, New York, 1976, p. 16.
8 Nogueira Pinto, *Portugal*, p. 189.
9 Otelo Saraiva de Carvalho, *Alvorado em abril*, Livraria Bertrand, Lisbon, 1977, p. 63.
10 See Norman Blume, 'SEDES: an example of opposition in a conservative authoritarian state', *Government and Opposition*, summer 1977.
11 Robinson, *Contemporary Portugal*, p. 170.
12 Interview with Francisco Pinto Balsemão, Lisbon, 12 December 1979.
13 Interview with Adelino Amaro da Costa, Lisbon, 11 December 1979.
14 *Ibid.*
15 Keefe, *Area Handbook*, p. 323.
16 *Ibid.*, p. 350.
17 *Ibid.*, pp. 354–5.
18 Robinson, *op. cit.*, p. 175.
19 *Sunday Times* Insight Team, *Insight on Portugal*, p. 68.
20 Robinson, *op. cit.*, p. 176.
21 Figueiredo, *op. cit.*, p. 72.
22 Malyn Newitt, *Portugal in Africa. The Last Hundred Years*, Hurst, London, 1981, p. 164.
23 Thomas H. Henriksen, 'Portugal in Africa: comparative notes on counter-insurgency', *Orbis*, Vol. 21, No. 2, summer 1977, p. 401.
24 Newitt, *op. cit.*, p. 220–1.
25 José Freire Antunes, 'Norton de Matos, um general do império', *Diário de Noticias*, 11 November 1980.
26 Henriksen, *op. cit.*, p. 409.
27 A good investigation into Cabral's death is provided by Basil Davidson's 'The men who killed black Africa's top guerrilla', *Sunday Times*, 8 April 1973.
28 *The Economist*, 27 April 1968, pp. 21–2.
29 Thomas H. Henriksen, *Mozambique. A History*, Rex Collings, London, 1978, p. 194.
30 One senior officer explained to the Insight team of *The Sunday Times* how a mark of sixteen out of twenty barely secured him entry into the Military Academy in 1953, while a decade later 'they were passing people with ten or less'. In the air force, we also learn, a place in the academy was so coveted in the 1950s that 'some 300 applications would be received for thirty places', a far cry from the mid-1960s, by which time these figures had been reversed. See *Sunday Times* Insight Team, *op. cit.*, p. 16.
31 *Ibid.*, pp. 16–17.
32 Douglas Porch, *The Portuguese Armed Forces and the Revolution*, Croom

Helm, London, 1977, p. 41.
33 Harsgor, *Portugal in Revolution*, p. 14.
34 Porch, *op. cit.*, p. 43.
35 Verrier, 'Portugal on the brink'.
36 Interview, Lisbon, 28 March 1977.
37 A. J. Venter, *Portugal's Guerrilla War. The Campaign for Africa*, Cape Town, 1973, p. 75.
38 Figueiredo, *Fifty Years*, p. 184.
39 Maxwell, 'Neat revolution', p. 30.
40 Richard Bourne, in *The Guardian*, 20 February 1968.
41 Robin Blackburn, 'The test in Portugal', *New Left Review*, September–December 1974, p. 9.
42 Harsgor, *op. cit.*, p. 13.
43 *Sunday Times* Insight team, *op. cit.*, p. 35.

9

'Entering the age of Aquarius'
Revolution, 1974–75

The Revolution of Flowers, April–September 1974

The Lisbon *coup* of 25 April took world governments completely by surprise. Perhaps unable to believe that a *coup* in dictatorial Portugal could ever be progressive, authoritarian Brazil and Spain welcomed the revolution. South Africa recognised the new government as early as 28 April even though the passage of a few months would quickly show that the upheaval would have disastrous consequences for white rule in Rhodesia and in southern Africa as a whole. Other non-communist but democratic Western states regarded the revolution as long overdue in a country as archaic as Portugal. However, little or nothing was known about the country's new military rulers or about the ideas that had motivated their action against a regime which the military had hitherto staunchly defended. The US embassy had not established any prior contact with the opposition and the CIA did not know what was happening outside the Tomás–Caetano cliques.[1] British intelligence (whose Lisbon desk had been occupied in wartime by Graham Greene and Malcolm Muggeridge) was similarly in the dark. One Western diplomat, observing the MFA shortly after 25 April, candidly admitted that 'we don't know why they are doing all this and we don't even know who most of them are'.[2]

Puzzlement also existed in the minds of the Portuguese, who suddenly witnessed the demise of a regime which, with all its faults, not a few had regarded as a permanent and reassuring landmark. In the remoter villages of Trás-os-Montes, in the north-east, news of the *coup* did not reach some communities until well into May 1974. But, generally, few tears were shed for the departing order. The prospect of a swift and amicable end to the unpopular colonial wars evoked nationwide rejoicing. Northern Portugal's hostility to the extreme leftist orientation of the revolution in 1975 should not obscure the fact that the fall of the undemocratic regime was broadly welcomed north of the Tagus. Oporto and a few of the other northern centres had been active strongholds of the democratic opposition during Salazar's time – opposition fuelled by Salazar's policy of locating major economic projects in the Lisbon conurbation to the detriment of other centres. In Lisbon, the most politically aware spot in the country and the scene of most of the drama of 25 April, the response of the citizenry to the *coup* was a joyful one. Soldiers were treated as conquering heroes and, besides being liberally plied with food and refreshment, many were given red carnations which became the symbol of the revolution in its initial euphoric phase.

The only incident to mar the carnival atmosphere of late April occurred outside the secret police headquarters in Lisbon when a nervy DGS man shot into a crowd milling outside the building, killing four people. Otherwise General Francisco da Costa Gomes, the new commander-in-chief of the army, was not far wrong when he claimed in May that the military had carried out 'the most dignified revolution in contemporary history'.[3] As the downfall of 'fascist' regimes went, the transfer of power from civilian reactionaries to military progressives was an extremely smooth one. MFA uncertainty about its own strength within the armed forces at large brought about the elevation of General Spínola as the first post-dictatorial head of state. Spínola was essentially a compromise figure who had appeared radical in the last months of the dictatorship by advocating a Portuguese commonwealth as a means of escaping from the thirteen-year war. Caetano had surrendered to him personally on the afternoon of the 25th, informing his successor, 'You must take care. You must keep control. I am frightened by the idea of power loose in the streets.'[4]

The next day, at a press conference in Lisbon, Spínola announced the setting up of a Junta of National Salvation (JSN) to help him run the country. It consisted of seven military officers – Spínola himself, Brigadier Diogo Neto and General Carlos Galvão de Melo of the air force, General Costa Gomes and Brigadier Jaime Silvério Marques for the army, and Captains José Pinheiro de Azevedo and António Alba Rosa Coutinho for the navy. Below the JSN there was a seven-man co-ordinating committee which comprised the main architects of the April *coup*, though not Major Otelo de Carvalho. The co-ordinating committee had no statutory powers, but its members were automatically drafted on to a Council of State which also contained the JSN, two Spinolist aides and five 'outstanding citizens', among them Professor Rui Luís Gomes, a veteran left-wing oppositionist and newly installed rector of Oporto University, Dr José Azeredo Perdigão, a wealthy liberal lawyer and director of the Gulbenkian Foundation, and Professor Diogo Freitas do Amaral, a member of the Corporative Chamber under the previous regime, and soon to found his own political party.

The formation of a provisional government three weeks after the coup would complete the new power structure, a confusing one in which it would soon become increasingly difficult to see where real authority lay. The MFA was not the government but, thanks to being the only strongly organised pressure group in the army, it was able decisively to influence the course of events from the outset. This was made clear on 26 April, when

Spínola unfurled a political programme which was based very much on the MFA's own original blueprint for a new Portugal. Among the measures announced were the abolition of the secret police, the Mocidade, the Legião and other remaining *Estado Novo* institutions, the removal of all civil governors, the abolition of censorship and the release of all political prisoners. Freedom of thought, expression and association (liberties which, in other words, allowed for political parties and trade unions) was guaranteed. It was announced that the solution to the overseas war had to be political, not military. Plans were drawn up to cleanse the armed forces of prominent supporters of the old regime (around twenty-five generals and admirals known as the 'rheumatic brigade' being forcibly retired in the next few weeks). Perhaps most important of all, free elections for a constituent assembly were promised within twelve months.

Late in April some of the exiled political leaders who would play an important role in the elections began to return. Mário Soares, lawyer to the Delgado family and leader of the Socialist Party (which had been founded in West Germany in the last year of the dictatorship), received an emotional welcome from supporters when the train bringing him back from Paris pulled into Santo Apolónia station in Lisbon. Soares soon took up the slogan 'O Povo está com o MFA' (The people are with the MFA'), which would dominate left-wing rallies for the first twelve months or so of the revolution. But only a short time before, in a memoir completed in 1973, he had stated fairly bluntly that:

> One knows what political intervention by an army means, however well it may be intended, and that nothing can be looked for but more and worse problems as a result.[5]

Soares was giving voice to the antagonism which has long existed between the military and the civilian political elite, the latter having been dominated by the legal profession through several historical epochs. The year 1926 had witnessed the triumph of 'militarism over attorneyism' and it remained to be seen what the outcome would be if the two professions dominating Lisbon politics once again fell out. All for the moment was sweetness and light between the holders of diverse political viewpoints who had been brought together by their opposition to a reactionary and blinkered dictatorship. This was demonstrated on 30 April when Álvaro Cunhal, the PCP general secretary, flew into Lisbon from Prague after fourteen years in exile. At Portela airport he was met by General Galvão de Melo, a conservative memeber of the JSN, who startled a disoriented Cunhal by telling him that Portuguese television was at his disposal that evening if he wanted to make a speech. Galvão de Melo, a dashing air force officer, who had a bodyguard consisting of a troupe of gypsies, would be one of the 'characters' of the revolution. He had resigned his air force commission in 1966 in protest at the fact that the government had purchased poor-quality planes which he considered were dangerous to anyone who flew in them.[6] This act of defiance earned him praise in Cunhal's *Rumo da Vitória* (*The Road to Victory:* a book in which he reveals the surprising extent of opposition to the wars in Africa on the part of ordinary soldiers during the 1960–64 period). Later, in democratic Portugal, Carlos Galvão de Melo would emerge as strongly anti-communist, as indeed did Jaime Neves and José Sanches Osório, the two MFA officers who toured the capital after 25 April with Jaime Serra, a PCP central committee member, inviting him to choose any building vacated by the old regime for the PCP's new headquarters.

The live-and-let-live atmosphere of the time is perhaps summed up by a comment Spínola made to Cunhal when they met:

> *Senhor douter*, I greatly respect your revolutionary past and your struggle against fascism, but now we can collaborate democratically because the MFA has already destroyed fascism and we do not really need any more revolution.[7]

This naive, almost touching statement reflected the political innocence of a man who was a competent soldier and a fine leader of men but whose experience of politics was extremely limited and whose natural ability in the Machiavellian art left much to be desired. Born on 11 April 1910 into a well-to-do landed family which farmed around Estremoz in the province of Alentejo, António Sebastião Ribeiro de Spínola chose the army as a career, graduating from military school with the rank of second lieutenant in 1933, the year in which the *Estado Novo* was formally established. His family, descended from Genoese merchants who had helped medieval Portugal to build its first navy, was a pillar of the conservative establishment. His father held a top post in the ministry of finance and, after his retirement in the 1950s, worked to revive the Portuguese Legion. In the Spanish Civil War the young Spínola commanded a detachment of Portuguese volunteers fighting on Franco's side; later he was sent by the Portuguese high command to Nazi Germany for training with the Wehrmacht.[8] In Berlin he picked up the habit of wearing a monocle in his right eye, which, along with his riding crop and African cane, became one of his chief trade-marks. Looking not unlike Erich von Stroheim, Spínola, a teetotaller and non-smoker, was decidedly conservative in his habits. During World War II he went to the Russian front as an observer with the German forces, and it was rumoured that his reports convinced Salazar that Hitler's cause was lost, thus strengthening Portugal's commitment to neutrality.[9] During 1958 Major Spínola was instrumental in maintaining public order in Lisbon without employing excessive force during Delgado's opposition bid for the presidency. Later, in the colonial wars, he made a habit of applying for tough military postings, something that won him the respect of the men who served under him. Unlike so many of his colleagues, Spínola was not an armchair general but one who was actually prepared to go into the combat zone and take part in operations against the enemy. By the early 1970s he was being described as the Montgomery of the Portuguese army, and foreign commentators were already marking him out as a coming man in Lisbon politics even before the 1973–74 crisis blew up. With a well oiled publicity machine playing up his achievements, Spínola displayed marked ambition as well as a certain contrariness: officers who incurred his displeasure were banished to dreary postings in the hinterland of Guinea-Bissau.

Spínola's proudest moment may have come on 15 May 1974, when he was inaugurated president in the Hall of Mirrors of the pink rococo palace at Queluz. More than a hundred foreign ambassadors were present, and this ceremony also marked the formation of a predominantly civilian government. Two long-standing opponents of the dictatorship, Raul Rego and Francisco Pereira de Moura, had been marked down as likely choices for prime minister. The MFA certainly then viewed these men – one a newspaper editor, the other a university professor – with much favour. However, Spínola chose as prime minister sixty-nine-year-old Adelino Palma Carlos, a wealthy business lawyer and former dean of the Lisbon University law faculty who had belonged to the anti-Salazar opposition but had never shown any great concern for social or economic issues. During his brief tenure as prime minister this gregarious but patrician figure showed himself to be a typical First Republic politician. He formed a fourteen-man government, all of them civilians, with the exception of the defence minister, Lieutenant-Colonel Firmino Miguel, a Spínola supporter. No fewer than five members of the new government had been students of both Palma Carlos and Caetano, which was one of the first indications of just how intimate and narrow the political elite would remain even in the midst of revolution. Four of the ministers were independent non-party figures. Two belonged to a new moderate centre party, the PPD (Popular Democrats), which called itself social democratic and was pro-European and progressive capitalist in outlook. The PPD had been founded in May 1974 by three of the leading dissidents in Caetano's National Assembly: Francisco Sá Carneiro, who became party leader and was minister without portfolio, Joaquim Magalhães Mota and Francisco Pinto Balsemão. The PPD would move rapidly to the right during the revolution, but at the outset its policies were very close to those of the Socialist Party, and 'in the first four months for many people (including future deputies) it was often a matter of chance or whim which of the two they joined'.[10] The PPD talked of socialism and called in 1974 for the nationalisation of monopolies and other key sectors of the economy. This use of left-wing rhetoric by politicians whose party would later be deemed

insufficiently socialist to warrant membership of the Socialist
International, alienated moderate liberals and conservatives, and
prevented the formation of a single moderate centre party in the summer
of 1974. Instead, during July a progressive conservative party emerged
called the Centre Social Democrats (CDS). Founded by Diogo Freitas do
Amaral, a thirty-two-year-old law professor and former academic
colleague of Caetano, it emerged from a plethora of right-wing groups and
survived because it steered clear of military plots and was very skilfully
led. During 1974–75 the CDS stood against the revolutionary tide and
refused to indulge in any left-wing posturing. Adelino Amaro da Costa, one
of its founders, was the first politician publicly to criticise the course of the
revolution, in a newspaper article published in June 1974.[11] To the left, the
CDS was a disguised fascist party: the heirs of the old regime in
democratic clothing.[12] The claim was not totally without foundation.
Many CDS leaders had been in the Caetanist bureacracy before 25 April
and the party's appeal was directed towards those groups which were most
content with the old order. Nevertheless, the CDS was progressive
Christian Democrat in orientation rather than reactionary, the party
favouring a mixed economy along west European lines. None of its leaders
entered any of the six provisional governments Portugal witnessed during
the revolution.

By contrast the Socialist Party (PS) would be a member of all but one of
these administrations. Three members, Mário Soares, Francisco Salgado
Zenha and Raul Rego, entered the Palma Carlos government as ministers
of foreign affairs, justice and social communications. From the outset the
Socialists would be hindered by the lack of a strong working-class
organisational base. Nevertheless, they had a formidable asset in their
leader, Dr Soares, a stirring orator and outgoing public figure who, in the
months to come, would show himself to be an extremely shrewd political
orator.

Two other parties represented in the cabinet were the Communists and
the Popular Democratic Movement (MDP). The MDP was an ambiguous
grouping which claimed to be a broad anti-fascist front, a role it had
certainly played before 25 April. However, after the *coup* it rapidly
emerged as a communist support organisation, despite attempts to
disguise its partisan image, and by the autumn of 1974 the supporters of
other political tendencies had abandoned it. Francisco Pereira de Moura,
the cerebral MDP leader, was minister without portfolio in the Palma
Carlos government. Once shorn of its neutral disguise the MDP came to be
described as the party of the 'recuperated', since it included many
communists who had left the party only to rejoin it after going through a
Trotskyite or Maoist phase. Miguel Urbano Rodrigues, the editor of *O
Diário*, the main communist daily newspaper, was one PCP militant who

broke ranks only later to rejoin the orthodox communist fold.

One of the early surprises of the revolution was the inclusion of the PCP in government. Álvaro Cunhal and Avelino Gonçalves, a veteran communist functionary, accepted Spínola's invitation to become minister without portfolio and minister of labour. For the first time since the end of World War II, communists were members of a major west European government. This deeply alarmed NATO circles, and Portugal was no longer made privy to certain classified information. Spínola tried to allay the fears of foreign governments, particularly Washington, by pointing out that the PCP had played no role in the *coup* and would probably be less dangerous inside than outside government. Perhaps the principal reason for bringing the PCP into government was to hold back the labour unrest that was the inevitable legacy of decades of depressed wages and appalling working conditions. With its base among the urban proletariat, the PCP seemed to be the one force capable of preventing industrial unrest from seriously damaging an already shaky economy. Cunhal, for his part, was prepared to be Spínola's policeman, since he feared a right-wing backlash in the face of major popular unrest, and he was anxious to present the PCP as an essentially moderate force to the nation at large, mindful of elections due to be held in 1975.

But, despite the PCP's best efforts, Portugal was engulfed in a gigantic wave of strikes during the summer of 1974. Industrial workers in the Lisbon and Oporto regions demanded a minimum wage of of 6,000 escudos per month, a forty-hour week and a more thoroughgoing *saneamento* (purging) of employers and managers who were connected with the old regime. Extreme-left groups, which were proliferating in Lisbon especially, also encouraged workers to institute self-management in enterprises where they had been locked out. The PCP was furious at seeing its lack of control over the working class so noisily displayed. It organised demonstrations against a strike of bakers, which it described as 'the most serious moment of the reactionary offensive'.[13] Indeed, the revolutionary wave that surged forth from the working class in 1974 was to find its most determined opponent in the party that was seen abroad as presenting the main threat of red revolution in Portugal. Refusing to place itself at the head of the popular movement of the oppressed, the PCP preferred to move its cadres sideways into positions of institutional power. Communists and MDP fellow-travellers took control of much of local government and the state media after 25 April 1974. These were areas which needed to be purged of large numbers of extreme right-wing sympathisers, and since the party was, initially, the only organised political force in the country capable of carrying out this task, no immediate friction occurred with other political groups. However, the newly created PS and PPD grew increasingly uneasy as the PCP began to seize control of other power-points. The party derived a lot of influence by gaining access to some of the vast archives of the secret police after 25 April. Given the number of people who collaborated with the regime in various ways, the information contained in the PIDE files was a powerful weapon in the hands of the PCP. General Galvão de Melo, who headed a commission investigating the PIDE, was determined to ensure that the communists would not be able to use it for their own ends and, interestingly, he would remain at liberty during the whole course of the revolution, despite his right-wing views. According to persistent Lisbon rumour, he remained untouched because he had taken the precaution of photocopying and dispatching to a safe deposit vault in Switzerland documents which allegedly compromised military figures in the new regime. Certain MFA figures were indeed vulnerable from this angle, since before their radicalisation they had behaved very brutally towards captured insurgents while in action in Africa.

Another matter which led to disagreement among the power brokers in the new regime was the fate of the *Estado Novo* leadership. On 26 April Caetano and Tomás had been flown to Madeira, where they were held in custody in a small palace. Of his own accord, Spínola decided to send Salazar's successors into exile rather than put them on trial, and on 20 May a Portuguese air force jet flew them to Brazil. (For a time Dr Caetano lived on the twenty-seventh floor of the São Paulo Hilton Hotel before moving to Rio de Janeiro, where he was professor of law at an exclusive private university until his death on 26 October 1980. He had vowed never to go back to Portugal, unlike his comrade in misfortune ex-President Tomás, who returned in 1978 and was sometimes to be seen shopping in the Chiado, the capital's main shopping centre.)

After disagreements about various aspects of government policy, the first major confrontation between Spínola and the MFA took place in July 1974. The president sought to capitalise on his mounting popularity, in the north especially, by getting permission for the holding of a referendum before 31 October in order to give himself popular legitimacy. Palma Carlos brought his proposal before the Council of State along with a recommendation that elections for a constituent assembly be postponed until the end of 1976. Both demands ran counter to the MFA's own programme, and not wanting to be responsible for a confrontation, the Council of State rejected them. Palma Carlos then resigned, along with the first provisional government, and Spínola sought to replace him with the outgoing defence minister, Firmino Miguel. The MFA rejected his candidate, and two of its own leading members, Colonel Vasco Gonçalves and Major Melo Antunes, emerged as likely candidates to succeed Palma Carlos.

Antunes, a shrewd, intelligent and widely read officer, Spínola dismissed as 'a dangerous communist'. If he had to choose between the two, he intimated, he would rather have Gonçalves, the most senior member of the MFA (in terms of military rank) and a wealthy man who ran his own engineering firm and had a large stake in a money-changing business founded by his father. Spínola considered that such an officer would hardly be predisposed to excessive political radicalism, which was a fair assumption. However, time would swiftly reveal Gonçalves to be a convinced Marxist and a committed supporter of the PCP. Aged fifty-three, he had spent much of his life in the artillery and served several tours of duty in the colonies. A rather aloof man, he suffered from insomnia as well as periodic fits of depression, and at other times he could become heated and overexcited, traits which would make him a very controversial figure when the revolution reached a climax in 1975.

Interestingly, Gonçalves was extremely puritanical, despite his political radicalism. After becoming prime minister, he spoke out angrily about the fact that since 25 April, pornographic literature had become a commonplace sight in shops and pavement bookstalls. The showing of the highly explicit film *Last Tango in Paris* on Portuguese television also failed to please him, but it was an uphill task to try and maintain moral decorum in a country which had emerged from fifty years of stifling social conformity. In vain did the PCP denounce a Lisbon revue of naked German blondes in black leather jackets as 'another CIA plot'.[14] Even Lisbon prostitutes felt sufficiently confident in the liberated atmosphere of 1974 to launch a campaign for their civil rights. On 28 May 1974 the *Diário de Lisboa* published their manifesto, in which it was pointed out that:

> they had to practise illegally what was the most ancient profession in the world and that although their lives were generally considered 'easy', this was far from being the case; the manifesto went on to demand the creation of a union where 'free from all puritan pressures, they could discuss the problems of their class'. Their main concerns were their exploitation by pimps, the need to protect minors . . . the promotion of a 'free pavement' aimed at 'developing tourism' and opposition to the 'scandalous activities of conservative colleagues who only practice in expensive nightclubs'. They offered their support to the MFA. For a period of a year, all ranks below that of lieutenant would only be charged half price.[15]

In a turbulent revolutionary atmosphere, law-and-order did not break down entirely. However, the police were unwilling to enforce the law too strenuously and they virtually disappeared from the streets during 1974–75. In Lisbon especially, policemen remained in their barracks or went on patrol in districts they knew would be free of trouble. Accordingly, the maintenance of the rule of law and the prevention of civil disorder soon became major priorities for the new authorities. During July 1974 a new militia, known by its acronym, COPCON (Operational Command for the Continent), was formed in order to preserve public order. Five thousand strong, COPCON was considered an elite force, since it included picked volunteers, the best shots, the best signals material and the finest light armour. Its commander was Otelo Saraiva de Carvalho, the chief architect of the April *coup*, who had been promoted to brigadier in July at the same time as he was appointed military governor of Lisbon. This represented a formidable array of power in the hands of the thirty-six-year-old ex-major. It had been Spínola himself who had personally awarded Carvalho his promotional stripes, but, not long before, the general had declared that he should never have got beyond the rank of sergeant. A warm and direct personality who was universally known as Otelo, Carvalho was the complete antithesis of Spínola and in fact had set out in life with the ambition of being an actor. This Mozambican-born officer, who had served in Guinea as a public relations man for visiting journalists and diplomats, had also been rather conservative in his viewpoint. A picture exists of him weeping over Salazar's coffin at the dictator's funeral in 1970, and in 1974, immediately after the *coup*, he issued a statement declaring that 'in Africa we want to achieve peace and self-determination, even if that includes having to fight against Frelimo and the PAIGC'.[16]

However, in the months after the *coup* the mercurial Otelo moved rapidly leftwards, from a position close to the PPD to one which placed him left of all the main parties, including the PCP. In his hands COPCON was a powerful weapon that was bound to put Spínola at some disadvantage in the event of a direct confrontation between the president and the MFA radicals. The issue that seemed increasingly likely to produce an open schism among the political soldiery was the future of the African empire. In a land of much rhetoric and little content, the MFA had drawn up a document which meant exactly what it said, above all in relation to the colonies. MFA soldiers wished to disengage from Africa as quickly as possible and transfer sovereignty to the insurgent forces they had been fighting. Much had obviously happened since 1968, when Salazar, asked how long it would take before Mozambique and Angola would be governing themselves, replied that 'it is a problem for centuries; within 300 to 500 years. And in the meantime, they will have to go on participating in the process of development.'[17]

After 25 April Spínola himself considered that the process of decolonisation might have to take a generation or more. He had not lent his support to the centurions of 1974 simply to bring about the dismemberment of Portugal overseas. Spínola believed in a pluri-continental United States of Portugal, but what he failed to see was that the downfall of the Caetano regime robbed the federal solution he had propounded in his book of any serious chance of success. It was the overseas question which brought him down as surely as it had toppled Caetano.[18] Spínola was unable to win support for his neo-colonial solution even from relatively moderate MFA officers. In government, both the PS and the PCP joined the MFA in advocating complete withdrawal from Africa, a view that triumphed over Spínola's gradualistic perspective in July–August 1974. In a historic speech relayed on television on 27 July he conceded the right of the people of Angola, Mozambique and Guinea to self-determination, and by September the latter territory had already been recognised as an independent state. Mozambique was next in line for independence, which would be conferred on 25 July 1975. The 150,000 white settlers, along with those Africans who had thrown in their lot with the Portuguese, were appalled at the prospect. In May 1974 white Mozambicans had founded the Independent Front for the Continuation of Western Civilisation (FICO: an acronym which means 'I stay' in Portuguese). However, the white community lacked the resolve to take matters into its own hands by declaring independence unilaterally as in Rhodesia, and most chose to leave during the traumatic months of final decolonisation. Portuguese settlers possessed little tradition of political activism, and even during the *Estado Novo* white separatism had been conspicuous by its absence, despite the major grievances settlers harboured towards the Lisbon authorities. The same was largely true in Angola, but here there were almost half a million Portuguese in a population of less than six million. Unlike Mozambique, the African nationalist insurgents were also split up into three competing movements based largely on tribal formations. So, at least for a few months, it did look as if Portugal might be able to retain some sort of stake in the largest and wealthiest of her overseas possessions. But the whites, despite their numbers and relative prosperity, did not possess a sufficiently strong political consciousness or 'Angolan' outlook to throw in their lot with the moderate African nationalist forces and decisively shape the future of an independent Angola. In July 1974 a new governor-general was sent out from Lisbon who worked to promote the cause of the Marxist MPLA led by Dr Agostinho Neto. Admiral Rosa Coutinho, a bullet-headed naval officer who had been humiliated by the tribal-based FNLA while their prisoner before 1974, was a convinced Marxist who soon became known as the 'Red Admiral'. That such a man was entrusted with the task of severing Portugal's connection with Angola indicates just how little the President was in control of events in mid-1974. At the end of July Spínola was heard to remark, 'I have just sold my country,' and, in a very dispirited frame of mind, he took himself off to the spa centre at Bussaco in the north to ponder how things had gone wrong. Soon only two outposts of empire would remain, the small territories of Macau and East Timor, both in the Far East.

In 1974, in the full flush of revolutionary enthusiasm, the MFA resolved to hand Macau over to the People's Republic of China. However, the Peking authorities were unwilling to incorporate this speck of the Chinese mainland, since Macau was an excellent source of foreign exchange and, through it, they were able quietly to import precious metals and other goods from countries which officially they had nothing to do with. In the end, the emissaries from Lisbon were rudely sent packing at the behest of Yo Hin, a wealthy entrepreneur acting as Peking's representative in Macau.[19] Unfortunately, the decolonisation of East Timor had few of these comic aspects and turned into a bloodbath in which 70,000 people, ten per cent of the population, are estimated to have perished between 1975 and 1977. The Portuguese deserve little credit for the way they handled the affairs of this small territory. Three antagonistic political groupings were left to fight it out in 1975, the radical Fretilin emerging as the dominant force. On 28 November 1975 it proclaimed the total independence of the Democratic Republic of East Timor. Within days the Indonesians invaded, fearing that East Timor could become a sort of Micronesian Cuba. Later the territory was incorporated into Indonesia itself, but local resistance continued for the rest of the 1970s, and the death toll due to famine, disease and massacre may now be of Cambodian proportions (relative to the size of the country), although the outside world has shown little interest.

Perhaps it might have been hard to avoid at least some of the chaos and bloodshed which accompanied the sudden end of 400 years of Portuguese rule in Africa and east Asia. Hoping to salvage something from the wreck, if only in Portugal itself, Spínola agreed to the suggestion of right-wing backers that a rally of the 'silent majority' be organised in his support on the afternoon of 28 September. The president hoped that a popular demonstration in Lisbon with people gathered from all over Portugal might give him enough strength to reshuffle the government and even abolish the MFA's co-ordinating committee. The organisers of the rally were mainly arch-conservatives in the newly formed Liberal, Progress, and Portuguese Nationalist parties, the last of these being dedicated to 'renewing the struggle interrupted by 25 April'.[20] As a prelude to the rally, a bullfight was organised in the Campo Pequeno by the right-wing Ex-serviceman's League on 26 September. The 15,000 crowd gave Spínola a standing ovation, while Premier Gonçalves was roundly booed. As the bullfight went on, the two men were seen to be having an angry disagreement in the presidential box. Gonçalves told Spínola, 'As you see, the ring is full of reactionaries.' At this Spínola exploded. 'Not reactionaries! Portuguese, patriotic Portuguese!'[21]

Matters came to a head on the night of the 27th, when Spínola summoned his chief opponents, Otelo and Premier Gonçalves, to his palace. Gonçalves was roundly denounced by the right-wing officers of the Junta of National Salvation, who were also present. One of them, General Diogo Neto, warned that 'If you open your mouth I'll smash your face.'[22] Later, when Otelo showed up, he was placed under virtual house arrest and told to phone his subordinates in COPCON with orders that they were not to hinder next day's rally. Otelo's detention indicates that Spínola may have had more in mind than a mere rally of the 'silent majority'. One source claims that he hoped to neutralise the MFA completely by arresting other members of its co-ordinating committee.[23] However, the events of this confused weekend are still not clear. One of the difficulties which the revolution presented to observers was how to distinguish an *intentona* (a planned attempt to seize power) from an *inventona* (the invention by the opposing side of such a plan to further their own interests). In the event, the power struggle of 27–28 September would end without bloodshed, as would most of the other revolutionary showdowns of 1974–75. Sensing from the tone of his voice that Otelo was speaking under duress, his COPCON aide decided not to carry out his instructions to dismantle the barricades which the left had placed on the roads into Lisbon to stop right-wing demonstrators entering the city. Once this became known in the Belém palace, Costa Gomes, the army chief of staff, began to side with Otelo, whom he persuaded Spínola to release. The 28 September rally was called off, and Otelo ordered the arrest of extreme right-wingers like Franco Nogueira and Kaúlza de Arriaga who had hitherto been at liberty. One of those detained after 28 September was the father of the radical Melo Antunes, a leading member of the Portuguese Legion. On being asked whether he wished him to be accorded any special treatment, Major Antunes was adamant that no exception should be made for his reactionary father.[24]

'Nobody to the left of us': October 1974–July 1975

Finding himself without power and likely to be elbowed aside by the MFA, Spínola resigned as president on 30 September 1974 after making a gloomy farewell speech to the nation. He was succeeded as president by the commander-in-chief of the army, General Costa Gomes, the man the MFA co-ordinating committee would have preferred to see as head of state from the first. Costa Gomes was born in 1914 in the picturesque town of Chaves in Trás-os-Montes. During the late 1960s Chaves was the scene of a little-known uprising which came about after an important football match involving the local team had been rigged in favour of the opposition. The town was seized by its inhabitants in an uprising which saw the local gendarmerie disarmed and reinforcements from Oporto compelled to retreat in some disorder. Civic peace was eventually restored only when the authorities agreed to a replay, the whole incident constituting backdrop to the 'hot summer' of 1975 as well as an indication that the old regime's backing for football as a tool of depoliticisation was a double-edged sword.[25]

Another famous scion of Chaves was General Carmona, Portugal's president between 1926 and 1951. Politics aside, Costa Gomes resembled Carmona quite closely, since during what would be a difficult term of office he proved a deft conciliator, able to head off confrontations within the military while keeping his own power base secure. General Costa Gomes's political philosophy was leftish, if vague, and he was nicknamed the 'Cork' for his ability to float with the tide. Although he was not apparently one of its 'submarines', the PCP welcomed his emergence; the failure of his moderate right-wing predecessor clearly indicated that the upper bourgeoisie had become disoriented after living through the long political ice age of the Salazar–Caetano era.

By contrast, the PCP showed itself far more astute in the revolution's initial phase. Long years of activity and struggle probably helped to make the PCP the most clear-headed force in politics, at least during 1974.[26] Unlike other parties, the Communists were careful never to argue with the MFA as it tightened its grip on the government. After 1974 it was no longer possible to obtain copies of Álvaro Cunhal's *O radicalismo pequeno-burguês de fachada socialista*, in which he delivered a violent attack on petty-bourgeois radicals. The MFA comprised some of the most successful petty-bourgeois revolutionaries seen in recent times, and it was deemed appropriate to keep Cunhal's principal contribution to Marxist theory under wraps, at least during 1974–75. No other party mouthed the main slogan of the revolution, 'The people are with the MFA', as often as the Communists. The party's apparent eagerness to please strengthened existing bonds between the PCP and the MFA. PCP members and the war veterans of the MFA shared a background of struggle and sacrifice – the officers abroad on behalf of the dictatorship, the party at home in opposition.[27] The Communists' dedication to efficiency, discipline and order appealed to the puritanism of MFA leaders, increasingly scornful of the high-living urban professionals who ran the other major parties. Portugal's communists could also offer important props which the inexperienced MFA lacked: political organisation, loyal support and credibility among the working classes.

After 28 September the MFA sought to legitimise itself further by creating additional power structures. At the top, a twenty-member Supreme Council was formed, composed of the President of the Republic, chairman by right, the Junta of National Salvation, the six officers in what was now the third provisional government, the commander of COPCON, and the seven members of the MFA co-ordinating committee. Below that came the MFA General Assembly, composed of delegates elected by the councils of the three services: the army, navy and air force.

The creation of these new bodies marked an important step in the institutionalisation of the MFA. By the winter of 1974 it had long ceased to be an underground pressure group and was well on the way towards becoming a new revolutionary elite, complete with its own military parliament in the form of its General Assembly. But what was to be the relationship of these new authorities to each other and to the civilian governmental structures? It was hard to answer this knotty question, since the MFA bodies were very *ad hoc* organisations whose powers and functions were never clearly defined. To Spínola this amounted to 'chaos and anarchy'.[28] To Major Vítor Alves it was 'teaching ourselves democracy'. Nevertheless, in some respects the MFA remained a very conservative force. At no point were the military rank and file encouraged to play a role in its formal activities. Had the leading MFA soldiers been willing to devolve power to the lower ranks, where political radicalism was strong, the Armed Forces Movement could perhaps have institutionalised itself in decisive fashion. However, MFA activists would shrink from such a fundamental revolutionary step. The membership of elected MFA bodies would at all times be largely decided by the officer corps. The MFA's own *Bulletin* declared that hierarchy was permissable, indeed vital, as long as it was 'a hierarchy of competence'.[29] It went on to say that 'the false idea of election campaigns within the military is definitely not on. There is not an army in the world where this is practised to any degree at all . . .'[30] Even a radical such as Captain Dinis de Almeida, who was closely linked with the most libertarian sections of the MFA, could remark (at the end of 1974) that 'a breakdown of discipline' was one of the most serious problems facing the army at the time.[31]

Politically inexperienced officers who were sometimes ill at ease in their new positions of eminence were not willing to transform the armed forces into a popular liberation army. That was too much of a leap into the unknown. They were, however, willing to countenance experimentation in other areas. In September 1974 Colonel Varela Gomes, a dedicated Marxist, began to reorganise the old psychological warfare section of the army, known as the Fifth Division of the armed forces general staff. His aim was to turn it into a propaganda task force capable of communicating the MFA's ideas for a new Portugal to society at large. In December 1974 Mário Soares would accuse the Fifth Division of trying to subvert his party by engineering a split at the PS annual conference and by encouraging an ultra-leftist faction in a bid to seize control.[32] However, its main claim to fame during the revolution was its pioneering of the ill-fated and now largely forgotten 'cultural dynamisation' campaigns in the northern countryside. For some time the most idealistic members of the

MFA had envisaged 'their organisation playing a role quite similar to that of the national liberation fronts against which they had fought in Africa'.[33] A particularly strong intellectual influence was Amílcar Cabral, whose PAIGC in Guinea-Bissau was particularly successful in winning popular support by seeking to modernise the tribal culture but 'within the history and conditions of Guinea'.[34]

Officers taking part in the cultural dynamisation campaign viewed rural Portugal, with its Third World poverty and medieval backwardness, as ripe for modernisation and change. However, their radical message was largely self-intoxicating. Once a team of army dynamisers had passed through a village there would be few permanent reminders of their visit. Often the typical programme of speeches, 'clarification sessions', music, army displays and literature distribution evoked an uncomprehending and sometimes adverse response. Villagers in the north were affronted when soldiers made attacks on the Church or disseminated information about birth control. In a society where girls are still chaperoned by their grandmother or aunt, much resentment was caused by soldiers taking up with local girls and failing to observe the traditional strict code of moral conduct. Drug-taking by a few soldiers also alienated prudish rustics, and in a few places, as for instance around Tomar, the dynamisers were stoned by irate villagers who felt that they would rather be left alone by the revolution. The same reception also awaited some of the leftist students who went north on self-appointed pedagogical missions. Very early in the 1974–75 academic year, all classes ceased in the universities owing to the purging of staff who had compromised themselves with the old regime. With no scholarly preoccupations, tens of thousands of students swelled the ranks of ultra-left groups in Lisbon or put together an alternative academic curriculum – a Chair of guerrilla warfare even being established at Coimbra University.

If the MFA had treated northern rural dwellers with greater sensitivity, then its message might have been more sympathetically received. For one thing, the dynamisers ought to have had the sense to back up their propaganda with a practical aid programme involving road repairs, bridge-building and the electricity supplies for remote villages. A 180,000-strong army was quite capable of these elementary tasks. However, the banishment of peasant ignorance and superstition was just too complex a feat for inexperienced officers only recently politicised themselves.

Civilian supporters of the MFA, led by Manuel Alegre and Fernando Piteira Santos, two non-party leftists, formed 'popular centres of 25 April', hoping that these would become the nucleus of an MFA party. But there was insufficient popular support for their efforts. Citizens who were drawn to politics preferred to join the orthodox parties. The three main ones, the PS, the PCP and the PPD, enjoyed phenomenal growth in the twelve months after the April 1974 *coup*. In the PS, an enthusiastic recruiting campaign won tens of thousands of new converts, until it was estimated that party membership stood at over 100,000 by April 1975. This represented a major mobilisation in a country of just over eight million people. However, in social origins the membership largely mirrored its leaders. Typically members came from the small professional and white-collar class and were lawyers, engineers, intellectuals, schoolmasters, artisans and doctors; Freemasons, a liberal elite force influential in politics before 1926, were an important element; the leadership was dominated by the urban bourgeoisie, which was a not unusual state of affairs in other European socialist parties. However, it was unusual for a party whose statutes declared that it was inspired by 'critical Marxism' to begin life with such a stratified membership.[35] The gulf between the party's advanced programme and its members' unradical social background was, as a result, perhaps bound to produce major internal disagreement.

At the party's second conference, held in Lisbon in December 1974, Dr Soares's position as leader was confirmed but he had to defeat challenges mounted by the social-democratic right and the revolutionary left. The latter current presented the most serious threat to his basically democratic socialist position. Manuel Serra, an ultra-leftist with a Resistance background, received 37 per cent of delegate support in key voting contests. Encouraged by this showing, Serra's radical current left the party and set up a Purified Socialist Front. This initiative came to nothing in electoral terms, and the whole affair was of considerable satisfaction to Soares. Bereft of a strong ultra-left that had voluntarily committed political suicide, the PS leader was able to secure internal acceptance of a programme with Marxist tinges but based on Western representative precepts. Santiago Carrillo, secretary-general of the Spanish communist party, was at the conference to attest to Soares's radical credentials. However, this gathering really marked the clear victory of a reformist perspective over a revolutionary one. It also witnessed the end of open party tendencies, hitherto permitted but no longer allowed under new rules.

One of the surprises of the Portuguese revolution was that an alliance failed to develop between the purveyors of military and civilian socialism: the MFA and the PS. On the surface both had much in common. In 1975 Mário Soares claimed that his party was the most left-wing in the whole of non-communist Europe, while the radical captains of the MFA applied the same yardstick to the army. If an alliance had arisen between them, much of the in-fighting of the later stages of the revolution could perhaps have been avoided and the chances of a major left-wing transformation in Portugal might have been dramatically increased. What were the obstacles militating against a PS–MFA convergence?

The degree and speed of political civilianisation was one issue which drove the PS and MFA apart, for as it increased its popular strength the PS made no secret of the fact that it wished the military to return to barracks as soon as possible so that party politicians and the voters could between them devise an open pluralist regime. Politicised soldiers disagreed. Hardly any wished to be politically superannuated so soon after tasting power, and many thought that close military involvement in the political process was essential for the destruction of right-wing authoritarian rule. Many MFA leaders were dismayed to find that the PS was dominated by the urban academic and legal elites. Some refused to treat it as a genuine socialist party at all. Military radicals were especially critical of its leader; Soares happened to be, among other things, the owner of a well known private school, a lawyer who had successfully avoided war service, and an associate of Jorge de Mello, one of the country's leading entrepreneurs. These were damnable offences in the eyes of a large number of MFA radicals, who reacted with increasing anger as Soares emerged as the best-known Portuguese figure on the world scene.

The PS interpretation of socialism differed from that of many elements of the MFA. Soares seemed content to strive for a Portuguese model of Swedish social democracy, with a large welfare state and extensive state control of the economy. His rhetoric in 1975 was usually more radical than the essentially social democratic make-up of his party, as its performance in government would later abundantly prove: in September 1975 Soares could explain to *The Times* that his programme 'was not meant to correct the most unjust aspects of capitalism but to destroy capitalism'.[36] The revolutionary elements of the MFA spoke in similar uncompromising tones but, unlike the PS, they believed indubitably in their radical creed. Radical officers considered Portugal almost as backward as some of her former colonial charges and sought to orientate the country firmly in the direction of the Third World. The cosmopolitan PS leaders disagreed totally, arguing instead that Portugal was geographically and culturally part of Europe and ought to join the Common Market.

Integration with western Europe, the Socialists believed, promised less chance of Portugal falling victim to authoritarianism of either the right or the left. Six months after the April *coup*, Socialist leaders were alarmed that there was a real prospect of a Stalinist state being formed on the banks of the Tagus. Relations between the major parties of the left, the PCP and the PS, became uniformly hostile once it was clear that the latter were outpacing the Communists in terms of popular support. Finally, in January 1975, a bitter conflict broke out over a PCP attempt to sanctify in law the monopoly role already exercised by the party in the trade union world. The PCP aimed to make the Communist-dominated Intersindical the only permissible union confederation. The party defended such a step by claiming that more than one union bloc would split the working class, making the defence of its rights more difficult. By contrast, PS leaders argued privately that the Intersindical affair was tangible evidence of the PCP's desire to grab key power points that would enable it to set up a communist-dominated state. Mário Soares demanded a pluralist union framework that would prevent Portuguese trade unionism being turned into a mere conveyor-belt for party directives. Eventually the conflict would only be settled by the MFA accepting a document which supported a single trade union but which included provisions that weakened PCP dominance.

The Intersindical controversy showed that the MFA, although left-wing, was not necessarily a PCP front. In February 1975 moderate elements within the movement gained heart from the results of elections to the MFA general assembly in which radicals of various hues like Vasco Gonçalves, Otelo and Melo Antunes failed to get elected. Shortly beforehand, on 10 February, President Costa Gomes announced that elections for a constituent assembly would be held in April. Several interesting clauses were inserted into the legislation governing the conduct of elections. Illiterate persons were able to vote but could not stand as candidates. Individuals who had held official political office during the *Estado Novo* were barred altogether from taking part in the contest. Portuguese living or working abroad could vote only if they returned to Portugal.

Meanwhile General Spínola had not been idle in the months following his resignation. Negotiations were carried on with a cross-section of political and military figures in the late winter of 1974–75 about how to avoid a communist take-over and resume the transition to an orthodox democracy. Through intermediaries Spínola consulted Dr Soares, who was his choice for prime minister in a shadow cabinet which he had prepared in readiness for the moment when he would regain political control. If the looming elections were postponed or rigged, two likely scenarios in Spínola's view, this was to be the moment for striking against the civilian and military extremists intent on establishing dictatorial socialism. The general felt that he was justified in using force against the present MFA leadership, who, in his view, were perverting the ideals of 25 April and going against the essentially moderate wishes of the people. Preparations for a *coup* got under way in February 1975, Spínola being encouraged by the degree of personal support he had within the officer corps as a whole. However, he overestimated the political indignation of the bulk of them, most still not wanting to get involved in politics if they could possibly help it.[37] News about his intentions also leaked out at an early stage. On 8 March Lieutenant Nuno Barbieri, one of the leaders of the Portuguese Liberation Army (ELP), an extreme right-wing group only recently formed, announced that plans had been drawn up by the Communists and the MFA to arrest 1,500 leading right-wingers, including Spínola, and then kill them in a *matança de pascoa* (Easter massacre). The rumour may have been a deliberate Communist provocation to get the conspirators to show their hand too early. Or it may have been an attempt by extreme right-wingers to double-cross Spínola, whom they blamed for the loss of Portugal's imperial patrimony.

Anyway, a panic-stricken Spínola left Lisbon on 10 March and headed north to the military base at Tancos, firm in the belief that the projected uprising (*atentado*) must take place now or never. The next day, Lisbon airport was taken by paratroopers from Tancos and the near-by RAL-I barracks came under attack from their planes. Interestingly, a crew from the Communist-dominated television station were on hand to film the whole scene, which was shown on television almost immediately afterwards. Some observers investigating the 11 March *coup* attempt have concluded that this was just too great a coincidence and communist manipulation has been suspected. In the event, Spínola's bid for power went off at half cock. Most pro-Spínola units failed to rally to his side, their commanding officers suspecting that the luckless general had fallen into a trap. Within hours the *coup* would splutter out altogether. The paratroop commander besieging RAL-I, where the First Artillery were based under the command of Captain Dinis d'Almeida, surrendered. Realising that the game was up, Spínola, along with his wife and eighteen officers, made his escape to Spain in helicopters. Interestingly, nobody hindered his flight even though it would have been possible for loyalist forces to apprehend him.

After the failed *coup* Spínola's Lisbon home was ransacked and copies of his book, the chief tract of the revolution a year before, were burned in the street. Employees occupied the domestic banks and refused to open for business until they were nationalised by the government. Decree-laws announced on 14 and 15 March 1975 transferred private banking and insurance to the public sector. The revolution was now proceeding at a rapid pace. The large private monopolies (which had owned many of the banks) were taken over by their employees in moves that were orchestrated by the Intersindical. CUF, a conglomerate listed as one of the largest companies in the world, employing 30,000 workers and accounting for more than 10 per cent of industrial production, fell to the state. Jorge de Mello, one of its co-owners, had been relatively sanguine about its future the year before. Rather naively, he declared in May 1974 that:

> our company is more than 100 years old and we have worked under regimes different from the previous one. I am confident that we can meet the challenge of adopting to new conditions. After all, private businesses flourish under socialism

in Scandinavia, Britain and Holland, don't they?[38]

The monopolies' links with the *Estado Novo* had been so intimate that even had the revolution not reached such a radical pass it is doubtful whether the 'robber barons' of pre-1974 could have weathered the transition to a new order. By the end of March 1975 some 50–60 per cent of the economy had fallen into the public sector, a transformation Salazar had made relatively easy by his long encouragement of a few huge conglomerates. Medium-sized industrial firms, hotels, fishing fleets and restaurants were also seized in tumultuous scenes that left no doubt Portugal was undergoing a major upheaval. At the entrance to one golf course in the Algarve, requisitioned by the army, a notice proclaimed, 'Open to anyone except members'.[39] These were not normal times. Ecstatic revolutionary soldiers talked about entering a new Age of Aquarius, and the Maoist UDP (Popular Democratic Union) could declare that 'only Albania is to the left of us'.[40] Interestingly, conservative parties like the Monarchist PPM were calling for 'communes with a king' in the spring of 1975, sentiments which convinced foreign observers that 'Portugal was clearly set on the road to becoming a socialist state'.[41] Incoming President Gerald Ford of the USA would shortly be making the suggestion that such a rogue elephant perhaps ought to be expelled from NATO, while Senator James Buckley, a conservative Republican, publicly declared that military action against Portugal was a serious option for NATO: 'There is nothing else now going on in the world – not in South East Asia, not even in the Middle East – half so important and ominous as the communist drive for power in Portugal.'[42]

Perhaps the most dramatic proof of communist expansion came from the province of Alentejo, where land occupations began after 11 March. Farm labourers, encouraged by far-leftists, seized the estates of absentee owners, which were then turned into vast collective farms with suitably proletarian titles such as Red Star and Catarina Eufémia Collective, the PCP thus commemorating one of its martyrs who had been shot by Salazarist police during an agricultural labourers' strike in the early 1960s. In less than six months several million acres of land were turned into collective or co-operative farms, a transfer of power which was given legal santion by the fourth provisional government, sworn in on 26 March 1975. Most of the revolutionary changes occurred in southern Portugal (in the Alentejo and the Lisbon area), which, during 1975, witnessed the most rapid extension of state socialism so far undergone by any non-communist European country.

These changes were accompanied by a further drastic overhaul of the MFA's own ruling structures. On 11 March, within hours of Spínola's failed *atentado*, the Junta of National Salvation (from which right-

wingers had been removed in October 1974) was wound up and a new
umbrella body, the Supreme Revolutionary Council (CRS), created.
Comprising among its twenty-eight members all the leading MFA
radicals, it assumed the right not only to veto decrees passed by the
cabinet but also full legislative powers. MFA militants, who had been on
the defensive in the weeks before 11 March, derived fresh confidence from
the popular upheavals of spring 1975. Ironically, the MFA could hardly be
regarded as responsible for the major structural changes in Portuguese
society witnessed in 1974–75. One observer has perceptively argued that
the main economic and political transformation took place because of the
absence rather than the presence of a strong central authority.[43] Not one of
Portugal's radical military factions would be able to cement its authority
in decisive fashion. Instead, with a kaleidoscopic collection of idealistic
officers, ambitious politicians and confused ideological sects jostling for
supremacy, it would become increasingly difficult to see where real
authority lay in revolutionary Portugal. In this situation the economy was
largely allowed to drift, and by the first anniversary of the revolution it was
already in grave difficulties. Industrial unrest, steep wage rises, the flight
of foreign capital and the traumas of decolonisation severely battered an
economy that had not been in the best of health anyway before 25 April.
Production dropped sharply as many firms went out of business and
emigrants proved unwilling to send their remittances back to Portugal in
its confused state. Complete disaster was perhaps staved off because the
soldiers had a precious asset in the foreign exchange reserves and gold
bullion which Salazar had carefully amassed during decades in power.

This financial cushion enabled the MFA to concentrate on hewing out a
political course for the country. On 11 April 1975 the reluctant but fearful
party leaders signed a pact with the MFA which gave it the right to veto
any decision taken by the constituent assembly and laid down that the
President of the Republic must be an officer, someone who could dissolve
any future legislative assembly in consultation with the cabinet and the
newly formed Council of the Revolution. This seemed to give the MFA
virtual control of the country for the next three to five years no matter what
the outcome of elections might be. Deeply pessimistic political leaders
feared that even these might be cancelled in the euphoria of the moment.
Certainly Alvaro Cunhal and Premier Gonçalves were privately
demanding that they be postponed on the grounds that the people were
insufficiently prepared for democracy. Opinion polls had revealed that the
PCP could only expect to win at best 15 per cent of the vote. However, most
of the leading MFA activists – above all, the moderate leftists Vítor Alves,
Melo Antunes and Vítor Crespo – were determined to press forward with
the elections, which were seen as a sacred part of the MFA's original
programme.

For the revolutionary soldiers directing the political process, the first elections in fifty years were of too symbolic importance to be sacrificed to the advancing revolution. Later the COPCON chief, Brigadier Otelo, would admit that 'in retrospect our biggest single mistake was to have allowed the elections to go ahead. Our downfall can be traced from them.'[44] However, at the time Otelo felt differently. He was determined to show that the Portuguese revolution was a uniquely libertarian and democratic event and that the MFA were not acting as PCP stooges. He was also mindful of warnings in the foreign press that one day the Communists might be in a position to bid for the MFA's own power. Otelo drew his civilian advisers from lapsed communists who belonged to radical left groups like the UDP and the Movement for the Socialist Left (MES), whose leading intellectual spokesman, César Oliveira, was in frequent contact with MFA radicals. Otelo himself was particularly close to the Portuguese Revolutionary Party (PRP) of Isabel do Carmo, a thirty-five-year-old endrocrinologist who believed that only through force could the proletariat take power. The Revolutionary Brigades, an armed wing of the PRP, possessed large caches of arms, and a PRP insurrection was thought to be on the cards at several points in the latter half of 1975. However, the ultra-left's importance was weakened by its endemic disunity and *penchant* for ideological squabbles. If a strong non-communist left-wing movement had existed, the MFA might have been more tempted to set up its own party, using ultra-left civilians as a shield. After his return from Angola, Admiral Rosa Coutinho actually proposed, in spring 1975, that a party representing the revolutionary spirit of the MFA might be founded after the elections, which after several delays were finally scheduled for 25 April 1975, the first anniversary of the *coup*. However, he was overruled by his colleagues on both the right and left. Already by now the MFA was too divided ideologically to take such a portentous step. Instead, leading members like Rosa Coutinho and Lieutenant Ramiro Correia urged the electorate to cast blank ballots as a demonstration of support for the MFA.

The Catholic Church also sought to give a lead to prospective voters. Priests throughout Portugal delivered sermons forbidding Catholics 'to vote for parties which by their ideology, objectives, prejudice and history have shown themselves to be incompatible with the Christian concept of man and his life in society'.[45] They also warned their flock against abstaining. In the event these admonitions were heeded, although voters may also have been just as influenced by the warning of the electoral commission on 15 April that registered voters who did not go to the polls without good reason would be forbidden for a year to hold national or local government office or to work for state enterprises.

91·7 per cent of voters went to the polls on 25 April, a day which passed off almost without incident, unlike the election campaign itself, in which

PPD and CDS meetings had been frequently attacked by ultra-leftists. There was a more or less uniform turn-out throughout the country, and the first results came from the village of Santar in the far north, well known for the quality of its *vinho verde* (sparkling green wine). Twenty-eight of the villagers' seventy-three votes went to the PPD, which was nineteen ahead of its nearest rival. Along with the CDS, the PPD would gain a clear majority in the rural north and centre, voters preferring to support the two parties which forty-eight hours earlier Lieutenant Correia had said he expected to wither away. The PPD also did extremely well in the island chains of the Azores and Madeira, winning over 50 per cent of the vote in both instances. Nationally, however, it was the PS which emerged as the clear winner, with 37·9 per cent of the total vote, compared to the PPD, in second place with 26·4 per cent. Having campaigned around the slogan 'Socialism, yes! Dictatorship, no!' the result was a major personal triumph for Mário Soares, the party leader, who dominated the PS election campaign. In every southern constituency except Beja the PS topped the poll, and in Lisbon it received 46·1 per cent of the vote. It came second in all the constituencies where it did not win, receiving its highest vote in Portalegre (52·4 per cent) and its lowest in Funchal, on Madeira (19·4 per cent). As for its chief rival on the left, the PCP, it could only manage 12·5 per cent of the vote, most of its support being derived from the Alentejo, the industrial centres of Barreiro and Setúbal south of the Tagus, and Lisbon. Over the rest of the country, the party could only achieve between 5 and 10 per cent of the poll, a result which greatly devalued its good southern performance. The PCP's stalking-horse, the MDP, also fared indifferently, winning only 4·1 per cent of the vote. But the Communist Party was relieved to see that none of the far-left parties in the contest did well, despite the amount of media time they were given in the campaign under the terms of a law which gave virtual parity to all the parties. Only the Marxist-Leninist UDP, with 0·8 per cent of the vote, was able to pick up a seat.

Broadly speaking, the results indicated a north–south/right–left polarisation, reflecting long-established differences between the two zones divided by the Tagus. The PS managed to bridge this divide by winning strong support in all social groups and gaining seats in every district on the mainland. MFA leaders could not hide their disappointment with the outcome, especially the small number of blank ballots (7 per cent) cast. Early on 26 April 1975 Rosa Coutinho was snapping at journalists, 'Go away! The MFA is not a political party and has nothing to fear from the results. I have nothing more to say.'[46] Soon after, Premier Gonçalves declared, 'We are profoundly satisfied with the results. The election will not decisively influence the revolutionary process.'[47] MFA leaders stressed the fact that the election had been for an assembly to draw up a new constitution, not for a fully fledged national parliament. When the constituent assembly convened afterwards, Professor Henrique de Barros, Caetano's brother-in-law and an elder statesman of the PS, was elected its first president. In the main the new body, like previous legislatures, was dominated by the professional and managerial classes. Even in the midst of revolution much of the electorate had demonstrated ingrained social deference, a high proportion of urban lawyers being elected as deputies. Indeed, the four main party leaders, Cunhal, Soares, Sá Carneiro and Freitas do Amaral, were all qualified lawyers, representing Lisbon constituencies, evidence that old political moulds were re-forming even after a moratorium of fifty years.

The behaviour of the PCP became noticeably more hard-line after April 1975. At the end of the month Álvaro Cunhal told the Lisbon paper *A Capital* that 'in a revolutionary process, the vote is not the only or even the most significant expression of the strength and influence of a party'.[48] On 13 June he was far more explicit to the Italian journalist Oriana Fallaci, to whom he declared in an interview, 'There is no possibility of a democracy like the one you have in western Europe. . . . Portugal will not be a country with democratic freedoms and monopolies. It will not allow it.'[49]

Candidates elected to the constituent assembly on 25 April 1975, by party and occupation (%)

	Communist	Socialist	Popular Democrat
Lawyers	7	28	33
Teachers and lecturers	10	15	13
Doctors	–	4	4
Engineers	3	5	4
Journalists/writers	–	7	1
Businessmen/managers	–	3	8
Other professional (incl. students)	–	4	11
Sub-total: professional and managerial	20	66	74
White-collar	20	17	10
Manual (excluding agriculture)	50	11	4
Agriculture (farmers and labourers and fishing)	10	5	3
Not classified	–	1	9
Total	100	100	100

Source: Ben Pimlott and Jean Seaton, 'Ferment of an old brew', *New Society*, 24 July 1975, p. 202.

In making this hardbitten statement Cunhal was going out of his way to reject the more accommodating, pluralistic and consensual political stance associated with Euro-communism. During the early summer of 1975 he poured scorn on bourgeois democracy and made less and less secret of the fact that he wished to create a militant Marxist state in western Iberia. Exactly when in 1974–75 this became an attainable objective in the eyes of party strategists is unclear. However, the leftward advance of the revolution undoubtedly radicalised a party whose long experience of repression had already predisposed it to militancy. Abroad, the post-1974 tactics of the PCP were viewed in more enlightened communist circles in Madrid and Rome as a political aberration, especially since the PS and the PCP constituted a ruling majority in Portugal. Others, on the broad left of European politics, chose to characterise Cunhal as an obedient Moscow hack whose 'long, bitter struggles with Salazar had moulded him into the image of his persecutor'.[50] As for the PCP itself, it appears to have regarded itself as being in a much stronger position than any other west European Marxist party since the time of Lenin and the Russian revolution. This is a debatable assumption, but it is certainly true that the PCP was much better placed than the French or Italian communists when they had found themselves in a pre-revolutionary situation at the end of World War II. No Allied armies of occupation were decamped in Portugal after 1974. Nor was the domestic military then a stronghold of reaction. Nor, in the wake of the Nixon–Watergate crisis did direct Western intervention in Portuguese affairs ever seem likely. Given these facts, the PCP viewed its behaviour in 1974–75 less as a desperate all-or-nothing bid for total power and more as a rational attempt to capitalise fully on an objectively revolutionary situation.

The fact that the Portuguese army was a battleground of different left-wing tendencies in 1975 undoubtedly encouraged a feeling of 'triumphalism' among PCP leaders. Perhaps less than a fifth of the MFA's peak membership of 2,000 officers were pro-communist, many of the rest being more inspired by Rousseau and Proudhon than by Marx and Lenin. However, each time military radicals advanced to the fore, displacing more moderate sectors, the PCP in its turn grew bolder. In May–June 1975 the MFA seemed poised for another leftward turn, with the non-aligned radicals pushing for the introduction of 'popular power' whereby self-governing neighbourhood commissions and revolutionary defence committees would bring authority down to the grass roots and bypass the political parties. This apparent consummation of the much-trumpeted MFA alliance with the people was rejected by a full session of the party's General Assembly on 26–27 May. However, General (formerly Major) Otelo, the main advocate of popular power, would not be put off, and at a further general assembly of the MFA on 8–9 July the radical left succeeded in securing the adoption of a radical plan providing for direct links between the military and the people and for 'popular participation in the march towards socialism through people's assemblies at all levels'.[51] In the event, 'popular power' would get off the ground only in Lisbon and surrounding working-class areas. Often elements of traditionalism were preserved in these brave new experiments. One investigator has found that although many more women than men were active at the base of the neighbourhood commissions, many more men than women had seats on the commission executive councils.[52] Another observer found that the existence of a radical militia, personified by Otelo's COPCON force, tended to dampen down proletarian self-awareness:

> By the early months of 1975, COPCON was being called out for pretty well everything – marital disputes being high on the list. At 3 a.m. a battered housewife would phone for help and COPCON would duly appear on the scene. There was a case in Ajuda of COPCON being called to rescue a stranded kitten
>
> . . .
>
> If COPCON existed to help them, why should the workers even begin to think of autonomous militant organisations on a class basis? In this sense, COPCON was an obstacle to the development of self-led groups concerned with workers' defence, groups which might have formed the nuclei of a workers' militia.[53]

The conservative reaction

The PS was strongly opposed to the 'popular power' scheme, half-baked though it was. However, publicly, in the early summer of 1975, it showed itself to be more concerned with the fate of *República*, a pro-socialist daily newspaper and the only one not dominated by the PCP. On 19 May 1975 the printers on the newspaper took it over, a move which prompted Dr Soares and his ministerial colleague Salgado Zenha to boycott cabinet meetings until the paper was restored to its editor, Raul Rego. The MFA vacillated over *República* and the PS whipped up a strident campaign against the PCP and its attempt to monopolise the press, although it had been ultra-left printers who had in fact seized *República*. Finally, on 11 July 1975, after nothing had been done to appease them, the Socialists resigned from the government and announced their intention of launching a campaign against encroaching Communist domination in Portugal. A better way of making his break with the MFA could hardly have been chosen by Soares. West European countries, which had remained discreetly silent during the Salazar era, raised a storm about the way civil liberties were being killed in newly democratic Portugal and the *República* affair became an international *cause célèbre*. In Portugal itself, on 15 July, crowds shouted their disapproval of MFA rule with such slogans as 'The people are no longer with the MFA' and 'Soldiers back to barracks'. These cries were heard at a monster rally which the PS staged in Lisbon, at which

Dr Soares made the resignation of Premier Gonçalves his price for returning to the government. This was the signal for a campaign of civil disobedience which acquired powerful momentum as a result of unrest breaking out in northern Portugal.

Here, until very recently, thousands of small rural capitalists had been convinced of the imminence of a second bolshevik revolution in their part of Europe, likely to sweep them to their doom. However, not all of them were resigned to this fate. The April election returns had shown village and small-town communities that, although geographically isolated, they were in the political mainstream, since the majority of Portuguese had opted for gradualist and non-revolutionary options. The resolve of many local notables was enormously strengthened as a result of this realisation. Inhibitions against challenging central government, reinforced by fifty years of strict political orthodoxy, were slowly removed, and in the second half of July serious violence broke out in many different parts of the north. The offices, cars and homes of PCP militants were the target of numerous attacks. Stalwarts of the old regime were able to come out and make common cause with moderate opponents of the incumbent leftist regime. Two underground movements, the Portuguese Liberation Army (ELP) and the Democratic Movement for the Liberation of Portugal (MDLP), helped to orchestrate much of the violence but a lot of it was also quite spontaneous. At the town of Rio Maior, a prosperous market centre just forty miles north of Lisbon, trouble arose after land seizures had crept up to the edge of the district. It was in fact the more developed and densely populated coastal zone which provided the storm centre for the unrest. Here there was greater ease of communication, better soil and more populated centres than in the inland north stretching to the Spanish border, where relatively few violent incidents were reported. In places like Trás-os-Montes and Beira Alta disappearing communities, poor quality soil and subsistence farming underscored a permanently depressed economy. But where wealthier peasants and small entrepreneurs tended to be in evidence anti-communist disorders were often at their fiercest, and in fact, within a seventy-five-mile radius to the north of Lisbon, there were more instances of trouble than in the whole of Trás-os-Montes.[54]

As the summer wore on, more heat was generated against the communist 'menace' than there ever had been against fascism. It was only with difficulty that troops rescued the PCP leader, Dr Cunhal, on 18 August when, along with 1,000 supporters, he tried to hold a meeting in the central Portuguese town of Alcobaça. The locals reacted with fury, and after a night of shooting and stone-throwing Cunhal was carried off in a state of collapse. This was seen as revenge for the way the fiercely conservative Archbishop of Braga, Francisco Maria da Silva, had been treated by pro-Communist customs workers at Lisbon airport while on his way to a diocesan conference in Brazil. Officials ordered him to strip after he was falsely accused of illegally exporting currency. Later, on his return to Braga, the archbishop assailed communism as hostile to God in a town-square speech on 10 August which was followed by the burning of the PCP headquarters in Braga. Even Dom António Ferreira Gomes, the liberal Bishop of Oporto, voiced open criticism of the revolutionary process, the unanimity of the protest from the north gravely worrying President Costa Gomes. In a speech to the MFA on 25 July 1975 he warned:

> The march of the revolution has accelerated faster than the people have the capacity to absorb it. ... We have in Lisbon an area capable of absorbing revolutionary advance but it stretches through an industrial belt of only twenty-five miles. The rest of the country runs the risk of losing connection with the front of the column.[55]

If the rural agitation had been confined to the north proper, government and MFA leaders in Lisbon would have been less concerned about the possibly grave consequences for the revolution. However, only the southern provinces of the Alentejo and the Algarve were relatively trouble-free. Elsewhere dissatisfaction with Lisbon's revolutionary government rapidly made itself felt. In the north, the pro-Marxist Lisbon daily press was rejected by those literate citizens who habitually took a newspaper. Most people instead relied for information about the political situation from foreign broadcasting stations such as the BBC world service in London.

On the island chains of the Azores and Madeira the degree of unrest was far greater than anything seen on the mainland. The demonstration by 30,000 islanders on São Miguel, the largest of the nine inhabited Azorean islands, on 6 June 1975 was actually the first public challenge to Portugal's left-wing military rulers. On the Azores and Madeira the island establishment of landowners, hoteliers and entrepreneurs had held on to their wealth after April 1974 and remained the most powerful social element. When it seemed that Portugal was destined for a left-wing future, a separatist movement emerged which was backed by conservatives who had previously been staunch defenders of Portugal's global empire. The leader of the secessionist Azorean Liberation Front (FLA), founded in 1975, was José de Almeida, a parliamentary deputy on the mainland before the revolution. During 1975 the Azorean separatists received active backing from North American business circles and were able to gain access to leading US politicians. When the separatists discovered that much of the US support was actually coming from crime syndicates in the expectation that an independent mid-Atlantic state could be easily manipulated and turned into a world gaming centre, they spurned the offered backing and began to mull over the dangers as well as the benefits of independence.[56]

Besides the fear of encroaching communism and the fear of losing property, several other factors accounted for the uniformity of the conservative protest in 1975. The survival in local communities of hierarchical forms of social relationships was not unimportant. Government failure to make provision for the needs of the small farmer in its reform programme must also be considered. This programme was almost wholly urban-oriented. The non-wage-earning peasant derived little or no benefit from the legalisation of trade unions, national pay increases, shorter working hours and other no less worthy reforms brought in after 1974. He often saw only the steep price rises which resulted from accelerating inflation. The behaviour of the PCP at local level also explains why such a varied cross-section of the rural population was so alienated by central government as to engage in civil resistance. Having taken over much of municipal government in 1974, PCP and MDP officials were soon being accused of directing jobs and favours to party comrades and of holding back agricultural credit from non-communist farmers. Another source of anger was the purported hold local Communist lawyers had gained over aspects of administration such as licensing and civil litigation. Country people also came to resent bitterly the Lisbon government's crash programme of immediate decolonisation in Africa. Hundreds of thousands of white Portuguese settlers, fearing the future, left Angola and Mozambique in 1974–75, many making their way back to the small northern communities from which they had emigrated in the post-war period. Often destitute and harbouring great resentment towards the new regime, the arrival of large numbers of *retornados* (literally 'returned ones') further strained the tense atmosphere in many parts of the countryside.

The rural revolt that occurred in 1975 has no obvious precedent in Portuguese history, excepting perhaps the Maria da Fonte uprising of the 1840s. While nineteenth-century rural Spain was convulsed by a series of Carlist wars, the Portuguese countryside remained politically dormant during most of this time. The same is true for the republican and Salazarist eras. Before 1975 no record of major antagonism between central government and provincial society has come down to us, although suspicion, ignorance, neglect and exploitation definitely underlay the relationship between the urban centre and the rural periphery. Accordingly, the 1975 explosion came as a shock to Portugal's revolutionary but still urban-oriented rulers, as well it might, for, in retrospect, the north's resistance to drastic modernisation could be said to have been far more nationally decisive than any of the past forays of Spanish Carlism. Generals Otelo and Fabião got a taste of the north's anger on 7 August 1975 when they were spat upon and booed in Oporto as they left their cars. Otelo had become a member of a triumvirate consisting of himself, Vasco Gonçalves and President Costa Gomes which had been formed on 25 July after the resignation of the fourth provisional government. However, it failed to function effectively or provide stability. By mid-summer Otelo already seems to have sensed that the game was up for the MFA radicals. After his return from a visit to Cuba in July, he talked frankly about his own shortcomings: 'I lack political co-ordinates. If I had them, I could have been the Fidel Castro of Europe, but I have a limited culture . . . This is the first revolution in which I have been involved in my life.'[57]

A few weeks of major violence made it apparent to many onlookers of the Portuguese revolution that the MFA was not about to institutionalise a Nasserite military regime. The Armed Forces Movement had proved quite incapable of facing up to the crisis provoked by the Socialist challenge. On 27 July 1975 Dr Soares was even daring to proclaim, 'Who chose these men? Little by little our revolution has been stolen from us.'[58] The MFA was unable to reply with a united voice, since it lacked a single recognised leader. Its chief spokesmen emerged as some of the most articulate and dedicated soldiers seen in recent times, but they also displayed alarming political naivety. By August the triumvirate had broken up, with Otelo urging Gonçalves to resign for the sake of the revolution. The crisis had taken its toll on the gaunt and morose prime minister. The crankiness which came over in his television appearances made him an object of ridicule in the north, where it was widely believed that he was deranged. On 8 August 1975 he had formed a fifth provisional government which would be the most pro-communist of all, since no other political grouping wished to be identified with an obviously sinking ship.

As deputy premier, he appointed sixty-eight-year-old José Teixeira Ribeiro, a professor from Coimbra University who had consistently declined cabinet posts under the previous regime but who was described in 1975 as a 'red Salazarist' because he had been a theorist of corporativism in the 1930s. On the very same day this government was sworn in, moderate socialist officers published a manifesto which became known as the 'Document of the Nine'. The document, largely drawn up by Major Melo Antunes, and signed by eight other prominent officers, rejected Russian-style communism and 'the social-democratic model of . . . western Europe because . . . the great problem of Portuguese society cannot be surmounted by repeating the classical schemes of advanced capitalism in our country'.[59] Instead the Nine called for 'a middle way' which would respect public opinion and lead to a gradual and peaceful transfer to socialism. They also attacked Gonçalves latest government, describing it as 'lacking in credibility' and 'manifestly incapable of governing'.[60]

Most of the signatories of the Document of the Nine were committed socialists, something which prompted the anti-Communist right to argue in the late 1970s that their initiative had been a PCP operation designed to avoid civil war while maintaining leftist influence in the army and the institutions of state. Claims and counter-claims like these about the behaviour of the main revolutionary protagonists in 1974–75 were legion in the democratic era. Many were fraudulent or merely sensational. But the whole story of the revolution has yet to be told, and a lot of surprises may be revealed in due course. As for the Nine in 1975, their document was circulated throughout the army and air force, where it gained the support of some four-fifths of serving officers. Very much on the defensive, Gonçalves made a desperate attempt to rally support with a speech to 10,000 communists at Almada, in the red belt south of Lisbon on 18 August. But his days were numbered and he was finally dismissed on 29 August by President Costa Gomes, who tried to soften the blow by making Gonçalves commander-in-chief of the army. This raised a storm of protest from the army as well as from the ever bolder Soares, who declared that the PS would not tolerate this appointment. In the end, it was not ratified and Gonçalves rapidly drifted into obscurity.

The new prime minister was fifty-eight-year-old Admiral José Pinheiro de Azevedo, the commander-in-chief of the navy and, until then, thought of as one of the more radical MFA leaders. Before the revolution Azevedo had been naval attaché at the Portuguese embassy in London from 1968 to 1971, a posting which for various reasons he did not find congenial. From April 1974 to September 1975 he cultivated a radical image and was thought to be close to the PCP, which had considerable influence in the navy. In spring 1975 Azevedo declared, 'I do not want any social-democrat in the navy,' a reference to Admiral Vítor Crespo.[61] Azevedo was in fact an opportunist who began to distance himself from the left as soon as its power was seen to be waning. Deep down, he had no real socialist convictions, as was demonstrated in 1976 when he joined the small right-wing Christian Democratic Party. After he became premier in September 1975 he even seems to have been in regular telephone contact with Commander Alpoim Calvão, leader of the underground right-wing MDLP, who was boasting in October 1975 that 'I shall eat my *rabanadas de Natal* [cinnamon Christmas cookies] in Lisbon'.[62] Mário Soares accurately summed up Azevedo as follows:

> Very direct, very frank, very emotional. Too emotional . . . He is certainly not cut out for politics. Among other reasons because, as a military man, he finds it difficult to listen to anyone else's point of view.[63]

The government formed by Azevedo on 19 September 1975 contained ministers from the PS, the PPD and the PCP. After three months of illness, during which the leadership of the PPD had been delegated to

Professor Emidio Guerreiro (an elderly radical with a long Resistance background both in Portugal and in occupied wartime Europe). Sá Carneiro returned to the political saddle on 24 September with a fierce attack on the MFA. At the PPD's national conference he accused it of 'having neither the legitimacy nor the competence to govern'.[64] Seeing its crippled state, the civilian political leaders lost all inhibitions about attacking the Armed Forces Movement, which was, by now, irredeemably divided. However, the new government was unable to establish control over the country. In Lisbon ultra-leftists still seemed to be making much of the running in the autumn of 1975. Huge revolutionary demonstrations occurred in the capital during August and September, swelled by thousands of sympathetic young radicals from other parts of Europe. A pact, known as the United Revolutionary Front (FUR), was even briefly established between the far-left parties and the PCP but it soon collapsed in acrimony.

Inside the armed forces, revolutionary feelings were spreading among the lower ranks of the army while the officer corps emerged as increasingly moderate. A radical military movement known as SUV (Soldiers United Will Overcome) emerged in August and was able to get its hands on large numbers of guns that disappeared from arsenals in military barracks. Captain Álvaro Fernandes, a senior member of COPCON, who had helped Otelo draft a manifesto for 'popular power', gave away upwards of 20,000 guns to military leftists in the autumn of 1975. The ingredients for a major confrontation obviously seemed to be present. On 27 September the Spanish embassy was sacked and burned after General Franco had ordered the execution of five political prisoners. The Azevedo government was unable to prevent acts of violence like this in what was still a revolutionary situation. Since COPCON was not discharging its original function of maintaining order, a new praetorian body, the Military Intervention Force (FIM) was formed on 29 September.

Gradually, professional military elements began to band together, and on 7 November FIM was able to blow up the transmitter of Radio Renascença, a Catholic radio station which had fallen into ultra-leftist hands. The next day 20,000 striking building workers beseiged the constituent assembly in the São Bento palace. Deputies were trapped along with an infuriated Premier Azevedo until the government finally capitulated before the strikers' demand for higher wages. On 20 November the government itself went on strike until President Costa Gomes and the army re-established order and authority. Talk of a Lisbon commune was rife, and contingency plans were drawn up to transfer the capital northwards to Oporto. In Rio Maior, during the third week of November, 20,000 farmers grouped in the powerful Confederation of Portuguese Farmers led by José Manuel Casqueiro, met and threatened to cut Lisbon off from the rest of the country by blocking roads and discontinuing food, electricity and water supplies. Eighteen months after the 25 April 1974 *coup*, there seemed a real danger of civil war, in which north and south, urban and rural Portugal, reactionary farmers and revolutionary workers would be the protagonists.

But on 25 November 1975 the revolution which had the rest of western Europe on tenterhooks suddenly fizzled out. Radical military units still outnumbered professional army forces in Lisbon but their level of disorganisation was such that they were easily neutralised after a confused radical putsch on 25 November. At the last minute the PCP decided to have nothing to do with their doomed effort, and commando units led by the tough Major Jaime Neves were able to mop up the remaining pockets of ultra-left strength inside the forces during the closing days of November. If they had been properly co-ordinated the left could perhaps have held Lisbon for some months but only at the cost of ultimate defeat and enormous bloodletting. Many of the MFA militants realised this, which may explain the half-hearted nature of their action on ˙25 November. Otelo, General Fabião and other radicals do not seem to have been involved but they were afterwards demoted or else removed from positions of authority. Colonel Ramalho Eanes, an unknown officer, who had largely been responsible for engineering the come-back of the moderates inside the army, became the new chief of staff. It was left to a disconsolate Captain Dinis de Almeida of the MFA left to remark with some justification that 'a thousand Maos and Lenins have betrayed us'.[65]

Notes

1 Harsgor, *Portugal in Revolution*, p. 22.
2 Maxwell, 'Portugal under Pressure', p. 20.
3 Sobel (ed.), *Portuguese Revolution*, p. 63.
4 Blackburn, 'The test in Portugal', p. 16.
5 Soares, *Portugal's Struggle*, p. 40.
6 José Freire Antunes, ' "Fazer o jogo" dos communistas', *Expresso*, 13 September 1980, p. 11.
7 Avelino Rodrigues *et al.*, *Portugal depois de abril*, Intervoz, Lisbon, 1976, p. 14.
8 *Current Biography 1974*, 'António Sebastião Ribeiro de Spínola', Wilson, New York, 1975.
9 Harsgor, *op. cit.*, p. 18.
10 Ben Pimlott, 'Parties and voters in the Portuguese revolution', *Journal of Parliamentary Affairs*, winter 1977, p. 41.
11 See *Diário Popular* (Lisbon), 26 June 1974.
12 Pimlott, *op. cit.*, p. 42.
13 Bill Lomax, 'The left in Portugal, 1974/75', in Graham and Wheeler (eds.), *The Portuguese Revolution*.
14 Kenneth Maxwell, 'The hidden revolution in Portugal', *New York Review of*

Books, 17 April 1975, p. 32.
15 See Mailer, *Portugal*, pp. 80–1.
16 *Keesings Contemporary Archives*, 20 May 1974, p. 26519, Longmans, London, 1974.
17 Bender, *Angola under the Portuguese*, p. 206.
18 Robinson, *Contemporary Portugal*, p. 200.
19 Murray Sayle, 'Red flags, running dogs, and air-conditioned horses', *New Statesman*, 26 May 1978, p. 703.
20 *Sunday Times* Insight Team, *Insight on Portugal*, p. 165.
21 Robinson, *op. cit.*, p. 217.
22 António de Figueiredo, 'About turn', *The Guardian*, 25 August 1975, p. 9.
23 Robert Harvey, *Portugal. Birth of a Democracy*, Macmillan, London, 1978.
24 Rodrigues *et al.*, *op. cit.*, p. 93.
25 Sra Amélia Pereira Hutchinson kindly provided this information.
26 Tom Gallagher, 'The Portuguese Communist Party and Eurocommunism', *Political Quarterly*, Vol. 50, No. 2, April–June 1979, p. 196.
27 George W. Grayson, 'Portugal and the Armed Forces Movement', *Orbis*, Vol. 19, No. 2, summer 1975, p. 353.
28 *Sunday Times* Insight Team, *op. cit.*, p. 185.
29 *Ibid.*, p. 196.
30 *Ibid.*, pp. 196–7.
31 *Ibid.*, p. 196.
32 Mário Soares, *Portugal. Quelle révolution?* Calman-Lévy, Paris, 1975, pp. 85–6.
33 Eusébio Mujal-Leon, 'The PCP and the Portuguese revolution', *Problems of Communism*, January–February 1977, p. 68.
34 Maxwell, *op. cit.*, p. 31.
35 Harsgor, *op. cit.*, p. 26.
36 Edward Mortimer, 'Dr Soares says his target is the destruction of capitalism', *The Times*, 23 September 1975, p. 5.
37 Harvey, *op. cit.*, p. 33.
38 *Time Magazine*, 13 May 1974.
39 John Torode, 'Lisbon letter', *The Guardian*, 25 April 1975, p. 17.
40 Robinson, *op. cit.*, p. 236.
41 Maxwell, 'Portugal under pressure', p. 20.
42 Sobel (ed.), *op. cit.*, p. 96.
43 See Ben Pimlott, 'Were the soldiers revolutionary? The Armed Forces Movement and the Portuguese revolution', *Iberian Studies*, Vol. 7, No. I, spring 1978, p. 20.
44 Harvey, *op. cit.*, p. 50.
45 Sobel (ed), *op. cit.*, p. 98.
46 *Sunday Times* Insight Team, *op. cit.*, p. 242.
47 *Ibid.*, p. 246.
48 *Keesings Contemporary Archives*, 2–8 June 1975, p. 27156, Longmans, London, 1975.
49 Quoted in Gallagher, *op. cit.*, p. 205.
50 Porch, *Portuguese Armed Forces*, p. 205.
51 *Keesings Contemporary Archives*, 8–14 September 1975, p. 27319, Longmans, London, 1975.
52 Chips Downs, 'Commissões de Moradores and urban struggles in revolutionary Portugal', paper presented at the ICGMP Conference on

Modern Portugal, University of Durham, New Hampshire, USA, 24 June 1979.
53 Mailer, *op. cit.*, pp. 237–9.
54 Gallagher, 'Peasant conservatism', p. 65.
55 *The Guardian*, 26 July 1975.
56 Details about the Azorean crisis is contained in Brian McTigue and Fred Strasser, '1975: Americanos, OAS e Almeida Reúnem–se em Paris para negociar a independência dos Açores', *Expresso* (review section), 14 November 1978, pp. 1–6.
57 Mailer, *op. cit.*, p. 312.
58 Sobel (ed.), *op. cit.*, p. 107.
59 Keefe, *Area Handbook*, p. 233.
60 Harvey, *op. cit.*, p. 66.
61 Rodrigues *et al., op. cit.*, p. 259.
62 *Time Magazine*, 6 October 1975.
63 Oriana Fallaci, 'Disintegating Portugal: an interview with Mario Soares', *New York Review of Books*, 13 November 1975.
64 *Keesings Contemporary Archives*, p. 27349, Longmans, London, 1975.
65 Robinson, *op. cit.*, p. 250.

10

Democracy's chance, 1976–81

Picking up the pieces: November 1975 – July 1976

The 1974–75 revolution had ended with a whimper, not a bang. If the PCP had deployed its forces on the side of the ultra-left on 25 November the finale might not have been so anticlimactic. One rumour prevalent in the mid-1970s suggests that Álvaro Cunhal backed off as a result of a US–Soviet deal whereby Washington allowed the Soviet-backed MPLA to triumph in Angola in return for a Moscow promise to restrain the Portuguese communists.[1] Whatever machinations accompanied the demise of the Portuguese revolution, it is clear that within a few hours of the November 1975 insurrection the balance of power had shifted decisively from the far left to the centre left. No anti-radical witch-hunt began, since the right was still very weak, and it was the divided forces of the left which had largely engineered their own fall.[2] Many of the original revolutionary heroes now found themselves in disgrace. Some, like Colonel Varela Gomes, Commander Ramiro Correia and Major José da Costa Martins, fled to the former African colonies.

Varela Gomes later returned, in 1979, but Commander Correia was drowned in a boating accident off the coast of Mozambique in 1977, while Costa Martins was arrested by the Angolans in June 1977 for his role in a *coup* bid against President Agostinho Neto of the Marxist MPLA, which had emerged victorious from the 1975 Angolan civil war.[3] Captain Álvaro Fernandes of Copcon, who had distributed thousands of army weapons to revolutionaries in 1975, was another casualty who, in 1978, tried to take his own life shortly after being arrested by the authorities on returning from France. But most of the hard left soldiers, like Vasco Gonçalves and Admiral Rosa Coutinho, faded into domestic obscurity. Surprisingly, there have been no insurrectionary ripples from the 1974–75 period. With the exception of a small terrorist group known as FP25, which attempted to kidnap the finance minister in 1980, Portugal has been spared the insurgency and terrorism which has convulsed much of western Europe from Belfast to Athens. No backlash occurred when Isabel do Carmo and other leaders of the revolutionary PRP were arrested in 1978 and, after a two-year wait, given heavy prison sentences on what some concerned jurists abroad saw as trumped-up conspiracy charges.[4]

Soon after 25 November *fados* (Portuguese folk songs) were heard on the radio. Beforehand, they had been banished 'on the grounds that they encouraged listlessness and fatalism and were therefore inimical to social progress and enlightenment'.[5] The once radical Bishop of Oporto surprised many when, in the revolutionary twilight, he singled out order as a greater priority than 'bread to eat'. Along with former radicals like Vera Lagoa, Bishop Ferreira Gomes had been alienated by the wilder excesses of the revolution, which its opponents afterwards referred to as the period of the PREC (*processo revolucionário em curso*). This is an ironic copy of the phrase that was used continuously by the MFA, who even abbreviated it and talked simply about the 'process'. Between September 1974 and November 1975, the period of the PREC, the air was thick with references to 'deepening the process', 'the rhythm of the process', obstacles to the process and any number of variations.[6]

After 25 November most of the PIDE operatives detained in 1974 were released unless, like Salazar's former henchman, Henrique Seixas, or the last head of the PIDE, Fernando Silva Pais, they faced grave charges. Outside prison they found that not all had changed, with some major roads, for instance, still named after pre-1974 leaders (one in Lisbon commemorating Duarte Pacheco, another, in Oporto, General Gomes da Costa). In the post-revolutionary atmosphere right-wingers on serious charges were treated more leniently than radicals. In 1977 *Le Monde*, the French newspaper, commented that Major Mota Freitas, the deputy police chief in Oporto (until implicated in right-wing bombings in 1976), 'had no difficulty in ignoring the warrant put out for him because of the solid protection he apparently enjoys'.[7] Conversely, investigators hunting for the PIDE murderers of General Delgado faced an uphill task. In 1976 Fernando Oneto of the Judicial Police died in rather mysterious circumstances after being dropped from the case. Thereafter the authorities seemed content to make an example of the former PIDE chief, Major Silva Pais. Although suffering from cancer, he was kept in prison until September 1979. He died in 1981 but his story had an ironic twist, since his daughter was then living in Cuba, where she was reputedly the mistress of Fidel Castro's brother Raúl, an important figure in his own right.

While the former stars of the *Estado Novo* and the revolution were drifting into obscurity, the military and civilian pragmatists in charge of the country by 1976 were very much preoccupied with devising stable and (hopefully) lasting political structures. Although challenged by right-wing officers like Colonel António Pires Veloso, Major Jaime Neves and Colonel Soares Carneiro, the group of officers known as 'the Nine' were able to maintain their political influence. Led by Majors Melo Antunes and Vítor Alves, they saw themselves as guarantors of democracy rather than as a revolutionary vanguard. This moderate rump of the MFA was instrumental in drawing up a new pact signed on 14 February 1976 whereby the military formally agreed to hand over power to civilians later that year. Under this agreement one MFA institution would survive the demise of the revolution: until at least 1980 the wholly military Council of the Revolution was to have a major say in the choice of cabinet as well as a blocking veto over legislation concerning defence and the socio-economic gains of the revolution.

The military's continued if much reduced influence in politics was buttressed by a new democratic constitution (much of it drawn up under the aegis of the left-wing jurist Jorge Miranda). Ratified by the constituent assembly in April 1976, it committed the country to assuring the 'transition to socialism through the creation of conditions for the democratic exercise of power by the working classes'.[8] Other statutes guaranteed the democratic conquests of the revolutionary process and decreed that the historic mission of the military was to oversee the peaceful transition to democracy and socialism.

This controversial document has been called the most radical constitution anywhere in the non-communist world. Its successful passage into law also demonstrated that the aftermath of 1974–75 could hardly be described as counter-revolutionary; just as there had been no real red terror in 1975, no white terror followed in 1976.

Instead, in an atmosphere of calm, plans went ahead for two sets of elections which, it was hoped, would complete the transition to democracy. April 25 1976 was earmarked for the first parliamentary general election and 27 June 1976 was set aside to elect a presidential head of state. The successful candidate would inherit wide powers, since, under the 1976 constitution, he could, among other things, dismiss a premier even if he had a parliamentary majority, or else appoint someone from outside parliament. The constitution (truly a quirky document) also laid down that only political parties could field candidates and that elections must take place four years after the first one, even if parliament had, in the meantime, been dissolved. The latter clause saddled the Portuguese with a plethora of elections at the end of the 1970s, while politicians were increasingly dissatisfied with the first one. In 1978 two former Socialists, José Medeiros Ferreira and António Barreto, challenged the current electoral legislation, declaring that groups, movements and even private persons ought to be given the right to stand. But in 1976 political leaders were too preoccupied with getting their parties into shape to worry overmuch about the awkward snares in the constitution. In the April 1976 general election the Socialists emerged as the overall winners, but with a reduced 34·9 per cent of the vote. Dr Soares's party was followed by the centrist PPD, with 24·3 per cent, and the right-wing CDS, up from 7·6 to 16·0 per cent. No large swing to the right had occurred, and (in alliance with the fellow-travelling MDP) the communist PCP was able to increase its vote from 12·5 to 14·4 per cent.

Afterwards, all attention was focused on the presidential elections, since it was not until they were over that the first constitutional (as opposed to provisional) government would be sworn in. Most political leaders were agreed on the need for a military president (at least in the short term) as the best means of staving off praetorianism. But who to choose? The military personalities of the revolution like Spínola and Otelo had more or less disqualified themselves, and the incumbent provisional president, General Costa Gomes, was not trusted by left or right. That anything could have happened is demonstrated by the fact that the radical Major Antunes was at one point even backing the candidacy of Admiral Azevedo, who (despite his leftist rhetoric) was in reality a devotee of the far right. In the end, the person chosen by all the main non-communist parties was General Ramalho Eanes, who, as a mere colonel, in November 1975 had been responsible for neutralising the far left.

The forty-one-year-old Eanes was a reluctant candidate, and it was only in April 1976 that he finally agreed to allow his name to go forward. Cold, austere and usually hidden behind a pair of dark glasses, his rather sinister appearance made him seem like a throwback to the pre-1974 past. His glum, laconic manner brought frequent comparisons with Salazar, while the left talked about the rise of a Portuguese Pinochet ready to turn the clock back to 24 April 1974. In Lisbon, during the summer of 1976, one English journalist thought the present writer hopelessly naive to read anything into the fact that Eanes had quoted Harold Laski and other democratic socialist theorists in his inaugural speech. However, in Portugal, politics especially are not always what they seem. In practice Eanes turned out to be a slightly left-of-centre officer who did not practise his Catholic religion and who would presumably have taken part in the 1974 *coup* but for the fact that he was stationed in Angola.

Three main candidates opposed General Eanes: the outgoing premier, Admiral Azevedo, standing as an independent; Octávio Pato, the civilian PCP candidate; and Otelo de Carvalho, standing on an independent far-left ticket. The 1976 constitution allows for a second ballot if the front-runner fails to get more than 50 per cent of the vote. But there was no need. With 61 per cent, Eanes won a landslide victory, Otelo coming a distant second with 16 per cent; Eanes won in every electoral district with the exception of working-class Setúbal, south of Lisbon.

Socialism again? 1976–78

On being sworn in as president, General Eanes resisted right-wing calls for a coalition and appointed a Socialist government even though the PS lacked an overall parliamentary majority; he also added the proviso that, should the experiment fail, an attempt would be made to form a more broadly based administration.

When the PS government, led by Dr Soares, was sworn in on 16 July 1976 it marked the completion of Portugal's two-year transition to democracy. Political conditions had stabilised during this period. However, enormous economic problems lay ahead for the new government.[9] Economic misrule before and after 25 April 1974, along with the traumas of African withdrawal, had left the country's economic infrastructure in chaos. With her foreign exchange reserves almost exhausted, investment from abroad almost gone, and emigrants still reluctant to send their earnings home, the PS government had to act decisively. Economic failure was widely seen as the greatest threat to Portugal's infant democracy. Nevertheless, disillusionment with the democratic process was hardly apparent. The electors (all first-time voters if under seventy) showed striking maturity in 1975–76, an eighteen-month period which saw two parliamentary, one presidential and one municipal election. Abstentionism, violence and major fluctuations in party support were signally absent from the scene. In the April and June 1976 elections an 83 and 75 per cent turn-out was recorded, respectable by southern European standards, high by north European ones. However, the parties hardly set a good example to the voters. Sharp antagonism between and within the major non-communist parties became the norm in place of the co-operation which had occurred in the revolutionary period. Dr Soares, the new premier, got off to a bad start in 1976 through his failure to persuade leading party figures to take on the three most difficult portfolios: finance, labour and economic co-ordination. In power for two years, the Socialist Party's inability to improve Portugal's economic performance badly dented its reputation with the voters. So did rumours of corruption and peculation in high places. No major scandals actually broke, but it was common knowledge in informed circles during the PS's two-year reign that party supporters were being drafted into the bureaucracy in large numbers, an ancient practice known in Portugal as *empreguismo*.

The job-seeking opportunists who flocked to join the PS after 1975 provided the bulwark of support for Dr Soares as he began to encounter difficulties from rival tendencies within the party. For most of its existence his government was in fact paralysed by internal divisions over economic policy, the centre-left advocating a policy of growth and the right supporting deflation and austerity. At the 1976 party conference left-wingers led by Aires Rodrigues Kalidas Barreto and the agriculture minister, António Lopes Cardoso, tried to assert themselves but were slapped down by the normally bland Soares, who acts ruthlessly when his personal authority is challenged. Afterwards the dissenters left the party but went their different ways. Lopes Cardoso formed a rival left-wing party, the UEDS, which performed abysmally (interestingly, its founding conference in 1978 was attended by Major Antunes of the Council of the Revolution).

In non-economic areas, it has to be said that the record of the PS was not without success. After revolution and years of dictatorship, the Soares government showed itself capable of maintaining order and discipline within a democratic framework. This was no mean feat, considering that wage levels slumped for certain groups of workers in 1977 and 1978 to pre-1970 levels. No backlash came from the communist-controlled trade union movement (whose name was changed from Intersindical to CGTP-IS in 1977), because Cunhal and his colleagues feared that this might prompt right-wingers in the army to make a bid for power. So the working class remained quiet, with the exception of a brief riot in a north-east mining district in 1976, involving Cape Verdian emigrants and local Portuguese. The Lisbon weekly *Expresso*, in its 8 October 1976 edition, described this as Portugal's first race riot, but it was very much an isolated event in a country where race relations are possibly more harmonious than anywhere else in Europe.

Portugal's ability to absorb newcomers was put to the test by the arrival of at least 700,000 white refugees from the *ultramar* in 1974–76. Embittered and susceptible to right-wing demagogues (like General Galvão de Melo, a member of parliament from 1976 to 1979), most of the *retornados* were set on their feet and integrated into the general community during the late 1970s. This is a small miracle for which a relatively poor country like Portugal has received scant credit. Much of the important work of rehabilitation was carried out by the Socialists between 1976 and 1978.

In view of *retornado* opinion, Dr Soares took a calculated risk by partially normalising relations with the Marxist regimes in Angola, Mozambique and Guinea-Bissau. This restoration of African ties was part of a wider global initiative which gave him an excuse to put his domestic troubles behind him and spend long periods abroad. Between 1976 and 1978 Portugal reaffirmed her membership of NATO, granted autamy to her Atlantic territories, renewed a forty-year alliance with Spain and, in April 1977, formally applied to join the EEC. However, the tangible benefits from Soares's foreign policy offensive were slight. EEC officials showed little willingness to ease entry terms for a country as poor in relative terms as Portugal, and a Marshall-type plan, which Western countries in 1975 intimated they would launch if Portugal rejected Marxist revolution, was simply not forthcoming.[10] The country was instead left to face its economic difficulties, which were stark. At the end of

1977 it had the worst unemployment (an estimated 25 per cent), balance-of-payments deficit and inflation in the whole of Europe. Bankruptcy seemed just round the corner when the Soares government called in the International Monetary Fund (IMF) late in 1978. Stiff terms (devaluation, deflation and a reduction of consumption) were offered in return for a large loan. Soares reluctantly accepted this classic IMF prescription but it was rejected by the other political parties, which in December toppled the eighteen-month government in a vote of no confidence.

The Socialist Party's experience in government was somewhat akin to the MFA's. Having been united in resistance to dictatorship, the pressures and responsibilities of office quickly combined to erode internal unity. By 1978 two ministers of agriculture and one foreign minister had left the party and more top members would follow. The later defections came from the right, despite the fact that Soares formed a coalition with the most conservative of all the main parties, the CDS, in December 1976. Coalition had previously been rejected, not least because single-party rule gave the PS control of patronage. Otherwise, the pragmatic Soares had no ideological qualms about arranging a marriage of convenience with the CDS.

However, it produced an angry reaction on the far right. Freitas do Amaral, the clever, bespectacled leader of the CDS, was openly insulted on the streets as a result of the pact. Nasty scenes occurred at extreme-right rallies organised on 1 December 1977 and 10 June 1978, respectively liberation day from Spain and the national day of Portugal. In the midst of the economic recession, extreme right-wingers gained adherents from among the country's middle-class youth, now facing the prospect of unemployment or else work far below their class expectations. After 1975 many middle-class adolescents quickly shifted over from the far left to the far right. In 1977 the press began to publish articles about Lisbon high schools which were virtually in the grip of militant right-wing pupils among whom Hitler and Salazar cults were flourishing.[11] In school elections, even in working-class towns like Barreiro and Setúbal, left-wing slates were routed. But leaving aside the ephemeral MIRN/PDP, organised by General Kaúlza de Arriaga, a strong counter-revolutionary force failed to emerge. With no history of party-building behind them, extreme right-wingers had been severely traumatised by the revolution and the loss of empire, while the CDS and PPD had quickly filled the vacuum on the constitutional right with their increasingly conservative policies.

At elections the far right has sunk without trace, and it is only through individual stunts that reactionaries have remained in the limelight. Attempts to erect a statue to Salazar in his native village of Santa Comba

Dão led to rioting with the police in 1978, and in the same year Manuel Múrias, editor of the incendiary *A Rua*, was sent to jail for a year for calling Premier Soares a liar. Two years later, with the triumph of Dr Sá-Carneiro's centre-right Democratic Alliance at the polls, Múrias proclaimed the death of the right, but this was premature. Before 1926 the undemocratic right was likewise electorally non-existent but that did not prevent it from seizing power. As long as post dictatorial Portugal continues economically and socially to resemble the pre-1974 period, then the authoritarian right will be of far more relevance than in other European liberal democracies.

However, in the short term, the ability of two parties like the PS and the CDS to co-operate in government weakened the right-wing claim that the Portuguese were inherently unsuited for democracy, as did the level-headed behaviour of ordinary people in the first five years of democracy. Eventually differences over agriculture caused the left–right coalition to break up in July 1978. The militant Portuguese Confederation of Farmers, led by José Manuel Casqueiro, organised demonstrations against the government's dilatoriness in taking action against the collective farms set up in the Alentejo during the revolution. With its supporters up in arms, the CDS took fright and indicated that it was leaving, which prompted President Eanes to dismiss Soares early in August 1978.

Frozen politics, 1978–79

In government Dr Soares had proved a nimble politician but a poor administrator. Like the politicians of the First Republic (some of whom he closely resembled), he was more concerned with rhetoric, abstractions and partisan politics than with the inglorious but necessary tasks of policy-making and economic reconstruction. At least up to 1980, this is a charge that could be laid at the door of the other party leaders too. *Personalismo* (loyalty to persons rather than to institutions or ideas) continued to play a divisive role in politics at a time when it was hoped that intrigue and factional in-fighting would give way to a concerted effort, on the part of major politicians, to tackle major structural problems in the socio-economic realm.

After 1976 hopes that the two largest parties, the PS and the PPD (renamed the Social Democratic Party, PSD, in that year) might form a coalition were quickly dashed. Both parties are only a few degrees to the left and right of centre, and together both would have enjoyed a clear parliamentary majority. However, intense personal rivalry between Dr Soares and the PSD leader Sá Carneiro destroyed whatever chances there were of a strong centre government emerging. It was the politicians' inability to compromise and agree which led President Eanes to take matters into his own hands in the middle of 1978. Having previously declared that 'Portuguese democracy is lucky to have such a man as Ramalho Eanes', Dr Soares, the dismissed premier, thereafter distanced himself from the head of state.[12] However, while the politicians squabbled, it was Eanes who kept the ship of democracy afloat. Before 1978 he had already demonstrated his presidential authority by calling individual ministers to the Belém palace without the premier's clearance and by appointing an independent commission (in 1977) to look into the troubled economy. Austere and shy, he proved a good target for right-wing cartoonists; in 1979 one of them, Augusto Cid, produced a best-seller which was eventually seized by the authorities.[13] But Ramalho Eanes was generally popular in the country, as was his new choice of premier in August 1978, Alfredo Nobre da Costa, an economic manager who was not a politician. A cabinet of moderate technocrats, who were also not full-time politicians, was sworn in on 10 August. This move angered parliament although it was constitutionally permissable. Nobre da Costa lost a vote of confidence but President Eanes would not be deflected from seeking a non-party solution to the political deadlock: none of the party leaders was capable of forming a government with majority support in parliament, and fresh elections were out of the question, as the voting register was being changed to accommodate the huge numbers of refugees from Africa. Once again, therefore, in October 1978, the president chose an independent prime minister. Carlos Mota Pinto, a Coimbra professor who had been a member of the 1974–75 constituent assembly, proved acceptable to parliament. His centre-right government was notable for including a minister of finance who had been a junior minister in the Salazarist 1950s and an information minister who had been a defence counsel for the PIDE and before that a police chief under Caetano.[14]

The Mota Pinto government rapidly became deeply unpopular as a result of introducing austerity measures on top of those imposed by previous governments and by July 1979 had lost its parliamentary majority. An exasperated President Eanes announced that a general election would take place before the end of the year. The decision was taken reluctantly, because any election held in 1979 could be only an interim one. Under the terms of Portugal's distinctive constitution, another general election would have to be held in 1980 to begin the next legislative term – even if parliament had been dissolved in the meantime.

To govern the country in the run-up to fresh elections, the president appointed a caretaker government headed by Maria de Lurdes Pintasilgo, the leader of the Portuguese delegation to UNESCO. This would be the third and last of the 1978–79 independent non-party governments. The new premier was a rather paradoxical figure: a radical Catholic who had been a member of the Corporative Chamber after 1969 and (according to her enemies) of the Mocidade before that. Her elevation was ample proof that all is rarely what it seems in the byzantine world of Portuguese politics, and that a politician's past record is no guide to future behaviour.

From the outset Senhora Pintasilgo met implacable opposition from the centre-right politicians, who, by 1979, were loudly accusing President Eanes of showing excessive partiality to the left, even though he had been elected with the support of the CDS and the PSD as well as the Socialists.

Dr Sá Carneiro was particularly scathing in his condemnation of the president. Having attempted to join the Socialist International in 1976, the PSD leader had led his party rightwards in the wake of the revolution, hoping to solidify a base among the rural and small-town Portuguese of the north and centre where the majority of the population live. An impulsive politician (known as the 'No. 1 Militant') and a tough anti-communist, Sá Carneiro, by 1978, was accusing the president of planning to set up 'a Yugolslav-style dictatorship'.[15] He also waged a strident campaign against the principal legacies of the revolution – the nationalisation of the banks, the 1975 land seizures in the Alentejo and the 'quasi-Marxist' constitution. But opposition came from many of his party colleagues, technocrats and lawyers, whose aim was to create a party of progressive capitalism based on the model provided by the West German Social Democrats.[16]

Sá Carneiro actually vacated the leadership of the PSD between November 1977 and July 1978. Nevertheless, he was able to return in triumph, owing to strong support from the rank and file. Most party members endorsed what others saw as Sá Carneiro's 'Poujadist' attacks on the leftist Lisbon establishment. This was impressed on the writer while he was travelling past Salazar's birthplace with a shopkeeper and his wife. These two party supporters patiently explained how they were Social Democrats as well as great admirers of Salazar. While retaining faith in the parliamentary process, Dr Sá Carneiro vividly expressed the aspirations of the large and mainly rural 'silent majority'. In April 1979 he established total dominance in the PSD when thirty-seven of its seventy-four deputies quit. Very quickly a new leadership emerged that was conservative, loyal to the party leader and close to the grass roots of the party.

Finally, in July 1979, Dr Sá Carneiro emerged as a major contender for power when it was announced that three of the centre-right parties were forming a coalition known as the Democratic Alliance (AD) to fight the approaching elections. Three parties – the PSD, the CDS and the royalist and ecology-minded PPM – agreed to draw up a common list of candidates, and a unified manifesto was produced which promised decisive action in areas where the PS had failed to honour election pledges. It also committed Portugal to staying in NATO, as well as pressing ahead with her application to join the EEC, and set as a goal the creation of a more market-based economy. Freitas do Amaral, the young, scholarly CDS leader, and Dr Sá Carneiro established a good working relationship, the former having remarked a few years before that 'the CDS is a party of the centre which says it is, and the PPD [since renamed PSD] is a party of the centre which says it is on the left'.[17]

The other party to form a united front in 1979 was the communist PCP, who (in alliance with the small MDP) styled themselves the United People's Alliance (APU). Since 1976 the party had recovered lost ground, gaining control of more than 250 municipal assemblies in local elections during December 1976. Activists must have been especially encouraged when the PCP won in the small northern town where the first party office had been destroyed in the 'hot' summer of 1975. In fact the post-1976 years witnessed a concentrated recruiting campaign which saw total membership rise from 113,000 in 1977 to 164,000 in May 1979.[18] The Italian PCI is now the only west European communist party with a higher concentration per head of population than the Portuguese party. Basically, inroads were made among hitherto unreceptive groups like northern sharecroppers by adopting a more nationally independent line, distinct from both the Euro-communist and Soviet models. This was not entirely an exercise in subterfuge. Relations between the Soviet communist party (the CPSU) and what had hitherto been regarded as the most loyal pro-Moscow party in the West became strained even before the end of the 1974–75 revolution. Dr Cunhal, the PCP leader, appears to have been disillusioned by the CPSU's decision to play a rather conservative role in the one revolutionary situation in recent European history (with the possible exception of May 1968 in France).[19] Cunhal apparently resented the fact that in 1975–76 the Brezhnev leadership appears to have backed the Italian communist view that the political future of Portugal lay with western Europe.

Thereafter, increasing emphasis was laid on a Portuguese road to socialism while general support continued to be extended to the Soviet Union in all international matters, including the Sino-Soviet dispute. In more prosaic matters, Cunhal has defended the total freedom of the individual artist and deprecated Soviet realism in art. The PCP leader is himself a painter of no mean ability, but liberalism in this area does not, as yet, indicate that the Portuguese communists are prepared to espouse the more pluralist doctrine of Euro-communism. Dr Cunhal continues to anathemise the more consensual communism of his Spanish colleague, Santiago Carrillo, while embarking on an electoral strategy which was in effect a repudiation of the 1975 line that a parliamentary system was inappropriate to Portugal because the middle class was not strong enough to act as a barrier against fascism.

In the realm of industrial relations the party's approach has also been more moderate, although it has been harried by the PS (whose trade union spokesman, Maldonado Gonelha, has attempted to form a rival Socialist union confederation to the mainly communist CGTP-IS). Above all, the PCP has surprised observers by employing non-violent protest rather than all-out resistance against government agents, who, in the 1976–80 period, were able to break up a large number of the 250 collective farms formed on seized property in 1975.

In the last quarter of 1979 the PCP waged a very effective campaign before the elections scheduled for 2 December. Having suffered defections, the PS was more subdued, and the Socialist strategy was to give maximum visibility to its fifty-five year-old leader, Dr Soares, who remained personally popular. However, it was the Democratic Alliance (with a handsomely funded campaign) which made the greatest impact, and on 2 December it gained a small but clear electoral majority. With 45 per cent of the vote, it won just over half the 250 seats in the National Assembly and thus acquired the overall majority which had previously eluded all other parties. Nearly all the AD's increased support was at the expense of the Socialists, whose vote slumped by 7·5 per cent to 27·4. In Lisbon, the largest electoral district, the PS vote had crashed from 50·0 per cent in 1975 to 25·8 per cent in 1979.[20] In Oporto the party's vote managed to hold firm, while in the north generally the pro-communist APU registered striking gains. On the north-west coast, the Oporto–Aveiro–Braga industrial zone, the party won five extra seats which helped to push its total vote up from 14·4 per cent (in 1976) to 19·0 per cent. In the strongly religious city of Braga, Vítor de Sá, a Communist historian, won a seat, evidence of local dissatisfaction with clerical dominance in a city known as Portugal's Rome; in Aveiro, to the south of Oporto, Vital Moreira, a young PCP member who has been seen as a possible harbinger of Euro-communism in Portugal, was returned for a conservative northern area.

Nationally, the results indicated that the north–south polarisation which had manifested itself in 1975–76 was much reduced three years later. Each of the main contenders for power did best (or, in the case of the PS, managed to hold its own) in the areas where it had previously been weakest. Without impressive advances in the radical south the AD would not have gained an absolute majority. Without its new-found gains in the clerical and smallholding north the PCP would still be far behind the Socialists.

Paradoxically, it is the latter who were most damaged by the erosion of regional divisions and the onset of voting on more class-based lines. Unlike the socialist parties in northern Europe, the PS support has not come predominantly from the industrial working class. In Portugal the proletariat has backed the PCP just as strongly at elections. To reach the position of being the strongest party in the country, the PS had to draw support from a cross-section of interests and classes whose loyalty was difficult to maintain in the harsh economic climate after 1976. But after the great setbacks of 1979 Mário Soares's party still continued to remain a polyglot force. Unlike the PCP or AD, it had no well defined geographical power base. Nor is it particularly strong within the trade union world. Here the PCP and the right-wing parties respectively control a majority of blue- and white-collar workers.

Sá Carneiro's year

After 1979 the PSD was the largest party in the new parliament as well as in the AD coalition. Accordingly, it was Dr Sá Carneiro who was asked by the president to form a new administration. Born in 1934, he came from a wealthy Oporto family with liberal traditions, although an uncle, João Pinto da Costa Leite, had been one of Salazar's longest-serving ministers. After resigning from the National Assembly in 1973, where he had been a liberal deputy, Sá Carneiro was involved in a serious car crash which necessitated major plastic surgery to the lower half of his back. He never fully recovered his health, which was perhaps one of the reasons why his own colleagues sometimes found him difficult to get on with. Nineteen-eighty would be a year of political triumph and further ill-luck for the premier, who in May would have to cut short a visit to Britain after being injured in another, less serious, car crash.

Dr Sá Carneiro had taken office at the head of the first majority government since the revolution, on 4 January 1980. His fifteen-man cabinet (nine PSD, five CDS and one independent) was notable for being the first wholly civilian government in the lifetime of Portugal's democracy. Even the post of minister of defence was given to a civilian, the able thirty-six-year-old Adelino Amaro da Costa, deputy leader of the CDS. This plump former civil servant proved to be a deft conciliator in a region where civil–military friction had hitherto been the chief bane of democracy.[21] The armed forces, generally, backed the strong pro-Western foreign policy of the AD government. Premier Sá Carneiro was the first European leader to enact sanctions against the Soviet Union following the 1979 invasion of Afghanistan. Pessimistic about the future, he believed that Europe stood on the verge of a nuclear war, and he was determined to place Portugal firmly in the Western camp. At home, the AD programme rested on three basic tenets: pragmatism, liberalism and Europeanism. Steps were taken to revive the bid to enter the EEC, although formidable obstacles stood in the way of Portuguese entry by the hoped-for target year of 1983. Portugal remains the poorest country in non-communist Europe, as the statistics make abundantly clear. For instance, the gap between

Hamburg in West Germany and the northern district of Vila Real was (in 1978) twelve to one as regards gross domestic product (and six to one between Vila Real and the west of Ireland).[22]

Appropriately, it was economic recovery that was the main goal of the AD government. Fully aware that fresh elections were due in October 1980 in order to begin a second four-year legislative term, Sá Carneiro devoted most of his time to improving his country's economic performance. By the time the Democratic Alliance took office, a savage IMF-inspired pay and credit freeze was already beginning to push inflation down. But in the next ten months the pace of recovery quickened as the trade balance improved, unemployment was reduced from nearly 20 per cent and inflation fell from 25 to 20 per cent. In the middle of 1980 the finance minister, Aníbal Cavaco e Silva, was able to cut income tax and authorise a rise in real wages for the first time in four years, moves which did the government's popularity no harm.[23] For its economic achievements the AD coalition received strong endorsement from Portugal's youth, which, badly hit by unemployment, had been the one group to be swayed by the anti-democratic message of the extreme right. There is no doubt that during his twelve-month spell in government Dr Sá Carneiro had sound achievements to his credit. This hard-hitting and sometimes capricious lawyer demonstrated real administrative talent and Portugal experienced a rare phase of good government in 1980. However, many of his plans were frustrated by the Council of the Revolution, the watchdog of the 1976 constitution, composed solely of non-elected members of the armed forces. It vetoed twenty-three pieces of legislation in 1980 alone, including a bill to denationalise the domestic banks and others designed to streamline the military.

Leftist officers led by Major Melo Antunes have had a majority on the Council of the Revolution even though the military as a whole are far less radical. During 1980 the Democratic Alliance accused President Eanes of being unduly influenced by this radical group and determined not to support him for a second term in presidential elections scheduled for December 1980. But first it had to get the second round of parliamentary elections out of the way. These were held on 5 October 1980 (the seventieth anniversary of the creation of the republic), with the AD confronted by the Communists and by a Republican Socialist Front formed by the Socialists with the 1979 PSD dissidents and Lopes Cardoso's small UEDS. Still led by the austere old bolshevik Dr Cunhal, the PCP ironically made a big play for the northern Catholic vote. At the end of 1979 he had even declared that:

Just like other citizens, the bishops have every right to their political opinion to be socialists, communists or whatever they want, but they ought not to confuse a public meeting with a church pulpit. In our party are to be found thousands of

Catholics and even some priests.[24]

Much of the PCP's drive for the traditional vote involved rather questionable tactics. Voters were reminded that Dr Sá Carneiro had recently left his wife to live with Snu Bonnier, a Danish woman who had business interests in Portugal. But this hard-hitting tactic rebounded on the Communists, since the premier won admiration for his honesty in taking his companion with him on the electoral trail, thus defying convention in what is still a very traditional, if not unduly religious, land. The PCP simultaneously accused Dr Sá Carneiro of financial malpractice. The story goes that he borrowed money from a bank which he did not repay, an oversight which the revolution effectively buried for a number of years.[25] His chief critic was the lawyer of the PCP daily newspaper, who, before 25 April, had written for extreme right-wing newspapers like *Ágora* and *Época* and in other more controversial ways had aligned himself very much with the *Estado Novo*; other extreme rightists also joined the PCP after 1974, being chiefly motivated by the wish to be on the side of those who looked likely to be in power. The PCP in its turn used these defectors to extend its hold on the state apparatus, to do special jobs, and to obtain information. Others, still on the right, can sometimes have close personal contacts with individuals of the opposite persuasion, so small still is the Lisbon political elite. One industrialist who began his business career by selling dried fish in the interior of Angola has written for the leftist *O Jornal* and is friendly with radical journalists although he is a shareholder of the extreme right-wing *A Rua* and an admirer of the chief practitioners of central European fascism.

The elections of 5 October showed that the PCP had overestimated the malleability of the electorate. The Communists lost ground for the first time since the revolution and the Socialists were unable to register any significant improvements. The results allayed fears that the 1980s were about to see the Italianisation of Portuguese politics, with a centre-right bloc confronting a national communist party which monopolised the left at the expense of non-Marxist socialism.[26] Instead the AD emerged with a greatly increased majority, the Socialists following in second place. At times the AD had appeared to be the only one of the parties with a coherent programme, capable of governing, and for the first time it made inroads among proletarian voters in the south; the new deputies included (for the CDS) Adriano Moreira, Salazar's minister of the *ultramar* in 1961–62.

Another sign that the revolution was fast receding into the background was the choice of fifty-two-year-old General António Soares Carneiro (no relation to Sá Carneiro) as the AD candidate in the presidential elections of December 1980. This officer played no role in the anti-fascist *coup* of 1974 and was the leader of a veterans' association of former commandos.

Opposition spokesmen made much of the fact that he had run a detention camp in Angola during the final years of the *Estado Novo*. But it also emerged that the man who had helped to set up the camp later became a prominent member of the PS, so the accusation was double-edged. Nevertheless, some inside the PSD (like the premier of the Azores regional government, João Amaral) felt that Sá Carneiro would have done better to choose a prominent civilian or else General Spínola, the hero of the revolution in its moderate phase, rather than a controversial military figure. However, it seems that General Soares Carneiro was chosen because the prime minister was confident that he would go along with his plans to reduce presidential power (and be a second Carmona, in the words of one journalist).[27] By now Sá Carneiro was making it plain that he wanted to abolish the Council of the Revolution, deprive the president of his right to sack a government even if it had a majority in parliament, and remove the constitutional prohibitions on private enterprise. To show the voters that he was in real earnest, the prime minister (along with Freitas do Amaral, the deputy premier), publicly announced that he was not prepared to hold government office under a future Eanes presidency.

The choice which Dr Sá Carneiro was presenting to the electorate was a stark one, since President Eanes had remained a popular figure despite the country's steady drift to the right. Although humourless, shy and lacking in political finesse, Eanes had won the approval of many Portuguese of different persuasions as an honest man who was quite clearly not a member of the political class of Lisbon lawyers or Coimbra University professors which (regardless of the political system in being) had long dominated the country. His opponents, with the exception of the AD challenger, lacked major public support. The right-wing General Galvão de Melo still youthful-looking despite his fifty-nine years, came over as a vain individual and was unable to rely on the *retornado* support he had cultivated after 1975. Another right-wing soldier, fifty-four-year-old General António Pires Veloso, turned out to be a rather stumbling figure despite having been hailed as the viceroy of the north by conservatives during the closing stages of the 1975 revolution. These two cancelled each other out, as did the far left's Major Otelo (fighting gamely without any party backing) and the Trotskyite POUS's Aires Rodrigues, a former PS politician who had become a lorry driver in his home town of Leiria during the late 1970s; the Communists stood a candidate, the colourless Carlos Brito, who, however, withdrew at the last minute in order to enable the party to back Eanes.

The Socialist Party too supported the president's re-election, even after Mário Soares resigned as party leader on 19 October 1980, being unable to back the man who had sacked him in 1978; observers reckoned that Soares withheld his support because he feared that victory by Eanes would make the president the effective leader of the Portuguese left now that the PS was in opposition. Soares even threatened to sit out the election campaign in Paris, a move which he ultimately had second thoughts about. But it is worth making the point that the present electoral system allows a deputy to neglect his constituents in the way Soares proposed to do. Portuguese electoral districts are very large, and if a leading politician enters government (or, as in the case of Álvaro Cunhal, is too busy with party work to attend parliament), then the next person on the party ticket takes his place in parliament. This electoral system is very confusing and is reckoned to be badly in need of reform.

With the country in some confusion about just who was supporting whom, the final election campaign of 1980 turned out to be acrimonious and bitter. Although he had no political experience, the AD candidate fought a quietly effective campaign, whereas Eanes (who refused to confront Soares Carneiro alone in a television debate) was involved in controversy about his role in the 1975 revolution.[28] Right-wingers and former military colleagues suggested that he may have been involved in the confused events of March 1975 (see p. 210). However, there was no doubt about the role he had played later that year in defeating the extreme left at the end of the chaotic revolution, and the president appeared to be ahead in the race when, in the final days of campaigning, news came through of the death of Prime Minister Sá Carneiro.

On Thursday 4 December the light aircraft in which the premier was hoping to fly to Oporto crashed in flames while taking off from Lisbon airport. All the passengers, who included the premier, his companion, Snu Bonnier, and his defence minister, Amaro da Costa, were killed instantly. Ironically, Dr Sá Carneiro's last words to the control tower appear to have been that 'this piece of junk will never get off the ground'.[29] Sá Carneiro, the archetypal man in a hurry, met his death in a land which is obsessed with speed and often contemptuous of machinery. Knowing his reputation for cutting corners, the staid deputy premier, Freitas do Amaral, was always careful not to travel any long distance with Sá Carneiro, whose intolerance of delay was legendary.[30]

An extraordinarily hard worker and rapid decision-maker, Sá Carneiro had a clear vision of the Portugal he wanted and his loss may well be a dear one for the country. One of his main aims had been to push through a programme of administrative reform, without which he felt it was impossible to get the country moving. With forty civil servants for every 1,000 people, Portugal's 400,000-strong bureaucracy is proportionately one of the largest in the world, and to the premier it was a dead weight on the country.[31] Perhaps his mistake was to feel that, to get things done, he must do them himself. This is possibly the stuff of which dictators are made, but in the past Sá Carneiro had shown himself strongly committed to democracy (at times when it was not prudent to be an outspoken democrat). Whether he was a pugnacious democrat or an autocrat in the making was a mystery that would not be solved after 4 December. On the 6th he was given a state funeral, the greatest, some said, in Portugal's history. For a time there was speculation that the presidential election would have to be postponed, but the electoral commission ruled that it ought to go ahead, as it had done in June 1976 when (in an uncanny dress rehearsal for December 1980's incredible events) Premier Azevedo was stricken by a heart attack within days of polling for the first presidential election.

Right up to the last minute observers were unsure whether the AD candidate would receive a large sympathy vote or whether stunned and fearful voters would play safe and endorse Eanes. In the event the latter was what happened. On 7 December six million voters went to the polling booths to give the incumbent Eanes a clear 56 per cent of the votes as against 40 per cent for General Soares Carneiro. With possibly 480,000 AD voters supporting the president, he received more votes in 1980 than he had four years earlier (but a smaller percentage total: this being possible because of the expanded electorate). In working-class Setúbal, the only electoral district which he failed to win in 1976, he won his best result in 1980, Major Otelo and the revolutionary left being completely routed.

One rather tasteless incident rounding off an altogether bizarre year occurred in the closing days of 1980 when Dom Eurico Nogueira, the Archbishop of Braga, intimated (during a discourse on the family) that someone like Sá Carneiro possibly had no right to a Christian burial, let alone solemn rites in Lisbon's Jerónimos monastery, because of his unsettled private life. Nogueira had succeeded the arch-reactionary Francisco Maria da Silva (1910–77) as Archbishop of Braga after the latter's death. He was head of the Portuguese Church and was also known as the Primate of the Spains. But his homily brought down upon him the wrath of the right (ironically conservative in social matters), who accused him of phariseeism and minimal Christian charity. The hapless archbishop (who is politically fairly progressive) was also accused of crypto-Marxism, and he was even indirectly rebuked by the Bishop of Oporto, António Ferreira Gomes, a Christian humanist who spoke up for the former prime minister. In death as in life, it seems, controversy will continue to surround the extraordinary career and personality of Francisco Sá Carneiro.

Quo vadis, Portugal?

It came as little surprise that the AD government resigned shortly after the election. Meanwhile the PSD, the linchpin of the coalition, embarked on the task of finding a successor. By 13 December the party had made its choice: forty-three-year-old Francisco Pinto Balsemão, one of the three original founders of the party, was elected leader and asked to form a government by President Eanes.

Balsemão is a newspaper editor who was born into a comfortably-off Lisbon family who were involved in textiles. He grew up knowing King Juan Carlos of Spain (who spent much of his boyhood in Portugal), and in style and temperament he closely resembles Adolfo Suárez, who from 1976 to 1981 steered Spain through the first five years of its experiment with democracy. A pragmatic politician known for his conciliatory manner and liberal outlook, Balsemão served as General Kaúlza de Arriaga's aide-de-camp in the early 1960s and later, in 1973, went on to found *Expresso*, the leading Portuguese weekly newspaper which he edited until 1979.

Belonging on the left of the PSD, it is possible that Balsemão would not have been chosen in 1980 had there been an obvious successor to Sá Carneiro from the centre or right of the party. He enjoys far better relations with the president and can be expected to provide a style of leadership (and perhaps policies) different from Sá Carneiro's; he is remembered for having said in 1975 that the PSD could be transformed into the civilian wing of the revolutionary MFA.[32] Later, in 1976, he declared that if the PSD became a party of the right he would leave it, and, indeed, in 1978 he seemed about to abandon the PSD because of its leader's intransigent policies. However, Sá Carneiro (who was a personal friend) pleaded with him to remain, arguing prophetically that in the event of his disappearance the party would require a stabilising influence to take over from him.[33] (Sá Carneiro seems to have been convinced that he would have only a short life, which is perhaps why he lived it so intensely.)

What happens to the PSD in the absence of Sá Carneiro remains very much an open question, since, for most of its existence, the party was largely his own personal vehicle. Nevertheless, the prime minister's tragic death relieved Portugal of the prospect of an immediate confrontation between the government and the president. Sá Carneiro's successor may well be able to reach an accommodation with Eanes over the constitution, which can be altered provided two-thirds of parliament approves. The PS and the AD together could secure this majority and the Socialists have agreed, in principle, to the need for constitutional revision.

In December 1980 Dr Soares resumed the leadership of the PS, but the party remains badly shaken in the wake of his quixotic decision to resign three months earlier. Relations with Eanes, whom he accused of 'Peronism' after his election triumph, still remain poor and he has fallen out with Dr Francisco Salgado Zenha, his former close colleague, and deputy leader of the PS. Ill-health prevents him from effectively challenging his leader but the party is divided between 'historicals' and *Soaristas* on the one hand and technocrats and supporters of the president known variously as ex-GIS or *melo-antunistas* on the other. During May 1981, at the party conference, Soares emerged on top against his rivals. His popularity among the party's rank and file was able to offset the fact that he enjoyed only minority support within the parliamentary party. But the party he now leads is a wreck and has far more in common with the pre-1926 republican groupings than with any European socialist formation.

Since his decisive role in the 1974–75 revolution Soares's reputation has taken a steep nose-dive and it is no exaggeration to say that, in its present state, the PS would be a menace to democracy were it returned to government. Although recent events have reinforced the truth of the saying that anything can happen in Portuguese politics and usually does, there is no sign that the PS will be lifted from the doldrums. Along with the Communists, it has presented virtually no opposition to the government in the National Assembly after the October 1980 general election, and often during the first half of 1981 the opposition benches were quite deserted.

The Balsemão government was unable to profit from opposition weakness because of growing disunity within the ruling conservative AD coalition. Premier Balsemão was assailed by right-wingers from within his own party, the PSD, angry that this moderate figure should be the successor to Sá Carneiro. If, with its overall majority in parliament, the AD government falls, then Portuguese democracy will have been gravely discredited. Without a strong moderate right-wing bloc, more extremist varieties are bound to step into the breach and the former Salazar regime can only grow in esteem, since at least it provided stability of a sort for thirty-six years.

Portugal's reborn democracy may shortly be approaching the crossroads reached by the First Republic at the end of World War I. Then, politicians failed to see the danger signs and the bickering between and within parties continued, with ultimately disastrous consequences. Today the heirs of the old bourgeois politicians of the pre-1926 republic are very much entrenched in the democratic system, and, in the battle with more sober and technocratic politicians, it is the former who have made the running so far. Perhaps politicians have been encouraged in their complacency by the fact that the army has been politically quiet since the revolution. There were no reverberations after the near-success of Colonel Tejero's *coup* attempt in Spain on 23 February 1981. Portugal has been spared the urban terrorism of Spain because she lacks a separatist problem (at least on the mainland) and because the far-left groups which act as a seedbed for terrorism elsewhere in Europe have very little support among the young or deprived, since they were badly discredited by their pusillanimous behaviour in the revolution.

Nevertheless, if liberty in Spain does perish once again, Portugal's own democratic prospects will have suffered a shattering blow. At the very least, the powers of the elected head of state will be greatly strengthened in the event of the party system falling apart completely. Already, in his second term of office, President Eanes remains as enigmatic a figure as before. The right distrusts his friendship with the radical members of the Council of the Revolution, as the following joke makes clear: 'Eanes says he is a Roman Catholic who does not practise. He doesn't call himself a Communist but *does* practise.'

Speculation was current in Lisbon during 1981 that Eanes had made plans to form a presidential party embracing the political spectrum. In London on 29 July 1981 for the wedding of the Prince of Wales, he had a much publicised meeting with Franco Nogueira, Salazar's respected foreign minister, which may indicate that he would like to be promoted as a champion of national unity. With the Council of the Revolution due to be wound up, his powers may also be increased substantially, since authority vested in the council is to be divided between the president and parliament, and there is no guarantee that the legislature will get the lion's share.

Within all the main parties, some outstanding politicians are to be found at middle rank who may ensure in the future that parliament is not eclipsed by a strong president or by openly undemocratic forces. These include the gifted economist Vitor Constancio, of the PS; Anibal Cavaco e Silva, another economist but from the PSD; Helena Roseta (PSD), the only woman prominent in Portuguese politics; Vital Moreira, who is sometimes depicted as a harbinger of Euro-communism in the PCP, and the very bright Francisco Lucas Pires of the CDS.[34] One independent who cannot be discounted is António Barreto, formerly of the PS, who in 1979 bowed out of politics, saying that he was a young man who might have a future in politics but who had a lot to learn and was going away to think and read: unfortunately, such humility is in very short supply among politicians in Lisbon at the moment.

While politicians engage in their power games the economy has been making only moderate progress. The frequent turnovers of government since 1975 mean that ministers often spend more time staving off the next political crisis than in tackling economic problems. Recovery in the economic sphere has been delayed by the international recession and by the rather limited range of products which a semi-industrial country like Portugal has to offer. A severe drought (the worst in 100 years) in 1980–81 further weakened the agricultural sector and made the country even more dependent than before on the import of foodstuffs. In 1979 Portugal was the USA's eighth biggest importer of corn, a dependence on external markets which helps to keep her balance of payments firmly in the red.

Agriculture still contributes only about 10 per cent of the gross national product although 30 per cent of the workforce is employed on the land. There are 800,000 small farmers, but only a tiny minority are real producers. Fishing is another industry which has great potential but which has been allowed to decline. Another drawback is Portugal's acute vulnerability to oil price movements. She must import about 80 per cent of her total fuel requirements, which only exacerbates the balance-of-payments problem. Domestic investment has also been slow because (right-wing critics say) the 1976 constitution, in discouraging private capitalism, has frightened off all but the most dedicated entrepreneurs.

The excessive bureaucracy to be found in Portugal is frequently singled out as a prime cause of her economic lassitude. To start an economic concern, would-be businessmen have to fight their way through a tangle of red tape. The over-centralisation to be found in Lisbon has encouraged corruption and waste. If more power and responsibility was given to local areas they would flourish, according to advocates of decentralisation. The social pressures of a small community would ensure that malpractice was not as flagrant as in Lisbon. But the bourgeoisie often says that ordinary people cannot be trusted if power is devolved to them. The elite has a low opinion of the masses, although it is a fact that ordinary Portuguese who emigrate, whether to the USA or to EEC countries, often come to be regarded as model citizens by their hosts. But it is surely a tragedy if people have to uproot themselves for their true worth to be recognised. Members of the professions with a stake in the present swollen bureaucracy say that the Portuguese will break the law if regulations and supervision are waived and people are required instead to act on trust. Even progressive lawyers react with great hostility when the need for such a top-heavy bureaucracy is questioned.

A gargantuan bureaucracy has always been a feature of the Portuguese state but two twentieth-century developments have served greatly to increase its scope. One was the onset of Salazar's corporative state in the 1930s: despite his reputation for cost-effectiveness Dr Salazar allowed the state sector to expand enormously in the name of corporatist principles. This baleful practice was continued after the revolution of 25 April 1974 when a new battery of laws to do with the nationalisation of domestic banks and industry created new bureaucratic empires. A few brief examples will serve to illustrate the ludicrous and sometimes callous extent bureaucracy has gone to in Portugal.

For many years, appointments like the nomination of a cleaning woman in a primary school have had to appear, first of all, in the *Diário de República*, the official gazette. Similarly, a foreigner recently discovered that if she wished to found a local animal welfare society she would have to travel miles to Lisbon to fill in lengthy forms for which payment was required. Animals themselves are not exempt. In the summer of 1981 a British satirical magazine generated much mirth when it relayed the chairman of the Portuguese parliamentary agricultural commission's announcement that all cows and oxen in the Algarve were to be issued with identity documents in order to foil livestock thefts. Less prosaically, widows of military officers in receipt of a state pension have to go to the local police station every year so that the local authorities can verify that they are living in 'a proper moral state'. No wonder one observer has dubbed the suffocating hand of bureaucracy as 'fascism in freedom'.

Stamped paper (which is not cheap) is the required currency a citizen needs even in the most trivial transaction involving the state. For illiterate people and rural folk, not surprisingly, the state is often something which is held in real dread. One man who singled out bureaucracy as a foe was the former premier, Sá Carneiro. However, his reforming efforts were terminated by his death in 1980, which some refuse to believe was a simple accident. Sá Carneiro might have been the twentieth-century Pombal. Instead he turned out to be a second Sidónio Pais.

Eight years after the fall of the *Estado Novo*, the time is long overdue for politicians to stop acting like lords of misrule and get down to tackling some of the country's most urgent social and economic problems. However, the fact has to be faced that no political party has so far emerged which, for a sustained period, has been able to capture the imagination of the electorate. This is perhaps just as true of the 1974–81 period as it is of the earlier republican and monarchist eras of parliamentary rule. In Portugal, during this century, periods of democratic civilian rule have been associated with austerity, chaos or depressed living standards. The authoritarian *Estado Novo* (1933–74) was inextricably linked with fierce exploitation of lower-income groups. In the medium and short terms the liberal republican regime (1910–26) and its post-1974 successor brought about no dramatic or irreversible improvements in ordinary people's living standards. The prevalence of short-lived minority governments may explain the unimpressive track record of Portuguese democracy. In the 1980s it will be interesting to see whether a government with an overall majority manages to open a more encouraging chapter in the story of the country's evolving democracy.

Notes

1 John Biggs-Davison, 'Counting the cost in Portugal', *The Spectator*, 2 April 1976, p. 8.
2 Tom Gallagher, 'Portugal's five years of liberty', *New Society*, 29 November 1979, p. 487.
3 *The Times* obituary, 19 August 1977, p. 14.
4 An interesting testimony from a PRP militant who turned state informant was

published in the Portuguese press at the end of 1980. See 'Assaltantes de bancos eram do PRP e armados pelo Copcon', *Expresso* (review section), 20 December 1980.

5   Robinson, *Contemporary Portugal*, p. 272.

6   The meaning of this phrase was kindly explained to the writer by Patricia Lança.

7   Marcel Niedergang, 'Presidential system in the making', *The Guardian Weekly* (London), 15 May 1977,

8   *The Constitution of the Portuguese Republic*, Article 2, Ministry of Social Communications, Lisbon, 1976, p. 17.

9   For detailed information on the performance of the economy in Portugal the London Branch bulletin of the Banco Totta e Açores can be recommended. Published up to six times a year, thirty-three bulletins had appeared by the end of 1980.

10 The *Guardian* published two editorials in which it criticised the parsimonious attitude of Britain and other European countries towards Portugal. See 'Portugal's futile friends', 30 November 1977, and 'The land we left in the lurch', 9 December 1977.

11 See, for instance, 'Liceu Dona Leonor, chocadeira fascista', *Diário de Lisboa*, 28 March 1977, pp. 10–11, and Fernando da Costa, 'Porque se refugiam os adolescentes', *Expresso*, 22 December 1978, pp. 6–7.

12 Robert Harvey, 'A revolution tamed: survey of Portugal', *The Economist*, 28 May 1977, p. vii.

13 Augusto Cid, *Eanes el estático*, Intervenção, Lisbon, 1979.

14 'Portugal: second time lucky', *The Economist*, 16 December 1978.

15 James Markham, 'Madrid, Lisbon and Socialism', *International Herald Tribune*, 26 January 1979.

16 This goal was supported in late 1979 by a future Portuguese premier, Francisco Pinto Balsemão. Interview with Dr Balsemão, 12 December 1979.

17 Robinson, *op. cit.*, p. 254.

18 Keith Middlemas, *Power and the Party. Changing Faces of Communism in Western Europe*, Andre Deutsch, London, 1980, pp. 211 and 371.

19 *Ibid.*, p. 259.

20 Ben Pimlott, 'European elections – Portugal', *West European Politics*, Vol. 3, No. 3, October 1980, p. 452.

21 *The Times* obituary, 11 December 1980.

22 John Cooney, 'Huge problems of transition in post-colonial world', *Irish Times*, 10 June 1978.

23 See the London Branch bulletin of the Banco Totta e Açores, Nos. 30–1, June and August 1980.

24 Carneiro Jacinto, 'A Igreja, o voto útil e os apoios externos', *O Jornal*, 26 October 1979.

25 In Britain the only major coverage of the financial controversy involving Sá Carneiro was a hostile story by Paul Foot, 'The mystery of the unpaid loan', *New Statesman*, 3 October 1980.

26 The late Adelino Amaro da Costa mentioned this fear in an interview with this writer in December 1979.

27 Óscar Carmona was the dictatorship's compliant head of state until his death in 1951.

28 This was indirectly triggered off by the publication of a book which gave a generally laudatory account of his role in the revolution. See José Freire

Antunes, *O segredo do 25 de Novembro*, Publicações Europa-América, Lisbon, 1980.

29 James Markham, *International Herald Tribune*, 6 December 1980.
30 Carneiro Jacinto, 'Eanes/Sá Carneiro: dois estilos', *O Jornal*, 30 December 1980, p. 7.
31 Vasco Pulido Valente, *O País das Maravilhas*, Intervenção, Lisbon, 1979, p. 277.
32 Fernando Antunes, 'Mota Amaral recusa substituir Sá Carneiro', *O Jornal*, 9 December 1980, p. 22.
33 Cáceres Monteiro, 'Francisco Balsemão: uma sucessão dentro da "dinastia"?', *O Jornal*, 12 December 1980.
34 Helena Roseta was one of the twenty-four women elected in 1980 to the 250-seat Portuguese parliament. Her sister is also a deputy for the PSD, as is her husband, Pedro Roseta. When thirty-four-year-old Sra Roseta was profiled in an English newspaper, it was revealed that a quarter of the adult female population was still illiterate, compared with a fifth of adult males. See Jill Joliffe, 'Speaking up from the back of the house', *The Guardian*, 17 August 1981, p. 8.

GLOSSARY OF POLITICAL TERMS

Africanista. Officer in the Portuguese army identified with military campaigning in Africa during the last phases of colonial expansion in the nineteenth century.

Aldeamento. A large settlement guarded by the Portuguese army before 1974 in which local African populations were sealed off from contact with guerillas.

Assimilado. African inhabitant of Portuguese territory who was regarded as sufficiently well educated to be granted full Portuguese citizenship.

Atentado. Military revolt, usually involving small numbers of people.

Baroẽs. The power brokers and men of influence in the political elite during the 1926–74 dictatorship.

Barraca. Shanty town.

Bufo. Informer of the PIDE (the post-1945 secret police). During the last hours of the dictatorship the names of the thousands of *bufos* who provided information were burnt, to prevent them falling into the hands of anti-fascists.

Câmara corporativa. The second chamber of Salazar's controlled parliament. It sat between 1935 and 1974.

Camarilla. Cabal or clique.

Casas do povo. Rural 'community centres' which were part of Salazar's corporative programme. The first was opened at the village of Barbacena in the Alto Alentejo by Salazar in 1934.

Castiço, Traditional counter-Reformation element in national life, often counterposed with the progressive *estrangeirados.* Salazar has been described as a typical *castiço.*

Catedradocracia. 'Aristocracy of the dons'. A reference to the number of academics (especially from Coimbra University) in Salazar's cabinet and in key political jobs after 1932.

Caudillo. Spanish term for political leader or strong man.

Conjura. Plot, conspiracy.

Dirigiste. French term denoting firm state control of the economy.

Dictablanda. Mild form of dictatorship associated with the rule of General Miguel Primo de Rivera in Spain between 1923 and 1930.

Duro. Hard-liner within the ranks of the Salazar–Caetano regime.

Eminência parda. Men of influence and often wealth who made up the political entourage of Salazar and later Caetano.

Escudo. Main Portuguese unit of currency.

Estado Novo. 'New State'. Name by which the authoritarian political system was known between 1930 and 1969.

Estado Social. 'Social State'. Name by which the Caetano regime was sometimes known between 1969 and 1974.

Estrangeirado. 'Foreignised', modern-minded Portuguese who will often have spent time abroad.

Excelentissimos senhores. The men of power and influence in Lisbon.

Flechas. Crack military units which infiltrated enemy positions in the 1961–74 colonial war.

Fontismo. Policy of growth through public works and communications schemes associated with António Maria de Fontes Pereira de Melo (1819–1887) of the Regenerator Party, who was prime minister for most of the 1870s and 1880s, the most stable era between 1820 and 1932.

Golpe d'estado. Military take-over.

Grémio. Association of employers in the corporative system between 1933 and 1974.

Intentona. A planned attempt to seize power.

Inventona. An 'invented' conspiracy.

Junta. Group organising a military conspiracy or forming a government after a successful seizure of power.

Latifundia. Large estates or farms found mainly in the Alentejo region and worked by landless labourers.

Latifundista. Owner of large estate.

Legião Portuguesa. Paramilitary group of civilians supporting the *Estado Novo* formed in 1936 and, before its dissolution in 1974, connected with the most reactionary sections of the regime.

Melo Antunista. Supporter of Major Ernesto Melo Antunes, who helped defeat the militant left in the 1974–75 revolution but played a radical role in politics thereafter.

Metropole. Mainland Portugal excluding the islands and former colonies.

Miliciano. Conscript officer.

Minifundia. Small-scale agriculture involving virtually only plots of land. Commonest in the Minho region of the north.

Mocidade. 'Youth'. Name of the youth movement which gave backing to the *Estado Novo* between 1936 and 1974.

Personalismo. In politics, owing allegiance to a person rather than to a party or ideology; awe and respect for an individual leader.

Pronunciamento. Broad-based military insurrection.

Retornado. Refugee who fled to Portugal from Africa at the time of decolonisation in 1974–75.

Rotativismo. Arrangement whereby the parties rotated in office between 1851 and the 1890s.

Salazarismo. 'Salazarism'.

Saneamento. Purges of people from office associated with the previous regime. It came into use in the 1920s and enjoyed special vogue after 1974.

Sidonismo. Pertaining to Sidónio Pais, President of Portugal in 1917–18.

Sindicato. State trade union formed after 1933.

Situacionista. Political supporter of the *status quo*, a phrase referring especially to supporters of the *Estado Novo*.

Soarista. Supporter of Mário Soares, leader of the Socialist Party after 1973.

Tubaronismo (from *tubarao*, shark). Denotes rapacious greed and was used by the opposition to describe the behaviour of some of Salazar's ministers.

Ultra. A dedicated supporter of the *Estado Novo* opposed to political liberalism, especially in the later stages of the dictatorship.

Ultramar. 'The overseas'. Collective term for Portugal's colonial empire.

União Nacional. 'National Union'. Name of the single political movement founded in 1930 and renamed National Popular Action (ANP) in 1969.

BIBLIOGRAPHY

1. Newspapers and journals referred to or consulted

Ánalise Social (Lisbon), *Atlantic Monthly* (New York), *Contemporary Review* (London), *Current Biography* (New York), *Diário de Notícias* (Lisbon), *Diário Popular* (Lisbon), *Economist* (London), *Expresso* (Lisbon), *Foreign Affairs* (New York), *Fortnightly Review* (London), *Government and Opposition* (London), *Guardian* (Manchester and London), *História* (Lisbon), *Iberian Studies* (Keele), *Index on Censorship* (London), *International Herald Tribune* (Paris), *Irish Ecclesiastical Record* (Dublin), *Irish Monthly* (Dublin), *Irish Times* (Dublin), *O Jornal* (Lisbon), *Journal of Contemporary History* (London), *Le Monde* (Paris), *A Luta* (Lisbon), *New Left Review* (London), *New Society* (London), *New Statesman* (London), *New Yorker* (New York), *New York Review of Books* (New York), *Observer* (London), *Orbis* (Washington), *Political Quarterly* (London), *Portugal Informação* (Lisbon), *Problems of Communism* (Washington), *A Rua* (Lisbon), *Socialist Register* (London), *Spectator* (London), *Studies* (Dublin), *Sunday Telegraph* (London), *Sunday Times* (London), *Tempo* (Lisbon), *Time* (New York), *Times* (London), *West European Politics* (London).

2. A note on reading

General works. A useful place to start is Richard Robinson's *Contemporary Portugal. A History* (London, 1979), which is an objective and scholarly work on the modern period. Without revealing many new facts about the dictatorship, it provides a balanced survey of events and major political and social trends. An invaluable source-book on earlier historical periods is Joel Serrão (ed.) *Dicionário de história de Portugal* (4 vols., Lisbon, 1963–71). Since its liberal-minded compilers were unwilling to provoke Salazar's censors by looking closely at the personalities, ideologies and movements which shaped Portugal after 1930, its sweep concludes with the fall of the liberal republic. Charles E. Nowell's *Portugal* (Englewood Cliffs, N.J., 1973) is one of the few general histories written by a foreigner before 1974 which manages to be neutral about the Salazar regime. Descriptive and short, it is a good introductory text which includes some interesting anecdotes. More ambitious is A. H. de Oliveira Marques's two-volume *A History of Portugal* (New York, 1972), which gives as much attention to economic and demographic factors as to political history and foreign relations. Although it will probably remain the most influential large-scale history of Portugal for some time to come, a number of claims about the *Estado Novo* may have to be revised. Undoubtedly controversial is V. G. Kiernan's 'The Old Alliance: England and Portugal', *Socialist Register* (London, 1973); this useful debunking exercise is a good counterweight to the literature in English on the subject, where the alliance is nearly always described in the most unctuous of terms.

Lawrence Graham and Harry Makler's *Contemporary Portugal. The Revolution and its Antecedents* (Austin, Texas, 1979) is an informative text in which various academics grouped in the International Conference Group on Modern Portugal (ICGMP) look at both the *Estado Novo* and the background to the 1974 revolution; António de Figueiredo, *Portugal. Fifty Years of Dictatorship* (London, 1975) is a useful critique of the toppled dictatorship by a Portuguese journalist in exile until 1974; an inspired but somewhat pessimistic look at Portugal in the liberal monarchy period is still in print a century after its appearance: J. P. Oliveira Martins, *Portugal contemporáneo* (2 vol., Lisbon, 1881). In Jacinto Baptista's *Caminhos para uma revolução* (Lisbon, 1975) the stifling atmosphere of *Estado Novo* politics is well conveyed through the personal odyssey of this journalist, who provides some neat vignettes of the dictator and his retainers. In a broader vein, worth recommendation is Charles Boxer's *The Portuguese Seaborne Empire, 1415–1825* (London, 1973), a monumental survey of Portugal's tri-continental empire during the first three centuries of Portuguese expansion.

Portugal 1900–26. The liberal era which extended up to 1926 in a long monarchical stretch and a briefer republican phase has been subjected to rigorous examination by several good professional historians in Portugal. Work was being undertaken and findings published before 1974, but the best monographs have appeared since then; Manuel Villaverde Cabral, *Portugal no Alvorada do século XX* (Lisbon, 1979), surveys the nature and extent of social and economic changes between 1890 and 1914 while not neglecting political developments; this is a well documented study which looks in painstaking detail at some of the major structural changes occurring in Portuguese society as one governmental system gave way to another. Vasco Pulido Valente, *O poder e o povo. A revolução de 1910* (Lisbon, 1976), is the work of a historian and polemical journalist who has been active in politics since the restoration of democracy: this work is a profile of the republican movement from the late 1880s onwards and it sheds much light on why it was able to topple the monarchy but not resolve its internal contradictions during the immediate aftermath of the 1910 revolution. The title of Douglas Wheeler's *Republican Portugal. A Political History* (Madison, Wis., 1978) is self-explanatory. It may be a long time before this definitive work by a North American historian may be bettered. Few would dispute that he has done Portuguese historiography a major service in this impartial study by rescuing the republican era from the sterile plane of polemical charge and counter-charge; a coherent picture somehow also emerges from the labyrinthine world of party-politics which Portugal knew before 1926. Carlos Ferrão's *História da I*^{a} *República* (Lisbon, 1976) is a traditional apologia for the parliamentary republic in which the author rejects the hostile interpretations that were common between 1926 and 1974; then anti-Republicans regularly depicted Portuguese Freemasonry as a troublesome and sinister element in politics particularly after 1910; in 1981 the veil was pulled from the craft for virtually the first time in a long and fascinating article by António Mega Ferreira, 'Maconaria portuguesa: ainda um ordem secreta', *Expresso* review section (21 March 1980), which explores its shifting fortunes from the 1920s to the present. António José Telo's *Decadência e queda da I República* (Vol. I, Lisbon, 1980) is a stimulating and lucid enquiry into how and why the republic entered into seeming irrevertible decline after 1919; it is largely a work of political history, while Fernando Medeiros's *A sociedade e a economia portuguesa nas origens do salazarismo* (Lisbon, 1979) pays more attention to the socio-economic aspects of what was turning out to be the concluding crisis of Portuguese liberalism.

The military dictatorship, 1926–32. Given the increased research being done on the first phase of authoritarian rule, the military dictatorship will probably soon cease to be the least-known stage of the forty-eight-year dictatorship. However, few full-length accounts of the 1926–32 period have so far appeared. Perhaps the best item to emerge after 1974 was Arnaldo Madureira's *'O 28 de Maio'. Elementos para a sua compreensão* (Lisbon, 1978). It provides a useful profile of the disaffected armed forces on the eve of the 1926 revolution but does not go much beyond the actual seizure of power by the 28 May rebels. Jorge Campinos's *A ditadura militar, 1926–32* (Lisbon, 1975) is solid but rather uninformative, since a lot of it appears to have been written in the restrictive times before 1974. H. Assis Gonçalves's *Intimidades de Salazar* (Lisbon, 1971) is a memoir by Dr Salazar's one-time secretary which is often revealing about the state of civil–military relations inside the dictatorial camp before Salazar's emergence as premier. Probably the best contemporary account of military rule in Portugal was provided by the Frenchman George Guyomard. His *La Dictature militaire au Portugal* (Paris, 1927) is written from a right-wing standpoint but is nevertheless properly sceptical about the performance in government of Portuguese officers. Two articles written during its lifetime but offering contrasting images of the military dictatorship are W. L. Smyser's sympathetic 'Dictatorship without a dictator', *Contemporary Review*, Vol. 138, No. 777 (September 1930) and the more probing work by the Spanish socialist politician Luis Araquistain, 'Dictatorship in Portugal', *Foreign Affairs*, Vol. 7 (October 1928).

Salazar. The Portuguese leader has been treated favourably by his many Portuguese and foreign biographers but few of the texts exploring his personality and record in government provide either balance or hard information. Still the most interesting study after more than forty years may be António Ferro's *Salazar. Portugal and her Leader* (London, 1939). Translated into a number of languages, this book is one extended interview in which Salazar is grilled by the author, a journalist sympathetic to the *Estado Novo*. Not all the questions were soft ones and several of the premier's answers are revealing and unexpected. Christine Garnier's *Salazar. An Intimate Portrait* (New York, 1954) is a light, impressionistic study of Salazar observed away from the cares of office by one of the few people permitted to enter his very private world. Another French writer, J. Ploncard d'Assac, presents a more ideological study of the Portuguese leader in his *Salazar* (Paris, 1967). Their sympathetic portrayal was balanced by a more sceptical treatment: Christian Rudel's *Salazar* (Paris, 1969). Appearing just before the dictator's death, Hugh Kay's *Salazar and Modern Portugal* (London, 1970) strives to be objective and detached, but in the end this English Catholic journalist finds little to be critical about in what nevertheless is a perceptive study. The same is true of Marcelo Caetano's *Minhas memórias de Salazar* (Lisbon, 1977), which makes light of the difficulties there undoubtedly were between the two leaders of the *Estado Novo* before 1968. Nevertheless, we learn much about internal politics during the *Estado Novo* period from Caetano's account. Less easy to assess is Franco Nogueira's massive *Salazar* (Coimbra, 1977–80) all but one of whose five volumes have appeared at the time of writing. Salazar's last foreign minister is unapologetic about most aspects of the chief's record while still being frank and critical in places. The style is elegant but dense; we learn much about Salazar's daily routine and relations with his colleagues but, often, damaging facts which could undermine this sympathetic portrayal are sidestepped. Finally, attention can be drawn to Salazar's collected speeches, *Os discursos* (Coimbra, 1944–67), which read well even though they are often excessively self-congratulatory.

The Estado Novo, 1932–39. The events and policies of the 1930s would shape Portugal until well after mid-century. This decade would be the most dynamic one in the history of the *Estado Novo* and appropriately it is the initial stages of the authoritarian experiment which have received most attention from academics and general commentators. A useful starting point is Manuel Braga da Cruz's *A democracia cristã e o salazarismo* (Lisbon, 1978), which presents the first detailed examination of the lay Catholic bodies that provided the undemocratic order with a large number of ministers as well as the dictator himself. João Medina's attractive and informative *Salazar e os fascistas* (Lisbon, 1979) tells of the challenge which the radical right briefly posed to Salazar in the first years of his premiership. Lopes Arriaga's *Mocidade Portuguesa* (Lisbon, 1976) describes the growth of the youth movement formed in 1936, when the *Estado Novo* was acquiring unmistakable fascist features of its own. By now, the corporative revolution launched in 1933 was reaching its climax, and most of Howard J. Wiarda's *Corporatism and Development. The Portuguese Experience* (Amherst, Mass., 1977) concentrates on the extent to which Portugal in the 1930s became a 'corporative' state. This is an important, if flawed, work by a North American academic who argues that the corporative drives after the 1930s were being duplicated elsewhere in the Luso-Hispanic world to different degrees. So Portugal's experiment with this other 'ism' was not a deviant or isolated case, although Professor Wiarda is rightly sceptical about the extent to which Salazar was committed to the corporative ideal. Philippe Schmitter's *Corporatism and Public Policy in Authoritarian Portugal* (London, 1975) treads similar ground but the writer is more prepared to admit that Portuguese corporativism was a sham exercise and his arguments are often more economical and precise than Wiarda's.

In the related field of constitutional development, two works offer contrasting studies. Marcelo Caetano's *História breve das constituições portuguesas* (Lisbon, 1971) looks at the different constitutions Portugal has had during her recent history and he quite neatly sketches the structural features of the political system that emerged after 1933. Jorge Campinos's *O presidencialismo do Estado Novo* (Lisbon, 1978) is similar in scope but offers different conclusions about the rationale behind the *Estado Novo*; he argues fairly convincingly that the New State took the institutional shape it did in order to facilitate one-man rule (by Salazar) and, as a case study to back up this argument, he looks at the head of state and his non-existent 'powers'. Maria Filomena Mónica's *Educação e sociedade no Portugal de Salazar* (Lisbon, 1978) is one other academic study of merit which looks at the way educational policy was influenced by crude political imperatives in the 1930s; much can also be learned here about the way society was becoming constricted and shaped by arcane values during the heyday of the 'national revolution'.

Solid analytical accounts of politics and society after 1933 have only recently begun to appear. Beforehand, works on developments in the 1930s were often either simplistic in approach or else eulogies of Salazar, if not outright examples of *Estado Novo* propaganda. Michael Derrick's *The Portugal of Salazar* (London, 1938) is one of the more level-headed contemporary accounts of Portugal in the 1930s to come from the pen of a foreigner. S. George West's *The New Corporative State of Portugal* (Lisbon, 1938) took the *Estado Novo* very much at face value, while J. J. Ryan's interesting essay 'Is Portugal totalitarian?', *Irish Monthly* (January 1940), absolved Salazar's Portugal of being in the Nazi fascist tradition. Quirino de Jesus's *Nacionalismo português* (Oporto, 1932) is perhaps the best exposition of counter-revolutionary thought to come from the pen of a Portuguese writing in the 1930s. Salazar's *Doctrine and Action. Internal and Foreign Policy of the New Portugal* (London, 1939) reads like a slick public relations tract more than forty years after its appearance, while Paul Descamps's *Portugal. La Vie sociale actualle* (Paris, 1935) is a useful text which looks at patterns of life and work, especially in rural Portugal: its overriding message is one of a 1930s Portugal which was steadfastly traditional and unchanging.

The middle years of Salazarism. The onset of the Second World War reduced foreign interest in Portugal, and it was not restored again until the last years of the dictatorship. In many important respects the middle years of the *Estado Novo* remain puzzling and enigmatic. Nevertheless, useful materials exist which enable us to explore the most stable phase of the long Salazarist era. On the Second World War period Fernando Queiroga's *Portugal oprimido* (Lisbon, 1976) is sensationalist in places but it reveals the methods the *Estado Novo* was prepared to use in order to forestall serious opposition. Some useful light on Luso-Spanish relations in the wartime period is shed in C. Halstead's 'Consistent and total peril on every side: Portugal and its 1940 protocol with Spain', *Iberian Studies*, Vol. 3, No. I (spring 1974). The effectiveness of the secret police and the extent and types of opposition generated are the subject of my 'Controlled repression in Salazar's Portugal', *Journal of Contemporary History*, Vol. 14, No. 3 (July 1979). In a pioneering article Hermínio Martins looks in closer detail at Salazar's motley opponents in his 'Opposition in Portugal', *Government and Opposition*, Vol. 4, No. 2 (Summer 1969), while Salazar's stage-managed elections are the subject of Philippe Schmitter's scholarly article 'Portée et significance des élections dans le Portugal autoritaire, 1933–74', *Revue Française de Science Politique*, Vol. 27 (1977).

Shortly before his death General Delgado, Salazar's leading opponent, published his *Memoirs* (London, 1964), a hastily written biographical essay (which supersedes an incendiary text, *Da pulhice do 'homo sapiens'*, Lisbon, 1932, in which, as a young airman, he emphatically endorses the counter-revolution). Henrique Galvão's *Santa Maria. My Crusade for Portugal* (London, 1961) is in many ways a more effective critique of the undemocratic order in Lisbon; it appeared at the same time as António de Figueiredo's moving *Portugal and its Empire. The Truth* (London, 1961), which explodes the myth of Salazar's civilising mission in Africa and is caustic about the *Estado Novo's* record at home. Equally damning is Peter Fryer and Patricia McGowan's *Oldest Ally. A Portrait of Salazar's Portugal* (London, 1961). This showed how out-of-step and archaic Portugal had become compared with the rest of Europe and is a first-rate survey of the country, written at a time when it looked as if internal contradictions were about to overwhelm Salazar's regime. Unlike other contemporary treatments, Fryer and McGowan provide a clear analysis of the dictatorship's economic policies. Other work in this field has been done more recently. R. Costa Reis and M. Rendeiro Júnior, in 'O Estado Novo e o "caminho da industria" ', *História*, No. 10 (August 1979), examine how the regime's economic priorities shifted away from self-sufficient nationalism in the post-war era. E. Baklanoff's 'The political economy of Portugal's old regime: growth and change preceding the 1974 revolution', *World Development*, Vol. 7 (1979), is a more general overview, while José Cutileiro's *A Portuguese Rural Society* (Oxford, 1971), which describes the rhythm of life in an Alentejan village in the 1960s, tells us much about how the *Estado Novo* impinged on the lives of ordinary people. Finally, Mário Soares's *Portugal's Struggle for Liberty* (London, 1975), is a helpful personal memoir which introduces the reader to the claustrophobic world of the opposition after 1945.

The end of Salazarism, 1961–68. In the 1960s the ageing dictator became more reliant on his ministers, and two articles examine this relationship along with the changing professional background and role of ministers. Paul Lewis's 'Salazar's ministerial elite', *Review of Politics*, Vol. 30, No. 3 (1978) is a broad outline, while my own 'Os 87 ministros do Estado Novo de Salazar', *História*, No. 28 (February 1981) examines in some more detail how the cabinet functioned in practice and what kind of pressure groups existed. J. Nogueira Pinto's two-volume *Portugal os anos do fim* (Lisbon, 1977) looks specifically at the last years of the *Estado Novo* and, while fairly sympathetic, tries to analyse why its power base was eroding. Some good anecdotes about Salazar and other notables are to be found here which give us an idea of life at the top in the undemocratic era. M. Harsgor's *La Naissance d'un nouveau Portugal* (Paris, 1975) is an overall survey of contemporary Portugal which is good on the political background to the 1974 revolution. Herminio Martins's article 'Portugal', in Giner and Archer's *Contemporary Europe. Class Status and Power* (London, 1971), provides a sharply etched description of Portuguese social structure as of the late 1960s. The colonial wars in Africa were coming to impinge on the domestic scene, and it was to this conflict that most foreign observers were devoting their attention. Perry Anderson's 'Portugal and the end of ultra-colonialism', *New Left Review*, Nos. 15–17 (1962), is a useful guide to social and economic developments both at home and in the *ultramar*, where the author seeks to explain why Portugal could not physically quit Africa like other colonial powers. John Sykes's *Portugal and Africa. The People and the War* (London, 1971) is a journalist's view of life at different levels of society in both the colonies and Portugal. Malyn Newitt's *Portugal in Africa. The Last Hundred Years* (London 1981) is an attempt to draw up a balance sheet concerning the final phase of Portugal's imperial role. Finally Lawrence Graham's *Portugal. The Decline and Collapse of an Authoritarian Order* (London, 1975) attempts to explain how one major outcome of the *Estado Novo's* blinkered colonial policies was the undermining of political unity and administrative cohesion at home.

Caetano's interlude. Sarah Bradford's *Portugal* (London, 1973) is easily the best guide in English to the politics as well as to the atmosphere of Caetano's Portugal. Although somewhat partial to the modified dictatorship, she often proves a cool and objective spectator, and her insights give us a helpful image of life just before 1974. Strangely, the Caetano period has not received serious treatment in Portugal, although censorship was much reduced in this period and it was the one closest to the democratic restoration. For the role Caetano's regime played in hastening its own downfall we have to turn abroad first of all. Keith Middlemas's *Cabora Bassa. Engineering and Politics in Southern Africa* (London, 1975) looks at the political and economic imperatives behind the grandiose hydro-electric scheme being created in western Mozambique during Caetano's time. Kenneth Maxwell's 'Portugal: a neat revolution', *New York Review of Books* (13 June 1974), says far more more about the political order preceding the *coup* in a sharp and impressive piece. Otelo de Carvalho's *Alvorada em abril* (Lisbon, 1977) is an account of the countdown to the 1974 revolution as well as of personal radicalisation brought on by the wars by the principal architect of the military take-over. António de Spínola's *Portugal e o futuro* (Lisbon, 1974) is wooden by comparison but was a far more influential tract: this appeal for colonial flexibility triggered off the final crisis of the regime after publication in Lisbon on 22 February 1974.

Revolutionary Portugal. A detailed examination of the military origins of the

1974 *coup* and how it was hatched and executed is provided by Avelino Rodrigues *et al. O movimento dos capitaes e o 25 de abril* (Lisbon, 1974). This team of journalists also wrote one of the earliest accounts of the way the subsequent revolution evolved in the 1974–75 period: *Portugal depois de abril* (Lisbon, 1976). A helpful attempt to put the downfall of the *Estado Novo* in historical perspective emerges in José António Saraiva's *Do Estado Novo à Segunda República* (Lisbon, 1974). Many of his readers would find comparisons with earlier upheavals fascinating, not least because the authorities had put so many obstacles in the way of disseminating knowledge about the recent past. Instant history was encapsulated in the middle of the revolution by an English group of journalists known as the *Sunday Times* Insight Team, whose *Portugal. The Year of the Captains* (London, 1975) offers a very readable and illuminating guide through the vagaries of revolutionary politics up to mid-1975. Kenneth Maxwell's two articles, 'The hidden revolution in Portugal', *New York Review of Books* (17 April 1975), and 'The thorns of the Portuguese revolution', *Foreign Affairs* (January 1976), are perceptive articles written at different points in the course of the revolution which can still be read with profit today. Ben Pimlott's 'Parties and voters in the Portuguese revolution', *Parliamentary Affairs* (winter 1977), traces the rise of a new civilian political order and cleverly distinguishes the main political parties, which could sometimes appear confusing, at least in name. J. Gaspar and N. Vitorino's *As eleições do 25 april. Geografia e imagem dos partidos* (Lisbon, 1976) is a detailed analysis of voting trends as exhibited in the 1975 constituent assembly elections. José Freire Antunes's *O segredo do 25 de novembro* (Lisbon, 1980) is an account of how the military radicals were finally expelled from power at the end of 1975, while Ben Pimlott's 'Were the soldiers revolutionary? The Armed Forces Movement, 1973–76', *Iberian Studies*, Vol. 7 (1978) is a more scholarly explanation of why the centurions ultimately failed to inaugurate a new revolutionary order. Hard to classify is Phil Mailer's *Portugal. The Impossible Revolution?* (London, 1977), which explains the demise of the revolution from an anarcho-syndicalist standpoint and throws out a number of stimulating views about the events of 1974–75.

Democratic Portugal. Written by the Lisbon correspondent of *The Economist*, Robert Harvey, *Portugal's Bid for Democracy* (London, 1978) is the best account of political trends since the revolution at present available in English. Keith Middlemas's *The Power and the Party* (London, 1980) contains an interesting chapter on the Portuguese Communist Party in which he claims that the PCP is motivated by a lot more than unreconstructed bolshevism. Carlos Roma Fernandes's *Portugal, Europa e o Terceiro Mundo* (Lisbon, 1980) is an intelligent discussion of the options open to Portugal in her bid to join the EEC, a topic which has been little debated even five years after Portugal first lodged her application in Brussels. Finally there is Vasco Pulido Valente's *O País das Maravilhas* (Lisbon, 1980), a series of essays and articles in which the Portuguese state and national political culture are critically examined and almost invariably compared with Anglo-Saxon models of government and society which the writer often finds have more to commend them: a very partisan judgement.

INDEX

Academic Centre for Christian Democracy (CADC): rise of, 31–2; Salazar and Cerejeira in, 49, 62–3; politically influential (1928), 49–50; members in political elite, 80

Acção Escolar Vanguarda (AEV), 85, 86

Action Française, 31

Afghanistan, 239

Afonso Henriques (1109–85), first king of Portugal, 2

Afonso, José, Portuguese folk-singer, 188

Ágora, r.-wing newspaper, 125

agriculture; early neglect of, 3; 19th c. reform frustrated, 16; wheat campaign of 1930s, 75; political influence of latifundists, 75–6; neglected under Salazar, 139–40; reforms overdue, 140; structural problems in 1970s, 247–8

Albania, 211

Albuquerque, Afonso de (*c.* 1460–1515), explorer and coloniser, 6

Alcobaça, 218

Alegre, Manuel (1937–), Socialist politician, 206

Aleixo, António (1899–1950), poet, 101

Alentejo: weakness of religion in, 127; becomes communist stronghold, 112, 211, 219; 1975 land seizures, 211; mentioned, 23, 159

Algarve: weakness of religion in, 127; mentioned, 219

Algeria, 175–6

Almeida, António José de (1866–1929), President of Portugal 1919–23, 21

Almeida, Dinis de (b. 1947), radical soldier, 186, 187, 205, 210; quoted, 224

Almeida, José de, Azorean separatist, 219

Almeida, Col. João de (1873–1953), r.-wing officer and colonialist, 42

Almeida Braga, Luis de (1890–1970), Integralist, 30

Alveira family, II

Alves, Major Vitor (1935–), MFA officer, 186, 187, 205, 212, 228

Alves Correia, Joaquim (1886–1951), theologian, 128

Amaral, João Bosco (1943–), Azorean politician, 242

Amaro da Costa, Adelino (1943–80): post-1974 politician, a founder of the CDS, 196; criticises the revolution (1974) 196; minister of defence, 239; death of, 243; mentioned, 171, 250 n. 26

Amélia (1865–1950), widow of King Carlos I, 19

Anarchists: displaced by communists in 1930s, 111; try to kill Salazar, 117

Andre, João da Costa, minister of Caetano, 173

Anglo-Portuguese alliance: origins of, 3; Portugal as client state of Britain, 9–10; Pombal's attitude to British influence, 11–12; reaffirmed (1910), 21; Britain plans to concede Port. colonies to Germany, 36 n. 8; in late 1930s, 87; and World War II, 102–5

Angola: banking system as political issue (1930), 51; rebellion, (1930), 53, 88; PCP supports independence for, 116; plan to transfer the Portuguese capital to, 116; harsh conditions of blacks, 124; call for a Jewish homeland there, 130; Salazar regrets oil discoveries in, 138; supports Delgado (1958), 147; black revolt in (1961), 150, 151–2, 155, 175; repercussions of revolt in Portugal, 151–2; pogroms (1961) against